The Philosophy of the Social Sciences

Also available from Continuum

The Philosophy of History, Mark Day

The Philosophy of the Social Sciences

An Introduction

Robert Bishop

continuum

Continuum International Publishing Group
The Tower Building
11 York Road
London SE1 7NX

80 Maiden Lane, Suite 704
New York, NY 10038

British Library Cataloguing-in-Publication Data
A catalogue record for this book is available from the British Library.

ISBN: PB: 0-8264-8953-2
       978-0-8264-8953-1

Library of Congress Cataloguing-in-Publication Data
A catalog record for this book is available from the Library of Congress.

Typeset by TechBooks International, New Delhi, India
Printed and bound in England by Antony Rowe Ltd, Chippenham, Wiltshire

Contents

List of Figures and Tables

Figures

Tables

Introduction

The social sciences have been of enduring interest. The Nobel Prize for Economics is widely publicized each year, psychologists appear ubiquitous in our culture – including TV sitcoms and movies – and political scientists are interviewed regularly in newspapers and magazines as well as on TV. Part of this interest lies in the fact that we want to know what makes us tick, why we are the way we are. But part of this interest also lies in the kinds of issues social science potentially can address and the worry that, try as they might, social scientists cannot help but bring personal and cultural biases to their research. These latter worries go right to the heart of some of the deepest issues in the philosophy of social science, the subject of this text.

This book is designed to serve as a comprehensive textbook for classes in the philosophy of social science for advanced undergraduate and graduate students at universities. My aim is to be accessible and stimulating to students in philosophy departments as well as students in social-science departments who are interested in the foundations of their disciplines. I focus on important conceptual and methodological questions in the social sciences in a way that identifies a number of often unexamined assumptions underlying the practice of social science, but which does not presume a substantial background in philosophy. These assumptions and issues are critically analyzed along with the key ways they shape the practice of research, the interpretation of findings, and theory formulation in social science.

Separate chapters are devoted to how the assumptions and issues discussed arise in psychology, rational-choice theory, political science and economics. I employ a broad conceptual framework for classifying modes of social-science inquiry affording readers a useful way to compare and contrast approaches to social-science research that often appear quite different or incommensurable. By the end of the book, you will have gained an ability to think critically about crucial aspects of social-science research as well as about the practices of specific disciplines.

With rare exceptions, there is more material in this book than is reasonable to cover in a typical semester for undergraduates. The design of the book is that a class will cover all the material in Parts One and Two and then select chapters of interest out of Parts Three and Four. Part One introduces the subject and covers important philosophical, historical and conceptual background serving as a foundation for the rest of the book. In particular, the conceptual framework of five different modes of social inquiry are introduced and discussed (Chapter 3).

The core of the book is contained in Part Two focusing on a sustained examination of the problems of value-neutrality in social sciences. What is unique about this section is its emphasis on how cultural ideals remain hidden away in social-science research, yet colour every aspect of social inquiry. Much of this material is very rarely discussed in the philosophical and professional literature on social science. This lack of attention is indirectly proportional to the influence these ideals have on social science.

Brief expositions of psychology and the behavioural sciences, rational-choice theory, political science and economics are given in Part Three. A chapter is devoted to each of the disciplines or perspectives, where the assumptions and issues discussed in the first two parts of the book are illustrated in each chapter.

Finally, Part Four discusses several issues in the philosophy of social science, some standard and some not. The material here deals with problems in the collection and sorting of data, free will–determinism dilemmas and scientific explanations in social science. The final two chapters in this last part are important for wrapping up the book and I would strongly urge that they be covered no matter what other choices are made. Chapter 16 deals in detail with a theme that appears throughout the book – the question of the similarity of natural science and social-science inquiry. The book concludes in Chapter 17 with a discussion of an alternative path to get beyond the stultifying options of objectivism or relativism that appear to plague our typical thinking about social inquiry.

A book of this nature is simply not possible as an individual endeavour. Rather, it is the product of much conversation and argument with friends, colleagues, students, texts and other interlocutors, far too many to name explicitly. But some do deserve special mention. Frank Richardson has been a true friend, mentor and inspiration. Our numerous conversations over the years have led to a number of the insights in this book that I consider revolutionary. He supplied a number of very helpful and insightful comments on several draft chapters as did David Lorenzo. Many of the ideas in this book were influenced by conversations with Harald Atmanspacher, Charles Guignon and Leonard Smith, often without their even realizing it. Special thanks to my students who read early drafts of the book as their textbook and offered lots of useful comments from the student's point of view. I would particularly like to acknowledge Sarah Douglas and Adam Green along with the editorial team at Continuum. They were most helpful and made the process of completing this book smoother than I ever could have imagined.

Part One

Conceptions of Science 1

This book is about exploration. The idea is to pull back the curtain to see what is going on behind research in the social sciences. What assumptions are being made? What concepts are involved? What makes social science tick? Just as the bulk of an iceberg lies below the ocean's surface, there is a great deal that lies below the surface of social-science research and practice. As we will see, 'out of sight, out of mind' does not have innocent consequences for the work of social scientists.

Exploring the inner workings and foundations of social science is a philosophical job. Usually, the first question such a job brings to many people's minds is: 'Why should we even be philosophizing about social science?' After all, these are established research disciplines. They are exploring and mapping the terrain of the social world just as natural-science disciplines are exploring and mapping the natural world, at least on the dominant view of these matters. What is there to say other than that social scientists use the methods of science to construct theories for purposes of explanation, prediction and control for the betterment of the human condition?

These are very good questions. The answers to them may contain a number of surprises for you, however. Many thinkers, both within and outside the social sciences, worry that these disciplines mostly produce 'wordy elaborations of the obvious' (Taylor 1985a: 1). More troubling, a number of people worry that instead of bettering the human condition, the social sciences actually contribute to some of the most unhealthy trends in contemporary (Western) societies: for example, hyper-individualism, social alienation, a narcissistic fascination with the self, overemphasis on instrumental control among others (see Richardson, Fowers and Guignon 1999).

Lying behind the question of why philosophize at all about the social sciences is a deeper philosophical question, one that is a central occupation of this book: are the social sciences like the natural sciences? Although a number of social scientists and philosophers assume that the natural and social sciences are quite similar (e.g., Kincaid 1996; Steuer 2002), there are reasons to think this is not the case. And if there are significant differences between social and natural science, then using methods and aims suited for natural-science inquiry might not only distort the social world we are trying to understand, but might also contribute to some of the modern sources of distress we all feel at numerous points in our daily lives. We will see that indeed there is evidence this is the case.

Another crucial question that has troubled many about the social sciences is whether they can genuinely be value-neutral. Many students, practitioners and critics of the social sciences are troubled about the latter's claim to be bias-free. They wonder that if the social sciences really are strictly neutral, how could such sciences be relevant to human affairs or contribute to personal welfare or a better society in any way other than as some kind of frighteningly manipulative behavioural technology? The natural-science ideal of pursuing a context-free science of human behaviour based on scientific laws appears to many to be thoroughly depersonalizing and in strong conflict with our ideas of what makes for meaningful living, such that this enterprise may, all things considered, be detrimental. For example, some observers argue that academic and clinical psychology does more harm than good (Cushman 1990; Hillman and Ventura 1992; Fancher 1995; Richardson, Fowers and Guignon 1999). We will see that these worries are well-founded as the problem of value-neutrality in the social sciences will be a central focus of this book.

Ignoring such questions – that is, not philosophizing about social science – does not make these issues go away. Rather, ignoring such questions can lead to a loss of confidence in the social sciences in particular and the entire enterprise of science itself. The theories and findings of social science turn out to be significantly coloured by assumptions about fundamental matters such as the nature of the world, knowledge and the good life – *philosophical* assumptions that are rarely acknowledged and largely unexamined. And we cannot accurately or honestly appraise social-science inquiry until we have teased out these assumptions, detected what we can of their influence, and begun the process of critically sifting them. On the other hand, thinking through these issues and assumptions does not lead to despair about social sciences either. Instead, I hope to show that by paying fuller attention to these matters we can think more clearly about what the social sciences ought to be about and how they might contribute to improving the human condition.

1. What is science?

Before we get started on our journey into the social sciences, I need to lay some foundations in place so we can think about these sciences and their relationship to the enterprise of science itself. Many people have asked themselves the question 'What is science?' without realizing they were posing a philosophical question. Analysing something is a quintessential philosophical task and answering the question: 'What is science?' requires giving an analysis of science as a particular kind of activity.

Answering this question, however, is far from straightforward as there are a number of possible analyses of science on offer. Historian of science David Lindberg (1992: 1–2) has identified eight distinct conceptions of science each of which has significant support among scientists, philosophers and historians:

Activity conception. Science is a mode of human activity by which we have progressively gained control over our environment. This view is closely connected with craft traditions, artisans and technology, and emphasizes that scientific practices grew out of our ordinary ways of coping with the world. Thomas Kuhn (1996) points out ways in which craft traditions and technological development were historically vital to the emergence of new sciences in the sixteenth to the nineteenth centuries. Even though we do not think of them as scientists, prehistoric people contributed to the growth of science as they learned how to engage in successful agriculture, to work hides and metals, and so forth. On this conception, science is a more reflective, systematic version of our ordinary practices (see Dewey 1933).

Theoretical conception. Science is a body of conceptual and theoretical knowledge, a connected body of concepts and facts. This conceptual body of knowledge is further useful for providing understanding or explanations of why things happen. To be scientific is to be theoretical as opposed to being 'applied' or focusing on technology say. Theoretical knowledge is considered as leading to and guiding technological developments. Proponents of this conception normally draw a strong distinction between science and engineering, but also acknowledge that not every theoretical body of knowledge is scientific (e.g., theology, philosophy). So further criteria are needed to distinguish scientific knowledge from other bodies of theoretical knowledge.

Universal-laws conception. Science is a search for universal, law-like statements expressible in a precise language (e.g., mathematics or). An example of such laws would be Newton's second law, $F = ma$, which states that the force on some object is directly related to the object's mass multiplied by the acceleration. Unlike the first two conceptions, this view expresses a goal for scientific activity: To discover or produce universal laws which can then be used to explain, predict and perhaps control the behaviour of objects.

Methodological conception. Science is a *methodology*; that is to say, it is identified as a particular set of procedures, usually experimental, for exploring and confirming/disconfirming hypotheses and theories about nature. A claim can only be considered scientific if it has an appropriate relationship to a recognized methodology or if the methodology can be empirically demonstrated to be reliable. Note that Thomas Hobbes and René Descartes also emphasized methodology as crucial to science, but argued that this methodology was primarily deductive rather than experimental.

Epistemological conception. Science is a special way of knowing and justifying knowledge claims; in other words it has a special *epistemology*. There is a unique kind of warrant supporting scientific claims so that what distinguishes the scientist is how and why she believes particular claims. Evidence is seen as crucial to justifying scientific claims and scientific practice is, in turn, viewed as possessing privileged ways of knowing and justifying knowledge. More extreme versions of this conception maintain that *only* science truly produces knowledge, a point of contention that sometimes flares up in 'science wars' between some natural scientists and some humanists and social scientists. In contrast, Emil Durkheim maintained that scientific and ordinary knowledge differ only as a matter of degree. So their analysis and justification would be similar, though scientific knowledge is often much more highly refined.

Content conception. Science has a particular content (not a special methodology or epistemology, but a special ontology[1] so to speak); that is to say, a particular set of propositions about nature reflected in disciplines such as physics, chemistry, biology, geography and so forth. This emphasis on special content tends to promote a patchwork view of science, meaning there is nothing in particular tying individual scientific disciplines together. In contrast, conceptions like the universal-laws, methodological and epistemological conceptions tend to promote a unified picture of science in that all scientific disciplines either share the same goal, methodology or epistemology.

Rigour conception. Science is associated with any procedure characterized by rigour, precision or objectivity. Under this conception engineering, crime-scene investigation, even military planning and theology may be viewed as scientific in the absence of any further distinguishing criteria.

Approval conception. Science is a label of approval designed to set apart what we wish to privilege. In its extreme form, this conception views scientific knowledge as purely socially constructed and ultimately no different from any other social phenomena except that we assign it special status.

These various conceptions are neither mutually exclusive nor completely overlapping, and each characterization picks out some feature of the scientific enterprise deemed important. The activity, content and approval conceptions – the latter in its less extreme forms – can be understood as connected to many of the other conceptions. For instance, the development and refinement of everyday practices into highly standardized methodologies perhaps connects the activity and methodological conceptions. Rationalists – those who believe that knowledge can be gained through reason alone – have tended to emphasize a theoretical conception of science while empiricists – those believing that most if not all knowledge is gained through the senses – have tended to emphasize a methodological conception, and both would understand rigour as necessary to the pursuit of science, but not as sufficient for characterizing science. Science's approval within a culture might be because of the rigour, methodologies and epistemologies involved.[2] The universal-laws conception focuses more on what appears to be an important aspiration or goal of the scientific enterprise, while the theoretical, methodological and epistemological conceptions focus more on the way the scientific enterprise is carried out (i.e., its practices). So these

Table 1.1 Eight Conceptions of Science.

Activity	mode of human activity
Theoretical	body of conceptual and theoretical knowledge
Universal Laws	search for universal, law-like statements
Methodological	a methodology
Epistemological	an epistemology
Content	a particular content
Rigour	characterized by rigour, precision or objectivity
Approval	a label of approval

latter three conceptions can be seen as appropriate means to pursuing the goal of attaining universal laws.

What all of these conceptions have in common is that they are various expressions of the need to seek out explanations, patterns or principles capable of bringing order, unity and meaning to our experience of the world around us. However, I should emphasize that there is nothing like a consensus on which of these eight conceptions represents the 'correct' view of science, or even on which conceptions should be grouped together. Most often, people flop around from one conception to another in their discussions of 'What is science?' without realizing it.

Furthermore, there is no consensus on whether all eight conceptions apply equally, if they apply at all, to the natural sciences as well as the social sciences. Or whether some are more applicable to natural sciences while others are more applicable to the social sciences, or whether the social sciences can even be viewed as conforming to any conception of 'science', whatever we mean by that term. Physics, chemistry and biology are taken to be paradigmatic natural sciences, while psychology, economics and sociology are taken to be paradigmatic social sciences. Some argue that social sciences should be similar in method to the natural sciences (e.g., Hempel 1965; Comte 1974), hence, to the extent that one (or more) of these eight conceptions characterizes natural sciences, it also characterizes social sciences. Others argue that 'the obsession with transforming social studies into natural sciences obscures, distorts, and suppresses the legitimacy of issues vital for theorizing about political and social life' (Bernstein 1976: 59), so if one (or more) of these conceptions of science is applicable to the social sciences, that conception must be understood quite differently as it applies to the latter sciences.

Suppose that we were to adopt a theoretical conception – science is a theoretical body of knowledge. If one thinks of physics or biology, it is immediately clear that these disciplines possess comprehensive, overarching bodies of theory and perspectives covering their various domains. By the lights of a theoretical conception, these disciplines surely count as sciences. In contrast, many commentators have noted how striking it is that, as compared with such natural sciences, there is very little in the way of widely endorsed systematic theory in psychology and other behavioural sciences (e.g., Taylor 1985b; Slife and Williams 1995; Richardson, Fowers and Guignon 1999). Perhaps the closest thing to such systematic accounts are familiar and influential personality theories like Freud's and its many successors, and particular broad orientations toward human behaviour such as behaviourism, existentialism and cognitive psychology. Still, the behavioural sciences exhibit enormous theoretical fragmentation. Should we judge these disciplines as sciences according to a theoretical conception?

The situation is equally difficult if we adopt a methodological conception – science is distinguished by a particular methodology. Natural sciences like physics and biology exhibit a high degree of methodological unity (or at least such unity is discernible without too much difficulty). They score well under a methodological conception, but what of the behavioural sciences? The various disciplinary branches of the latter are methodologically fragmented. Not only that, but even within the major disciplinary branches the situation resembles hundreds of tiny, relatively isolated islands of theory and/or research. Inquiry within them is being pursued independently, often with quite different methodologies, and with no obvious prospect of them ever being integrated into any coherent picture (see Koch 1981; Staats 1991; Yanchar and Slife 1997). Do the behavioural sciences qualify as science under a methodological conception?

Such debates as these are further examples of quintessential philosophical questions addressed to the social sciences. Indeed, whether the social sciences are of a piece with the natural sciences or are different in kind, along with the normative question whether the social sciences *ought* to be of a kind with the natural sciences, will be key concerns raised in these pages. By the time you reach the end of this book, you should be in a position to think through these questions and at least formulate some tentative answers.

2. Some standard conceptions of theories

Usually when one thinks about science, the idea of theories comes quickly to mind. Indeed, the theoretical conception of science emphasizes just this idea, namely that scientific knowledge is somehow embodied within theories. But what is a theory? This is another question that is almost purely philosophical in nature and for which, again, there is precious little consensus outside the intuition that theories are systematic bodies of knowledge.

2.1. Logical positivist or received view

One conception of theories, most popular in the first half of the twentieth century, is known as *the positivist*[3] or *received view*. The core idea is that theories are bodies of statements anchored by universal, context-free laws (universal-laws conception). The meaning of a theory is contained in the sentences constituting the theory similar to the way the meaning of a book is contained in the sentences constituting it. However, logical positivists emphasized the form such statements should take – that laws and other scientific statements should be formulated in a precise language (e.g., some form of logic). The laws can be thought of as axioms for an axiomatic system that could then be connected to other statements through logical relationships (usually deductive, but sometimes inductive). So a theory, on this view, is really some kind of axiomatic, logically coherent system of statements (sometimes called propositions).

Additionally, there are bridging statements or coordinating definitions connecting the formal statements of the theory with empirical consequences. This would allow experimental tests of the theoretical statements. Under this positivist conception, theories are viewed as having a logical structure with empirical implications. Hence, theories, were taken to be formal descriptions of facts, observable relationships among facts, and generalizations about facts and their relations. Explanations of observed phenomena were to be framed in terms of laws (see Chapter 15) and, in turn, laws were thought to be subsumed under more general laws. The most fundamental level of theory – usually taken to be physics – ideally would consist of a small number of general laws from which all other laws and phenomena could be derived.

Logical positivism, the influential philosophical movement behind this conception of theories, is more an epistemology than anything else and its view of theories reflects that emphasis. The basic underlying 'scientific epistemology' is very similar to what Francis Bacon (1561–1626) advocated: science starts by making particular observations, moves to empirical generalizations of these observations uncovering enduring patterns. These observations and generalizations are all formulated using a vocabulary of observational terms describing the behaviour of the phenomena under investigation. Later a theoretical vocabulary is introduced by definition and universal laws or generalizations are formulated in some formal language. The laws are supposed to ultimately provide an explanation for the observed phenomena and are linked to the observational statements through bridging statements. This epistemology is taken to parallel the more fundamental process of language learning: humans are viewed as first acquiring an observational vocabulary, which they extend by pointing to similar things and naming them, then later acquire a theoretical vocabulary. This is very much a 'bottom up' approach to knowledge.

As formalistic as it sounds, logical positivism had enormous appeal in that it seemed to offer pristine, ahistorical standards for knowledge, a kind of Archimedean point for discriminating truth from error or illusion. It appeared to offer certainty and the kind of bias-free knowledge we have come to expect from the scientific enterprise. However, as we will see over the course of the book, there are a number of problems with these appealing ideals.

This tradition collapsed for well-known reasons (Kuhn 1996; Miller 1987; Suppe 1977): (1) The logical vocabulary used in these positivist analyses was too limited to accurately capture the structure of scientific theories.[4] Furthermore, the emphasis on the form statements about the world take was almost completely disconnected from actual scientific practices. (2) The variety of rules of inference[5] worked out in such analyses could neither endorse the inferences scientists make nor accurately reconstruct those inferences. (3) The idealizations employed in such analyses were far too simple to reflect the subtlety of scientific theory and practice. (4) The assumption in such analyses that objective data existed from which theories and their structures, methods of confirmation and modes of explanation could be in some sense read off from the data seriously underestimated the subtle interrelationships among theory, experiment, fact and interpretation (we will see examples of this throughout the book).

2.2. Semantic view

An alternative view of theories, known as the *semantic view*, is that they are collections or families of models, where the emphasis is not on the form of statements, but rather on the meaning or content of the models. This view of scientific theories seeks, at least to some degree, to more closely pattern itself after the practice of scientists. There is no distinction between theory and model, so, in contrast to the received view, the meaning of a theory is to be found in the family of models rather than any sentences used to describe the models. In the most popular versions of the semantic view, theories are identified with a set of models such that they may be described in a variety of ways. One can say that a theory is a class of models, mathematical or physical objects say, but even the latter are usually taken to be amenable to formulation as a mathematical system. For example, under the received view, Newton's equation of motion, $F = ma$, is considered to be a universal law of motion, one we now know is false. In contrast, on the semantic view, this equation is an abstract model that can be used to construct concrete mathematical models of real-world systems such as cannon balls shot from a cannon. Newton's equation, along with his other laws of motion, are viewed as principles for model construction, rather than laws. The models of a theory, then, might be related to each other in some logical sense, or related in some weaker sense such as resemblance (the precise nature of this relationship is still very much an open question).

Models, and therefore theories, are not true of the world. Rather, they are similar[6] to real-world systems in specified respects and to limited degrees of accuracy. Therefore, models do not aim to describe all aspects of the phenomena within some intended domain. Rather, the most important aspects of the phenomena are abstracted for analysis and description. It is assumed that these are the crucial features and that all other aspects of the phenomena have negligible influence on these crucial features. So there is a very strong idealization assumption at work in the semantic approach. A theory, then, is adequate to the phenomena just in so far as it adequately characterizes the behaviour of these phenomena in terms of the identified crucial features when the phenomena are sufficiently isolated to behave as the theory predicts. The empirical parts of models are identified as candidates for representing observable phenomena. Hence, there is still a distinction between theoretical and empirical structures (or between theoretical and observational vocabularies if one wants to stay close to the linguistic analyses of logical positivism). Under the semantic conception, observed regularities are related to or embedded within (in more or less sophisticated ways) the models of relevant theories. When this can be successfully achieved, then the models are said to apply to those phenomena observed in the world, and we can explain and predict the phenomena covered by the models.

Of course, there are various questions that can be raised regarding the nature and validity of the idealizing assumptions that go into the formulations of the models. How does one go about identifying and distinguishing crucial from insignificant features? One of the ways this is accomplished is through controlled experiment, seeking to establish which features have large effects on a system's behaviour and which ones have little or none. The idealization assumptions involve throwing out the 'insignificant features', but are they really negligible in every context?[7] There are also problems clarifying what auxiliary assumptions must be brought in to achieve empirical adequacy and how these additional assumptions are to be justified.

2.3. Kuhn's view

A third influential conception of theories derives from Kuhn's (1996) analysis of science and is radically different from the previous views. He articulated a conception of scientific practice that has been very influential among philosophers and historians of science, and which played an important role in the downfall of the received view of theories. For instance, one of the points Kuhn emphasized was that natural-science inquiry was much more creative than the kind of wooden, algorithmic approach of logical positivism could take into account.

Kuhn makes a basic distinction between normal and revolutionary science. Normal science amounts to problem solving done under the direction of a fixed, accepted *paradigm*.[8] One way in which Kuhn characterizes a paradigm is as 'universally recognized scientific achievements that for a time provide model problems and solutions to a community of practitioners' (Kuhn 1996: x). In Kuhn's storyline, a particular scientific discipline starts out in a pre-paradigmatic state, where there is little or no agreement about the subject matter, what counts as evidence, what the key problems and exemplars are. Eventually, the discipline coalesces around a paradigm, a dominant set of achievements or exemplars. These exemplars represent techniques and strategies for problem solving and an organized collection of such exemplars may be taken as representing a theory. But such a theory should not be equated with a paradigm (roughly speaking, theories are constructed within paradigms). The exemplars provide the paradigm for normal-science problem solving (perhaps through explicit rules, tacit rules or no rules at all) and scientific theories of a given discipline are dependent on the reigning paradigm in that discipline. While a theory may represent some amount of systematic order, it need not necessarily have an axiomatic or logical structure (indeed Kuhn doubted that scientific theories ultimately were such structures).

The business of normal science is to make the dominant paradigm more determinate and precise as well as to apply it to new problems. Revolutionary science, in contrast, has to do with the proposal of a new paradigm for some branch of science where, seemingly, everything is up for grabs. The reigning (but perhaps failing) paradigm and the new paradigm are 'incommensurable' in Kuhn's most extreme description. The meaning of incommensurable here is that there is no basis for comparing the two paradigms because there are no concepts, knowledge, methods or even data that are shared between the two paradigms. So once scientists adopt the new paradigm, there might not be any overlap with the predecessor paradigm – the two would be as different as apples and oranges from each other. Therefore, Kuhn, in his more radical moments, sometimes maintained that scientific knowledge was not cumulative across scientific revolutions (e.g., Kuhn 1996: 2–3, 92–96).

Theory development and theory change, on this view, are dependent on paradigms, but this view has been strongly questioned as involving: (1) relativism (no grounded or independent standards by which to judge when an old paradigm should be abandoned in favour of a new one), (2) incommensurability (a shift in paradigms introduces a corresponding shift in the meaning of theoretical terms such that there may be very little if any relationship between the old and new meanings) and (3) 'irrationalism' (no criteria exist to judge whether a shift in paradigms represents progress, regress or is merely different). These three points have left a number of people with the impression that irrationality lies at the very heart of science. However, Kuhn in his more reasonable moments appears to take back or undermine the kinds of relativism and irrationalism he sometimes espoused in his more radical moments.

There is no consensus among philosophers of science about these or any other conception of theories. The logical positivist and Kuhnian views have been the most influential in the social sciences. Considering these three conceptions of theories, however, we face yet another philosophical question. The natural sciences form the background for these analyses of theories, but do any of them genuinely apply to the social sciences? Is theorizing in the social sciences the same kind of activity as in the natural sciences? Throughout the book we will see indications that there are important differences between theorizing in the natural and social sciences, but ought there to be such differences? One of the goals of this text is to help you judge what answers you should give to these questions.

3. Social sciences as pre-paradigmatic

One feature of Kuhn's picture of science that has been applied to the social sciences is his concept of paradigm mentioned above. Kuhn took pre-paradigmatic sciences to be ones where no reigning paradigm existed. There would be no theoretical and methodological coherence to such disciplines, but, rather, a kind of 'every scientist for themself' mentality, if you will, where there are several isolated islands of theory and methodology, little agreement on what the key problems are, as well as an unfocused view of the objects of inquiry. His description of pre-paradigmatic sciences looks very much like the description of behavioural sciences we encountered earlier and, indeed, Kuhn thought of these as well as all of the social sciences as still in a pre-paradigmatic stage (Kuhn 2000; see Chapter 16, sec. 2).

This view of the social sciences suggests to many that the reason the social sciences still lack such coherence is due to their being relatively young compared to the natural sciences. After all, so the idea goes, it took physics centuries to achieve something like its first paradigm. How can the social sciences be expected to achieve paradigmatic status so soon after their beginnings?

There are at least two problems with this line of thinking. First, if, as many believe, the social sciences find their beginnings in the systematic thought of Hobbes, then it is arguable that many of the social-science disciplines are centuries old. Perhaps the social sciences have not received as much sustained effort as the natural sciences over the same time period, but there were plenty of people engaged in attempts to study and quantify human behaviour. In 1738 Daniel Bernoulli introduced the concept of utility (Chapter 10, sec. 1) to describe people's preferences, Pierre-Simon Laplace discussed the application of probabilities to social phenomena in the 1800s, and in the 1830s Adolphe Quetelet studied the existence of patterns in observed data ranging from the frequency of different methods for committing murder to the chest size of Scottish men (he actually coined the term 'social physics'). So it is not the case that the study of social phenomena is relatively new. Second, very recent scientific disciplines in the natural sciences like microbiology have achieved paradigmatic status, on Kuhn's analysis, within decades, not centuries. So the age of a discipline is neither a necessary nor sufficient condition for it to have failed to produce a paradigm.

One can argue that additional reasons for not achieving paradigmatic status might be: (1) the social sciences have received far less sustained effort relative to the natural sciences or (2) the social sciences are vastly more complex than any natural science. If these are the crucial factors – and many have pointed to them as explanations for why the social sciences are still pre-paradigmatic – then the only crucial differences between the natural and social sciences are that the latter are more complex than the former and/or the latter have received much less attention than the former. As far as the complexity defence is concerned, it is not clear at all that this has any bearing on the problems of the social sciences. After all, so the response goes, science has made clear progress in all other extremely complex phenomena (e.g., biology and ecology), so why should any of the social sciences be any different if complexity were the only issue? Sheer complexity plus lack of enough time or sustained effort together might explain the pre-paradigmatic nature of the social sciences, but as we have just seen, much time and effort have been put into the social sciences.

However these arguments play out, notice they assume that differences between natural and social inquiry are matters of degree, not matters of kind. But there may be a much more significant reason why the social sciences look so pre-paradigmatic with respect to the natural sciences. As suggested in the next section, the social sciences may be crucially different from the natural sciences. If the subjects of study in the social sciences are significantly different, then the strict application of natural-science methods to social-science inquiry would likely result in just the kind of theoretically and methodologically fractured picture we see in many of the social sciences. Moreover, as indicated earlier, trying to fit the social sciences into a natural science mould is likely to maintain or even exacerbate the very problems of the human condition we are trying to understand and treat.

There are two further issues raising questions about this paradigmatic analysis of the social sciences. First, are paradigms really the appropriate way to conceive of scientific activity? As Kuhn conceived them, paradigms are focused with a great deal of uniformity; and, in his more radical moments, thought to have nothing in common between predecessor and successor paradigms within the same discipline (i.e., there supposedly would be no knowledge from a predecessor paradigm that would be carried forward into a successor paradigm). But this is too wooden a picture of paradigms, as Kuhn himself admits in his less radical moments (e.g., Kuhn 1996: 129–30, 169). Can a more relaxed conception of paradigms do the work Kuhn expects or does the notion then become too elastic to make useful distinctions?

Second, Kuhn's analysis of paradigms takes place wholly within the natural sciences and is illustrated by natural-science examples. To simply apply the same form of analysis to the social sciences looks to prejudge the issue as to whether the natural and social sciences are similar enough to each other. This happens to be Kuhn's (2000) view (and we will examine it in Chapter 16), but there is substantial controversy here, and it is far from clear that the social sciences should be conceived along these lines. Calling the social sciences pre-paradigmatic, for instance, suggests that the social sciences will undergo the same kind of transformation as the natural sciences at some point. But is there any reason to expect this? Not unless we have already established that the social sciences really are fundamentally the same as the natural sciences. Because to expect social sciences to form paradigms like natural sciences is to assume there is nothing significantly different between these sciences rendering the notion of paradigm irrelevant or problematic when applied to social inquiry.

4. Empirical versus interpretive approaches to understanding

In an insightful essay, entitled 'Peaceful Coexistence in Psychology', Charles Taylor (1985a: 117–38) distinguishes between two broad approaches to understanding in psychology that are applicable to the social sciences in general. The first approach focuses on brute data and Taylor calls its practitioners 'correlators'. This approach is driven by the aim of univocal (admitting of only one meaning) intersubjective agreement and has three key components: (1) reliance on 'brute' data, that is, data that are available to the scientist without the need of any interpretation (put differently, the experiments carried out to produce the data must be replicable by anyone and not just those who hold a particular viewpoint), (2) reliance on operations carried out on the data that are also interpretation-free or admit of only one meaning ('univocal operations') and (3) physicalism, that is, physical parameters and variables are the appropriate candidates for brute data (because physical parameters and variables are thought to be univocal). Evaluative judgements, that depend on someone's viewpoint or interpretation, are never beyond interpretive dispute and cannot meet the first two criteria. Hence, they cannot serve as appropriate scientific data on this approach. Correlators generally are searching for universal laws of human behaviour, follow particular methodologies and hold a particular epistemology (as we will see later).

Data, here, serve a dual role. First, data constitute the domain of observed phenomena for which theories are constructed. These theories are taken to provide explanations for these phenomena and to offer predictions for what kinds of phenomena to expect. Second, data provide the evidence that either confirm or undermine our theories. So data serve both as the targets of scientific theorizing and as evidence for the success or failure of theories. If data admitted of more than one meaning, they most likely could not play this dual role in any way where we could draw principled distinctions between success and failure of our theories, clearly interpret what our theories mean, and so forth. If the data of the social realm admit multiple meanings, then there is no one fixed, stable meaning. Without this kind of stable meaning, how would it be possible to formulate theories about such phenomenon and then test whether the theoretical explanations and predictions were accurate if there are shifts in or disagreements about meanings?

A simple example of a correlators approach proceeds as follows. A questionnaire is developed where various attitudes are objectified as statements of beliefs to which a person assents or dissents (e.g., standardized course-evaluation surveys). This can be done by giving the respondent a selection of responses ranging from 'strongly agree' to 'strongly disagree'. These responses are assigned different values or weights based on a scale that must be validated for the attitudes in question (e.g., regarding the course they have just completed). A statistical analysis can then be applied to show the degree of correlations between respondents' overt expressions of attitudes as identified through objectified propositions and desired outcomes (e.g., their expected grade in the course). The responses to such questionnaires are treated as brute data just like someone's raising their hand, while the statistical methods of data analysis uncovering the correlations are supposed to be univocal data operations. No interpretation is seemingly needed.

Taylor contrasts correlators with what he calls 'interpreters'. The latter recognize that human beings are self-interpreting beings – about which I will have more to say – and that the sources of our actions are usually intimately tied to our feelings, what we take to be significant, the way we see the world, and so on. In other words, very little if any social-science data generated by human action is interpretation-free, hence the need for an interpretive approach in social-science inquiry. As Taylor puts it, 'acts and feelings . . . are partly characterized in terms of the thoughts, images, intentions, and ways of seeing of the people considered' (Taylor 1985a: 120).

As Taylor characterizes them, correlators and interpreters are caricatures or extremes for kinds or modes of social-science research (see Chapter 3). Very few investigators actually fit these characterizations, but they prove useful for uncovering possible differences between natural and social sciences. For example, how do we identify an action? As correlators, we would characterize actions by their overt, observable features and look for regularities. However, actions are identified in virtue of purposes and intentions. If you offer me a box of chocolates, it makes a difference to the act of my reaching my hand out if I am doing so to select a chocolate or if I am tying to stop the box from falling. A more difficult example would be trying to decide, without understanding her vision of things and sense of what she is doing, if a person is simply attempting to save face or if she is genuinely expressing indignation.

The situation is similar for feelings. Take shame as an example. A feeling of shame occurs when a person has done something that is dishonourable or demeaning in some way that is connected both with her sense of herself as well as her sense of the traditions and expectations of her society. Her understanding and appraisal of this feeling of shame is due to the meaning things have for her, involving her values and ideals, a moral vision she has of herself, and what she takes to be the important concerns for her as well as her current understandings of her social surroundings and the subtle influences of these surroundings, many of which are largely unnoticed by her. So shame is not merely a matter of efficient causation.[9] A person's meanings and way she sees things as well as the social surroundings act as formal causes.[10] Without these formal causes, the situation or act would not be deemed shameful by her.

This means that the data of psychology – for example, acts and feelings – as well as other social sciences are indelibly interpretive because they are constituted by meanings, both those of the individual persons as well as those of their societies. So the correlator's first requirement is violated because the data can never be brute, that is interpretation-free – the interpretations and feelings of people constitute their actions. According to Taylor, we cannot understand what a person is doing apart from her feelings and intentions. And without brute data, there can be no interpretation-free data operations, procedures or methods, so the second requirement characterizing the correlator's approach looks to be of limited applicability at best. Furthermore, physical variables, like quantifying overt acts, will not do as candidates for brute data if there are no brute data, so the correlator's third requirement looks problematic as well.

Throughout modern times critics and thoughtful observers of social science have thought that the correlator's approach was a rather distant, detached way to study the intimate, human realities of life. The worry is constantly raised that this natural-science approach actually distorts rather than clarifies everyday life and that interpretation is crucial to understanding human and social behaviour (see Chapter 2). Along these lines, a different way of seeing the difference between correlators and interpreters comes out in thinking about the idea of engaged agency. Taylor (1993) discusses two different conceptions of being engaged, or world-shaping. The first conception is characterized by the way efficient causes impinge upon us due to the kinds of bodies we have.

Suppose I am lecturing in a classroom. At this moment I cannot see the wall behind me because the light refracted off its surface cannot reach my eyes. My physical disposition and the physical properties of light are currently juxtaposed such that my channels of efficient causation shape my perception and, hence, my world and my engagement with it. Those sitting in the audience, by contrast, are in a position to see the wall behind me. In this sense the dispositions of our bodies are shaping our perceptions of this room differently. Call this a *weak sense* of embodiment or world-shaping, where the characteristic feature is how my surroundings are related to my body in terms of efficient causation (e.g., the transmission and reception of photons).

The second conception of engagement, or world-shaping – I will refer to it as the *strong sense* – has at least three aspects according to Taylor. First, to say that we are engaged in this strong sense means that understanding such an experience necessarily draws upon concepts only making sense against the background of the particular kind of bodies we have. Even to understand what it is for something to 'lie to hand' or be 'out of reach' requires being an agent with our bodily capacities. This is to say, that the very nature of experiencing things in the world as human beings is largely constituted by our particular *form of embodiment* and not in the main by efficient causal relations. Seeing a small child crying over the loss of a favourite toy certainly makes use of efficient causation in the sense that photons refracting off the child reach my retinas and sound waves from the child's crying reach membranes in my ear. However to interpret what has happened to the child and its significance for her, as well as to know how to comfort her in this situation, derives from my embodied experience as a person feeling what is happening to her. Furthermore in order to comfort the child requires my embodiment with the particular capacities of a human being (e.g., warm hug, soft and soothing speech, confident and encouraging manner).

There are other aspects of engagement, notably the ways a person's world is shaped by her form of life – her everyday practices and beliefs. For example, if someone views the world as a playground for her desires, she is going to act differently than if she sees the world as a collection of traditions, meanings and opportunities from which she can learn and grow. Also, a person's history – family upbringing, community customs and traditions, contingent events in life – affects how she sees the world and engages in action. These features mediate or shape our actions; but as well, our actions and interpretations of these features shape them in turn. In these senses, strong world-shaping pictures our engagement with the world around us as up close and intimate. By contrast, weak world-shaping pictures us as disengaged from the world, observing and acting at a distance.

These three ways in which our world is shaped, Taylor argues, are qualitatively different from the world conceived of as shaped merely by efficient causation. The shaping due to a form of life or history is more akin to formal rather than efficient causation. The kind of body I have, the kind of history I find myself in, the form of life I practice, all three provide the context from which my actions as a person are intelligible because they condition the kinds of self-interpretations I have. In contrast, if it makes any sense to talk this way, the world of an electron is shaped purely by its efficient causal interactions with its surroundings (e.g., the presence or absence of electromagnetic fields). My body, my history and my form of life supply meanings for me and shape the kinds of involvements and concerns I have. There is nothing analogous to this in the case of the electron interacting with its environment. It has no meanings or self-interpretations derived from bodily experience, social history and way of life.

All actions take place within and are made intelligible by some background without which actions cannot be the kinds of things they are. Under the correlators' approach, this background amounts to only the physical–biological world and the efficient-causal structures taken to constitute this world. Under the interpreters' approach, the background for actions is not only the physical–biological world but also the intentions, beliefs, feelings and viewpoints of the actor as well as her cultural–historical background.

I take it that this is what is supposed to constitute the crucial difference between the subject matter of social sciences – people and their institutions – and the subject matter of natural sciences. The subjects of social-science inquiry 'talk back', 'change their minds' as it were, and 'view the world' in different ways at different times which have no correspondence with the objects of natural-science inquiry. If this is right, then it looks as if studying humans using only empirical and formal methods – like correlators – means treating them as connected with their surroundings through efficient causation of the same order as we see with rocks, amoebas and computers, but perhaps only in a more complex way.[11] Interpreters argue their approach can take fuller account of the many other ways in which we are connected with our environment, particularly the social and political, by explicitly taking into consideration how people see their various situations.

Generally, correlators maintain that their approach offers the only hope for achieving the kind of intersubjective certainty in the social sciences that has thought to have been obtained in natural science.[12] As such it is recognized that actions and feelings are not amenable to study under this approach, so alternative levels of analysis are sought – information input, cognitive processing, output – that are, hopefully, physically quantifiable so as to proceed with social-science inquiry in a mode as close to that of the natural sciences as possible. This would typically be done by finding correlations between appropriately identified quantified variables.

Interpreters, on the other hand, will insist that the self-interpretations of people are crucial to understanding human activity and that the truly scientific approach to this problem is to strive for the degree of intersubjective certainty that is appropriate for the subject of study rather than deciding in advance that a model for inquiry based on the natural sciences is the only appropriate way to conduct social-science research. In other words, interpreters recommend a different conception of science than that presupposed by correlators.[13]

These two approaches look to be quite at odds with each other, particularly since correlators demand that nothing be a matter of interpretation (is this not just another interpretation offered in place of the others?). But then it would be impossible to say what the correlations discovered under this approach mean or even what the true nature of the correlations are. On the other hand, Taylor argues that room for correlators can be made within the approach of the interpreters based on different subdisciplines within psychology each having differing aims.

He begins with a rough typology of psychological research. The first category is the study of *infrastructure* – the necessary physiological conditions for the exercise of human capacities. Here, the correlator's approach seems largely unproblematic in that the objective is to study the relationship, say, between various physically defined variables (e.g., state of body chemistry) and psychological states (e.g., feeling of hunger). The second category is the study of *competencies* – the structure of these capacities and their development. Here, too, there is room for some empirical measures (e.g., intelligence tests or quantification of kinds and levels of operations children are able to perform at different stages of development). The third category is the study of *performance* – the motivated activity of exercising capacities for some purpose. Here, we must go beyond simply studying infrastructure and competency, but rather focus on the self-understandings of people. Hence, the entrance of interpretive approaches as the main avenues of inquiry since the subject matter of this category does not fit the assumptions of the correlator's approach.

Taylor's proposal, then, is that infrastructure studies are correlational, performance studies interpretational, and competency studies combine the two in the sense that the structures under investigation can be formalized and empirically investigated to a large degree but may also involve interpretation at various points (though Taylor is largely silent on how this interaction between correlators and interpreters would take place). This proposal, and the accompanying typology, is not to be understood as the final word or as setting firm boundaries; rather, this is as much a diagnosis of the correlator's strengths and weaknesses relative to the types of phenomena marked out by the three domains, principally the infrastructure and performance domains, as it is a proposal for real cooperation.[14]

5. Taking stock

In the previous section, we reached what is probably the major question in the philosophy of social science: namely, are the differences in subject matter treated by natural and social science a matter of degree (human beings and social structures are merely more complex than electrons and amoebas), or a matter of kind (self-interpretations, meanings, values, involvements and concerns are qualitatively different from quantifiable attributes like mass, charge and chemical ratios). These differences are palpable and debates about them very much alive. Taylor's proposal represents a kind of accommodationist approach, but others would reject this and advocate a strictly correlator's or interpreter's approach. Part of the purpose of this book is to help you to evaluate the nature of the social sciences and formulate some conclusions about these differences.

Before we go on to look at some historical background in the next chapter, I would like to point out that these debates about the differences between natural and social science are not just abstract, academic debates. We will see later that these debates really matter to the outcomes of social-science research, sometimes in ways that are deeply disturbing.

For further study

1. Which conceptions of science seem to go naturally together? Which ones, if any, appear to be inconsistent with others? Why?

2. Compare and contrast any two of the three conceptions of theories discussed in sec. 2.

3. Which of the three conceptions of theories seems best suited to social inquiry? Why?

4. Explain the differences between weak and strong world-shaping. Give some examples of each.

5. What do you take to be the strongest reason in favour of the natural and social sciences being similar? What do you think is the strongest reason against this similarity? Which reason do you consider more convincing and why?

Recommended reading

R. Giere, 'Theories of Science', in *Science without Laws* (Chicago: University of Chicago Press, 1999), pp. 22–61.

T. Kuhn, *The Structure of Scientific Revolutions* (Chicago: University of Chicago Press, 3rd edn, 1996).

C. Taylor, 'Peaceful Coexistence in Psychology', in *Philosophical Papers*, vol. 1: *Human Agency and Language* (Cambridge: Cambridge University Press, 1985a), pp. 117–38.

—'Engaged Agency and Background in Heidegger', in C. Guignon (ed.), *The Cambridge Companion to Heidegger* (Cambridge: Cambridge University Press, 1993), pp. 317–36.

Historical and Philosophical Roots of the Social Sciences

2

Chapter Outline

As with almost any topic discussed in this book, one could start with Plato and Aristotle as two of the earliest systematic thinkers on politics, society and human behaviour. Their thinking and analysis of such social phenomena were very much focused on what makes for the best society and had a clear ethical thrust. Beginning with the early modern period, there is a trend away from this kind of ethically charged social analysis and towards the conditions for society and for human action. With this trend, the notion of the good or best society drops from explicit view and is replaced by the causes and conditions underlying social reality.

The goal of this chapter is to present a brief history of the roots and development of social science. Any presentation such as this must necessarily be highly selective, but there are particular themes I want to emphasize that will recur throughout the book. Giving even a brief historical overview is helpful for setting the stage and providing a feel for how things have come to be in the social sciences. For the most part, the figures I present are representative of the various developments in the social sciences, but each in his own way is also a seminal contributor to these disciplines.

1. Thomas Hobbes

The early modern scientist and philosopher[1] Thomas Hobbes (1588–1679) is considered by many to be the founder of modern political science and also holds some claim to being the founder of the social sciences. He had a deep admiration for and some involvement in the emerging scientific methods of what we now think of as modern natural science, though not so much the experimental methods. Rather, Hobbes was enamoured of deductive methods, those seeking to deduce the workings of things from some basic first principles in combination with true definitions of the basic elements. The model for this deductive approach to science was geometry – for example, starting with some fundamental axioms, one applies deductive logic to build up the entire system of Euclidean geometry. Though this deductive approach was to go out of favour shortly after Hobbes' time (and return in a new guise in early twentieth-century philosophy of science), it clearly informs his philosophical thought about human and social reality. For example, though probably not an atheist, Hobbes insisted on categories related to material/physical realities (largely matter and motion) in his analyses of human nature, political thought and morality. His political and social theorizing has a deductive structure beginning with definitions of human perception and reasoning, moving to a picture of human motivation and action and resulting in a deduction of the possible forms of political relations as well as their relative desirability. Through this deductive method, Hobbes refined what have become key concepts for the social sciences such as society, the state, citizenship and power. Furthermore, he attempted to define these concepts in a way that would be independent of any particular traditions or contexts.[2]

This mechanical–deductive presentation of Hobbes' views may not necessarily mean he held a mechanistic view of human nature, that is, that human nature is somehow only the product of more rudimentary physiological and psychological mechanisms. There are points in Hobbes' writings suggestive of human beings as mechanical objects, programmed as it were to strictly pursue self-interest (see below) so that the only incentives capable of modifying human behaviour are pleasure and pain. On the other hand, some hold these passages to be mostly metaphorical, particularly given that the sciences necessary to underlie these mechanical pictures were either non-existent or far too underdeveloped to secure a literal picture of the inner workings of human beings. There are passages in Hobbes, however, where he seems to think that he has provided the foundation for developing just these kinds of sciences and that it was possibly just a matter of proving more theorems to connect his matter-in-motion picture of matter with psychological motivation and perception.[3]

Whatever one thinks about Hobbes' ultimate view of human nature, he maintains that science is the most reliable means of forming beliefs; contrasting strongly with less reliable means of forming beliefs, human judgement in particular. Hobbes believed science – 'the knowledge of consequences' (1994: ch. V) – offered reliable knowledge about future outcomes where human judgement often failed. Thus, he sought to set his political theory on a firm, scientific basis and to work out the deductive consequences. This effort is largely responsible for the attribution to Hobbes of a leading role as the founder of modern social sciences and political science in particular.

Unfortunately, his view of science, based as it was on crude mechanistic principles and deduction, was not even very plausible in his own day, much less very influential on the development of modern natural science. Part of Hobbes' picture of social–political interaction is a crude commitment to individualism; that is, political interactions must be analysed in terms of the actions of individuals and then deducing the consequences of these latter individual actions and interactions. Although this kind of individualistic picture of social and political reality re-emerged later (see sec. 3 below), Hobbes failed to reach the level of 'scientific certainty' in his theorizing, though his determination to create chains of logical reasoning for his theoretical conclusions would serve as an influential model for later developments in the social sciences (and show up in logical positivist analyses of science described in Chapter 1, sec. 2.1).

Another Hobbesian legacy for the social sciences – and another reason many cite Hobbes as an important founder of modern social science – is a perceived emphasis on self-interested rational choice in Hobbes' account of human motivation. Although self-interest and rational choice have played important roles in such areas as political science, economics and game theory (see Chapters 10, 11 and 12), attributing this emphasis to Hobbes is a controversial matter of interpretation. In favour of the self-interested, rationalistic interpretations, Hobbes is sometimes given to making point-blank claims about the self-interest of human beings and their deploying of reason to avoid death and advance themselves (e.g., 1998: 3–7). Against these kinds of interpretations of Hobbes are two factors. First, the purely self-interested picture of agents presents a false view of human nature. We often engage in self-sacrifice and other actions that go against self-interest, and Hobbes seems perfectly aware of these human tendencies, showing no surprise that we often do things that are not motivated by self-interest.[4] Second, Hobbes often invokes motives that go beyond or against self-interest, such as pity and honour, and maintains that we often have difficulty judging what our interests really are. In other words, he has a much more sophisticated view of human action than the purely self-interested accounts make him out to have. Whatever the outcome of the interpretive dispute regarding Hobbes' thought on self-interest and rational choice, interpretations emphasizing self-interested agents have inspired the development of several lines of inquiry within a number of social sciences as we will see.

2. Auguste Comte and Wilhelm Dilthey

Although other figures contributed significantly to the development of social science after Hobbes,[5] Auguste Comte (1798–1857) was one of the first to exclusively apply the methods of natural science to the study of social phenomena. He believed that human behaviour must obey strict laws like billiard balls must obey Newton's laws of motion (universal-laws conception). Presumably laws governing human behaviour have a similar source to those governing the behaviour of natural objects like billiard balls. With these laws in hand, the perfect society could then be engineered. Comte maintained the only legitimate models for knowledge were the natural sciences with their empirical methods and the formal disciplines of logic and mathematics. This ties in closely with Comte's view that society goes through three stages of development:

(1) Theological: where our reflections on ourselves and our place in society are in terms of direct reference to God.
(2) Metaphysical: where universal rights of people are grounded in some plane higher than human authority, though this plane had no reference to the sacred except metaphorically.
(3) Scientific: where people find solutions to all problems, social and otherwise, in the methods of natural science, logic and mathematics.

Hence, for Comte, the social sciences could not be distinct from the natural sciences, logic and mathematics if they were to truly be 'scientific'.

Comte coined the term 'positive science' for his strictly natural-science approach restricted to the study of facts and laws (and leading to logical positivism). He also coined the term 'sociology', and analysed such phenomena as the division of labour and how it leads to a shift in social bonds from similarity to interdependence. He believed sociology would be the last and greatest of the sciences, somehow including and integrating all other sciences into a comprehensive whole. While sociology would be methodologically of a piece with the natural sciences, he recognized an important limitation of quantitative and empirical analysis when it comes to social phenomena: 'Social phenomena, being more complicated still, are even more out of the question, as subjects for mathematical analysis. It is not that a mathematical basis does not exist in these cases ... but that our faculties are too limited for the working of problems so intricate' (1974: 59). Note that the distinction between sciences such as physics and chemistry, on the one hand, and sociology, on the other, is one of degree, not of kind – in his view, humans simply do not have the ability to make the mathematics of social behaviour tractable (but God could do it).[6] Nevertheless, Comte believed that social scientists should pursue the search for universal laws and that the methods of the natural sciences were the appropriate methods for this search.

Comte's views serve as an important link between Hobbes and contemporary natural-science approaches to the social sciences via the mechanical–deductive interpretation of the latter's views on human actions and social interactions. In Taylor's categorization, Comte would be a correlator, and many look to him as the founder of sociology as a scientific discipline. He emphasized the discovery of causal laws of behaviour whereby social events could be predicted or explained, and the need for empirical justification of those laws.

The social theorist Wilhelm Dilthey (1833–1911) reacted strongly to the 'natural science turn' of Comte (and John Stuart Mill [1806–73], whom Comte influenced) regarding human behaviour. Instead of seeking for universal laws via empirical observation, Dilthey emphasized historical contingency and changeability, focusing more on the meanings and interpretations social actions had for the actors. He argued that the natural sciences view objects 'externally' as meaningless material things possessing no 'inner' capacity for experience and intentionality (e.g., atoms, rocks, stars). The attempt to explain events by subsuming them under general laws requires the ability to treat the world as a collection of decontextualized objects which may occur in various causal relations. In turn, treating things as mere objects presupposes a capacity for abstraction in which all meanings and values are removed from what is experienced (Chapter 5, sec. 3). In this way the things we study are encountered as inherently meaningless spatio-temporal objects governed by laws. As Dilthey puts it, we can see the world around us as a collection of objects regulated by laws only 'if the way we experience nature, our involvement in it, and the vital feeling with which we enjoy it, recede behind the abstract apprehension of the world in terms of space, time, mass and motion' (1976: 172). In other words, this objectified worldview is Hobbes' picture of the world as nothing more than matter in motion.

Dilthey's interpretive approach to social phenomena – itself heavily influenced by the thinking of German philosopher Friedrich Schleiermacher – involved three steps: experiencing, expressing and understanding. He emphasized the role of experience – an emphasis shared with British empiricist philosophers David Hume and John Locke – and believed all science was experiential. But in contrast with the empiricists, Dilthey maintained that all experience ultimately must be traced back to our own consciousness and historical setting. The foundation is our immediate lived experience which is tied together by meaning. But at this first stage, our experience is still pre-reflective or unanalysed. These experiences, in turn, come to creative expression or realization in human lives. These expressions take the form of ideas, judgements, conceptions and actions, as well as articulations through words and gestures like works of art, literature or even theorizing. The result of reflective understanding of these experiences and actions would then lead to grasping the meanings of human actions and events as well as their context. In this way, Dilthey sought to keep social inquiry rooted in a historical, interpretive approach as opposed to the empirical approach advocated by Comte. However, Dilthey did see empirical research as necessary to guard against speculative metaphysical theorizing about life (e.g., Georg Hegel).

Dilthey would be an example of an interpreter in Taylor's categorization, and argued that social sciences like psychology, history and sociology were distinct from natural sciences because the former crucially involved meanings and interpretation whereas the latter did not. In his view, the natural sciences aimed only at description and explanation of concepts and phenomena, while the social sciences aimed at understanding concepts and phenomena. For him, social sciences were about uncovering the meanings of social events whereby they would be explained, though they could not be predicted, and he emphasized that methods of interpretation were appropriate for discovering those meanings. In contrast to Comte, Dilthey believed there was a fundamental unbridgeable gap between the natural and social sciences. Yet, he thought that social science should aim for objective descriptions or interpretations of the inner life and experience of people that were equal or superior to the natural sciences.

3. Emile Durkheim

Emile Durkheim (1858–1917) is also considered by many to be the founder of modern sociology, partly because he was the first to be accorded academic status as a sociologist. He emphasized the collection of empirical data to support theoretical speculations and argued that sociology was distinct from other social sciences like psychology. However, Durkheim did maintain that, just as every natural event finds its explanation in a lawful connection to some natural fact, like natural phenomena and forces of nature, every social event finds its explanation in a lawful connection to some social fact, like social phenomena and social forces (universal-laws conception). The pattern of explanation is roughly the same, though he argued that social facts did not reduce to natural facts. The task of social sciences, then, is to discover causal laws describing the links between social facts and human behaviour. He was much influenced by Comte regarding methodology in the social sciences, and thought of these sciences as positivist in Comte's sense.

In contrast to Hobbes, who believed society arose out of individuals, Durkheim maintained that society was prior to the individual. Indeed it is the social facts that make people what they are in any given society. Durkheim believed that these social facts were the subject matter of sociology. Social facts, in his view, were unique and distinct from physical facts and, hence, must be studied on their own terms even apart from physiological and psychological phenomena. Social facts are like patterns of conduct serving as guides or channels of behaviour that are external to individuals, functioning like group norms, mores and folkways. These behavioural guides are learned in the family and other socialization/educational avenues, become internalized in the consciousness of individuals, and subsequently govern behaviour. Furthermore, social facts, on Durkheim's view, were determined by other social facts: 'The determining cause of a social fact should be sought among the social facts preceding it and not among the states of individual consciousness' (1950: 110). He maintained that social facts were not reducible to psychological and physiological facts.

Durkheim believed that the self-interest of humans (an important theme in Hobbes, recall) could only be held in check by external constraints provided by society.[7] In his view, the more one has, the more one wants because the satisfaction of needs or desires only stimulates rather than fulfills those needs and desires. Durkheim referred to the external forces moderating self-interest as the *collective conscience*, by which he meant our common social bonds expressed in shared ideas, norms, beliefs and ideologies. These bonds are institutionalized in social structures as well as internalized in individuals, and are the most important sources of social order.

These sources of social order come under threat by the growing division of labour as societies grow, become more complex, modernize and industrialize (Durkheim 1960). According to Durkheim, early societies exhibit what he calls *mechanical solidarity*, a deep sense of likeness stemming from a largely homogenous society. Men and women engage in similar daily tasks and activities, have similar experiences and interact via relatively few social institutions (e.g., a hunter-gatherer society, where there is little variety in conscience tasks or experiences). The homogeneity of the collective has such force that little opportunity for individuality and deviance exists. In such societies, Durkheim argued, there was a high level of social and moral integration, a strong sense of role or place within the social order, shared moral and spiritual values, where people tended to identify themselves as members of a group rather than as individuals.

As societies become more complex, according to Durkheim, a division of labour develops, where individuals play more specialized roles. Consequently, people become more dissimilar from each other in terms of their daily tasks and activities, undergo different social experiences, take on different material interests, values and beliefs. In this way, the division of labour erodes the mechanical solidarity of society, weakening social bonds and order as people have less in common. In turn, however, people become more interdependent on each other for survival and for the meeting of needs and desires. Durkheim called this latter form of solidarity *organic solidarity*, and viewed it as a direct by-product of the division of labour. He thought that the growth of individualism was an inevitable result of the increasing division of labour, and that this individualism developed at the expense of the common values, beliefs and sentiments associated with mechanical solidarity. Hence, in contrast with traditional societies, in modern societies, Durkheim argued, people tended to identify themselves as individuals first, rather than as members of a group. Indeed, he believed that as individualism progressed, people's sense of community and common identity increasingly weakened. The social bonds forming the collective conscience progressively weakened to the point where social values and beliefs no longer provided coherent or consistent guidance for the behaviour of everyone in society. Durkheim, and others, observed that the industrialization and mechanization of eighteenth- and nineteenth-century Europe deepened these conceptual differences between pre-modern and modern societies.

As society is organized around shared beliefs in individualism, there is less 'top down' guidance for collective action as found in pre-modern societies in the sense that social bonds are less effective at channelling individual behaviour. This change in social factors has implications for how individuals think and act. Durkheim acknowledged that this diversity of norms and values had potential to free people from oppressive traditions and the hierarchy of family, church and community. But such diversity also creates problems, one of which he identified with self-interest. As the social bonds weaken and perhaps break, individuals no longer have strong external restraints on their self-interests. Durkheim argued they would increasingly tend to seek satisfaction of their needs and desires with little or no thought to the possible effects their actions would have on others. People would be more likely to ask, 'Does this meet my needs?' rather than asking, 'Is this moral?' or 'Is this right?' Individuals, though interdependent on one another for survival, are basically left to their own devices for meeting their needs and desires, leading to deviation from expected social behaviour, social isolation and stress.

4. Max Weber

Max Weber (1864–1920), rivals Durkheim in the minds of many as the father of modern sociology and offered an approach to understanding human action that, in some sense, combines the interpretive emphasis of Dilthey with the empirical emphasis of Comte. In essence, Weber believed that natural-science methods could be employed to uncover the causes of events in the social realm, but ultimately rejected the thoroughgoing positivism of Comte and Durkheim. Weber maintained that an interpretive method should be employed to discern the meaning of the events and causes uncovered by empirical methods because people's actions are largely defined by their experience and what they see themselves as doing – that is, by their own self-understanding directing their behaviour. He might be viewed as representing an accommodationist approach between correlators and interpreters in Taylor's categorization (Chapter 1, sec. 4).

Weber viewed sociology as a comprehensive science of social action. In his words,

> Sociology . . . is a science concerning itself with the interpretive understanding of social action and thereby with a causal explanation of its course and consequences. We shall speak of 'action' insofar as the acting individual attaches a subjective meaning to his behavior – be it overt or covert, omission

or acquiescence. Action is 'social' insofar as its subjective meaning takes account of the behavior of others and is thereby oriented in its course. (Weber 1968: 4)

Initially, Weber focused on the subjective meaning we attach to our actions and interactions with others, distinguishing four types or sources of motivation for social action. The first, *zweckrational* (roughly 'technocratic thinking'), is action where the means to attain a particular goal are rationally chosen. An example of this kind of means–ends rationality is the selection of a university education as the most effective way to obtain a good job with the end goal of achieving material wealth and success.

The second, *wertrational* (roughly 'value-oriented thinking'), is also a form of means–ends rationality, but where the goal itself is not necessarily rational though the means to pursuing the goal are. The values informing these goals come from religious, ethical, philosophical perspectives or some other kind of community or context. Goals and means tend to be evaluated in terms of ultimate human values such as social justice or human flourishing. Examples of *wertrational* would be someone attending university because she values the life of the mind or seeking salvation through following the teachings of a prophet.

The third, *affective action*, is based on a person's emotional state rather than the rational sifting of means and ends. Feelings and sentiments can be very powerful motivations for human behaviour, such as going on a trip with friends in order not to feel left out or moving to a new city to be with one's girlfriend.

The fourth, *traditional action*, is action guided by custom or habit. People engage in this kind of behaviour perhaps because it is always done in a particular way, and this kind of action can be carried out completely unreflectively. Many students attend university simply because that is the expectation of their peers and community, or a son may take over the family business from his father because the business has always been handed down that way.

In Weber's picture, human behaviour is typically caused or channelled by a mixture of two or more of these four motivational categories. But his four-fold categorization also supplies a way to distinguish modern from pre-modern society, with the characteristic feature of the former being an emphasis on the efficient application of means to achieve ends at the expense of tradition, values or emotions. Indeed, the evolution of modern society looks to track very closely with the increasing emphasis on *zweckrational* and diminished emphasis on traditional action. One of Weber's enduring interests was to trace the factors at work in this *rationalization* of Western societies, of which he identified two: the growth of industrialization and bureaucracy.

For Weber, bureaucracy provides a particularly compelling example of a distinctive feature of modern society. In his conception, bureaucracy is the rationalized (*zweckrational*) coordination of human action with the aim of efficiently achieving set goals (think of a modern state organizing and coordinating an economy so as to achieve efficient wealth distribution or particular unemployment targets). As modern societies become more complex and populations grow, we become more dependent on bureaucracy for coordination and control. At the same time, the growth of bureaucracy threatens to undermine our freedom as we potentially become mere cogs in the bureaucratic machines. Democracy can also be threatened by the growth of bureaucracies as both the electorate and elected officials are effectively unable to know much of what bureaucracies are actually doing.[8] Weber's studies of bureaucracy laid the foundation for a field known as organizational sociology.

Underlying bureaucracy is the seemingly relentless process of rationalization, a feature Weber thought central to the thrust of modern societies. Rationalization, according to Weber, is the process of the practical application of knowledge to achieve desired goals, as human behaviour becomes increasingly dominated by *zweckrational*. Both physical and social environments progressively become coordinated and under control to achieve desired ends, ends that are often tied more to ideals of efficiency and effectiveness than to traditional sources such as religious or moral perspectives.

As Weber describes it, rationalization is associated with secularization, depersonalization and the routinization of many aspects of life because more and more elements of the natural and social environment fall under the purview of means–ends reasoning. As life becomes increasingly dominated by *zweckrational*, our picture of human character changes. Values such as individualism, efficiency, effectiveness, self-discipline, materialism and quantifiability/calculability become more highly prized at the expense of wider, more meaningful values playing key roles in traditional societies. These features contributed to what Weber called the 'iron cage of modernity' – as more activities of life are brought under the domination of *zweckrational*, life is robbed of its romance and savour. Increasingly, we feel as though we are just cogs in the machinery of bureaucracy, which promotes the feelings of isolation and alienation so prevalent in modern society. Weber foresaw and feared how the increasing domination of zweckrational led to depersonalization, emotional isolation, a shallow social life and a loss of the sense that anything can be absolutely worthwhile. As society becomes modernized and rationalized, it becomes de-traditionalized and our social bonds are broken down so that we increasingly become like helpless pawns in the bureaucratic machine rather than members of a community.

Rationalization is the fundamental element of Weber's social theorizing. It leads to an increasing division of labour, the growth of bureaucracy and the mechanization of society. Weber believed rationalization also fostered the secularization of society in the following sense. People in pre-modern or traditional societies took for granted that they belonged to a hierarchical and meaningful cosmic drama. As a result, men and women acquired meaningful roles to play in everyday life as well as a sense of place in the cosmos. The collapse of such traditional visions of a meaningful cosmic order went hand in hand with the rise of rationalization, according to Weber. The cosmic narrative of a universe steeped in meaning was progressively replaced by the mechanized narrative of the cog in the machine as societies became organized under *zweckrational* rather than traditional values and beliefs, and people found their place in a bureaucratized effort aiming at efficiency in the distribution of goods and services among other goals set by those in power. Rationalization transforms rational action based on values, or actions motivated by traditions or emotions into predominantly means–ends action. So under the action of rationalization, the universe became 'disenchanted', as Weber famously put it, with meaning now being found in the roles men and women play in the organization of society orchestrated under *zweckrational* rather than in some overarching religious, moral or metaphysical order of the universe (compare with Comte's three stages of social evolution).

5. Taking stock

One observation from this quick historical survey is the diversity of approaches to social-science inquiry practised by some of the seminal figures in its history. This diversity has been the source of several different approaches to social science that are still with us today as we will see shortly. Moreover, buried within this diversity is a tension that has existed in social science since its beginnings. On the one hand, there has been a tendency on the part of many social scientists to give explanations of human action in natural-science terms, to seek for empirical generalizations and universal laws as the basis for behaviour (correlators). On other hand, others have argued that such approaches to mapping human behaviour leave the everyday realities of living out of the picture at best, or distort these realities at worst (interpreters). Weber struggled with this tension more deeply than almost any social scientist before or since. He saw the distinction between empirical theory and the normative perspectives of people as the expression of an unbridgeable gap between fact and value. He wanted social inquiry to be both truthful (or accurate) and morally relevant, but the divide between facts and values seemed to stand in the way of bringing these aims together. This tension will become more apparent in the remaining chapters.

This diversity among the intellectual pioneers has also bequeathed several problems that are part and parcel of social-science practice as well as philosophical analyses of social science. Comparing Comte and Durkheim, on the one hand, and Dilthey on the other, we see that one problem is the stress on empirical research versus interpretation, that is, correlators versus interpreters. Which is more crucial for understanding social phenomena: amassing empirical data and fashioning theories, or getting a fix on the meanings and motivations guiding actions? Or are both necessary for understanding human actions and social institutions? If so, then it sounds as if the social sciences turn out to be a mix of science and values, so to speak.

There are two typical responses to this potentially troubling entanglement of science and values. One is to make a sharp distinction between the so-called context of discovery and context of justification, first proposed for other purposes by Hans Reichenbach (1938). In the context of discovery, intuitive, speculative or value-laden guesses as to possible explanatory hypotheses are allowed. However, claims to knowledge can only be confirmed in the context of justification. Values might enter into the first context, but not the second. Though seemingly a tidy solution, it fails to do justice to Kuhn's widely accepted contention that even in the natural sciences there is 'no neutral algorithm for theory choice, no systematic decision procedure which, properly applied, must lead each individual . . . to the same decision' (1996: 200).

The second response is more sophisticated and increasingly influential. This approach admits the indelibly value-imbued character of our accounts of human activity or the 'social determination of truth' (Lukes 1987) and goes on to embrace the thoroughgoing relativism such a view implies (we will see examples of this later). The philosopher Richard Rorty recommends this approach as offering an upbeat kind of 'ungrounded hope' that 'gives mankind an opportunity to grow up, to be free to make itself, rather than seeking direction from some imagined outside source' (1987: 253–54).

In spite of its stress on the historical embeddedness of social inquiry, this second response may not acknowledge fully how intimately cultural and moral values are implicated in the articulation of social knowledge. One might argue that even though Rorty asserts that all our constructions of social reality and our own identities are thoroughly 'ungrounded' and revisable, his own thought seems still to presuppose some version of the 'classical liberal belief that a society designed as a neutral matrix to promote freedom . . . will naturally lead to the public good' (Guignon and Hiley 1990: 357). In other words, even this kind of thoroughgoing anti-foundationalism may turn out to be inseparable from substantial ethical commitments, a possibility we will explore later. Are there any genuine alternatives to a choice between a strict scientism versus a relativistic interpretive swamp? Are these the only possibilities for conceiving of social inquiry?

Closely related, a second problem emerging from these early pioneers is the degree to which social science inquiry *must* be committed to value-neutrality. The core idea of value-neutrality is that the theories and methods or research and data collection must all be value-free or objective in the sense that they presuppose no moral or religious commitments, are not informed by feelings or sentiments and so forth (the requirement of univocality we met previously). The thrust of Comte's and Durkheim's approaches is to incorporate such neutrality by modelling their inquiry on the natural sciences. In contrast, Dilthey explicitly maintains that focusing on values and meanings is crucial for arriving at genuine understanding of social phenomena. Weber also believed there was an important role for such an approach, but ultimately was unable to square an honest, forthright treatment of values with a value-free commitment to objectivity. Value-neutrality crucially underlies the approach of Taylor's correlators. On the other hand, interpreters see striving for value-neutrality in all aspects of social science inquiry as distorting the very subjects of that inquiry. Are values in social science inquiry an all or nothing affair, or is there some legitimate role for values here?

A third problem is typically referred to as *methodological individualism* versus *methodological holism*. Weber introduced the concept of methodological individualism[9] as an assumption crucial to the social sciences, but it can already be found in Hobbes' analysis of human action and interactions and of the political system. The key idea is that social phenomena are only explainable in terms of how they result from individual actions, which, in turn, are to be explained in terms of the motivations of the individual actors (recall Weber's four sources of motivation for action). In contrast, Durkheim maintained methodological holism, the thesis that individual actions are primarily explained by large-scale social events and forces that are not reducible to the motivations and actions of individual actors. Here, we clearly see a tension between individualism, on the one hand, and social bonds, on the other. Which one is more important in understanding human actions? Does this question harbour a false dilemma forcing us to choose between only two somewhat limited options?

These three problems appear over and over again in discussions among social scientists as well as among philosophers who concern themselves with the social sciences. Accordingly, we will discuss them at length. A fourth problem, much less discussed by contemporary social scientists and philosophers is the rise of means–ends reasoning/action often called instrumental reasoning/action. Durkheim and Weber both discuss the trend away from what might be called traditional forms of action, where reasons, means and goals are evaluated in terms of values and sentiments deriving from larger moral, religious or cultural perspectives, and towards *zweckrational*, with a focus on efficiency and effectiveness of means for achieving given ends. This transition leads to a strong emphasis on instrumental knowledge and control that, as we will see, has some disturbing consequences for social-science research as well as for institutional and governmental policy founded and informed by such research.

As a preliminary remark, I would like to point out that this contemporary emphasis on control and instrumental knowledge does not have its origin in the practice of science as such. Rather, it derives from the Greek distinction between magic on the one hand, and science (in its pre-modern form) and religion on the other. The former as a practice – at least in ancient Greece and the wider West – was an attempt to impose the will of an individual on the natural world or to circumvent the natural order. The latter practices were attempts at understanding which exhibited balance between individual and collective goals and values (Jordan, Montgomery and Thomassen 1999; see particularly the essays by Jens Braarbig and Einar Thomassen). The latter practices, including early scientific ones, were largely consistent with traditional modes of reason and action. But a number of intellectual transformations during the early period of the Enlightenment – the story is quite complicated – led increasingly to viewing science, philosophy and other practices through a *zweckrational* lens. The Enlightenment (seventeenth and eighteenth centuries) was an intellectual and social movement emphasizing the application of reason through philosophy and science for the betterment of the human condition, materially, intellectually and spiritually. The notions of mastery and control over nature and ourselves is a dominant theme of Enlightenment thinking. Thus progressively science took on the colour of control and instrumentality originally associated in the ancient world with magic (quite an ironic twist!)

Restricting ourselves to the 'three fathers' of modern sociology, given their differences, it may seem puzzling that these three figures would be competing for the role of founder of the discipline. Perhaps it is better to see them as founders of influential research traditions or approaches in sociology and the social sciences more broadly: Comte (arguably Durkheim should be considered here as well) as the founder of an empirical-science tradition, Dilthey as the founder of an interpretive-science tradition, and Weber as a founder of an approach combining the two. Helpful as this might be, such a categorization is still too coarse for our purposes. In the next chapter I will introduce five modes or models of social-science inquiry, providing a schema that I believe is adequate for categorizing any research approach in any social-science discipline. Each mode has its strengths and weaknesses. Hence, an approach employing one of these models in any given social-science discipline will inherit these strengths and weaknesses. Therefore, this schema will be very useful for us in analyzing various social-science disciplines and their practices.

For further study

1. What are the strongest points of contrast between Comte and Dilthey? How are these related to the question of whether natural sciences and social sciences are similar?
2. Explain *wertrational* and *zweckrational*. Give an example from daily life of each kind of action.
3. What is rationalization and how has it transformed modern society? Give an example where rationalization has transformed a domain of life formerly dominated by traditional or *wertrational* action.

Recommended reading

A. Comte, *Introduction to Positive Philosophy* (Indianapolis: Hackett, 1988).

W. Dilthey, *Wilhelm Dilthey: Selected Writings* (Cambridge: Cambridge University Press, 1976).

E. Durkheim, *The Rules of Sociological Method* (trans. S. A. Solovay and J. H. Mueller; New York: The Free Press, 1950 [1895]).

T. Hobbes, *Leviathan* (ed. E. Curley; Indianapolis: Hackett, 1994 [1651/1668]).

M. Weber, *Max Weber on The Methodology of the Social Sciences* (eds and trans. E. Shils and H. Finch; New York: The Free Press, 1949).

Five Modes of Social Inquiry

3

Chapter Outline

In the previous chapter, we saw that a number of key contributors to the founding and formation of the social sciences took widely divergent approaches to inquiry. That divergence continues in the contemporary scene. Thomas McCarthy has observed that in the social sciences one finds 'a whole range of rational practices, some looking like textual interpretation of historical narratives, others trying to look as much as possible like natural-scientific rationality' (1988: 237). Instead of a disordered picture of social-science inquiry, it is possible to bring some organization to the highly fragmented picture of theory and research findings presented by these disciplines.

In this chapter, I describe five broad modes or models of social science inquiry: (1) natural scientific, (2) descriptivist, (3) critical, (4) postmodern or social constructionist and (5) hermeneutic.[1] These five modes are not only helpful for identifying research efforts; they are also helpful for diagnosing why so many efforts of the past two centuries aimed at understanding human behaviour have met with so much difficulty.

1. Natural scientific

Comte and Durkheim endorsed applying natural-science methods to the study of social phenomena. This is the *natural-scientific* mode of social inquiry. The mainstream consensus on research in the social sciences is that the natural sciences provide the best, perhaps the only, model for inquiry. This means the social realm should be treated as a part of nature just like electrons, molecules, amoebas and rocks are, and social phenomena should be studied by methods analogous to those in any other natural science. This approach to inquiry assumes that empirical theory is the gold standard of social-science knowledge, so to speak.

The goal of empirical theory is not just amassing correlations among various behavioural, psychological and situational variables. Though this is important, genuine scientific knowledge or explanations should go beyond mere correlations to produce universal or context-free laws of psychological and social behaviour derivable from a few assumptions and definitions concerning the realm under investigation (essentially Comte's picture of social science). An example would be attributing government agencies' tendency to perpetuate themselves and expand to three key factors: (1) people who have jobs do not like losing them, (2) people habituated to particular skills do not welcome change and (3) people who have become accustomed to exercising power do not like relinquishing such control – they tend to want to expand their power (Hempel 1965: 235–36). Or explaining why farmers in the 1930s drought in the Dust Bowl region of the USA – parts of Colorado, Kansas, New Mexico and Oklahoma – headed west to California in terms of 'universal hypotheses' like 'populations will tend to migrate to regions which offer better living conditions' (Hempel 1965: 236). Ideally, these laws and regularities should be empirically confirmed through controlled experimentation. The resulting theory would put these laws to use in establishing explanations and produce precise prediction of future behavioural and social events (involving the theoretical, universal-laws and methodological conceptions of science). Such empirical knowledge, then, represents the instrumental power to manipulate events in the social realm for the goal of achieving desired outcomes or advancing human welfare.

A further feature of the natural-scientific model is a sharp distinction between facts and values. This fact/value split is part of the objectivism that permeates natural-scientific conceptions of social inquiry: Scientific knowledge is about facts, not values. Instead, values are typically treated as only subjective feelings, attitudes or preferences about objective states of affairs. It is important to note that this split paints a picture of the world and its workings that many will welcome and many will abhor. In this picture, there is little if any place for moral or spiritual realities or meanings except possibly as whimsical or even dysfunctional fantasies that need not be taken seriously (e.g., Comte's third stage of society, where all questions are answered scientifically).

Indeed, if facts and values are separable in this manner, then it is possible to take an indefinite number of value positions towards any given fact. To the extent that scientists consider these 'subjective' factors, they tend to treat them as an order or flow of events linked to antecedent causes or subsequent effects in the 'objective' world. These subjective factors may exist, but they are mainly conduits for or by-products of forces and influences in the objective world. Often, this linkage takes the form of propositions like the following:

> If an agent desires *a* and believes that *b* is a means to attain *a* under the circumstances, then the agent will attempt *b*.

If you are thirsty (a desire) and you believe that drinking water from your fridge will quench your thirst, then, if you are at home, you will get the water from the fridge and drink it. Your desire for water and your belief that there is water in the fridge that will quench your thirst cause you to drink the water in the fridge provided you are at home. Your behaviour is the effect of prior causes, your subjective desires included.

In contrast to inner feelings and values, the objective world is viewed as a collection of material objects devoid of meaning, but which can be mapped profitably by empirical investigation. Such a view fits very nicely with the domination of *zweckrational* and the disenchantment of the world Weber describes with trepidation (Chapter 2, sec. 4). Instead of a meaningful cosmos, objects of the world are to be viewed as standing in causal relations to one another and are to be represented and understood with experimental methodology and explanations grounded in laws.

An analysis of natural-science inquiry is not exhausted by its experimental and explanatory methodologies; it also has a distinctive epistemology (epistemological conception) that can be traced back at least to Descartes (2000) and Bacon (2000). The world is viewed as a realm of (mind-)independent objects to be known through appropriate methods rather than from custom, sacred texts or other traditional sources of authority. Descartes' contribution to this epistemological picture, identified as unique by many commentators, is a strong inward turn, where genuine knowledge results from correct inner representations in our minds of an external, independent realm of objects (e.g., beliefs about antecedently existing external objects). The application of reliable methods is then supposed to generate well-justified beliefs producing objective knowledge that is distinct from anyone's personal or subjective wishes or evaluations.[2]

This epistemology presupposes what can be called a *subject-object ontology*, where a sharp distinction is made between a subject and her inward states of awareness and feeling, on the one hand, and a mind-independent realm of objects external to her. On this picture, our experiences of beauty, any sense of relevance to our purposes, and any notions of goodness or badness are regarded merely as products of our varying interpretations and purposes, which are located in and confined to a private, purely subjective realm. Meanwhile, things and events in this independent world – including agents and their actions – stand abstracted away from any of the rich experiences or meanings of everyday life. Thus they are seen as merely standing in efficient causal relations to one another and to ourselves. The world and its objects – us included! – become *objectified*, if you will, with the social scientist occupying a disinterested viewpoint somehow detached from any values so as to give a strictly neutral account of social reality 'out there'. The social scientist is pictured as taking on an *outsider's* perspective, a viewpoint standing above or apart from the social arena (Fig. 3.1). This kind of objectification ignores or abstracts away from most of the meanings, evaluations and purposes constituting so much

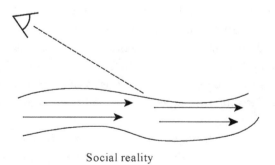

Social reality

Figure 3.1 Outsider's Perspective
The outsider's perspective, a supposed detached, objectifying, value-neutral viewpoint outside of social reality.

of our everyday lived experience (see Chapter 5, sec. 3). Instead, it concentrates on cause–effect relations among events for the purposes of producing generalizations and context-free universal laws applicable to these cause–effect patterns.

This combination of ontology and epistemology as the path to true knowledge shows up in mainstream social science's insistence upon the use of correlational and experimental methods regardless of the subject matter under investigation (recall Taylor's correlators, Chapter 1, sec. 4). The natural-science approach seeks secure knowledge of a realm of human events that is independent of observers or the accounts of social scientists, even though observers are also part of that realm. For example, it appears in the privileging of formal relations in Lawrence Kohlberg's (1984) influential theory of moral development. Kohlberg takes the highest level of morality to be the ability to apply highly abstract, formal principles to concrete situations (looking suspiciously similar to natural-science methodology and epistemology).

To borrow an example of Richardson and Fowers (1998: 468), subjects with what some psychologists call an 'internal locus of control' (i.e., they usually believe they can influence the course of events by their actions) typically persist longer in trying to solve difficult problems in laboratory settings than those lacking such a locus. Here is an example of a persistent correlation between behaviour and beliefs. However, the presence of such correlations alone do not tell us whether this belief system really causes such persistence, or if both of them are co-effects of other unknown factors, psychological or physiological. On the natural-science model of inquiry, such questions ultimately can only be answered by further controlled experimental work, leading to the development of genuine empirical theory to explain these enduring patterns.

This, then, is the correlator's picture of social science; however, so far it has fared relatively poorly. There is little disagreement among perceptive observers that even after decades of tremendous and often methodologically sophisticated effort, mainstream social science's achievements, even when evaluated by its own favoured standards, are paltry at best. Especially when compared with the accomplishments of natural-science. However, there is much less agreement about what this troubling situation actually means. Some think we should stick with and refine our methods, redoubling our efforts because there simply has not been enough time to reach the right level of refinements to achieve substantial success. In contrast, others argue the evidence is almost overwhelming that mainstream approaches are significantly off track (recall Dilthey's negative reaction to the natural-science turn of Comte).

Serious doubts have arisen within and without the social-science arena about whether these ideals of empirical theory and true value-neutrality (see Chapter 6) ever have or ever could be achieved in accounts of human activities in their real-life social and historical setting. Brent Slife and Richard Williams (1995: 180–94) point out that this mainstream approach to social science is based on a strict dichotomy between theory and method: theory or ideas are confirmed or rejected by the best available methods. However, these authors cogently argue that it is impossible to sharply differentiate between theory and method in this way, because there are no theory-free approaches or methods. Some methods might be consistent with some theories and inconsistent with others, but they all presuppose a number of things about what the world is really like, what truth about it would resemble, and what is worth knowing in the first place. Without these assumptions we could not even know we needed methods, let alone which ones would serve our needs. When these assumptions are taken for granted, any other view of the world than as a realm of determinate objects or of knowledge as consisting in anything other than laws of human behaviour can seem hopelessly fuzzy, immature and 'unscientific'. But once they are questioned – and once we consider the possibility, as many critics argue (e.g., Gergen 1982), that to date we have developed no genuine empirical theory of the human realm – they begin to look quite arbitrary. Methods cannot easily serve as *independent* tests of our theories or beliefs (Kuhn 1996). Such methods assume things about the world, human understanding and the purposes of social inquiry that it is simply dogmatic not to call into question.

Increasingly refined arguments have been mounted to the effect that the great difficulties of social science in attaining genuine empirical theory are a result of its epistemological ideal being inappropriate for its subject matter (e.g., Gergen 1982; Taylor 1985a; 1985b; Vaughan, Sjoberg and Reynolds 1992; Richardson, Fowers and Guignon 1999; I will have more to say about this later). There are also worries about the durability of patterns of human action – the targets to be explained by laws – in that such patterns appear subject to significant alteration because we change our social practices and values over time (we will return to this worry often).

Furthermore, Peter Winch (1958; 1977) argues compellingly that explaining human action, in both everyday life and social inquiry, means giving an account of why people do the things they do – their reasons, motives and goals – by reference to the intersubjective rules or standards that constitute their particular 'form of life'. He maintains that the acceptability of such an account depends on its making sense to the social actors themselves. If so, then social-science explanations of behaviour are different in kind from explaining nature or society via context-independent general laws. Human activity, according to Winch, consists more in cooperative activities guided or channelled by common meanings and shared values – Durkheim's social bonds – than in radically self-interested behaviour following causal laws. After all, people are socialized to see themselves as distinct individuals in our modern individualistic society similar to the way they are socialized to see themselves as gaining identity from their tribe or group in traditional societies. Indeed, from an early age people in Western societies are taught a very detailed set of rules and customs about how to live successfully within an individualized context. Change the social context, and the rules and customs taught to children will change as well. This is not the kind of situation we expect if context-free, universal laws hold sway in the social realm (see Chapter 13).

Many commentators sympathetic to Winch's views have moderated his position by stressing that the explanation of an action may be more sophisticated than people can normally be expected to grasp, and need only be meaningfully connected to agents' own intentions and beliefs (e.g., Taylor 1985a). It is the meanings we live by and the goals we seek that actually shape or determine the patterns of our lives, even if we often cannot fully or accurately articulate what they are. Others (e.g., Bernstein 1976) have pointed out that nothing in Winch's critique denies that uncovering correlations among factors in the social realm may help identify those patterns and elucidate some of the dynamics of human activity in various ways. For instance, such correlations may show that people say one thing and do another in a way that calls for a deeper interpretation of their conflicting motives, self-deception or rationalizations.

The essence of many of these critiques of mainstream social science is that natural-scientific models of scientific explanation fail to capture what goes on in behaviour when meanings and purposes play a crucial role in constituting personal and social reality. A lucid characterization of this situation is Roy D'Andrade's (1986) depiction of social inquiry as studying ' "imposed" order based on "meaning" rather than on natural or physical order . . . [Such imposed order] creates meaning and is created by the attempt to convey meaning.' It is an 'arbitrary order, which can change rapidly and varies from place to place and time to time' (1986: 22). An example of imposed order would be language, which creates meaning and is created by the attempt to convey meaning. Or consider norms for appropriate dress and behaviour, which structure the significance and context for activities like ballroom dancing versus a sock-hop. In other words, human actions and emotions, indeed our very selves, in contrast to events in the natural world, are symbolically structured in these sorts of ways. Put another way, human action is structured by meanings rather than context-free laws. This imposed order may actually render some aspects of human and social behaviour predictable to some degree. But a perfectly predictable society would be a perfectly conformist society, not necessarily one governed by context-free laws of behaviour. And laws governing personal and social behaviour – if any exist – would be dependent for their existence on the feelings, attitudes and values of the actors (we will see this idea again later). Personal interpretation, then, enters into the very definition of the phenomenon under study by the social sciences, rendering the aspirations expressed in the universal-laws conception of science inappropriate for social inquiry.

Most of these critics would agree that it is pointless and potentially harmful to insist on an either/or choice between correlational and interpretive approaches in social inquiry. The upshot of their critiques, however, is that such correlations are not even approximations to strict empirical theory and universally applicable laws of human activity. Empirical methods drawn from natural scientific modes of investigation may have their place in social inquiry, but empirical theory and universal laws look to simply be irrelevant.

2. Descriptivism

Insights of this sort concerning meaningful human action have been incorporated into what Bernstein (1976) calls *descriptivist* approaches of social inquiry, which emphasize that social science mainly describes purposive human action in a meaningful, intersubjective lifeworld. Descriptivists seek to describe the personal and social meanings structuring human life on its own terms rather than explain human life as the products of universal laws and efficient causes.

Such approaches, a growing but still minority viewpoint in social science, show up, for example, in phenomenology, social anthropology, ethnomethodology and a broad array of 'qualitative' research approaches. Winch's approach, briefly described above, falls into this mode of social inquiry as do the approaches of Alfred Schutz and the historian and philosopher R. G. Collingwood (Bernstein 1976). Some sort of descriptivist approach has seemed the only plausible alternative for many critics of mainstream social science. The key intuition is that we should describe meaningful human action or lived experience on their own terms rather than reduce them to deterministic universal laws. And the vocabulary appropriate for describing human activity is not one consistent with such context-free laws. For instance, the appropriate vocabulary for describing human actions might be in terms of feelings and desires, where reference to 'laws of behaviour' are as irrelevant as descriptions in terms of 'hate' or 'hope' would be to explaining the movement of physical bodies.

To briefly elaborate Winch's approach as an example, human actions cannot be understood or appropriately described apart from the reasons and motives humans have for their actions. Nor can these reasons and motives be understood or adequately described apart from identifying the forms of life and rules or standards governing life in their particular society. Given these forms of life along with the reasons and motives, the meaning such actions have for the actors can then be discerned and described. Universal laws are never needed nor do they appear relevant for such descriptions.

A number of social scientists and philosophers (e.g., Giddens 1976; Taylor 1985a; 1985b) argue that social inquiry is characterized by a *double hermeneutic* – that is, they are doubly interpretive. Views of scientific inquiry like Kuhn's acknowledge the first half of this double hermeneutic in emphasizing that a science's theory and findings are shaped in crucial ways by the investigators' interpretive framework of assumptions, conventions and purposes. Natural sciences share this 'single hermeneutic' with the social sciences – that is, they both involve these interpretive aspects of a scientist's research framework. After all, terms like 'gravity' and 'chlorophyll' come from us, not from nature, just as terms like 'anxiety neurosis' and 'intermittent reinforcement' come from social scientists, not from everyday parlance – unless, of course, we have been reading a lot of psychology books! Descriptivist approaches to social inquiry, begin to take account of the other half of this two-way interpretive street, namely that in the social disciplines the object of study is the same sort of activity or being that carries out the inquiry. That is, social scientists are actors engaged in an intelligent, social activity of studying intelligent, social activities of fellow human beings. Put another way, the interpretive nature of social inquiry is a two-way street. Social scientists are people who are deeply shaped by their societies while their practices of social inquiry reshape those same societies.

The natural sciences do not have anything like this; a physicist studying the behaviour of electrons is neither like the electron (the object of study) nor behaves like an electron. That is, human activity and the behaviour of electrons are different in kind. In contrast, the social scientist is a self-interpreting being who is always trying to make sense of and cope with her world (social science is one way we do this), studying other self-interpreting beings who are trying to make sense of and cope with their world. The subjects under study in social inquiry talk back in ways that rocks and volcanoes cannot, and studying them means paying very close attention to the things they say to us with their words and deeds. In this sense, descriptivist approaches appreciate that human actions and emotions are symbolically structured aspects of social reality, namely that order in the social realm is imposed by meaning and interpretation rather than by universal laws. Descriptivists take this contrast with the objects of study in the natural sciences seriously. They are pointing out something we can all sympathize with because in everyday life we are always seeking to understand the meanings and attitudes of others (e.g., 'Can I really trust my friend in this situation?')

Moreover, social scientists are in every respect a part of this same reality, even as they are investigating other parts of it. The activity of research is a human activity like any other actions in which humans engage (activity conception). Thus, at the heart of social inquiry there is a mutually influencing interplay between the meaning-laden activities of self-interpreting beings and the interpretive framework of investigators. Through wide-spread dissemination of social-science results, people might come to see themselves the way social-science researchers do! Equally troubling, such investigators also could absorb the cultural ideals of their research subjects into their research framework and then pass those ideals on as outcomes from their research (Chapter 8).

Proponents of natural-science modes of inquiry are likely to complain that descriptivist approaches focusing on meaningful action are suspect. Focusing on meaning rather than causal mechanisms looks like a kind of wishful, non-rational, even somewhat immature desire to characterize human action and the social world in terms that are comforting, soothing or supportive. Such desires would lead to descriptions having questionable epistemic value (how would we get evidence to ground objective knowledge claims?) and questionable practical benefits. These desires would interfere with or perhaps obscure more disciplined, useful accounts focusing on laws and mechanisms of behaviour.

Characterizing human action in terms more congruent with the self-understandings of people, however, does not necessarily involve a soft, sentimental, merely comforting or self-deluding approach to behaviour. Much literature and the texts of the world's great religious traditions convey the sorts of meanings that are felt by many to be embedded in human action and practices. These writings often describe the human condition in starkly realistic, tragic and uncomplimentary or unconsoling terms. Sometimes they uncover new paths to meaning through deep interpretations of the dark side of life, sometimes not. Often, they are anything but flattering. Moreover, a case can be made that natural-science approaches tend towards being utopian (e.g., Skinner 2005), unrealistic or naive about the human condition. Natural-science approaches can downplay human limitations, exaggerate the possibilities for control over circumstances and direction in life, ignore existential dilemmas and contribute to ethical confusion in ways to be explored more fully below.

Although acknowledging this interplay or double hermeneutic, descriptivist views of social inquiry do not take it fully onboard. Once they opt for meaningful descriptions rather than natural-science explanations as the goal of inquiry, they are faced with a tough question, namely: 'What characterizes a good description?' This is a pressing question, to say the least, because a little reflection shows that every description is necessarily partial and selective. And that selectivity may very well reflect the particular values or interests of the social scientist or his or her community. But most descriptivist writers continue to insist that they are providing not an arbitrary, but a thoroughly objective, characterization of lived experience or human activity. So, as with natural-science modes of inquiry, descriptivist modes still presuppose a subject-object ontology and epistemology that places the observer/describer at a vantage point largely detached from the social reality under description. In other words, descriptivist approaches also adopt an outsider's perspective similar to natural-scientific approaches. But taking the two-way interpretive street seriously implies that no such outsider's perspective is genuinely possible.

For reasons to be explored more fully later, this objectifying viewpoint looks to be neither possible nor desirable. In the descriptivist view, as in natural-scientific approaches, the social scientist is pictured as detached from the social reality under description (Fig. 3.1). In fact, she, is culturally embedded and thoroughly a part of the same social reality, contrary to her ontological and epistemological assumptions. Recall Weber's point that a person's actions are directed by their self-understandings of their situations and what they see themselves as doing. One implication of this feature of action is that there is no value-neutral, objective description available to the social scientist (Weber never fully grasped this). When I raise my hand in a meeting, I am not just moving air molecules around nor flexing my muscles. I may be signalling that I want to ask a question or I may be voting for the male candidate. My action is defined by my understanding of the situation in the meeting and my way of seeing what I am doing.[3] Others can only correctly identify my action as voting if they understand my action under the description it has for me. In fact, they may understand my action better than I do, perhaps seeing me actually displaying sexist attitudes by voting for the man rather than the woman (my self-understandings certainly can be subject to various distortions and rationalizations mediated by social fads, unconscious biases and the like). But even this interpretation of my action must first presuppose my own self-description to move beyond it. In this sense, at least initially, we must understand an action in its own terms under the description it bears for the person. And this self-understanding of the person and her action necessarily involves her own value commitments and her concerns about what is at stake as well as her interpretation of her situation.

It seems clear that one cannot give an insightful description of others' actions from a thoroughly detached or neutral position. One has to be involved or get involved to a meaningful extent in the situation, even if mainly as what anthropologists term a 'participant observer'. One has to develop a real feel for the situation and people one is attempting to describe, imagining what it is like to be them and how events impact on them, maybe asking them questions or even letting them challenge one's ideas and interpretations of them. An attenuated but often quite powerful version of that questioning and challenging can take place in one's own inner dialogue, without any overt exchange, between oneself and the other person or culture. These activities are familiar to all of us. They play a central role in our constant efforts to get to know or better understand strangers, friends or family members in everyday life.

If this is true, however, the descriptivist mode of social inquiry runs into big problems. First of all, social scientists will always bring cultural concerns and commitments to their work of understanding. They must start out interpreting others in their own terms and categories, and can never escape them entirely. To escape them entirely would not mean being objective so much as inhuman. Naturally, social scientists will always want to be as accurate and unbiased as possible in their accounts of social phenomena. But this does not mean disengaging from all or much of one's human sympathy and connection with the object of study, as if one were trying, as it were, to avoid bias by only looking at the phenomena through the wrong end of a telescope! Rather, it means trying not to operate from unworthy or inappropriate motives, like deceiving oneself or others, manipulating the account for selfish or ideological purposes, and the like. Ironically, the ideal of neutrality and strict moral disinterest for which so many strive is appealing largely because it reflects substantial values such as openness to, respect and tolerance for the great variety of forms of life – a caring, concerned and very substantial ethical perspective to say the least (Part Two)!

Secondly, social scientists will not only bring their cultural biases and meanings to their work of interpreting and explaining human action but will be *influenced* by their interaction with their subjects and by their biases and values. A kind of conversation will take place between investigator and subject matter in which both may be changed, often unpredictably, in small or large ways. Once again, we are familiar with this process in everyday life, as students, teachers, parents, friends or fellow citizens. How could a rich and humane social science be anything other than a living part of this process? In any case, social inquiry turns out to be both a lot messier and more interesting a process than descriptivist approaches, to say nothing of natural-science approaches, have appreciated.

Nevertheless, descriptivist viewpoints make important contributions to debates about the nature of social science, yielding valuable insights into the inherently social and moral texture of human life. They suggest that human action is not reducible exclusively to *zweckrational* but, rather, largely consists of cooperative practices and institutions embodying shared understandings of life. One or another set of intrinsically meaningful values, giving us things to do and be that are worthwhile in themselves, always orients our activities, pre-reflectively shaping our experiences and practices long before we begin consciously to deliberate about such matters even if we eventually engage in *zweckrational.*

Helpful as these contributions might be, Bernstein (1976) argues descriptivist approaches founder when it comes to explicating normative dimensions of social theory and practice. This conception of how social science might characterize its subject matter, as more purposeful and meaningful than natural-scientific views allow, leads to a distressing and seemingly irresolvable paradox. Winch may speak for many descriptivists when he writes movingly that the study of other cultures 'is closely linked with the concept of wisdom. We are confronted not just with different techniques, but with new possibilities of good and evil, in relation to which men may come to terms with life' (1958: 103). However, as Bernstein points out:

> Such a 'wisdom' is empty unless it also provides some critical basis for evaluating these 'new possibilities of good and evil.' Certainly we can recognize that there are forms of life which are dehumanizing and alienating, and we want to understand precisely in what ways they are so; to insist that philosophy and social theory remain neutral and uncommitted undermines any rational basis for such a critique of society. (1976: 74)

3. Critical social science

Some social scientists – often called *critical social scientists* – take this evaluative edge of social inquiry seriously. Their attitude might be characterized in this way: 'If interpretation, values and a moral thrust are inescapable, and if attempts to avoid them only mean that we end up surreptitiously advocating values that may be questionable, then let us get our moral values right and do our best to serve human freedom and welfare as best we are able'. According to critical thinkers, social science cannot just be descriptive if we are not going to end up rationalizing and reinforcing the status quo. Rather, we should dig deeper into the status quo looking for hidden biases and agendas, bringing them to light, and subjecting them to a serious critique. Ideally, as a result of their research, investigators should change or develop their views and values, and communication of their findings should, if possible, influence society for the better. Commitments and values of some kind influence not only the topics researchers choose to investigate, as Weber emphasized, but the conclusions they reach as well (examples of this will be discussed later). Thus, commitments and interpretations become forces influencing social life just like motivations, ideologies and points of view shape the events of everyday life. Recognizing and clarifying such often hidden or unacknowledged influences lying at the heart of social science is a chief characteristic of critical social scientists.

Critical theory has its roots in Karl Marx's critique of classical political economy as hiding underlying ideological distortions of reality. Because critical theorists believe all social theory and research findings are inescapably interpretive and evaluative, they think there is a crucial difference between the social and natural sciences – the latter do not study objects capable of self-interpretation nor do they involve ethical evaluation of states of affairs. Critical thinkers also maintain that both natural scientific and descriptivist approaches to social inquiry are severely limited in at least two ways. First, both approaches deny or ignore the moral commitments or ideological beliefs animating their own theorizing and interpretation of research findings. Different as they are, both approaches aspire to objectivity and value-neutrality, but cannot attain such lofty heights because this viewpoint itself is driven and animated by its own substantial moral commitments that often remain unacknowledged, while influencing all aspects of social inquiry (see Part Two).

Second, because of their commitment to value-neutrality, both natural-scientific and descriptivist approaches are unable to fully explore some of the most interesting features of human action. Especially those revealed in the many contradictions or inconsistencies pervading human life. Consider an environmental activist advocating living in harmony with nature who turns to violence to advance her aims. Or ordinary citizens who claim to be dedicated to democracy but usually do not bother to vote. Or parents who justify their failure to set needed limits on their children out of concern not to 'thwart' or 'hurt' them. The possibilities are endless. Social scientists' commitment to value-neutrality prevents them from doing anything more than just describing these inconsistencies. To do more than simply observe and report would involve interpreting and evaluating the sources of these tensions and contradictions in social currents and human motivations. But this is to be inescapably involved in ethical evaluation about the human goods or moral evils involved, just the kind of judgements that are off-limits in natural-scientific and descriptivist social inquiry. The insight to be expected from such approaches, argue critical social scientists, necessarily cannot be very deep or illuminating because deep analyses of this ethical kind are shunned.

Critical social scientists' analysis of objectifying approaches to social inquiry are deeper than just plumbing the limits of such approaches just mentioned. They also offer an illuminating diagnosis of 'what's going on behind the scenes' of such research often locating the problem as one of hidden or *disguised ideology* (e.g., cultural ideals that go unnoticed by social scientists and social actors). A particular way of life may contain contradictions because the self-understandings or beliefs of the social actors involved contain systematic distortions (e.g., Freudians and Marxists diagnose these distortions as stemming from various kinds of repressions and rationalizations). For instance, accounts aiming at objectivity and neutrality are very likely to portray oppressed workers as happy campers and grim workaholics as proud citizens all the while rationalizing the status quo and evading important questions about justice and human well-being. People do not necessarily say or own up to what is really going on in their lives, and will often say what they think is expected of them or what they think is 'safe'. So merely describing their behaviour will not clue us in to the genuine plight of the oppressed worker, the frightened conformist, the submissive and intimidated abused spouse, or the compulsively driven workaholic. Delving into the contradictory nature of human actions, so critical theorists maintain, inevitably involves invoking values and ideals. The great danger, according to critical perspectives, is that social scientists unwittingly will reproduce the blindness and rationalizations of the hidden ideology of social actors and cultures in their 'objective' presentation of data and theorizing. In other words, they will blindly or inadvertently reinforce and perpetuate serious human problems (see Chapter 8).

While critical theorists are concerned with familiar evils and injustices, they have also focused on new forms of domination and corruption unique to a modern technological society (e.g., Habermas 1971; 1991; Horkheimer 1974; Bernstein 1976; Held, 1980). Jürgen Habermas, in particular, has argued that modern Western culture is built largely upon a damaging confusion of culturally meaningful activities and shared meanings, on the one hand, with means–ends reasoning and technical mastery (*zweckrational*) on the other. This leads society to tend to collapse the cultural and moral dimensions of life into merely technical and instrumental considerations (recall Weber's process of rationalization). We will explore this 'instrumental turn' more fully in Part Two, but the key point for the moment is that far from being value-neutral, the objectivist outlook celebrating strict means–ends reasoning actually contains an implicit value system or ideology hidden beneath the surface. Following squarely in the tradition of the Enlightenment, such an outlook sees itself as doing battle with ignorance, superstition, dogmatism and arbitrary authority with the goal of promoting an understanding of human rights, freedom and dignity – significant values most of us share in some form. So on the surface, objectivist approaches to social-science inquiry treat all values as merely subjective and limit knowledge to the findings of objective methods all the while holding substantial commitments undermining any such claims to objectivity and value-neutrality. Social scientists, whether natural scientific or descriptivists, have not avoided ideology and moral advocacy, but (unwittingly) smuggled them in through the back door.

Critical social scientists and theorists constantly ask: 'How can we be sure that our perspectives, arguments and research are not distorted by ideological commitments lying below the surface?' This question is important because apparently nothing human beings do is fully free of hidden biases and all forms of knowledge are coloured by particular cultural ideals and conventions. The spirit of their approach is to bite the bullet, accept the inevitability of ethical commitment and advocacy, and welcome the opportunity to press on with liberating individuals and seeking a fuller social justice. A significant minority of contemporary social scientists identify deeply with this robust and committed viewpoint as to what social science is or should be all about.

However, this approach is bound to make many people nervous. The very commitments to social justice and the freedom of all that this view embraces can make their own approach seem somewhat narrow or dogmatic. Do we not risk arbitrariness in advocating a particular view of justice and liberation? These are familiar problems for a modern Enlightenment-based moral outlook of this kind. Such an outlook places heavy emphasis on human rights and tolerance. But how far should we go in tolerating what may seem to us like dogmatism or intolerance? What about more conservative cultural or religious viewpoints? Are they just flat out wrong or merely different from the strongly liberationist and anti-authoritarian bias of critical social science? If we are uncomfortable condemning them outright – after all, we strongly believe in freedom and tolerance – does that not make our theory and research, with its own particular kind of ethical slant and advocacy, look more like just another political voice in the wind rather than any kind of generally valid social science? Even if we embrace most of critical social science's ideals, we might still feel that there are other sorts of cultural, moral or spiritual values that are also important, and that need to be in the picture if a society is going to be able to sustain its commitment to a wide degree of tolerance and respect for human rights (Etzioni 1994; Sandel 1996). Should other values of this sort also infuse our research and theory in the social sciences? What would that look like? Especially when as individuals and a society we are uncertain and confused about how individual freedom and deep loyalty to a community or tradition, liberal and conservative values, or spiritual values and a hatred of dogmatism can coexist or mesh in a reasonable way. If they can.

For critical theorists, like Habermas, a key question for practical life as well as social science is: 'How, in modern times, can we reach agreement about matters that are at least partly moral or evaluative without falling back on dogmatism and arbitrary authority?' Critical social scientists are opposed to endorsing the social-constructionist alternatives discussed below, which they see as abandoning the idea of an ethically serious social science and adopting an 'anything goes' attitude. Often, critical theorists assume that their ethical and social programme of unmasking domination and striving for greater procedural and distributive justice in a modern context is entirely sound or sufficient for answering such questions. Procedural justice is concerned with making and implementing decisions according to fair processes (e.g., ensuring that a fair trial takes place by impartial and consistent application of the law). However, procedural justice can become rather abstract and formal, and critical theorists such as Habermas tend to emphasize procedures and abstract ethical principles that are supposed to be neutral to all interests and visions of the good life.[4]

As some sympathetic critics have pointed out (e.g., Taylor 1985b: 231–36; Warnke 1987: 130–34), critical social scientists tend to embrace much of the modern formalist ethical outlook they decry in objectivist approaches to social science. This focus on formalist approaches and procedural concerns is unlikely to have any genuine impact on, say, overcoming subtle racial biases or our 'predatory' attitude towards the environment. Moreover, Taylor (1985b: pp. 230–47) argues that all such modern 'formalist' approaches fail to do justice to the fact that no society or tradition strictly limits itself to procedural principles. Societies and traditions always give comparable weight to other substantive and sometimes conflicting ideals of maturity, character, honour, the social good, loyalty to tradition, existential meaning and the like. This makes moral and political discussion both a lot messier and more interesting than formalist views suggest.

Critical social science does force us to face up to the inescapable presence of moral or spiritual values in interpreting and explaining human action and social life. And these approaches make it clear how social inquiry itself has to be seen as part of life, not something bleached of its humanity that tries to make sense of our very humanity at a great distance from it like natural scientific and descriptivist approaches. Still, we are left with some enormous problems to solve. Habermas' formalism and residual individualism (albeit a very social and dialogical kind of formalism and individualism) still contain an element of striving for a kind of objectivity that hopes to escape from the fact that we, even as social scientists, are always tied to and shaped by our history and cultural contexts. If we give that up and accept what we might term a thoroughgoing relativist view of all our activities, we are left with a great puzzle as to how we can make sense of there being better and worse, or more or less valid interpretations of human activity. It is tempting to give in to a complete relativism and proclaim that in the differences of views and values among people and societies, all we have is a naked clash of one arbitrary bias with another. But it is also possible to conclude that our human situation and its limitations – lacking an outsider's view – means that we can neither escape coming to reasonable convictions about better and worse interpretations nor ever claim final or certain truth for them. One of the last two approaches to social inquiry I will cover calls for an unqualified relativism, the other, instead, advocates a strong dose of humility.

4. Postmodern/social constructionist viewpoints

A different kind of critique of the culture of individualism and *zweckrational* of modern societies is offered by a number of thinkers loosely grouped together

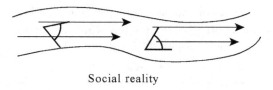

Social reality

Figure 3.2 Insider's Perspective
The insider's perspective, where social reality can only be viewed by those immersed in it.

as *postmodern* theorists. The perspectives championed by postmodernists are perhaps best characterized as a combination of forms of analysis, sensibility and intellectual condition. These thinkers, somewhat like Habermas and other critical theorists, seek to restore a sense of people as embedded or contextualized in a historical culture – we only have *insiders'* perspectives available to us (Fig. 3.2). Unlike Habermas and many critical theorists, the postmodernists reject any attempt to define a universal standard or procedure for critically evaluating our values and practices. To them, that sort of critical theory is simply another example of modern Western society's setting its own way of life up as a kind of absolute and arbitrarily insisting all cultures and peoples be judged in terms of its ethnocentric viewpoint. Postmodernists also reject any attempt to 'get beneath' the shifting sands of history by identifying metaphysical grounds, infallible methods or universal moral standards for judging our beliefs. Any such standards, they argue, amount to projecting a particular community's viewpoint onto others because there are no such standards apart from what communities choose to adopt. Basically, most of our philosophical and scientific traditions have mistaken what is culturally or historically stable for something supposed to be eternal and universal. Instead, postmodernists believe social order and meaning is always local and contextual. As a result, 'society' actually refers to a heterogeneous, fractured entity. This picture of society parallels postmodernists' contentions that knowledge is local and contextual rather than universal.

Postmodern thinkers acknowledge that people are self-interpreting animals and usually think that, as such, we have often engaged in practices enabling us 'to act as if [we] had a whole series of different natures in the course of history' (Dreyfus 1987: 65). Postmodernists argue human nature does not transcend culture – that is to say, there is no objective, relatively fixed human nature as many pre-modern and modern philosophers and scientists thought. Social-constructionist psychologists, like Philip Cushman, tend to argue that this picture of a fixed, ahistorical human nature has several deleterious effects such as promoting 'a culturally disrespectful and damaging psychological imperialism abroad' and numerous 'attendant miseries at home' (Cushman 1990: 599). Hence, by postmodernist lights, any attempt – scientific or otherwise – to use the concept of a fixed human nature as some standard by which to judge individuals or societies, or to conceive of a more humane or just social order, is deluded at best and destructive at worst.

According to postmodernists, rather than a self somehow independent of culture, culture explains and interprets what it means to be a human self, shaping our natures and identities. Cushman maintains that 'cultural conceptualizations and configurations of the self are formed by the economies and polities of their respective eras' (1990: 599). Philosopher Richard Rorty puts it this way: there is 'no criterion that we have not created in the course of creating a practice, no standard of rationality that is not an appeal to such a criterion, no rigorous argumentation that is not obedience to our own conventions' (1985: 28). Along with this, postmodern thinkers typically view science as simply one more way of knowing, having no superiority over other ways of knowing (extreme version of the approval conception).

4.1. Social constructionism

The most prominent philosopher representing this branch of postmodern thought is Rorty (1982; 1985), who also has much to say about the social sciences. He maintains that there are no vocabulary-neutral facts or criteria we can use to judge one vocabulary or description of events as better or truer than another. Rather, we only have sets of irreconcilable 'language games' with their own internal criteria and rules. This means that no approaches in the social sciences are any better or any worse than any others. Moreover, on Rorty's view, social science cannot offer descriptions of events superior to any other descriptions that might interest us (e.g., aesthetic, religious, ironic), because any particular social-science description only reflects a particular vocabulary or language game that we might choose.

A good example of social constructionism in the social sciences is psychologist Kenneth Gergen (1982; 1985; 1994). He argues that the terms in which we understand the world are social constructions because these terms are produced in our historically situated interactions with each other (1985). According to Gergen, Western culture has made individual minds the 'critical locus of explanation' in psychology and much of the social sciences in general (1994: 3).[5] But this is just a social construction, according to him, because inquiry into the historical and cultural foundations of 'various forms of world constructions' indicates that 'psychological processes differ markedly from one culture to another' (Gergen 1985: 267). Hence, he thinks many of the theories and findings of social science distort psychological phenomena by pretending that the world, self and psychological processes have a transhistorical or essential nature. In other words, psychological phenomena are just one way – namely, our way, which is both ethnocentric and erroneous. The subject-object ontology and epistemology underlying natural science view psychological phenomena as objects from a distinctly Western culture-laden standpoint – hardly the kind of objective, value-neutral perspective to which mainstream psychologists aspire.

Gergen believes social constructionism can help us get beyond this distorting 'subject-object dualism' and chauvinistic ethnocentrism (1985: 270–72). On the constructionist view, reports or descriptions of a person's experience turn out to be 'linguistic constructions guided and shaped by historically contingent conventions of discourse'. There is no correct method warranting findings objective, no procedures yielding truth. Instead, on the social constructionist view, 'the success of [our] accounts depends primarily on the analyst's capacity to invite, compel, stimulate, or delight the audience, and not on criteria of veracity'. There is no real difference between everyday life and social theory in the sense that all our concerns, whether practical or theoretical, are socially negotiated. There is no subject-object split, but only subjects immersed in the play of cultural/social conventions.

This kind of constructionist view sounds irrational and relativistic, but Gergen and Rorty believe such charges are misplaced. First, our practices and values can evolve only gradually through a (loosely) coordinated social effort because there is a stability to our understandings and meanings due to an 'inherent dependency of knowledge systems on communities of shared intelligibility' (Gergen 1985: 272). In other words, because knowledge and values are socially shared and conditioned, they are restrained from changing chaotically or whimsically because cultures are inherently slow to change. Still, there is nothing objective about American society or the world that stands in the way of US citizens waking up tomorrow and rushing headlong towards a fascist culture. Second, if we are not hiding behind a facade of objectivity or value-neutrality, we are forced to acknowledge that our theory and practice 'enter into the life of the culture, sustaining [particular] patterns of conduct and destroying others'. Hence, 'such work must be evaluated in terms of good and evil' (1985: 272) and because these standards for good and evil exhibit social stability, they can serve as rational standards for evaluative judgements.

Although these standards, too, could be subject to very rapid change. Finally, Rorty (1985) thinks this sort of relativism will not lead to social fragmentation or loss of personal direction. Rather, it frees us to experience a deepened sense of 'solidarity' by undermining dogmatism and fostering a positive sense of connectedness and shared purpose with fellow travellers of our particular way of life.

4.2. Michel Foucault

In contrast to the rather upbeat view of cultural embeddedness offered by Gergen and Rorty, Michel Foucault (1979; 1980a; 1980b) presents a darker though perhaps more realistic perspective. Foucault focused on power and relations of power, particularly as expressed in social institutions. There is no overarching truth or falsity in any field of knowledge for Foucault; instead, 'truth' is an effect resulting from the 'rules' of the power relations that create and constitute a particular form of life or field of knowledge. The power relations he typically had in mind are not matters of explicit consent nor violent coercion. Rather, they are the myriad ways people are constrained to act together within a particular, ultimately arbitrary system of 'power/knowledge' (for Foucault there is little difference between these two). On Foucault's analysis, what we might call domination or justice are simply 'truth effects' within our cultural rules; that is, what we take to be truth is simply the effect or consequence of the rules of some institution or social-science discipline. Cultures and institutions evolve in contingent ways, so there is no necessity or direction to these evolutions. Hence, systems of 'power/knowledge' are largely arbitrary.

On Foucault's view, relations of power might be exercised positively to produce forms of life or fields of knowledge as well as negatively to repress or dominate. The kinds of domination and forms of justice in previous eras are neither more or less dominating or morally superior or inferior as compared with any others, including our own, only different. For Foucault, there is no historically discernible direction for such forms of power, no sense of moral or intellectual improvement, no 'progress'.

Foucault refers to the social sciences as the 'dubious sciences'. Although they purport to aim at truth, in fact, they really turn out to classify and manage people in line with the current cultural regime's view on what a normal and healthy population is.[6] The social sciences subtly enable the kind of detailed surveillance and control that Foucault thinks modern societies exert in the service of their favoured ideals of acceptable and unacceptable behavior. Foucault attempts to detail how modes of domination and discipline form human beings into the modern individuals we take ourselves to be. He stresses how particular practices, often mediated by an external authority figure (e.g., psychological counsellor or priest), bring individuals' active self-formative processes in line with the current regime of thought (Foucault 1980b). Since their rise in the eighteenth and nineteenth centuries, Foucault agues that the social sciences, along with the church, the military, the school, the prison and the clinic, have been part of regimes of power/knowledge. These regimes have introduced new ways of maintaining public order and social control that did not previously exist, and social scientists have played a leading role in creating these new ways.

An example might be how therapy clients, in either individual or group settings, are led by a therapist to scrutinize themselves until they 'find' particular problems or tendencies. They are then persuaded to take responsibility for managing or eliminating these desires. In this way, Foucault thinks, the self-formative capacities of people are enlisted in the service of conforming to current norms of health and productivity. One does not have to agree with everything in Foucault's analysis to see the potential problems raised by such a situation. For instance, there are indications that therapists tend to rate client therapeutic improvement in terms of the degree to which clients take on therapists' ways of thinking, including therapists' values (Kelly 1990). In other words, therapists' notion of improvement/lack of improvement are tied up with therapists' values. To the extent that these values reflect the psychological community's definitions of acceptable/unacceptable behaviour, the potential for enforcing 'truth' in personal beliefs and behaviour is very real.

As another example, in his *Discipline and Punish: The Birth of the Prison* (1979), Foucault traces the development of disciplinary technologies of power. He also traces the corresponding changes in discipline and punishment practices as well as the development of relevant social sciences which provide the necessary classifications for the penal regime. Hence, there is a kind of scientific imprimatur for the regime itself, but the related social sciences are seen as largely constructing notions of self and practices rather than *discovering* some independent social realities (see Chapter 13).

On Foucault's analysis, emotionally isolated modern individuals are trained to adapt to being a cog in the social and economic machinery, to do without lasting social ties, and to criticize only themselves and not the prevailing social order for their problems in living (compare Weber's take on rationalization slotting people into their proper roles in the social machine). In this way, one can imagine citizens of a society being 'kept in line' without their conscious awareness of the role power relations play in shaping their lives and forming their very selves.

What Foucault offered in place of objectifying mainstream social science or the ethical discussion of critical theorists, is the practice of *genealogy*. Genealogy seeks to uncover the likely origins of these rules of power. This mode of analysis is supposed to reveal how the rules' deceptive claims to truth actually arose from historical accidents and not from a supposed universal nature of human beings. His study of the development of the modern penal system is an example of his genealogical approach at work. Yet, this genealogical mode is highly detached objectifying the fields of practices involved with regimes like the penal system. Foucault presents a highly depersonalized picture of these practices in his attempt to portray how power actually functions in such concrete settings.

Toward the end of his life Foucault began to articulate a more positive ethic beyond merely engaging in the detached genealogy of ultimately equally dominating regimes of truth. He wanted to indicate how a lack of any fixed or universal human nature could lead to our ceaselessly creating and recreating ourselves as works of art (Foucault 1982). However, given the arbitrariness identified by Foucault in these matters, it is unclear how he could have justified this direction. Why not adopt nihilism, existentialism or a religious leap of faith as legitimate responses to the denial of a fixed human nature?

4.3. Assessing postmodernism/social constructionism

Both these as well as other versions of postmodern thought have the virtue, along with critical theory, of helping unmask troubling modern pretensions to exaggerated autonomy, certainty and control. Many have also felt that these approaches provide new, helpful tools for illuminating individual and social behaviours and for explaining experiences in ways not available to scientistic, rationalistic or instrumentalist ways of thinking (e.g., Flyvbjerg 2001). Nevertheless, these postmodern views are seriously flawed.

One thing to notice about social-constructionist accounts is their paradoxical picture of the human self. The self is simultaneously radically determined by historical influences yet radically free to reinterpret itself and social reality as it wishes for its own self-invented purposes. This is an ultimately implausible view. How would such historically embedded beings ever get free of culturally determining forces to radically reinvent themselves in this way? Do they step outside this stream of influences to an ahistorical point and then choose the selves they will become? Or do they somehow harness this stream of forces,

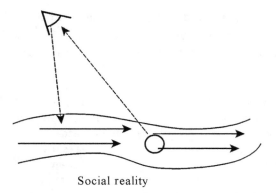

Social reality

Figure 3.3 Manipulating Social Influences
How does a self wholly embedded in a flow of cultural and historical influences rise above or manipulate this flow to reinterpret or change itself?

using it to launch themselves in a new direction not determined by this stream (see Fig. 3.3)? Postmodern writers are not clear on how this self-construction works, but their picture of agents reproduces the detached picture of self and world found in the subject-object ontology and epistemology constructionists repudiate. The self that is supposedly capable of such reinventing somehow is able to stand apart from the social order choosing which interpretations and meanings it wishes to take on, implying such selves are absolutely free from the historical flow in which they are supposedly embedded.

Another tension in these postmodern views has to do with objectivity itself. On the one hand, Rorty, Gergen, Foucault and others emphasize that there is no outsider's perspective on social reality. This means there is no objective or perspective-free standpoint for observing and analyzing social phenomena. On the other hand, these writers are making claims to some kind of 'truer perspective' along with commitments to relative evils and goods (e.g., apartheid is bad, freedom is good). But how is this superior view on offer to be justified on any basis other than from some outsider's vantage point? Why are the perspectives postmodernists and constructionists offer not simply that – perspectives that are neither better nor worse, neither clearer nor cloudier than any other perspectives? By their very lights, postmodernists are committed to saying that there is no qualitative moral difference between apartheid and democracy, for example.

Postmodernist thinkers often suggest that denying all metaphysical and moral universals frees us from dreaded tendencies toward dogmatism and domination (e.g., Rorty). However, what is to keep such free selves from abandoning our society's ideals of freedom, universal respect and toleration in favour of shallow diversions or some comforting new tyranny? In times when democracy is appearing increasingly vulnerable to internal as well as external pressures, such questions become particularly acute. As Richardson and Fowers put the point:

> We are asked by postmodern theory to believe that when such ideals as freedom and respect for human life are taken seriously, they are dangerous illusions. Unfortunately, however, the social constructionist recommendation that we escape this danger by evaluating our moral beliefs and values in terms of their 'pragmatic implications' severely clashes with what we seem to mean by genuine commitment or taking responsibility in everyday life. One wonders if constructionist thinkers have really thought through what it would mean, for example, to collapse the distinction entirely between feeling guilty merely from the fear of disapproval versus remorse from violating one's personal moral standards. Taken literally, that would mean adopting an inhuman and quite destructive amorality. However, it is more likely that it means we are being asked to endorse postmodern relativism as the most humane and authentic viewpoint, one that actually will help undermine irrational guilt and dogmatic beliefs. Nevertheless, even though [such a viewpoint] is quite sincere, it seems utopian and naive. The loss of credible conviction and sense of purpose it entails would seem more likely to lead to individual apathy and social atomization (if not despair and violence) than to enhanced solidarity. Such thinkers seem to believe that their own hard-won character and cultivation will spring up automatically in others as a result of embracing relativism. Also, they are embroiled in the contradiction of treating all moral values as purely relative or subjective in order to promote [particular] moral values, such as human solidarity, which they do not appear to view as purely relative or optional. (1998: 484)

Foucault's writings, in particular, reveal a dark side to the kind of cultural play on individuals that postmodernists emphasize, raising the frightening spectre of social science as a 'technology' for manipulation and control. On the constructivist view, there certainly is no particular reason to think that the cultural stability of values and practices alluded to by Rorty and Gergen is always good or somehow promotes human welfare. Rather, there seems all the more reason to worry about the results of social-science inquiry and on what basis such results can be put to use for the common good.

5. Contemporary hermeneutics

Contemporary philosophical or ontological *hermeneutics* (e.g., Gadamer 1975; Warnke 1987; Taylor 1989; Guignon 1991; Ricoeur 1992; Richardson, Fowers and Guignon 1999) does not conceive of sharp divisions between a person on one side, and the body, others and the world on the other. In other words, it does not presuppose a subject-object ontology and epistemology. Rather, hermeneutics sees the meanings we live by as permeating and shaping the practices and institutions of others and the world 'out there' much as they belong to our 'inner' life. The way we experience everyday life, values and meanings are both in us *and* in the world around us. When we see a hotel or restaurant blown up, and men, women and children maimed and killed, we recognize something bad has happened right there and not just in our mind.

In some sense ontological hermeneutics seeks to combine insights from the other modes of social-science inquiry in an attempt to get beyond the seeming impasse between the scientism of many natural-science approaches and the raw relativism of constructionism (Chapter 17). Hermeneutics heartily takes on the natural-science approach's virtues of healthy scepticism and commitment to some form of objectivity, accuracy and reproducibility. It values descriptivism's emphasis on the richness and irreducibility of meaningful human action, though it rejects the possibility of giving an objective, value-neutral description of human action (no outsider's perspective is available to us). It endorses the general thrust of critical theory's drive to lay bare hidden assumptions and disguised ideologies, but is suspicious that procedural justice and formalist ethics can really address the problems raised by ideologies. While it abhors postmodernism's moral relativism, hermeneutics agrees with these thinkers that there is much modern hubris in the critical-social-science approach and that human action is interpretive.

Hermeneutic philosophers and social scientists acknowledge that actions and knowledge of actions are historically conditioned and inescapably interpretive. Hence, they usually view natural-science and social-science inquiry as separated by a gulf (Chapter 1, sec. 4; Chapter 16, sec. 2), where interpretation is crucial to social inquiry, but not to natural science.[7] Understanding and explanation in the social sciences for hermeneutic thinkers always reflect some degree of creativity and interpretation that is neither bound by some objective order of facts (or metaphysics) nor is thoroughly relativistic. And they think that denying this kind of creativity and interpretation in social-science inquiry contributes greatly to both the fragmented character of these sciences as well as their tendency to simply offer wordy elaborations of the obvious.

Dialogue is a key feature for contemporary hermeneutics, distinguishing it from other modes of inquiry. Conversation is the central model for thinking about and investigating human action and interaction because dialogue is one of the central processes of interaction and growth in human life. Simple examples from everyday life like talking with friends or family show how often such conversations lead to new insights about ourselves and to new ways of looking at our situations in life as well as our world – for both us and our conversation partners. Similarly, reading a book often leads us to reflect on ourselves and our way of life, perhaps leading us to see our past and future in a new light which, in turn, leads to a new interpretation or change in our view of who we are now and where we are going in life. Television programmes and movies we watch, music we hear, artwork we see and a myriad other channels of influence also affect us in such ways. These are ordinary experiences we have in life and philosophical hermeneutics tries to pattern itself as closely as possible on these kinds of everyday realities of human life in its conception of human motivation and action. Nor is there one true, right or correct insider's perspective on the hermeneutic picture. Rather, we have to put several insiders' perspectives in conversation with each other to fill out an accurate picture of human motivation/actions.

In addition, the family, community and society in which we grow up provide us with numerous interpretations, meanings and values from early on in life. We find ourselves 'up and running' with these interpretations and values (Heidegger's 'thrownness'), shaping much of who we are as persons. As we mature and become reflective, we begin to re-evaluate and rework these interpretations and meanings in new, creative ways, rejecting some, personalizing others. On the hermeneutic view, social forces are not seen as deterministic in the strong sense that postmodernist writers often envisage.

How does the hermeneutic view avoid the extremes of objectivism and relativism? Hermeneutic thinkers are not necessarily opposed to absolutes. There may be absolutes in the form of persistent natural patterns or moral universals, but hermeneutic thinkers recognize that absolutes are not uninterpreted or univocal (i.e., admitting only one meaning). Any absolutes always admit multiple meanings or layers of meanings. So there is no naked objectivism on this picture of reality. On the other hand, not everything goes with interpretations. If there are natural laws, these laws limit the kinds and range of interpretations about them. Or think of the Ten Commandments or the golden rule as moral universals. 'Thou shalt not kill' cannot be interpreted in just any way one chooses. It makes no sense, for instance, to interpret this universal as saying nothing about killing whatsoever, nor as saying we cannot kill anything no matter the situation (e.g., self-defense, invasion). On the other hand, the commandment perhaps places limits on capital punishment and is relevant for determining what makes for just war. So even moral absolutes admit of multiple interpretations, but the range of interpretations is limited and some are better or fuller than others. Again, there is neither naked objectivism nor raw relativism (cf. Chapter 17).

Like postmodern approaches to inquiry, hermeneutics repudiates the subject-object ontology and epistemology found in so many modes of social inquiry.[8] Natural-science, descriptivist and critical approaches either explicitly or implicitly abstract objects of investigation away from subjective qualities (like our feeling of attachment toward some object or some person; see Chapter 5, sec. 3). Hermeneutics recognizes that these meanings and attachments are part of our everyday lived experience, including our shifting desires, values and purposes. Moreover, hermeneutic thinkers recognize that these desires, values, purposes and significance are not mere subjective attitudes towards objective facts. Meanings and significances of a situation are not reducible to the feelings and responses of the people involved in the situation. For instance, a disgraceful action has the characteristic of being humiliating whether the person who performed the action has the appropriate feeling or not. That is why we can say, 'You ought to be ashamed of yourself'. Similarly, it is because situational imports are the grounds for our feelings that emotions can be mistaken or irrational – as occurs when people feel ashamed of something they have no reason to feel so. The desires, values and goals of Genghis Kahn, Adolf Hitler or Osama bin Laden are not merely subjective responses to meaningless realities in the world, but really exist as part of the reality of our world and have genuine consequences.

So to 'regard the world as it is independently of the meanings it might have for human subjects, or how it figures in their experience' is to limit inquiry to a fairly narrow investigation of human actions and concerns (Taylor 1989: 31). This kind of detached, limited approach has proven useful in many areas of natural science and is not without its usefulness in the social sciences. However, hermeneutic thinkers believe there are other avenues to knowledge and understanding of social phenomena, which can be more insightful than natural-science methods by, as it were, picking up what objectification and detachment throw out. By closing the distance between the investigator and the investigated – the subject and the object – and by fully acknowledging the force of the double hermeneutic, hermeneutic social scientists believe that we can learn and understand more about people and their actions than by the pursuit of correlation studies alone. This means rejecting the subject-object ontology emphasizing correct representations of an independent reality, acknowledging that social scientists are part of the social fabric they are studying and that this social fabric has an influence – for good or for ill – on their research and results.

Hermeneutic approaches to social inquiry have received much less attention and consequently are much less fleshed out than the other modes. However, some outlines can be traced briefly here. Such thinkers are committed to re-placing the subject-object ontology and epistemology dominating most of social-science inquiry with a historically embedded view of agency drawing on such notions as engaged agency/strong world-shaping to fill out this alterna-tive. In this sense, hermeneutic approaches are better able to avoid the return of a stark subject-object picture of social reality than social constructionists or critical theorists. Hermeneutic social scientists and philosophers offer an interpretation of what human beings are like not from some vantage point outside human practices and history – what Thomas Nagel calls the view from nowhere (1989) – but from within.

Such an insider's account begins with the insight that human beings are 'self-interpreting animals' (Berlin 1962; Taylor 1985a; 1989). This is the idea that the meanings we hammer out in daily life largely make us what we are. In other words, genetic and social influences as described by objective natural science are not completely responsible for our behaviour. Instead, life has more of a narrative character, with our genetic and social influences providing af-fordances for possible storylines we might 'write' for our lives. In working out these narratives, we sometimes employ abstraction and objectification to forge knowledge of enduring patterns or lawfulness regardless of our evaluations of these events, including knowledge of means–ends relations. We sometimes take a distanced stance towards our ethical reflections, stepping back so to speak from less worthy attachments and passions to better do the right thing as we see it. However, there is a more fundamental and practical kind of understanding that people hammer out together; that being our mutual understandings of events, social realities and the actions of others, involvements that affect us much more intimately than universal laws and abstract methods can capture. In particular:

> Historical experience changes the meaning events can have for us, not because it alters our view of an independent object, but because history is a dialectical process in which both the object and our knowledge of it are continually transformed. Thus, for example, both the meaning of the American Revolution and my lived understanding of freedom continue to be modified in the dialogue between them. So we are immersed in and

deeply connected to this process rather than essentially detached from it as scientistic, descriptivist, and even postmodern approaches all tend to suppose. (Richardson and Fowers 1998: 490)

The model of ongoing conversation or dialogue is important to hermeneutic philosophers and social scientists. Indeed, conversation is the model for how many of them see the interaction between natural-science and interpretive approaches to understanding human experience.[9] Usually when one thinks of integrating two different approaches, there is a serious question to be addressed: 'On what basis are the two approaches to be integrated?' With respect to mainstream and interpretive approaches, are we to integrate them on the basis of the mainstream view? Some interpretive view? Or a third supposedly neutral view? Simply to raise this question reveals that the model of integration is hardly an unbiased way to bring multiple approaches together as one of the approaches more or less subtly ends up establishing the basis for all future interactions.

Just as conversation between two people opens them to mutual influence from each other, this model of cooperation between hermeneutics and other approaches allows for mutual give and take, mutual influence of these perspectives on one another rather than the dominance of one over the other found in integrationist models of interaction. Correlational studies surely have a place in the study of human agency and interactions, helping us detect enduring patterns or regularities that might otherwise go unrecognized. But the role that such processes and patterns play in our lives, the meaning they have for us, and the nature and direction of our efforts to cope with or alter them, are determined by the place they come to occupy within unfolding individual and social narratives. Conversation looks to be a good model for bringing the strengths of these different approaches together.

But by proposing the model of conversation between mainstream and hermeneutic approaches, hermeneutic thinkers, perhaps only implicitly, acknowledge that natural-science approaches are actually more interpretive or more open to interpretation than they often lead us to believe. By this I do not have in mind the mainstream's almost always unspoken commitment to neutrality, fairness, tolerance, respect, liberal individualism and other values composing a substantial moral framework, which are inconsistent with a pretence to objectivity and value-neutrality (this viewpoint will receive closer scrutiny later). Rather, I mean that the very notion of conversation between two partners presupposes that both partners are in possession of meanings and interpretations, some of which must be shared for conversation to take place, and that these meanings and interpretations are open to change as a result of conversation. In other words, Taylor's characterization of correlators as being solely animated by their reliance on brute data and univocal methods mis-represents to some degree at least some portion of mainstream social-science research. Otherwise, dialogue would not be as attractive a model for bringing hermeneutic and natural-science approaches together (the conversation would likely more closely resemble a monologue rather than genuine dialogue).

6. Taking stock

In this overview of the various modes of social inquiry, every approach has something to offer for gaining purchase on social phenomena. Each mode has various distinctives, some emphasizing empirical practices, some emphasizing interpretive practices (and among the latter taking distinctive approaches to interpretive practices). Regarding the founders of social science surveyed in Chapter 2, Hobbes and Comte would clearly fall under the natural-science mode of inquiry, though Hobbes would endorse deductive methods while Comte would endorse empirical ones. Although Dilthey's approach is de-scribed as hermeneutical ('interpretive'), he would not fall under contempo-rary hermeneutics (none of the founders do, but Taylor falls in this category). Rather, his interpretive approach follows from Schleiermacher, where the goal is to put oneself into the position of feeling what another person feels, seeing things how another person sees things, to understand (*verstehen*) the motives and values of another person. Dilthey falls most naturally under the descrip-tivist mode, seeking as accurate an interpretive account of people's behaviour as possible. Durkheim and Weber, in contrast, both fall under natural-science and descriptivist modes, incorporating key aspects of both approaches in their work. None of the founders really departed from the subject-object/fact–value splits, with their emphasis on values and interpretation as subjective.

Interestingly, and somewhat surprisingly, mainstream as well as descrip-tivist, critical and postmodern approaches largely share a commitment to a subject-object ontology and epistemology. Only the hermeneutic approach looks to be thoroughly explicit in rooting out and replacing this ontology and epistemology with some kind of alternative (even if this alternative currently is not fully developed). However, one might question this move. After all, if the subject-object ontology and epistemology, along with an objectifying tendency, are so pervasive, might this be reason to suspect that they play an important role in scientific inquiry and that significant losses might be incurred if we give these up? No doubt some losses will be incurred, but as we will see over the coming chapters, a subject-object ontology and epistemology are as much *moral ideals* as they are scientific ones. As such, they also exact a rather high price that has gone largely unnoticed by social-science practitioners.

For further study

1. Pick one of the five modes of social inquiry and explain it as briefly as you can. What is the strongest objection to this mode? Can the mode be modified to meet this objection without transforming it into one of the other modes? Why or why not?
2. Explain the subject-object ontology and epistemology. Even though natural scientific and postmodernist modes of social inquiry are radically different, in what way do they both share this ontology and epistemology?
3. How might this analysis of five modes of social inquiry help explain the theoretical and methodological fragmentation of the behavioural sciences described in Chapter 1?

Recommended reading

R. Bernstein, 'Conceptual Analysis and the Language of Action: Peter Winch', in *The Restructuring of Social and Political Theory* (Philadelphia: University of Pennsylvania Press, 1976), pp. 63–74.

F. N. Kerlinger and H. B. Lee, *Foundations of Behavioral Research* (Belmont, CA: Wadsworth 1999).

F. C. Richardson and B. Fowers, 'Interpretive Social Science: An Overview', *American Behavioral Scientist* 41(1998): 465–95.

Part Two

Cultural Ideals I: Instrumental Reason

Chapter Outline

As I have described things so far, *zweckrational* along with the subject-object ontology and epistemology (see Chapter 3, sec. 1) are pervasive in social-science analyses of personal and social behaviour. Also, I have hinted that all may not be well with these concepts, so it is time to examine them more closely. Interestingly, these concepts are related in a way that helps explain their often unacknowledged dominance in social-science inquiry. The way in which they are connected also suggests some possible alternatives for social inquiry as well as perhaps addressing the worry raised at the end of the previous chapter about losing too much if we give up on the subject-object ontology and epistemology.

1. Instrumental picture of action

According to Weber, the signal characteristic of *zweckrational* is its means–ends structured reasoning. Given some already established ends or goals, such as improving student test scores or protecting increasingly fragile marriages, *zweckrational* emphasizes rational examination and choice of the most effective or efficient means for achieving these goals. Such means–ends reasoning is often useful or necessary, like explaining the quickest route to the nearest post office when someone asks, or deciding the most effective and safest way to lift a heavy load.

The rise of means–ends reasoning, which emphasizes, efficiency or effectiveness of means as the predominating picture of rational thinking and action, has much to do with the rise of utilitarian ethics and the marginal revolution (Chapter 12, sec. 1) in economics (not unrelated phenomena) in the 1800s. Briefly, utilitarian ethics focuses on the maximization of the happiness or welfare of an individual or group of individuals ('the greatest good for the greatest number'). The action(s) bringing about the maximum possible happiness or welfare are those judged to be the most ethical. The rise of marginalist thinking in economics has much to do with conceiving consumers' and producers' choices as involving trade-offs among different consumable goods and different means of production. Marginalists emphasized thinking systematically about optimal or maximizing choices of means for a given end. Hence, a profit-maximizing employer might respond to an increase in wages by minimizing labour costs through outsourcing as much of the production process as possible. These kinds of means–ends rationality proved very influential in the development of the modern picture of rational action. Also, this picture fits well with a subject-object ontology, viewing the world as a collection of potential means to a subject's ends.

The worries about *zweckrational* raised by Weber as well as critical theorists like Horkheimer and Habermas is that such means–ends thinking comes to so dominate society that other equally or more important features of life get squeezed out. This would leave us with a picture of human action that is largely or perhaps exclusively *instrumental* – all actions are merely means or instruments for achieving our aims with little if any thought for the morality of our actions, the other possible reasons for acting, or the worth of our aims.[1] As Jon Elster, succinctly puts it, 'actions are valued and chosen not for themselves, but as more or less efficient means to a further end' (1989: 22), where the ends are not evaluated for their worth.

But there is more to this instrumental conception of human agency than just the emphasis on means–ends reasoning. In this picture of agency, while being simultaneously immersed in the efficient causal chain of events – indeed these chains of causal events impinge upon and flow through us – agents are pictured as somehow turning back on this causal flow using the knowledge of such causal chains to intervene in and alter the future course of events to suit their purposes. Imagine the chains of causes and effects as a river, where causes lead to effects, which are causes for further effects, and so forth. It is this flow of causes and effects in which we as agents are supposedly trapped. But on the instrumental picture, the agent is also somehow able to manipulate this flow by intervening in the causes and bringing about effects suited to his

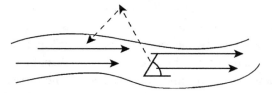

Figure 4.1 Instrumental Picture of Action
Suppose social reality is dominated by chains of efficient causes and effects. In the instrumental picture, an agent is assumed to somehow manipulate these causal chains to bring about desired outcomes.

purposes (see Fig. 4.1). Social scientists, for instance, produce knowledge of the cause–effect relations determining self-esteem that they, or social planners or individuals, can then use to manipulate these relations to increase self-esteem.

Such a conception of agency appears to be consonant with the ideals of many social scientists. They imagine applying value-free theory and results – supposedly mapping the efficient causal chains governing human behaviour – to the concerns of individuals and groups so that they may more effectively change or otherwise enhance their lives according to their purposes or pursue policies supportive of their conception of the good life. This feature of instrumental action is deeply connected to our prized value-neutrality (Chapter 6) and plays an important role in free will – determinism dilemmas in the social sciences (Chapter 14).

In turn this kind of instrumental agency or rationality derives its plausibility as an account of human behaviour primarily from two sources: a scientific ideal and a family of cultural ideals. Regarding the scientific ideal, because instrumental reason appears to fit well within a physical world of efficient causal interactions, it rests comfortably with much of mainstream social science's mechanistic pictures of the world and action. Viewing agents as operating through efficient causation acting on a world conceived of as an interconnected web of efficient causes presents a strongly compelling picture of action in the world amenable to scientific study.

The instrumental picture does afford a plausible image of fit between action and world in at least some areas of practical life (e.g., determining the most efficient route for a trip). This image of things also has the advantage of being much in harmony with a modern scientific outlook on the world, including its emphasis on technological solutions to humanity's problems (e.g., Comte's third stage of society). In short, the instrumental picture of action appears to be consonant with what many take to be our best understandings and practices in science. Moreover, focusing on efficient causation allows social scientists to attempt to design controlled experiments to test relationships among, for example, environmental factors, beliefs and behaviour. And if the contributions of these various elements turn out to be measurable and predictable, then there is the possibility of using this knowledge for human betterment in the form of improvements in therapies, management techniques, learning strategies, organizational structures, public policy and so forth.

2. Instrumental agency, the subject-object ontology and autonomy

Not only is an instrumental picture of agency cosy with a scientific picture of the world, it also fits well with and is reinforced by the subject-object ontology presupposed by so much social inquiry. Agents are conceived as sharply distinct from the world, including the social realm the self inhabits, and this allows agents to take on a largely instrumental relationship between self and world (Taylor 1985a: 187–212; Slife and Williams 1995). The agent is 'in but not of' the social realm so to speak. If one assumes the events in both the physical and social realms flow as sequences of efficient causes and their effects, this meshes well with the conception of agency as mainly concerned with an individual's manipulation of those causes to produce desired outcomes. On mainstream views, chains of efficient causation in the social realm are studied by the social sciences and objectified as independent objects standing in causal relations to one another. Then the results of such studies can be put to use to achieve those value-laden outcomes. There appears to be a concrete fit between the way the world seems to work and the conditions needed for successful instrumental action, on the one hand, and the purposes or goals for which instrumental action is employed on the other. The chains of causes and effects mapped out by social science are thought of as value-neutral means to achieving individual or social goals. This is one way the fact/value distinction comes to expression in social inquiry. The physical and social worlds are represented as objects external to us while values are our subjective attitudes towards these external objects. The kind of knowledge social science discovers is *instrumental* knowledge, the knowledge of causes in the social world that can be manipulated according to our subjective desires and values.

Beyond this apparent 'scientific fit', the instrumental picture of action and a subject-object ontology are mutually reinforced by substantial commitments to autonomy and individuality, ethical ideals characterizing modern Western societies (recall Durkheim's and Weber's discussions of the transformation of pre-modern societies to modern ones). On the instrumental picture, agents are largely motivated by self-interest and more or less consciously evaluate alternative courses of action based upon their preferences (this is essentially Hobbes' picture of individuals engaging in rational choice on the self-interested interpretation discussed in Chapter 2, sec. 1). Societies, then, tend to be conceptualized as aggregations of individual actors exercising instrumental rationality yielding some form of collective rationality at the group level (Chapter 10). In limited, highly structured settings, where actors are engaged in strategic reasoning based upon preferences for outcomes, this picture of agency does have some applicability and plausibility. It is the apparent success of this picture in these limited settings that gives it apparent validation as an appropriate conception of action for all settings. In essence, the instrumental picture of action views actors as engaged in roughly the same kind of means–ends reasoning when they are trying to construct the shortest route for a trip as when they are dealing with the quest for meaning or the surprise of love.

Ideally, according to the instrumental picture, actors engage in means–ends reasoning, deliberating among the means independently from or untainted by social context, cultural values and roles, history or other larger perspectives, even apart from what others (will) think about them. Furthermore, agents' purposes are usually portrayed as ideally deriving from inbuilt inclinations or personal choices of the individual, not from some wider cultural, moral or spiritual community to which the individual belongs or with which he or she identifies. This reflects a crucial concept of self-determination premised on a sharp dichotomy between drawing our purposes and motivations out of ourselves and being unreflectively or oppressively subordinated by the purposes of others. So this notion of agency incorporates a profound aspiration to autonomy and separateness distinctive of modern Western culture. As Ronald Dworkin describes this ideal: 'A person is autonomous if he identifies with his desires, goals, and values, and such identification is not itself influenced in ways which make the process of identification in some way alien to the individual' (Dworkin 1989: 61).

At the core of most of these notions of autonomy is the idea of a person's capacity to exercise the power of self-government. Historically, the notion of an autonomous person was developed in analogy with the sovereign self-government of individual nations. But it has proved difficult to pin down the exact nature and conditions of self-government in the context of human action. Certainly autonomy involves external conditions which are identified relatively easily, such as having the right or privilege to live our lives free of interference from the state or other people. But it also involves internal conditions, such as the psychological capacity for self-government just mentioned. Identifying some of these internal conditions – freedom from compulsions, say – seems to be a relatively straightforward matter. But others are quite controversial. Robert Kane (1996) argues that genuine freedom involves our being 'ultimately responsible' for and the 'ultimate cause' of at least some values, choices and actions. This means that if one is held responsible for immoral acts issuing from his or her character, then one must have been responsible for forming this character at least at some point in the past. Some will find this kind of 'ultimate responsibility' essential to meaningful free will; others will find it to be an otherworldly, unintelligible mystification (see Chapter 14, sec. 3). But most of the thinkers on either side of this argument embrace some conception of autonomy as self-determination. This typically involves such things as the absence of internal and external constraints, the ability to make our own decisions and to chart our own course in life, an exercise of individual responsibility, and thus the possession of human dignity.

At bottom the instrumental picture assumes what Taylor calls the 'punctual self', that is, a self viewed as free and rational to the extent it has fully distinguished itself from the natural and social worlds and is able to treat these worlds instrumentally for the goal of securing the welfare of itself and others (Taylor 1995: 7). The punctual self is pictured as disengaged from the physical and social realms in two respects. First, the punctual-self picture involves what I called weak world-shaping (Chapter 1, sec. 4), where interactions between self and world are structured purely in terms of efficient causation. This is the kind of self that is ideally suited to exercising instrumental action in a world of efficient causes.

Second, the punctual self is disengaged in such a way that it is ideally free or unsubordinated, a kind of 'sovereign self' (Dunne 1996) able to manipulate these realms as it pleases. Any overlap between self and world, then, is seen as compromising not only the individual's autonomy, but also her integrity, dignity and other values associated with liberal individualism (Chapter 5). This profound aspiration to autonomy and separateness is certainly an epistemological ideal as expressed in the subject-object ontology, but clearly it is a moral ideal as well. It reflects and is reinforced by the intense liberationist or anti-authoritarian temper of modern Western culture, where 'to be free in the modern sense is to be self-responsible, to rely on your own judgment, to find your purpose in yourself' (Taylor 1995: 7). From this perspective allowing a religious community or influential persons to significantly shape a student's choice to become an inner-city schoolteacher rather than an engineer or a lawyer, say, runs the risk of subordinating her desires to some authority outside herself. This strong autonomy streak in modern Western culture dates back to the Enlightenment and seeks to liberate people from superstitions, unexamined prejudices and potentially bad authorities to make individuals the captains of their own souls. The Enlightenment ideal of autonomy sees us as casting off custom, tradition and authority so we can be autonomous, self-defining individuals.

Being free from superstitions and illegitimate authorities are worthy goals as far as they go. And the Enlightenment ideal of autonomy has proven attractive to many over the centuries as a way of assuring people's individuality and autonomy. And autonomy looks attractive because it seems to empower individuals, enhancing their freedom, dignity and ability to live their own lives. But this emphasis on autonomy comes at the expense of lasting social ties and obligations – after all, one cannot be autonomous and bound to others at the same time. Viewpoints celebrating personal autonomy usually push an untrammeled self-actualization which ultimately fails to satisfy, and which encourages efforts at mastery and control over the world around us. But this encouragement often backfires, turning us into slaves of the things over which we have achieved dominion like time, labour and even cell phones!

Furthermore, overemphasizing autonomy runs a high risk of deteriorating into a clash of will against will, power against power due to a one-sided emphasis on autonomy and separateness. In order to prevent such catastrophe, the modern moral outlook supplements this uncompromising stress on autonomy and self-interest with a serious commitment to respecting individual dignity and rights. So the instrumental picture and the drive for autonomy that animates it, are tied deeply to many of our cherished values such as liberty, dignity, tolerance and individuality. In other words, the instrumental picture of action is united with a powerful set of moral values in the modern Western outlook. Indeed, without these surrounding liberal values, the instrumental picture of action, as well as the ideal of autonomy, would lead to the crass treatment of other people as mere means to our desired ends.

Moreover, the drive for autonomy reinforces the instrumental picture of action. To be a sovereign, self-determining individual is to be able to do whatever is required or best to get you what you want (not what someone else wants for you). In turn, the instrumental picture of action reinforces autonomy. The ultimate autonomous individual is the punctual self, who has complete instrumental control over the natural and social worlds as well as features of herself, and who can manipulate these resources as means to achieve her chosen ends.[2] Meanwhile, as mentioned above, the instrumental picture of action also reflects and reinforces scientific practices such as objectification, explanation in terms of efficient causes, and a subject-object ontology and epistemology. And these practices, in turn, tend to reinforce the instrumental picture of action. For instance, the subject-object ontology pictures actors as being separate or detached from the natural and social worlds. When combined with mainstream social science's emphasis on efficient causation, the natural picture of action appears to be an instrumental one.

To make the instrumental picture of action more concrete, let me give some examples from behaviourism, psychodynamics and cognitive theory (Chapter 9). First, on the behaviourist analysis, any seemingly altruistic or self-sacrificing behaviours are simply the result of stimulus–response–reinforcement patterns due to external stimuli. The assumption is that we will relate to people only so long as they provide us with positive reinforcement. Once we begin receiving negative reinforcement from a person, our relational behaviours toward that person will change markedly. Reinforcement is the fundamental governing factor for all relationships, making them instrumental in that we pursue relationships only insofar as we obtain pleasant outcomes for ourselves. Once the outcomes turn unpleasant, the relationship changes. At the same time, behaviourism also views us as able to freely choose which and what kinds of relationships we want and to change our relationships however best suit our purposes. We are supposedly fully immersed in stimulus–response–reinforcement cycles while simultaneously able to step outside these cycles and channel them to suit our needs and desires.

In Freud's psychodynamics the influence of the sexual instinct is pervasive. This implies that other people serve mainly as objects of gratification. Furthermore gratification plays a crucial role in the development of a person. Every action we undertake, no matter how noble to our conscious mind, is, in large part, an attempt to meet past and present unmet gratification needs, making all our relationships with others instrumental in that others serve as objects for our gratification (we, in turn, serve the same function for them). Relationships, then, are largely means for meeting our needs and desires (clearly a *zweckrational* approach to relationships!) At the same time, psychodynamic theories assume that we can somehow step outside of or turn back on the various interacting and counteracting 'forces' within our psychic 'apparatus' to transform our behaviour and view of the world.[3]

On the cognitive analysis, we are complex information processing systems. The assumption is that our relationships with other people are the results of logical processing on information inputs along cost–benefit or other lines of analysis. This implies that our relationships with others are instrumental in that such behaviours are the result of rational calculations regarding the input we receive from relationships and what is considered best or beneficial for us regarding our relationships (an information technology version of 'It's all about me!') At the same time, cognitive approaches assume that we can somehow manipulate or change our input–processing–output scheme for these desired purposes.

3. Critique of instrumental reason

When laid out in this manner, efficient causation and instrumental action in social science begin to look like axioms of inquiry assuring rigorous scientific propriety. The focus on efficient cause–effect relations and their manipulations provides possible targets for potentially brute data and univocal methods as well as for controlled experimentation leading to possible goals of empirical theory or accurate, objective descriptions of personal and interpersonal dynamics. Some have objected that this 'scientific' picture comes at a great cost in that this description makes social science and its accounts of human life sound thoroughly dehumanizing. But vague worries about dehumanization are insufficient to call into question a potentially rigorous, axiomatic approach to scientific inquiry.

In the context of understanding human behaviour, however, such axioms, look arbitrary, anything but value-neutral, and offer little purchase on dealing with the intimate details of human living. In my view, there is no better place to begin to see this arbitrariness than the influential 'critique of instrumental reason' in the work of the Frankfurt school (Horkheimer 1974; Bernstein 1976; Held 1980) and Jürgen Habermas (1971; 1991) in particular.

As pointed out in the previous chapter (sec. 3), Habermas argues that modern Western culture largely conceptually confuses culturally meaningful activities (e.g., voting or religious rituals) and shared meanings (e.g., notions of patriotism or dignity), on the one hand, with instrumental reasoning and technical mastery on the other (focusing almost exclusively on knowledge and techniques for bringing about desired ends). The contrast can be seen in the following way. An instrumental viewpoint focuses on the most effective or efficient means for obtaining some goal or desire. Its purpose – its aim – is technical mastery leading to producing a desired outcome. In contrast, a *wertrational* viewpoint focuses on our goals and purposes as well as the sources of these goals and purposes. It aims not at obtaining or fulfilling these goals and purposes, but at the well-lived life and how our goals and purposes fit into a conception of excellence in living.

To transmute meaningful pursuit of living well into matters of mastery and technique is fundamentally to confuse *wertrational* and *zweckrational*. This confusion leads society to tend to collapse the cultural and moral dimensions of life into merely technical and instrumental considerations (the very thing Weber warned about as *zweckrational* took hold on more and more features of society). As a result, in social inquiry and public policy, according to Habermas (1971: 254), we imagine applying theory to practice chiefly as a matter of applying principles uncovered by empirical science in a manipulative or instrumental manner to produce desired results (this indeed is the stated goal of much of social science).

Suppose we understood the conditions protecting and nurturing good marriages. One might think it plausible that we could adjust environmental influences and counselling techniques to better facilitate families staying intact and flourishing, and to promote higher marital satisfaction. Marriage, then, becomes a means toward achieving desired ends like maximizing self-actualization or achieving a satisfying life. However, this view tends to collapse various cultural and moral dimensions of marriage into merely technical and instrumental considerations focused on effectiveness and efficiency for pursuing our individual and, perhaps, policy preferences (see Chapter 8). Marriage is now transmuted into an instrument, focusing on what is considered best or beneficial for the spouses and children rather than on any deeper meaning of love or sacrifice or the cultural role of such an institution.

The critical theorist Max Horkheimer (1974) explored the contradictions and adverse consequences of overemphasizing instrumental reason at the expense of wider cultural or moral values. He argued that the modern outlook glorifying instrumental reason actually turns into its opposite or an 'eclipse of reason'. Scientific neutrality dictates that we concentrate on discerning lawful means–ends connections among events, which are supposedly 'objective', and regard social and moral values as merely subjective and irrelevant to scientific inquiry (similar to the view of positivist philosophy in the first half of the twentieth century). But viewing agency as exclusively instrumental leads to a situation where we have 'on the one hand, the self, the abstract ego emptied of all substance except its attempt to transform everything in heaven and on earth into means for its preservation, and on the other hand an empty nature degraded to mere material, mere stuff to be dominated, without any other purpose than that of this very domination' (1974: 97). In other words, the personal, social and physical worlds are reduced to mere raw materials for an individual's manipulation in order to achieve some pre-selected purposes. This implies that other people are eventually reduced to being mere means for domination and manipulation to meet an individual's needs or desires. Examples of acting instrumentally in everyday life would be seeking to help others so you feel good (rather than helping others for the sake of being a caring, decent person) or telling someone the truth to gain their trust (rather than telling the truth as part of being a truthful person).

Many social scientists and biologists invoke an instrumental picture of action to explain the evolution of cooperation and society (e.g., Axelrod 1984). Given that these social scientists and biologists assume that our interests do not go beyond our self or our family or relatives (biologists call this 'kin selection'), why would unrelated people ever help each other? The answer given is 'reciprocal altruism' – we aid our unrelated neighbours when they are in need because they are then more likely to aid us or our kin in the future. In everyday parlance, we call this 'You scratch my back and I'll scratch yours'. But notice that this explanation for the evolution of cooperation and society is explicitly instrumental. Instead of helping others for the sake of being a caring, decent person, or out of a wider sense of moral or spiritual obligation, we help them because of the expected future benefit we or our kin will receive. The intent of this instrumental explanation is not that we consciously think along these instrumental lines. Rather, we have internalized this instrumental relationship between action and future expected benefit and now rationalize our altruistic behaviour as being of a fundamentally different moral character than – according to the theory – it actually is.[4]

This conceptual picture, however, does not really match so well with everyday life. Generally, people do not make decisions in the highly idealized manner pictured by the instrumental perspective with its detached, subject-object split. Instead, we usually seek out the advice of family and friends, draw upon the traditions and values of our communities as well as larger moral and religious perspectives, open ourselves up to the influence of media and authority figures (rightly or wrongly) and actually do care deeply about what others think of our choices and actions. People living together must intentionally discuss norms, values, interests and ends, as well as means. For example, decisions and actions taken to cope with risks in everyday life are not the results of strategic or rational calculations, as the instrumental picture would have it, but are taken with larger values such as fairness, equity and solidarity in mind (Short 1984). Too narrow a focus on strategic reasoning about means tends to undermine important ends like fairness and equality. Focusing purely on strategically efficient means does not guarantee fair distribution of social and material goods, and neither does a *zweckrational* emphasis on means–ends guarantee equality among persons. Rather, the calculating rationality of self-interest – where means tend to be the only real point of deliberation – often lead to morally unjustifiable abuse and domination. Questions about how fair or equitable our means are tend to be minimized in the instrumental picture even though they are values that, in the liberal Western tradition, we view as important and worthwhile.[5]

The almost exclusive focus on instrumental action among mainstream and some other kinds of social-science researchers both reflects and encourages Western culture's emphasis on gaining control over natural and social processes in order to enhance human well-being, dignity and other worthwhile goals. Doubtless this increased capacity for control has often benefited us. But a key shortcoming of this elevation of technical mastery over culturally meaningful activity and shared meanings is that, even as we grow in instrumental prowess, we progressively lose our ability to evaluate the worth of ends on any basis other than personal preference or sheer desire (e.g., choosing to stay in a marriage or pursue a divorce because of my own desires for self-fulfilment). As a result, too many spheres of life have become heavily coloured by a calculating, instrumental viewpoint which discerns means–ends relationships, performs cost–benefit analyses, and seeks to maximize, as an end in itself, our control or mastery over events. As society becomes increasingly rationalized (Chapter 2, sec. 4), we find it increasingly difficult to distinguish between practical and technical powers. We often see prudential, moral and political concerns through a lens of technique and technology (e.g., asking 'What's the best way to get what I want' rather than 'Is it genuinely good for me or my community?')

Moreover, as everyday life becomes increasingly dominated by an instrumental picture, our social life is weakened. Our sense of mutual obligation and belonging as well as our social involvements are replaced by or transformed into means for individuals to achieve or fulfil their personal preferences.

American secondary-school curricula, for instance, routinely emphasize scientific, technological and instrumental proficiency while tending to ignore weighty issues of care, mutual obligation and social responsibility. This is no value-neutral curriculum. By ignoring many of the values that parents are trying to teach their children, schools send the message to students that these values do not matter as much as instrumental prowess and control.

The instrumental picture, then, far from being objective or value-neutral, actually represents a vision of the good life as a quest for mastery and control devoid of deeper or wider contextual meanings: in short a search for means without due consideration of the nature of ends (e.g., marginalizing *wertrational*). Unfortunately, as critical theorists, argue, this focus on means at the expense of ends weakens our ability to reason together about the inherent quality of our way of life and about what goals or ends we might best seek. This is a powerful source of the social fragmentation, loss of community and increased sense of personal alienation complained about by so many cultural critics in recent decades. Furthermore, as the means of control and influence grow, life gets more organized and complicated at the same time that we lose the ability or basis on which to set priorities and impose needed limits. In this way, critical theory tries to illumine the sources of our tendency to despoil the environment, our fascination with power and control to the neglect of other important values, and our stressful, overextended lifestyles.

In contrast, mostly we cooperate with, deliberate with, contend with, or seek to influence one another concerning shared cultural, ethical, aesthetic or religious meanings (Habermas 1971; Taylor 1985a; 1985b). We pursue activities and meanings not primarily for their instrumental value in gaining control over events, but for what we take to be their intrinsic worth (e.g., *wertrational*). These intrinsic values and cherished ends shape and direct our instrumental activity, not the other way around (Taylor 1989). So Weber's fears about the rationalization of all of life, though perhaps largely realized in the approach to inquiry of most social scientists, appear less well-founded regarding how people go about their daily lives. To conceive of human action as fundamentally instrumental, then, is tragically to confuse quintessential and important human capacities with narrow technical powers and, thus, distort much of the business of human living. The practical situations we face in everyday life are mostly matters of prudence, insight, moral judgement and wisdom, not mere matters of applying correct value-free methods or successful techniques.

Consider situations like understanding how to comfort a small child or knowing when and how to show deference. Our responses in such situations are played out within a complicated and rich social context. This context simultaneously shapes our options and actions through the influence of subtle cues that are largely unnoticed by us and are tacit rather than explicit in contributing to our sense of the situation. Often our responses take place in interaction with others, and take embodied forms, such as a hug or standing a pace further back from my wiser companion. On the instrumental picture, the response of something like 'getting deference right' is mainly a matter of right technique and appropriate calculation. The response is then a matter of going from one configuration (e.g., shaking hands at half arms' length) via an appropriate set of rules to another configuration (e.g., standing a pace further back) based on past and present information and 'encoded' social rules.

But showing deference has little if anything to do with applying rules to configurations. Deference is an action constituted by my sense for what ought to be done given a feeling of humility. My feeling of humility in the presence of a wiser person has to do with my sense of how we are related socially, as well as with the traditions and expectations of my society regarding how a person of her status is to be appropriately treated (Bourdieu 1977). These traditions and expectations are not completely internalized, but are defined in relation to constantly changing social contexts; hence they do not function as rules (e.g., Dreyfus and Dreyfus 1988). My understanding and appraisal of this feeling of humility is due to my sense of the situation and the meaning things have for me. This sense or meaning reflects my ideals, purposes and concerns as a social being. But their influence usually shows up in the form of an immediate feeling for or perception or appraisal of the situation and the sense of an appropriate response to it that bears little resemblance to calculating outcomes, searching for the right technique to produce them, or explicitly applying pragmatic rules of action.

Still, one might object that all actions, including showing mercy or deference, can be understood as ultimately instrumental, as more or less consciously designed to bring about some outcome, payoff or reward. But at least three strong lines of argument can be levelled against the view that instrumental action can be taken as fundamental, in spite of its appeal to many in an individualistic and pragmatic age. First, as already noted, a great many philosophers and cultural critics have argued that conceiving human action as largely instrumental is at the root of many of the social and emotional confusions and pathologies of our kind of modern society (Horkheimer 1974;

Barrett 1978; Habermas 1991; Gadamer 1975; Lasch 1991; MacIntyre 1981). In Horkheimer's words, it brings about an 'eclipse of reason' because we lose the ability to reason or deliberate about the worth of the ends we seek and can only assess means–ends connections as more or less efficient or effective. This promotes a one-sided orientation toward mastery and control that encourages undue shallow self-seeking and narcissism, precludes a greater sense of moral direction or integrity, undermines cooperation and compromise, and generates a frenetic pace of life that discourages a sense of healthy limits and weakens our capacity for any sort of rest and repose. Over the years, a number of psychological theorists (e.g., Fromm 1975; Schumaker 2001) have suggested that just such a way of life, not individual or family pathology per se, is the source of much of the anxiety, depression and interpersonal problems in the modern world. For instance, this focus on mastery and control de-emphasizes our shared meanings and social bonds, leaving us emotionally isolated and alone to cope with the increasing stressfulness of modern life in a *zweckrational* world.

Second, despite the appeal of the instrumental picture in an individualistic and pragmatic age, it actually is quite counter-intuitive and affords a distorted picture of human experience, motivation and action. Taylor undermines the idea that humans simply desire particular outcomes or satisfactions in living. Rather, we always or 'inescapably' make higher-order or 'strong evaluations' (1985a; 1989). Even if only tacitly or unconsciously, we evaluate the quality of our desires and motivations and the worth of the ends we seek in terms of how they fit in with our overall sense of a decent or worthwhile life, even if the terms of these evaluations vary widely across societies and eras. Taylor (1989) further argues that although theorists or ordinary social actors may endorse a utilitarian or existentialist outlook according to which the ends or ideals that guide actions are ultimately arbitrary – that is, either given desires or mere subjective preferences – on closer examination they are often quite dedicated to liberating individuals from irrational or moralistic viewpoints that hamper their living, and may devote considerable energy or even make sacrifices to promote human welfare in this sense. Such ideals and activity reflect commitments or a sense of integrity that they clearly do not regard as merely subjective and instrumental!

In line with this view, Alistair MacIntyre (1981) argues that the most basic and important kinds of human action are not 'technical activities', which aim to produce whatever results or satisfactions someone just happens to desire, but 'social practices' of a qualitatively different sort. Social practices do not achieve 'external' payoffs or consequences for which, all things being equal, any means will do. Rather, they realize 'internal goods' that are inseparable from acting out of a particular motivation or character. Charles Guignon defines authenticity in similar terms:

> Authentic agency has a different quality than does inauthentic agency. Our ordinary, inauthentic ways of living often have an instrumentalist, 'means-ends' structure. We do things in order to achieve social approval or to attain the awards that come from having acted properly. Given such a means/ends orientation to life, we tend to live as strategic calculators, trying to figure out the most cost-efficient means to obtaining the ends we desire. In contrast, as authentic, you experience your actions as contributing to the formation of your life-story as a whole. Life then has what we might call a 'constituent/whole' structure: you act for the sake of being a person of a particular sort, and you experience your actions as constituents of a complete life that you are realizing in all you do. In this sort of life, the ends of acting are intrinsic to the action, not external rewards that might be obtainable without performing this action. (2002: 98)

Perhaps most fundamentally, the very concept of instrumental action depends upon a deeper foundation for its applicability, a point going back to Durkheim and organic solidarity. For such action to be possible presupposes stable, organized communities and societies, where a network of beliefs, values and ways of seeing things is already up and running drawing people together in moral solidarity and informing and shaping the actions open to them. As Sir Isaiah Berlin (1962) eloquently argued, such social structures are the results of neither formal calculation/analysis nor empirical methods, but are the shared understandings and meanings of self-interpreting beings. Our instrumental action is always understood and interpreted within this larger value matrix and depends upon such a matrix for its viability.

Finally, suppose the objection was weakened to say that any human action *can* be redescribed as largely instrumental. Although even this claim is contentious, it might, indeed, be possible to describe each sentence in James Joyce's *Ulysses*, for example, as the result of instrumental reason, but to do so simply would make no sense. Put differently, to do so would render Joyce's text as well as the lived experience of Leopold Bloom unintelligible. Hence, it is not the case that *any* human action *always* can be redescribed as largely instrumental in character.

4. Taking stock

So there are deep cultural reasons – cultural ideals – for why the only conception of reason that seems to make sense is instrumental – determining the most efficient or effective means to achieve a desired end.[6] Similarly, for why the only conception of action that seems viable is that of technical application, manipulation and control. These are not mere scientific, objective pictures of human rationality and action. Rather, they are historically developed, culturally conditioned ways of seeing and thinking about rationality and action. In this sense, the instrumental picture of action represents simply another value-laden view of what human action might be.

One response to these objections against the instrumental picture of action is that all the hullabaloo about shared values and meanings, unavoidable references to larger moral and religious perspectives and the like can all be taken into account in filtering and informing the preferences of agents. The instrumental picture can account for all of this by packing it into how people arrive at the ends they seek while they remain largely strategic in terms of their deliberations over the means to achieving those ends. Certainly such influences are at work in the ends people seek. But this response renders the instrumental picture of action unfalsifiable because any expression of behaviour can always be reconstructed along these lines. As Karl Popper emphasized, unfalsifiability (see Chapter 10, sec. 4.4) is the hallmark of an unscientific theory (even if the criterion does not tell us positively what counts as scientific). So to take this response literally is to admit that our conceptualization of human action is not open to any possible falsification from experience.[7] But the whole point of social science adopting an instrumental picture of action is to forge scientific theories and explanations for behaviour, so making the picture immune to any counter evidence is headed in the wrong direction for a scientific approach. Moreover, taking this move literally also means that our theoretical picture of agency amounts to 'wordy elaborations of the obvious' (Taylor 1985a: 1). The trivial result that every person acts for a reason. This is not informative to say the least.

Another problem with taking this response literally is that it presupposes a strong distinction between facts and values. Instrumental reasoning about means is closely aligned with the realm of facts (e.g., most efficient, effective or optimal means for achieving a given goal) while the formation or adoption of ends is closely aligned with the realm of values. This kind of distinction cannot possibly be right, however, as it presupposes that all 'real' questions about individual and social action can be answered on the basis of empirical or formal methods as well as begging the question on instrumental rationality. As Berlin (1962) and Bernstein (1976), among others, have argued, the meanings constituting social and political reality can neither be comprehended nor addressed adequately if there is a strict break between facts and values. We are self-interpreting beings and as such our beliefs and feelings, the understandings we have of ourselves, the way things seem to us and so forth are constitutive of the actions, practices and institutions composing social and political life. Thus, values and understandings cannot be neatly segmented off from political and economic institutions or any other spheres of social life because the latter are largely constituted by interpretations involving individual and shared norms, values, meanings and so forth. The banking system and financial markets, for instance, are very efficient mechanisms for achieving particular economic ends, but such institutions – not to mention economies – are built on a base of shared values and norms. If we change our values and norms, then the banking system and markets will no longer serve as efficient economic mechanisms. Facts and values blend together in modern life in ways that make the idea of neatly separating them a chimera.

So instrumental reason, along with a subject-object ontology and epistemology, harbours an unacknowledged commitment to a punctual view of the self. Such a view of the self is part of the reason why we find these pictures of action, ontology and epistemology bundled together so often in the social sciences. In addition, as I have indicated, the punctual view of the self reflects a deep ethical commitment to autonomy which, in turn, reinforces a punctual view of the self. So there is also a substantial ethical ideal – also largely unacknowledged – acting to reinforce what passes for scientific ideals of human inquiry – instrumental agency along with a subject-object ontology and epistemology.

This kind of 'package deal' raises serious and troubling questions about value-neutrality in the social sciences that we will look at shortly. Here, I want to raise a concern that we will address more fully in the coming chapters, namely that instrumental rationality with its pretence to value-neutrality and objectivity is the only kind of rationality amenable to 'scientific investigation'.

One form this concern might take is that instrumental agency, nevertheless, is the only *empirically accessible* form of agency that a science can study. To abandon it, then, would supposedly render human agency beyond the reach of scientific investigation. However, this objection simply repeats the problems I have raised; namely, that in order to 'scientifically study' behaviour, we must reduce it to some manageable minimum ultimately bearing limited resemblance to everyday human behaviour, all the while importing some hefty assumptions about the nature of the self as well as some substantial ethical ideals. If we were to grant the restricted notion of empiricism lying behind this objection – that only instrumental reason is empirically accessible – the social sciences would have to consciously restrict themselves to understanding a subdomain of human behaviour quite limited with respect to our full range of activities, ways of knowing, interests and concerns, a subdomain that in many ways is trivial compared to what we really care about. This represents a conception of empiricism limited to measurable, quantifiable magnitudes; whereas, from a broader empirical perspective, human activity as we experience it is clearly more than quantifiable behaviour.

More importantly, many, such as Richard Miller, maintain that (1) 'value judgment plays no legitimate role in justifying a scientific explanation' and (2) 'that explanations using concepts that are not inherently evaluative are always to be preferred, for scientific purposes, to moralizing explanations' (1987: 109). In other words the whole thrust of the 'scientific method' is to expunge values from our theories and explanations. In natural sciences such as physics, these requirements appear quite plausible. An explanation for the motion of a pendulum, for example, does not rest directly upon a value judgement and can be described using non-evaluative terms. Nevertheless, even in physics, the research community's adjudication between two equally empirically adequate and conceptually sound hypotheses may be carried out in terms of values such as simplicity, elegance and the like, as well as other 'non-scientific' types of values and beliefs. Another example would be medical sciences, where concepts such as good health, normal state, disease and the like presuppose an evaluative component.[8]

Social scientists might think that there are always alternative non-evaluative concepts and terms with which to recast 'moralizing explanations' as Richard Hare (1963), Gilbert Harman (1977) and John Mackie (1977) among others have argued. Taylor (1989) demonstrates convincingly that such alternatives *do not* always exist in the social and behavioural domains. Even the types of questions we raise and answers we propose take place within a larger moral web of indispensable background practices and values (Root 1993: 205–28). Attempts to avoid such value-laden descriptions are, themselves, value-laden positions, albeit emphasizing a different set of values (Root 1993).[9]

Consider an example developed by Robert King (1973: ch. 3).[10] Suppose we happen across a man who is pumping poisoned water into the water system of a house where some people are gathered plotting an unjust war. On a neuro-physiological account, we could at best understand how the brain directs the hand to hold the pump and the arm to work the pump causing the poisoned water to enter the water system. What he is doing – namely pumping – would be apparent, but we would not yet understand *why* the man was doing so. The typical psychologist's appeal to past events might illuminate some of these motivations, but we will later see reasons to question whether such explanations are not coloured by determinism and other value commitments in a way that often 'explains' such actions by explaining them away, or eliminates the very human agency it seeks to illuminate (Chapters 9; 15). Suppose we ask him why he is pumping the water and he replies, 'To poison the people living there'. We persist in asking why to which he then responds, 'They are plotting an unjust war and by killing them, I will prevent that war from happening'. Why does he want to prevent such a war? 'Because I want to promote world peace and prevent unnecessary suffering'. If pressed further he might answer that he is 'working for the kingdom of God'.

Now we really can say that we understand not only what the man is doing, but also why he is doing it. Notice that the series of questions forces the man to continually re-identify and reinterpret what he is doing within an ever broadening context. Pumping poisoned water is a means to an end (poisoning people) which is, in turn, a means to a further end (preventing an unjust war) which, in turn, is a means to a higher end and so forth until we get to his ultimate end: serving the kingdom of God. This multi-layered set of intentions and values are crucial to understanding why the man is carrying out this action. Furthermore, note that the explanation for why he is pumping poisoned water provides both illumination and satisfaction that we have grasped, to some degree, the grounds for his action. Notice also that the explanation relies upon inescapably moral concepts, the elimination of which would destroy the adequacy and intelligibility of the explanation.

The possibility of ineliminable evaluative judgements in the social sciences, of course, raises alarms about how biases and corruption can be properly cordoned off from our social-science research. And it is these worries that have driven many to seek value-neutral approaches to social inquiry. We will see in the next three chapters that such value-neutrality is a myth and that we really do need some better way to come to grips with how and why values enter into social inquiry as well as how to keep values from corrupting or impossibly biasing such research.

For further study

1. What is the instrumental picture of action? How is it both a scientific and moral ideal?
2. Describe autonomy. What role does this cultural ideal play in social inquiry?
3. Summarize the critique of instrumental reason. How is this critique relevant to social science?
4. Evaluate the responses to the critique of instrumental reason.

Recommended reading

R. C. Bishop, 'Cognitive Psychology: Hidden Assumptions', in B. Slife, J. Reber and F. Richardson (eds), *Critical Thinking about Psychology: Hidden Assumptions and Plausible Alternatives* (Washington: American Psychological Association, 2005a), pp. 151–70.

M. Horkheimer, *Eclipse of Reason* (New York: Continuum Publishing, 1974).

C. Taylor, 'Cognitive Psychology', in *Philosophical Papers* vol. 1: *Human Agency and Language* (Cambridge: Cambridge University Press, 1985a), pp. 187–212.

Cultural Ideals II: Political Liberalism and Liberal Individualism

5

In the last chapter, we saw how an instrumental conception of action as well as the subject-object ontology and epistemology underlying much social inquiry are connected to a powerful ethical ideal central to Western culture: autonomy. However, this is not the only cultural ideal at work in this package of assumptions. They also have a deep connection to individualism, another hallmark of Western culture.

Individualism comes in many forms. In this chapter we will explore these varieties and how they come to expression in social-science research. After we have done so, we will then be in a position to look anew at debates about the supposed value-neutrality of the social sciences, beginning with an interesting connection to a scientific practice known as abstraction.

1. Political liberalism

The congruence between viewing human action as instrumental and all objects in the world – social actors included – as related only or largely via chains of causes and effects also reflects a profound aspiration to individuality. In its stark autonomy, the punctual self is a unique individual first and foremost. Likewise, autonomy is tied to some of our most cherished values in Western society like respect and tolerance for individuality. Indeed the concept of autonomy makes little sense in the context of a pre-modern society where, as Durkheim noted, a person's identity is found in the group or society first and is governed by social bonds (Chapter 2, sec. 3). Western democratic traditions are built, in part, upon the liberal values that a person's individuality be respected, that her individual rights be protected, that her individual freedoms remain unfettered and that her individual values be tolerated. These kinds of liberal values are unintelligible in the traditional societies Durkheim described.

At the heart of such liberal values lies an important political ideal, *political liberalism*. According to this ideal, the state should not support one conception of the good life – to seek happiness, to live with honour and integrity, to become rich and famous – over any other, nor favour any particular religions, sexual mores and so forth. To advocate or enforce some conceptions of the good over others restricts and threatens autonomy and individuality. So government should be neutral to all such conceptions, allowing individuals the freedom and opportunity to pursue their own visions of the good. But this stance of neutrality towards all conceptions of the good is another vision of the good – the good life as neutrality towards and respect for all conceptions of the good that anyone might pursue.

Michael Root (1993) has identified political liberalism as an underlying or unifying theme among the social sciences. As he argues: 'Most social scientists believe that their methods and findings should be neutral and silent as well' with respect to competing visions of the good (1993: 1). This is the kind of picture Weber has of the neutrality of social science research (Weber 1949). The upshot is that:

> According to a liberal philosophy of the social sciences, social scientists (in their capacity as social scientists) should not attempt to influence their subject's judgments of the intrinsic superiority or inferiority of any conception of the good life or justify their methods on the basis of any such judgment.

> When they conduct their research and offer their findings, the social scientists should be nonpartisan and silent on the question of what morally ought to be. (Root 1993: 1–2)

The social sciences, however, cannot avoid being partisan with respect to competing conceptions of the good. Theory choice and construction, data collection and categorization, as well as explanation in these sciences, lie far from this non-partisan ideal in that these practices cannot be carried out in the prescribed value-neutral fashion. Developmental theories like those of Lawrence Kohlberg (1984) or Carol Gilligan (1993) are well-known examples. The 'mature' stage of development in these theories either implicitly or explicitly presupposes value judgements about the moral and political competencies of people (Root 1993: ch. 3).

One might hope to circumvent many of these value-judgement problems by adopting value-free methods for the collection, categorization and analysis of data. However, such value-free methods are far and fleeting (see Chapter 13). For example, the classifications used in the study of human activity reflect the social, legal and political interests of the subjects of study, the ways in which 'communities of men and women have chosen to organize and regulate their lives', rather than natural kinds that are somehow already given to the scientist by nature (Root 1993: 152). Furthermore:

> Although the standards of goodness for the data in the social sciences are intended to be value-neutral, they pass moral and political values from sites like the office and the school to the data scientists collect when they test, interview, or survey their subjects. (Root 1993: 5)

The social scientist's choice to use such categories for the collection, categorization and analysis of data then reflects and passes through the (often unacknowledged) value judgements underlying these classifications; and the results of such research, then, tend to pass back through and reinforce these value judgements to the communities which are the targets of such research (Chapter 8; Root 1993: ch. 7).

Moreover, to the extent that social scientists strive to be neutral towards all conceptions of the good in their research, they are pursuing and (at least surreptitiously) advocating a significantly morally laden position – namely, political liberalism. Political liberalism encourages us to keep functions like education and research separate from political action and advocacy. The government should not use its near monopoly on education or its position as the main funding source of science to dictate or recommend how citizens should live their lives. Mainstream social science sees itself as falling in line with this political ideal. It ostensibly offers objective, value-neutral research that, while separate from any education or advocacy functions, can be put to use for those purposes by others. However, in pursuing this ideal, social-science research cannot be neutral, but subtly advocates and reinforces political liberalism as an ideal way of life for all.

The problem here is not that there is something wrong with political liberalism as an ideal. Many of us would be unwilling to give up this ideal. Rather, the point is that social inquiry ends up subtly (sometimes not so subtly) advocating a particular vision of the good. So it pretends to be value-free when it actually is not.

2. Liberal individualism

Root's analysis of these and other examples is trenchant, showing that try as it might, social science cannot escape value-laden judgements. Furthermore, his analysis shares much in common with critical theory's emphasis on disguised ideologies. In this case, the disguised ideology is the political philosophy of liberalism. But as helpful as Root's analysis is, there is a deeper layer of individualism underlying political liberalism, identified as *liberal individualism* (Bellah et al. 1985; Richardson, Fowers and Guignon 1999) that encourages social science's attachment to instrumental action and a subject-object ontology and epistemology along with political liberalism.

Liberal individualism is a thoroughly modern moral outlook. Recall the picture of pre-modern societies discussed in Chapter 2. In those societies, people took for granted that they inhabited a meaningful cosmic drama, bringing a sense of belonging and purpose in the midst of the uncontrollable and tragic aspects of human life. This meaningful sense of place or station in life may indeed often have been achieved in ways that appear, by our modern lights, to have resulted from people being subordinated to false or superstitious beliefs, unjust hierarchies or other forms of tyranny and domination (as Durkheim acknowledged). The rise of modern society brought about massive changes in this social topology. The development of modern science, Enlightenment philosophy, industrialization and bureaucratization shared various interrelations. These tightly interlocked cultural developments adopted natural science's tendency to ignore or abstract away from the rich appearance of things, including the values and meaningful relationships of our ordinary experience in the pursuit of pure knowledge (sec. 3 below). These practices of abstraction allow science to regard the world in an objectified way, that is to say, as made up of inherently meaningless objects in causal interaction with one another (more on that below).

In modern Western culture, such developments led to a deep split between 'objectivity' and 'subjectivity', between the meaningless flow of chains of efficient causes studied by science and our experiences of things like beauty, purpose and goodness. The latter are often viewed as human constructions, the products of our varying interpretations and purposes. This idea of subjectivity gave birth to our distinctive modern emphasis on personal inwardness and inward depths, an emphasis on the individual, and much of our modern focus on individuality, rights, dignity and freedom flow from this emphasis.

This profound aspiration to individuality and separateness is certainly an epistemological ideal captured in the subject-object epistemology and ontology underlying natural-scientific and descriptivist points of view (Chapter 3, secs. 1–2). But this aspiration is at least as much a *moral* ideal. Like autonomy, it reflects and is reinforced by the liberationist drive of modern Western culture, where any undue influence on a person is viewed as compromising their individuality.[1] Here, we see the basis for liberalism individual's tenacious defense of individual rights and freedoms from interference. Of course, a raw individualism would run the risk of devolving into a kind of one against all clash of individuals pursuing their own life projects. Such a dark outcome is mitigated by emphasizing respect for individual dignity, rights, freedom, the rule of law, tolerance and other substantial moral commitments so as to protect individuals' pursuit of their own conception of the good life in such a way that they do not fall into a chaotic free for all.

Liberal individualism is a fundamental though largely ignored assumption colouring much research and theorizing in the social sciences (Richardson, Fowers and Guignon 1999). Robert Fancher (1995) argues that modern psychotherapy systems actually surreptitiously promote a liberal individualist view as opposed to the more pre-modern notion of a station or place in life. Schumaker notes that most cognitive therapists 'still persist in locating depression-generating cognitions within the individual, simultaneously overlooking culture as the source of most cognitions' (2001: 53), reinforcing an individualist view of people and depression.[2] Conceptually, liberal individualism can be analysed into components: an ontological component plus one of three versions of how the ideal comes to expression in both theory and society.

2.1. Ontological individualism

It is no wonder, then, that contemporary Western society, particularly in the USA, has come to be characterized by 'a concentration, persistent, if not feverish, upon one's thoughts, feelings, wishes, worries – bordering on, if not embracing, solipsism: the self as the only or main form of (existential) reality' (Coles 1987: 189). Robert Bellah and colleagues (Bellah et al. 1985: 143) christen this *ontological individualism,* the widespread modern notion that the basic unit of human reality is the individual person, who is assumed to exist and have determinate characteristics prior to and independent of his or her social existence. Conceptually, the characteristics of people are pictured as formed in a completely asocial way. On this view, also known as social atomism (see Chapter 9, sec. 3), social systems are understood as artificial aggregates of individuals set up to satisfy the needs of those individuals. Ontological individualism as liberal individualism forms the cornerstone of a modern way of life with its stress on personal autonomy and self-realization, its sharp distinction between public and private realms (e.g., public vs. private morality), and its tendency to privilege and idealize relatively distant, mainly contractual ties between individuals who cooperate or compete for ultimately individual ends.

These sensibilities fit hand in glove with the ideal of social-science methods and findings being value-neutral which could then be applied instrumentally to any notion of the good life. On the instrumental picture, such theorizing and results supposedly represent value-neutral means for the pursuit of individual aims and projects, self-actualization, and other forms of enhanced welfare. Indeed, despite ongoing philosophical debate over methodological individualism versus methodological holism in the social sciences (Chapter 7), ontological individualism forms a core assumption of mainstream social inquiry (Part Three).

2.2. Utilitarian individualism

Over the course of the modern era, liberal individualism has taken several distinct forms. Bellah et al. identify two main forms of modern individualism. The first they term *utilitarian individualism* which 'takes as given certain basic human appetites and fears . . . and sees human life as an effort by individuals to maximize their self-interest relative to these given ends' (1985: 336). It assumes that the ends of human life are either inbuilt pleasures and satisfactions, or whatever goals and desires a person just happens to prefer. Human thought and action are essentially tools for effectively and efficiently pursuing survival, security and satisfaction. The ego in classical psychoanalytic theory (Chapter 9, sec. 1.2) is almost a pure utilitarian, pragmatic calculator of such limited gratifications as are possible under the heavy constraints of social living. As well, the vast majority of theories in rational choice and economics picture agents as rational calculators seeking to maximize their self-interests (Chapters 10; 12).

2.3. Expressive individualism

The second form of individualism Bellah et al. identify is *expressive individualism* which is guided by the belief that 'each person has a unique core of feeling and intuition that should unfold or be expressed if individuality is to be realized' (1985: 334). It is these core, inbuilt feelings that guide one's development, that should be respected and nurtured. This form of liberal individualism arose out of the Romantic movement of the late eighteenth and nineteenth centuries as a reaction against the overly rationalistic, calculating, deadening aspects of utilitarian perspectives. Romanticism celebrates closeness to nature, instinct, mythical consciousness, as well as beauty and art. Romantic notions have a large presence in the world of psychotherapy exemplified in client-centered, humanistic and gestalt among a host of other therapeutic approaches. They are expressed richly in Heinz Kohut's turn against the classical Freudian viewpoint. In Kohut's (1977) theory, the self, far from the beleaguered, calculating ego that Freud depicted, becomes, if properly nurtured, an artist of its own life. The self follows a universal 'narcissistic line of development' from birth to maturity, its goal being a 'healthy narcissism' including pride, assertiveness, vitality, joyfulness, creativity and, eventually, mature wisdom and acceptance of one's mortality (1977: 171–73). Both meaningful social ties and life-guiding values play a more significant role in Kohut's view than Freud's, since empathic parental 'self-objects' are essential to this development and 'twinship experiences' with others are an enduring part of a full life. But such relationships and values are primarily instrumental, serving mainly as means to the end of self-enhancement or what Kohut calls an 'intensification of the inner life' (Cushman 1990).

2.4. Existential individualism

A third type of liberal individualism has been termed *existential individualism* (Richardson, Rogers and McCarroll 1998: 500; see also Richardson, Fowers and Guignon 1999: ch. 5). It is a reaction to the heavily scientific, technical and conformist tendencies in modern society. However, it is also sceptical of the expressivist idea of getting in touch with core feelings or impulses as the main way to find integrity and direction in one's life. Instead, existential individualism values a kind of self-creation like Sartre's formulation of existential freedom. This involves repudiating any notion of pre-given inner directives or objective values as inauthentic 'bad faith'. Instead, on this view, we can take a kind of total responsibility for the basic choices that 'invent' the ultimate values and 'fundamental project' of our lives as a whole. We create our own values and self from scratch, so to speak, there being no fixed or ultimate nature to human beings. Along with this, we should strive to realize both our own practical freedom and – though it is not clear why – that of all others as well. Recent postmodern or social-constructionist views in various social sciences, though sharply critical of what they call 'self-contained individualism', also reflect many of the themes of existential individualism (recall the radical freedom social constructionists ascribe to the self: Chapter 3, sec. 4).

Numerous modern therapy theories incorporate a version of this ideal of existential freedom (e.g., May 1958; Yalom 1980). For instance, Roy Schafer's (1976) radical revision of psychoanalytic theory incorporates an original version of existential philosophy. He rejects the tendency of many therapy theories to 'disown responsibility' for our actions by attributing them to inner or outer causes other than our own choice – my feelings, hang-ups or 'inner-child' made me do it. And he insists that we should accept our ultimate responsibility as authors of our ourselves, others, and our world through what he calls 'optional ways of telling the stories of human lives' (Schafer 1981: 41). Schafer celebrates the 'joyfulness' and 'integrity' of this kind of freedom and autonomy.

2.5. Liberal individualism as disguised ideology

Liberal individualism operates like a disguised ideology in social inquiry similar to the air we breath. We live out and experience individuality and values like fairness, dignity, tolerance and the like. Most all of us bristle when we see someone treated unfairly or get angry when we see someone's dignity diminished. Liberal individualism to a great degree describes how we see the social world, the way things are or ought to be for us. And it is no different from how social scientists see their research subjects and practices. Liberal individualism and political liberalism figuratively are the air social scientists breathe. Just as we rarely notice air as we go about our daily life, so social scientists barely notice how liberal individualism and political liberalism come to expression in or colour their inquiry. The practising social scientist simply sees her subjects of inquiry as individuals deserving of respect, tolerance, dignity and the like, as if that objectively is the way people are (in contrast to beings finding their identity largely in their allegiance to tribe or group as in premodern societies). But these ideals are constitutive of the Western societies so many social scientists inhabit and study – such societies would not be what they are without such individualist ideals. And when social scientists study individuals, groups, institutions and so forth in such societies as if this were objective social reality, these ideals and values transparently pass through social inquiry in the form of the questions to be answered, the categorizations to be deployed, the data to be collected, the methods to be used as well as the analyses to be given.

Their differences aside, the various versions of liberal individualism all share a notion of the punctual self in their anti-authoritarian aspirations for individuality and freedom. The world, physical, psychological as well as social, represents a set of raw materials for the self to instrumentally shape and manipulate for its own purposes and welfare. On all versions of liberal individualism, these purposes are portrayed as ideally deriving from within the self, otherwise the individuality and integrity of the individual risk being compromised. And the instrumental picture of action fits neatly with this strong emphasis on individualism. Instrumental knowledge provides the means aimed at most efficiently or effectively attaining the desired ends of this largely self-contained individual. Given social scientists' desire to deliver value-free results to be applied towards achieving any of these desired ends without presupposing a set of ends in advance, an instrumental picture of action would naturally come to be seen as the value-neutral way of providing these means while also seeming to fit seamlessly into the liberal individualist picture ('tread not on me!'). After all, for a utilitarian individualist instrumental knowledge is the key to most effectively maximizing his welfare or securing his highest desires. Or for the existential individualist, viewing the natural and social worlds as resources to be manipulated instrumentally is crucial to her project of radical self-creation.

On the other hand, if the instrumental picture of action is valid, then it is natural to be some kind of liberal individualist. Not only does the instrumental picture of action turn the natural and social worlds into raw materials for individual projects, it also includes the ability to turn back on and manipulate the cause–effect patterns in these worlds. There is no better way to ground utilitarian and expressivist or existentialist individualism and to provide a suitable framework for action in pursuing individual goals and desires.

These cultural ideals of liberal individualism and the instrumental picture of action are not without their consequences, however. Take contemporary religious views in a modern Western society like the USA. Many observers have noted that contemporary forms of spirituality here have 'little to do with morality, social institutions, or political power', traditional concerns of the world's great religious traditions. Rather, what really seems to matter for many religious people in Western societies today 'are the inner experiences of isolated individuals, cultivated and evaluated largely by those individuals' (Jones 1997: 21). Other observers have noted how Americans, for example, frequently report that religion is a key source of personal satisfaction, as if spirituality is a means to their end of self-fulfilment (Bellah et al. 1983). Yet, how could people under the sway of liberal individualism and an instrumental picture of life see spirituality in any other way?

The instrumental picture of action and the individualism that animates it, are tied deeply to many of our cherished values such as liberty, dignity and individuality. In other words, the instrumental picture of action is deeply reinforced by, and in turn reinforces, a powerful set of cultural and moral ideals. It also reflects and reinforces scientific practices such as abstraction and efficient causal explanation, along with a subject-object ontology and epistemology. In this way, the instrumental picture of action looks to be highly plausible and unquestioned in its role as a fundamental premise of social science's view of agents (and increasingly of the average participant in Western societies). So much so that social scientists rarely recognize that they are presupposing such cultural ideals in their research. Their disguised ideology remains unacknowledged because social scientists do not see themselves as enmeshed in the ideals of their social arena.

The liberal individualism supporting the instrumental picture of action is a decidedly partisan, deeply ethical point of view. It privileges a particular conception of the good life, namely one that emphasizes values such as individuality, dignity, justice, fairness, liberty and creativity in the service of maximizing individual welfare or pursuing individual desires. These are deeply prized, substantive value commitments that few of us would be willing to give up easily. However, this picture of the good life is not without its problems. As Philip Rieff has so powerfully put it, similar to the critical-theorist critique of the instrumental picture of action (Chapter 3, sec. 3), this ethical vision tends to leaves us with the problem of 'being freed to choose and then having no choice worth making' (1966: 93).

However worthy these values might be, the point is that social science, in the name of pursuing so-called objective, value-neutral methods and results, is anything but free of weighty ethical commitments. Its theorizing, methods of data collection, categorization and analysis, and other practices are saturated with these value commitments (e.g., freeing people from false authorities or to lead more effective lives – which in the eyes of many social scientists are virtually the same thing!) Likewise, the results social scientists publish pass these values back through to society, reinforcing the instrumental–individualist conception of the good life. A conception that many argue leads inevitably to social isolation, alienation, troubling emptiness, and that has been traced to the foundation of many of the psychological problems for which people seek counselling (e.g., Cushman 1990; Hillman and Ventura 1992; Fancher 1995; Richardson, Fowers and Guignon 1999). The double hermeneutic (Chapter 3, sec. 2) lives indeed.

Perhaps more importantly, there is a deep tension between these two ethical poles of radical self-interest of individualism, on the one hand, and deep obligation to respecting the rights of others, on the other hand, in this individualist–instrumentalist picture. The moral stance of liberal individualism represents an ethically serious vision of eliminating dogmatism without abandoning our obligations to others. This often comes to expression in such notions as procedural justice and the maintenance of a neutral stance toward various versions of the good life so as not to trample on fundamental values like dignity, liberty and individuality. This represents a substantial commitment to a vision of the good life that is much needed to overcome the corrosive effects of a one-sided focus on strictly instrumental action that would tend to lead to a morally unacceptable situation of people treating each other strictly as means to their own selfish ends. The instrumental picture of action and liberal individualism need each other.

As such, this individualist–instrumentalist stance is seriously committed to human dignity and rights as morally superior or good in themselves. However, there is nothing preventing the ideal of a principled neutrality toward all notions of the good life from extending to these basic values of liberty and human dignity as well. Such a neutrality would undermine their credibility and strip them of any possibility of rational defence. After all, if we are committed to the ideal of strict neutrality, we cannot offer moral arguments in support of these values. The most we can offer in their support are instrumental considerations, but these instrumental considerations only hold so long as these values serve our instrumental needs. Moreover, under this instrumentalist cast, given that the punctual self treats even commitments to human dignity and justice as means to its own and others' welfare, what is to prevent punctual selves from distancing themselves from such liberal values and adopting other means that might appear more expedient to their ends? A slide toward moral relativism and social fragmentation seems an inevitable consequence of this theoretical view of agents. An unexamined commitment to liberal individualism and the instrumental picture of action looks destined to undermine precisely the values we cherish and likely to perpetuate the 'disease' of social fragmentation, emptiness and alienation in our social-science 'cures'.

3. Abstraction and the lifeworld

Before turning to a discussion of value-neutrality proper as well as trying to draw out some alternative to liberal individualism and the instrumental picture of action, it will first be helpful to show how instrumentalism is also connected to a particularly important scientific practice known as *abstraction*.

3.1. Two modes of abstraction

As I have suggested, the instrumental picture of action gives a limited view of human activity. We have also seen that this picture is tied deeply to strong cultural ideals of autonomy and individualism. Furthermore, I have indicated that it is consonant with a 'scientific' perspective often characterized variously as disengaged, impersonal, neutral, objective, third-person, disembodied, mechanistic and the like. But many philosophers and social theorists advocate another picture of human activity, namely a holistic perspective on human action more consonant with ordinary lived experience and with the conception of who we are and what we are about that is implicit in such everyday experience. This latter point of view is often variously characterized as engaged, personal, situated, subjective, first-person, embodied, humanistic and so forth. These two points of view or pictures of human action are often taken to be opposed to one another, but perhaps this need not be the case. To begin to see why, I first want to contrast the instrumental picture and its relationship with the scientific practice of abstraction with the more holistic everyday world of practical agency and then indicate how these two perspectives are related to each other.

One of the core motivations behind the instrumental picture is positivist (Chapter 2, sec. 2), to be sure: keep meanings and values at a distance, treating them as subjective, in order to objectify and 'properly' explain human behaviour. Additionally, the instrumental picture has an interesting relationship to the scientific practice of abstraction that also serves to reinforce social science's adherence to an instrumental picture of action and objectification.

Abstraction plays an important role in scientific practice and involves two aspects. One aspect is related to idealization or simplification in the sense that the scientist studying a particular object abstracts away or disengages from the original physical context in which the object arises so as to study its core properties that may be masked because of the complexity of the original context. For example, physicists often treat the hydrogen molecule in isolation as a harmonic oscillator (e.g., two masses attached to opposite ends of a spring) or as interacting only with its nearest neighbours. The key idea is to isolate the properties in question from the rest of the environment and analyse them in as context-free a manner as possible. This aspect of abstraction stands in stark contrast to the Aristotelian conception of objectivity, which emphasized studying objects in their concrete contexts rather than objects abstracted from such contexts (McMullin 1965; Daston 2000).

The second aspect of abstraction in scientific practice is related more directly to abstracting away or disengaging from the context of everyday, embodied experience to study particular properties apart from our experience or perception of those properties and their influences. An example would be ignoring qualities such as colour or heat when studying electromagnetic vibrations. Colour and heat have more to do with the particular way our bodily senses interact with electromagnetic radiation. The key idea is to isolate the properties in question from our embodied state. Engaging in this kind of abstraction does not at all mean freeing ourselves from our ordinary human concerns and interests relating to the properties in question, from their meaning for us, or from the background knowledge and practices in which we and they are embedded. It simply means that to a great extent we have the remarkable capacity to abstract away from those features of our pre-reflective embodied outlook (e.g., colours, smells and other appearances) which could and in the past often did distort our view of physical reality. This process of abstraction has become an indispensable element of scientific practice for those disciplines dealing with impersonal properties of reality.

Carried to an extreme, the aspiration of abstraction in the first mode – disengagement from the physical context – leads to viewing an object in complete isolation from any other element of physical reality. In the second mode – disengagement from embodied experience – carrying the aspiration of abstraction to an extreme represents a supposed purely neutral stance toward an object, completely free from 'subjective distortions' (hence, we have a connection with the subject-object ontology and epistemology). Pursuing abstraction to the extreme in both modes leads directly to the subject-object ontology and the epistemological ideal of the punctual self whose context, thoughts, feelings and values are completely removed from the standards and methods of knowledge discovery.

But abstraction in either of its aspects can never be carried out free from all context. For instance, all objects of study – even in the natural sciences – have an indispensable complex of relationships to the scientist (e.g., a space–time location with respect to the scientist, a location within the body of theories in use by the scientist, a location within the scientist's concerns and so on). Furthermore the amount of abstraction in either mode is tied to our purposes (e.g., the kinds of questions we are seeking to answer). As noted above, in order to understand the nature of electromagnetic vibrations and radiation, it is appropriate to abstract as fully as possible in both modes given the kinds of questions being asked. In pursuing an explanation of colour perception, however, scientists cannot disengage fully from the physical context in which colours are presented (because the phenomenological appearance of orange can change based upon the surrounding colours) nor from the bodily experience of colour perception and perceptual reports (because this is what we are trying to understand). These limitations on abstraction were well recognized (if only implicitly), for example, in the practice of eighteenth- and nineteenth-century scientists studying colour perception (Daston 2000).

In the social sciences, the first mode of abstraction – disengagement from physical contexts – is not of primary importance, though it does show up in various kinds of simplified experimental arrangements such as the simple tasks designed to isolate various cognitive capacities.[3] However, the second mode of abstraction – disengagement from subjective features of embodied existence – leads to objectification, abstracting away from all value judgements to focus on the efficient causal chains describing behaviour as in the instrumental picture of action, a picture involving only weak world-shaping (Chapter 1, sec. 4). Again, the ideal of value-free goals and methods, it is thought, should yield law-like connections between causes and effects in human behaviour,[4] the knowledge of which could then be applied for any number of purposes according to any number of value judgements. The key point is that the results of social science be abstracted away from such value judgements and purposes in order to not be 'infected' or obscured by the presence of such subjective features of human life.

In this way, the social sciences parallel natural sciences such as physics very closely. Physicists seek to isolate various chains of cause and effects (e.g., water molecules flowing through a pipe) to conduct precisely controlled experiments and map all the pathways of these chains. Likewise, social scientists try to treat various aspects of human behaviour in as isolated a fashion as possible attempting to quantify and map its causal paths. And just as physics keeps subjective factors isolated away from its experimental and theoretical practices of understanding these causal chains, so, too, does social science in the guise of objectivity and value-neutrality. Put in a very crude, but not wholly unfair way, social science seeks to treat the behaviour of agents by treating them as much like law-governed molecules of physics as is possible (recall Comte's vision of social science: Chapter 2, sec. 2).

Not surprisingly, the practices of abstraction – even in the natural sciences – are neither context-free nor value-free. Abstraction can only be carried out against a set of background knowledge and practices with respect to particular purposes of embodied agents. Indeed such a background is presupposed by the very idea of disengagement. Even the attempt to understand a thing neutrally requires that we take a particular stance toward the thing. That is to say, we must be involved with the thing we are studying in particular, limited ways. To abstract to the 'neutral' view requires that we have at least some awareness of the context in which the subject of study is situated and that we have a purpose which abstraction serves. Background understandings and practices are necessary for us to be able to distinguish what is relevant from what is irrelevant in the process of idealization and decontextualization in addition to understanding what it means to adopt a disengaged stance in the first place. For an object treated in a neutral way to be intelligible is for the object-treated-neutrally to be situated in a *way of understanding* that is a form of coping with and being concerned with things in our world for particular human purposes (what other purposes could there be?). Although many elements of scientific practice in natural science appear to proceed as if from an aperspectival standpoint, even if such a standpoint were available to us, our practices would still not be separated from our situated, practical agency (Taylor 1989; van Fraassen 1993; Torretti 2000). The practice of abstraction, disengaged as it attempts to be, still requires engagement with the world.

Obviously the ideal of a 'manageable minimum' lies behind both aspects of abstraction, so that scientific descriptions represent our best attempts to describe our world given our intellectual limitations and our purposes in the face of almost overwhelming, tremendously complex and often highly variable raw experience. Our understanding is always partial, limited and inexact even in our best theories and models (Taylor 1985a; 1985b; Auyang 1998; van Fraassen 1993; Teller 2001). This is trivially true in the sense that there is always more to know than our models and theories contain. More importantly, however, any standpoint we adopt – be it that of maximum abstraction in both aspects or some other standpoint – always hides or ignores some features of reality while illuminating others. In order to make a scientific analysis, we have to cut into our raw, complex, variable experience seeking to find some tame chunk we can hope to understand. Selections of where and how to cut are value and interest driven, always excluding other possibly valuable interests.

For example, most laws and models in physics (like Newton's laws or the harmonic oscillator) focus on the factors crucial to particular events. Such laws and models are stated for systems typically closed to outside interventions (whether of a physical nature or due to human agency) and the number of factors involved in the relations among the elements of the system are typically kept small. Both modes of abstraction are at work in such laws and models as they are idealizations away from the larger context of myriad physical influences (e.g., a tremendously complicated environment) and exclude the perspectives and agency of embodied beings (e.g., no human interventions as influences). Additionally, the laws and models of physics so abstracted also represent idealizations of the very objects we are trying to isolate through both modes of abstraction in the following sense. They represent a balance between what we are capable of understanding and calculating versus what we are interested in understanding and find relevant about the objects themselves. In other words, after pursuing both modes of abstraction as far as possible, we have to further simplify our laws and models to make them minimally manageable. So every such law and model represents a description that actually departs from 'the truth' about the objects in question in ways that render the descriptions inherently inexact, and which hides or ignores other aspects of the objects that may be crucial to other interests and purposes (Auyang 1998; Teller 2001). And, as social scientists are quick to admit, human behaviour is much more complicated than the behaviour physicists are trying to study!

Furthermore, these physical laws and models are typically mathematically precise and allow for the determination of any forces or magnitudes when all other relevant factors are known precisely and the context is properly restricted via abstraction. But this is to say that the laws and models of physics are *context dependent* in that they require us to move from one context rich in physical and human interactions and interrelationships to a more limited context through abstraction and further idealizations.[5] Specifically, these laws and models are context dependent in a particularly important sense relevant to social science: namely, all laws and models in physics are specified in the absence of human agency or influences. So to seriously push similarities between abstraction in the natural and social sciences to the extreme, social scientists would have to attempt to understand agency by abstracting away from all human influences, a rather paradoxical way of gaining objective, value-free distance on one's object of study!

3.2. The paradox of abstraction

It is at this point that a paradox of abstraction arises. In social and political activity, context is crucial to the actions of self-interpreting beings. However, if the natural-science ideal is context-free laws and theories (e.g., like the universal-laws conception of science), then our very approach presupposes that we abstract away from a crucial factor constituting the very activity we wish to understand – we have to give context-free explanations of context-dependent actions! But then we cannot explain our subject of study. Consider the example of gift-giving. There is no context-free way to specify what is a gift because the very notion of a gift and the practices surrounding gift-giving are dependent on particular societies. It looks like seeking context-free principles of explanation is horribly mismatched to social and political phenomena.

One might try the so-called second-order approach, where scientists take the social constructions and contexts as given and look for context-free relations among those structures. In economics, for example, this amounts to taking socially defined elements like money, property, a banking system and economically oriented desires like maximizing profit as given, that is fixed elements of the economic order among which to search for laws and regularities. But the problem here is that there is nothing within such a theory to account for or predict how or when people will change any of these socially constituted elements, so there really are neither laws nor context-free principles available even for a second-order approach attempting to approximate natural science ideals.

This paradox is driven by abstracting away from concrete contexts in social and political life with an exclusive focus on seeking efficient causal connections among events as the basis for developing context-free laws. The contexts themselves resemble examples of formal causes crucial to constituting meanings and actions. One way in which the fascination with context-free principles of explanation might be tempered is to incorporate other notions of causation into social-science theorizing (see Chapter 6).

Note that there is also a connection with the role of theories and issues of realism. Recall that there are different conceptions of theories – axiomatic, semantic, paradigmatic. Much of the drive for context-free laws and theories is a holdover from the received view (Chapter 1, sec. 2.1) that gets carried forward into other accounts of not only the structure, but also the role of theories. Should they be predictive? Explanatory? Both? The social and political realms present a challenge to unreflectively carrying forward our natural-science ideas about what constitutes a theory and its role into social-science practices.

Furthermore, there is the related issue of what are we to take as real in our social-science theorizing? If we follow natural-science ideals, then as realists we would be committed to saying that the abstract, context-free social and political structures of idealized theories would be the real elements of the social and political realms. This seems quite at odds with the crucial role contexts and self-interpretations play in these realms. In the social sciences, we start with an understanding of what things actually mean to people. Abstraction conceals large parts of this experience and meaning and, therefore, gives a quite narrow, bleached-out picture of what we want to understand. How is this denuded theoretical picture supposed to correspond to the reality we actually inhabit?

3.3. The lifeworld

In contrast, our everyday experience includes sights, sounds, smells, tastes, contexts, interruptions, surprises and so forth integrated in a holistic and dynamic unity. Furthermore, this experience is tied together by meaning – it makes sense to us. However, both modes of abstraction seek to cut as many strands of this dynamic relatedness and holism as possible down to some bare, manageable minimum. Let me call engaging in these kinds of abstraction taking a *theoretical stance*. This stance abstracts away the richness and unpredictability of everyday experience and objectifies a narrow range of events upon which it chooses to focus. The theoretical stance assumes (implicitly or explicitly) that humans can know valid and important things in a way at least partly independent of physical context and embodiment (the two modes of abstraction). It partially attenuates our relationship to this wider relational reality often for worthwhile purposes.

But even the theoretical stance represents a *human* activity that only has meaning for persons pursuing answers within some field of questions – that is, all human activity is for some purpose. Moreover, all human activity – even adopting the theoretical stance – takes place in a complex physical and social-historical world. So even in the midst of pursuing abstraction, we are always embedded in a holistic lifeworld. Our theoretical stance is embedded within a *practical stance* made up of the various ways we seek to cope with and live meaningfully in our world. Cultivating this practical stance is more a matter of developing character, exercising judgement and gaining insight, and less a matter of formulating laws or explicit general rules and applying techniques as we see from examples like expressing deference (Dreyfus and Dreyfus 1988; Richardson, Fowers and Guignon 1999; Flyvbjerg 2001). Indeed, the prudent use of such laws, rules, and techniques depends upon the prior existence of such character and judgement.

So even when engaging in abstraction, our relationship to our wider environment, including our involvement with and dependency upon other people, institutions and culture in large part constitutes who we are as agents who may engage in the practice of abstraction. This complex of physical–social–historical interrelations is the fundamental and inescapable arena of human action. Adopting the theoretical stance exclusively, often touted as the ideal for social science, breaks or seriously distorts this unity of our arena of action. It attempts to reduce all concepts and relations to the vocabulary and ontology of a science which approaches its subject matter mainly by way of abstraction and objectification. However, in doing so it ignores or obscures the fact that taking the theoretical stance is but one of a number of ways that humans, based upon their interests and purposes, approach their world to make sense of and cope with it. So, again, we see that the aiming for strict objectivity and value-neutrality is far from value-free.

One might still argue that the theoretical stance – the disengaged, 'objective' perspective – is the true or truer perspective, but why think this is justified? To begin with, the ideal of 'objectivity' driving the disengaged perspective is, as I have indicated, as much a morally motivated ideal as an epistemological one; in its instrumental form, it represents a particular understanding of the good and worthwhile life. The theoretical stance is another 'insider's' perspective among others and may be an important one for various purposes, but not necessarily 'truer'. It is far from neutral and cannot be divorced from our purposes as engaged agents situated in a complex, multifarious world. It is an often useful mode of engagement with the world, but no more than that.[6]

Furthermore, just because the natural sciences aim at maximum abstraction does not imply that the knowledge gained by their methodologies is somehow truer than knowledge gained through other modes of knowing in other domains. The truth or falsity of natural-science knowledge is often limited to its abstracted, idealized domain.[7] The theoretical stance contributes to our understanding of ourselves and our world, but it by no means exhausts these understandings. To take a 'down home' example, I can know you as a person only by entering into a personal relationship with you. In the absence of such a relationship, I can only know your behaviour by observation and inference (at a considerable distance). Certainly this amounts to legitimate knowledge claims about you and, as such, can even be shown to be either true or false in many instances (e.g., that you leave your home at the same time every day). However, this knowledge is abstract and limited by its distance from you as a person. This does not mean that upon entering into a relationship with you, knowledge of regularities and patterns in your behaviour and reactions is rendered irrelevant. But which regularities and patterns are interesting and important, what they mean, why they are sustained, and how I feel I should relate to them is determined largely by my grasp and appreciation of what you are all about as a person. This only comes through personal involvement with you, and the accompanying risks, vulnerabilities, pains and delights of that relationship.

Finally, one might think that the theoretical stance is always truer because, in the natural sciences, abstracting away from bodily experience removes distortions allowing us to grasp phenomena like electromagnetic radiation clearly. Our bodily experience of light and heat often mislead us as to the true nature of such phenomena. Similarly, so one might think, we need to abstract as far away from context and bodily experience as possible in order to see social phenomena clearly. But what is good for natural phenomena is not necessarily good for social phenomena in the sense of being a truer picture of those phenomena. Consider a personal account of grief such as C. S. Lewis's in *A Grief Observed* (2001), which almost makes us experience what grief feels like from the inside. What does a study of grief that treats it from a distance – as psychological or sociological accounts do – add to our knowledge or experience of grief? Certainly not a 'truer' account. Perhaps the latter adds knowledge of similarities or some generalizations about the experience of grief and the grieving process that we do not get from such a rich, highly personal account. But this in no way makes the theoretical perspective on grief any truer. It is simply another perspective that adds something to our knowledge of grief found in Lewis's personal story, but does not somehow supplant or replace that personal knowledge. As argued here and in Chapter 4, striving for this abstracted, theoretical stance in the social arena actually often introduces distortions rather than frees us from them. So the results of adopting the theoretical stance in social science are not the same as in the natural sciences.

4. Taking stock

The instrumental picture of action, along with a subject-object ontology and epistemology, harbours an unacknowledged commitment to a punctual view of the self. Such a view of the self is part of the reason why we find these pictures of action, ontology and epistemology bundled together so often in the social sciences. In addition, as I have indicated, the punctual view of the self reflects deep ethical ideals such as autonomy and liberal individualism, ideals which, in turn, reinforce a punctual view of the self. So there is also a substantial ethical component – also largely unacknowledged – acting to reinforce what passes for scientific ideals of human inquiry – instrumental action along with a subject-object ontology and epistemology. This kind of 'package deal' raises serious and troubling questions about objectivity and value-neutrality in the social sciences to which we now turn.

For further study

1. What is political liberalism and how does it show up in social science?
2. Explain ontological individualism. How is it related to Hobbes' picture of society?
3. Describe the three versions of liberal individualism. Which one do you see as most dominant in society?
4. Why is the combination of autonomy, liberal individualism and the instrumental picture of action unstable?
5. What are the theoretical and practical stances and their relationship to each other?

Recommended reading

R. Bellah, R. Madsen, W. Sullivan, A. Swidler, and S. Tipton, *Habits of the Heart: Individualism and Commitment in American Life* (New York: Harper & Row, 1985).

F. Richardson, A. Rogers and J. McCarroll, 'Toward a Dialogical Self', *American Behavioral Scientist* 41(1998): 496–515.

M. Root, *Philosophy of Social Science* (Oxford: Blackwell, 1993).

The Myth of Value-Neutrality

6

The upshot of the previous two chapters is that the social sciences are far from value-neutral. At least they are far from neutral as they are currently practised. Two questions about the supposed value-neutrality of social inquiry remain to be addressed. The first is an ontological question. Can the social sciences be value-neutral? Is there an approach to social inquiry that genuinely is value-free the way we think natural-science inquiry is value-free?[1] The second question is normative: Should the social sciences be value-neutral? Is a value-free approach the right or appropriate goal for social inquiry?

In previous chapters, I have written as if objectivity and value-neutrality always go together. Here, I will suggest that there is a sense in which objectivity can be separated from value-neutrality. This will be part of the key to answering the ontological and normative questions about social science.

Part of the answer to these two questions also involves answering a third question, a practical question: is there a genuine need for social inquiry to be strictly value-neutral? In one sense, this question seems to be a no-brainer. Of course we want social inquiry to be free of biases just as we expect natural-science inquiry to be bias-free. Otherwise, it seems impossible to escape some kind of advocacy, however implicit, in our social inquiry and results. Such research would, therefore, be tainted and only of limited use to those whose vision of the good life fit with the biases reflected therein. At least this is the kind of worry Weber (1949) expressed. Clearly, this is political liberalism shining through as a disguised ideology of social science (Root 1993). It is an explicitly value-laden position the majority of social scientists support and public administrators and policy officials want. But do we need what many thinkers argue is impossible to obtain? Is it not possible that, following critical theorists, by exposing underlying biases in social inquiry we can gain a kind of objectivity about how that very research may bear the limitations of its biases and, hence, what its applicability or validity for our social purposes might be?

1. 'Traditional debates' about value-neutrality

Let us begin with two examples of social-science research that are often treated as if they are strictly value-neutral (both in the way such research is carried out as well as the correlations discovered). The first example is discovery of correlations between voter attitudes and voter behaviour. Thinking of our correlators (Chapter 1, sec. 4) as seeking brute data and univocal methods for the moment, political scientists often take such correlations to be value-free in the following way. Actions identifiable as voting usually conform to institutional rules like showing a voter-registration card, stepping into a booth and pulling the lever (or pressing a button, punching a hole or marking an oval on a form) for a particular candidate or proposition on the ballot. Afterwards, the voter's attitudes can be recorded by means of an anonymous questionnaire by giving their responses to various objectified statements of beliefs as well as how the person voted. A statistical analysis is then applied to show the degree of correlations between voters' overt expressions of attitudes as identified through statements on the questionnaire and their voting behaviour.

The responses to a questionnaire are viewed as brute data just like the actions of pulling a lever, while the statistical methods of data analysis uncovering the correlations are supposed to be univocal data operations. No interpretation is seemingly needed. Of course, there are further value-laden questions about these correlations. What do these correlations mean? What do voters see themselves doing when they engage in the act of voting? How do they see the situation or what is at stake when deciding how to pull the lever? These questions cannot receive an answer from simply carrying out more correlation studies, so it seems that to go further with interesting analysis of voter behaviour crucially involves interpretations of voters' meanings and experiences that admit of multiple possible understandings. There is also the problem that the very categorization the political scientist invokes – namely prescribing particular physical behaviours purely by institutional rules and translating values, meanings and points of view into lists of propositions for assent or dissent – already carries with it various interpretations and cultural ideals of the scientist (e.g., political liberalism and liberal individualism are already presupposed in this whole project in Western democracies).

Another example of supposed value-neutral research is the description of patterns among variables such as a rough correlation between high self-esteem and better test scores. This might also be assessed by means of a questionnaire giving a list of statements to which students assent or dissent and these results correlated via statistical means with actual student performances on exams. However, the meaning or concept of self-esteem depends on a host of values and cultural affordances. In Western culture with its emphasis on individualism and inwardness, self-esteem appears real and meaningful for us – it is a feature of our social reality. But consider the cultural situation of mediaeval knights, where ideals of chivalry and honour somewhat lost to us were important. The idea of self-esteem would make little sense to them. So seeking correlations between self-esteem and something like student grades is far from the kind of objective, value-free research it is presented to be. Furthermore, simply locating this kind of correlation does not tell us whether boosting self-esteem without addressing actual achievement is a good way to improve student's grades. Nor do such correlations tell us to what extent higher self-esteem or better grades are worthwhile goals to pursue.

Weber famously argued that values do affect the social scientist's choice of problems and her considerations about how any causal laws discovered in the social arena might best be applied. Furthermore, any concrete knowledge of social reality always involves the particular point of view a social scientist takes. However, Weber maintained, while the social scientist's research framework is influenced by a number of values, the results or truth of her investigation are not similarly influenced. The results should be valid or applicable for all, not just for the person engaging in inquiry with a specific framework. One reason he thought this is because social science could at least discover persistent causal relationships like those between voter attitudes and voter behaviour (even if it could not produce exact mathematical laws like natural science). These causal relationships should, in principle, be independent of the values informing the social scientist's research framework (though whether we take them to be significant patterns requires a value judgement – significance has to do with how we see things). One does not have to follow critical theorists or postmodern critics like Foucault in every detail of their views to see that the possibility of research results escaping unscathed by values – whether those of the investigator or those of the subjects of investigation – is quite remote. Most of these 'persistent causal relationships' in social life are dependent on the values and meanings of social actors and their institutions and, as such, are apt to disappear or change when those values and meanings change (e.g., the non-existence of self-esteem in pre-modern societies and its emergence in modern societies).

Ernest Nagel (1961: ch. 4) argues that values enter into social science not only in problem selection but also in the evaluation of conclusions, the identification of what is a fact, and the assessment of evidence as well. Nevertheless, he maintains, one sees these same influences of values in natural-science inquiry, so social-science research can still produce unbiased conclusions like the natural sciences. The key distinction in Nagel's analysis is between *appraising* value judgements, which express approval/disapproval, and *characterizing* value judgements, which estimate the degree to which some feature is present. A neutral social science would, like the natural sciences, admit characterizing value judgements – indeed, one can argue that an important part of scientific research is making just such estimates of what factors are present in a situation and their relative roles in behaviour – but be devoid of appraising value judgements. But this distinction in judgements depends on the fact/value distinction. Nagel argues as if this distinction can always be made, but his appeal to some instances where we can disentangle facts from values is not evidence that we can always do so nor that it is wise to always do so (see below).

Nagel acknowledges, however, that social scientists often carry appraising judgements into their work. And while it is worthwhile for scientists to uncover and state their biases as explicitly as possible, we are often unaware of some of our most significant biases. Rather, these biases 'are usually overcome, often only gradually, through the self-corrective mechanisms of science as social enterprise' (1961: 489–90).[2] Certainly it is the case that sustained scientific practice can root out errors and biases, but Nagel's confidence in the 'self-corrective mechanisms' of social inquiry is likely to be overblown. First, the model for self-correction Nagel has in mind is natural science and unless natural and social science are sufficiently similar, it is far from clear that there are appropriate self-correction mechanisms in social inquiry. Indeed, neither mainstream nor descriptivist modes of social inquiry have anything in their arsenals to deal with the subtle effects of disguised ideologies. Second, and more troubling, if descriptivists, critical theorists, constructionists and hermeneutic thinkers are right (Chapter 3), the very fact that humans are self-interpreting beings – both social scientists and their subjects are meaning sponges if you will – presents very stubborn obstacles to achieving genuinely value-neutral forms of social inquiry. There is no methodology for detecting the cultural ideals and meanings of the social arena under investigation and screening these out from being simply passed through social inquiry as results of scientific research (Chapter 8). For example, how would we detect the hidden ideology of liberal individualism in the voting and self-esteem examples given earlier? Finally, as we have already seen, the very drive to make social science value-free is, itself, a substantial value-laden position (e.g., political liberalism, liberal individualism), calling into question the very possibility of social inquiry ever being value-free. Though scientists might like to stick only with characterizing judgements as Nagel advocates, their surreptitiously carrying forward cultural ideals like political liberalism and liberal individualism represents tacit appraising judgements endorsing these ideals. The problems of value-neutrality in social science are much deeper than analyses like Nagel's assume.

A more recent theme in value-neutrality debates comes from feminist analyses of social inquiry and culture. Naomi Weisstein (1971), for example, has argued that the conclusions of psychology regarding the behaviour of men and women are deeply influenced by the social conditions and expectations under which they live. If culture characterizes women as emotional, weak, inconsistent, nurturers, intuitive rather than intelligent, as suited only for particular roles and so forth, then women's lived experience and behaviour will be different due to subtle and not so subtle forms of bias. For instance, hiring a male over an equally qualified female candidate because 'she won't be able to lead anyone', or male graduate students treating a female graduate student as their secretary. On the other hand, if women are characterized as intelligent, reasoning, strong, competitive, with qualities like empathy, intuitiveness and so forth, their lived experience will be quite different. In this sense, psychology, by simply taking society's characterizations of men and women over uncritically, tends to pass off behaviour under social expectations as behaviour due to innate natures. Similar to critical theorists, Weisstein urges challenging prevailing theories and cultural expectations as well as transforming men's and women's perspectives. Hence, biases could possibly be rooted out and our psychological and social pictures of men and women be made more accurate.

As Alison Wylie (1992) points out, however, many feminist theorists have saddled social inquiry about women with an a priori limit that it must remain forever bound within female experience. But to do so undercuts the very power to raise and transform the consciousness of both men and women regarding social expectations and their roles in guiding or dominating behaviour. The aim, consistent with Enlightenment aims, is to ultimately free people from false and oppressive ideals guiding their behaviour, so keeping such social inquiry confined to female experience also keeps it from taking on the transformative function feminist theorists want it to have. There is much to be admired in such transformation of consciousness, but many feminist analyses of how to go about freeing ourselves from social biases focus more on achieving this from a fixed point of view (some form of feminism or uniquely female perspective) with little on offer in the way of how this point of view could be put into conversation with other points of view, both traditional and otherwise, so that better understandings of our biases and expectations could be achieved.

2. Cultural ideals and the ontological and normative questions

Clearly, the typical debates about value-neutrality in the social sciences do not 'get to the bottom' of the core issues: the role cultural ideals play in social inquiry as disguised ideologies. The majority of debates about value-neutrality revolve around the possibility of being value-neutral; that is, that there is nothing presenting an in-principle unremovable obstacle from social inquiry being value-free though it may be difficult to achieve this in practice. However, as we have seen in the previous two chapters, the aspiration to value neutrality, if it could be fulfilled, would simply be another value-laden standpoint for conducting social inquiry.

First, the very ideal of a value-neutral social science is an expression of a substantial political ideal – political liberalism. Far from being a value-free point of view, this liberal ideal contains a potent vision of the good life as neutrality toward all possible conceptions of the good. Hence, the aspiration toward value-neutrality in social inquiry, as in natural-scientific and descriptivist modes, represents a significant commitment to liberalism, hardly a value-free standpoint for social science.

Second, most social inquiry presupposes an instrumental picture of agency along with a subject-object ontology and epistemology. But this package of assumptions, as we have seen, carries with it deep commitments to liberal individualism and autonomy, as well as values such as liberty, individuality, tolerance, respect and so on: all part of the furniture of modern Western culture. Again, what looks like the best bet for achieving objectivity and value-neutrality is, itself, a value-laden, biased point of view for social science.

A very plausible reason why this value-laden standpoint is treated as value-free in social science is the critical-theorist notion of disguised ideology: the ideals and ways of seeing social reality animating the instrumental agency/subject-object ontology package in social inquiry lie below the surface, unacknowledged by social scientists. But just because they are unacknowledged does not mean they are somehow denuded of influence. On the contrary, just like a motor, though lying out of sight, powers a car, so disguised ideologies colour all of social-science practice from problem selection/definition to research methods and the interpretation and application of results (so 'out of sight, out of mind' does not apply here).

It is hard to escape the conclusion that hidden *moral* motivations as well as scientific ones have moved many capable minds in the social sciences to pursue this package deal. Largely unknowingly, they have smuggled in at least as many value commitments as they have tried to keep out. And in pursuing this package deal, social scientists often have forged accounts of human action that fail to do full justice to the reality of their subject matter, focusing almost exclusively on instrumental action (*zweckrational*) and practising as much abstraction away from rich human contexts as possible. Furthermore, I have suggested that this package deal along with its motivations and commitments, has not always been helpful and perhaps has often been harmful to the pursuit of knowledge and understanding in the social sciences.

Conceiving of human behaviours as somehow law-governed, in the way that say the interactions of molecules are law-governed as the universal-laws conception would direct us to do, overlooks the self-interpretive character of human agency (Berlin 1962; Taylor 1985a; 1985b; Richardson, Fowers and Guignon 1999). Similarly, it tends to undermine the meaningfulness of the enterprise of social science itself as a source of insight into human dynamics and as some sort of aid in the conduct of human action. Clearly, social science is driven by an abhorrence of ignorance, superstition and political tyranny, and is motivated at its core to find knowledge of human behaviour that can be employed to liberate and improve people's lives for the better – this is part of what autonomy and individualism are all about. Unfortunately, its prevalent focus on explaining behaviour as instrumental in a context-free manner under the guise of value-neutrality obscures or even denies many important dimensions of the human lifeworld and human experience, including its own morally motivated, intentional efforts to fashion a credible and useful science of individual and social behaviour (Bernstein 1976; Taylor 1985a; 1985b).

So the answer to the ontological question – can the social sciences be value-neutral? – clearly is no. It simply is not possible to avoid serious value commitments in the conduct of social inquiry. Worse, more often than not, cultural ideals like political liberalism and liberal individualism operate as disguised ideologies, pervading social inquiry and any supposed value-free results.

But there is a second question about value-neutrality, the normative question: should the social sciences aim for value-neutrality? Answering this question initially seems to present us with a distasteful dilemma. By answering 'yes' we commit ourselves to pursuing a particular vision of the good for social science as well as advocating substantial values and ideals. By answering 'no', however, we are admitting that social inquiry should simply remain biased. It looks like we are simply throwing up our hands and giving up all hope of objectivity in social inquiry.

Perhaps there is a way to avoid this distasteful dilemma. So far we have been proceeding as if value-neutrality and objectivity always go together: that is, that to be objective in social inquiry is to be completely free of bias, seeing things clearly from some supposed value-free vantage point (outsider's perspective). Given this kind of vantage point does not exist, does this mean we have to give up things like objectivity and accuracy, wallowing in biases as we muck around in the social arena searching for understanding?

One way to lessen the severity of the dilemma, if not diffuse it altogether, is to bite the bullet that only insiders' perspectives are available to us and reconceive objectivity. Instead of trying to conceive objectivity along the lines of a 'view from nowhere' devoid of values, objectivity is that quality of perspective we gain when we put differing approaches to social inquiry and differing conceptions of the good into conversation with each other.[3] Each perspective might then become enriched by the interpenetrating influences of other perspectives as well as seeing its own commitments more clearly and more deeply. In this way, particular perspectives in social inquiry not only become more aware of their own biases, but also the biases of others, allowing for a fuller understanding of the meaning and potential usefulness of social research.

Consider a simple example highlighting ordinary social processes of conversation, the kinds of processes that have been largely overlooked as pervasive influences shaping the direction of human action.[4] Suppose you are at a meeting where a controversial decision is under discussion. You enter into the debate and argue clearly for the position that seems to make the most sense to you, appears to reflect your own best values, illustrates what you believe is at stake in the decision and cast your vote accordingly. As you leave you are feeling quite good about your thinking on the matter, how you voted, and that things turned out the way you wanted. Later, in conversation with a friend, you turn to discussing the meeting and describe the deliberations, your reasons for arguing and voting as you did, what you felt was at stake and so forth. However, she replies, 'Gee, that's not how I see it at all', and proceeds to cast fresh light on the issues, mentioning various facets, consequences or values you had not taken fully into account. After the conversation (perhaps even during), you find yourself thinking about what she said, revising your sense of what really was at stake, questioning what your true desires and motives were at the time, wondering or doubting if you lived up to what you take to be your own best values on that occasion, and perhaps even rethinking some of those values. Whatever the outcome of this conversation with another and yourself – it could, in the end, either harden your defences or enrich your sensibilities – you will have been changed or influenced, possibly in some significant way. The steady accumulation of such events over time adds up to much of the reality of a human life and, like practising deference, is not in the main characterizable as instrumental action.

The suggestion I am making here is that you have gained some more objectivity on your own best values and your motives for action as well as those of your conversation partner. She, likewise, has also gained new appreciation of your view of things as well as her own. You now have a more accurate picture of your and her values (she likewise). Similarly, social scientists by engaging differing perspectives on the model of conversation can also gain in objectivity and accuracy about the values animating their own research frameworks, the values and ideals they are surreptitiously passing through their research as value-neutral 'facts' of the social landscape. As well, they can better see the biases and ideologies at work in the perspectives and research of other social scientists, getting a clearer picture of false claims or wrongful biases. The result may be the need to ruthlessly root out some values we all agree are bad (e.g., subtle forms of racism or sexism). This need not always be the case, however, as a deeper understanding of the values at work in various aspects of social inquiry may shed light on positive, creative ways in which research can be performed and how it can inform everyday living, education, counselling and public policy. If the core ideal of objectivity is to get clear on what is really happening, an outsider's perspective, as we have seen, too often distorts what is going on in social reality. Therefore, objectivity cannot be the same as the value-neutral outsider's perspective as so many social scientists and philosophers take it to be. The kind of honesty, fairness and detachment that arises in bringing your point of view into genuine conversation with others is what makes intellectual community possible and illuminates all the points of view in question. It is difficult to imagine what more social inquiry could want from our insiders' perspectives.[5]

Social scientists and theorists have only begun to map and analyse such conversational realities and influences (Gergen 1985; Richardson, Rogers and McCarroll 1998). But such influences represent just the sort of historical forces and social processes that, if brought centre stage in the social sciences, will illuminate human life as it is actually lived as well as challenging our thinking about value-neutrality and its problems in useful ways.

3. An alternative to instrumental action and subject-object ontology/epistemology

I want to sketch a possible direction for pursuing alternatives to the instrumental picture of action and the subject-object ontology and epistemology that comes along with it. This package deal is one way the social sciences avoid falling into relativism, but if we give these up, can we still avoid that fall (see Chapter 17)? To start off, consider different modes of understanding in which we might be engaged in social inquiry.

3.1. Types of understanding

Social science seeks for understandings of our world and behaviour. To understand something fundamentally is to bring some form of interpretation to the thing which illuminates it, makes sense of it, clarifies it and so forth, appropriate to the kinds of questions we have about the thing we wish to understand. To say that social science as a practice is basically interpretive (and, perhaps, predictive in some respects as well), according to Taylor, involves three characteristics (1985b: 15–17):[6]

1 The categories of 'sense' or 'coherence' – meaning – must apply to the objects of study.
2 The 'sense' in question must be at least relatively distinguishable from its expression or embodiment – the same meaning is often capable of alternative expression.
3 This 'sense' must be for or by a subject.[7]

Characteristic 1 is obviously crucial to any kind of understanding activity, whether in the sciences or other disciplines. Unless it is possible to 'make sense' of the events, patterns, processes and other happenings we are studying, understanding them in any form is hopeless. The kinds of questions we want to ask regarding the object of study give us the ability to say if something 'makes sense' or is 'nonsense', is coherent or incoherent, so for the categories of 'sense' and 'coherence' to fail to apply to something would require the impossible situation of something existing for us outside all possible questions and concerns we might have.[8]

Characteristic 2 occurs in the practice of social science (among other disciplines) in many forms. What are taken to be 'scientific truths' are always capable of being re-expressed in terms of theories, experiments, models, pictures, metaphors, aphorisms and their various descriptions. These 'scientific truths' are, among other things, meanings we attach to the phenomena we study (in the sense of the modes of understanding described below) enabling us to understand and, in at least some instances, predict and manipulate those phenomena. The so-called law of diminishing returns in economics is an example here; this principle admits of various interpretations but also its applicability depends on the kinds of shared values, norms and institutions at work in a society giving structure to a particular economy and giving sense to what is meaningful activity. In addition, we can distinguish between a given situation or action and its meaning in terms of the kinds of descriptions we give, one of these descriptions being characterized in terms of its meaning for a subject (e.g., scientist investigating a behaviour). Multiple descriptions or re-expressions bring different emphases and different insights that serve to illuminate the phenomena in question.

Characteristic 3 is obvious in that it is human investigators in the social sciences who, based on individual values and purposes as well as the values and purposes of their research communities, choose which phenomena to investigate, which questions to ask, which methods of inquiry to pursue, what categories to bring to the data collected, how to apply the knowledge gained and what counts as significant in each of these choices. At a more general level, the whole notion of science as a practice (activity conception) points to the fact that it is an activity that *we* find meaningful.[9] Furthermore, this meaning things have for us (like the particular behaviours we are studying) is related to a web of meanings other things have for us. In other words, the meaning a thing has for us is partly constituted by other meanings other things have for us. For example, the meaning of a word is partly defined in relation to its synonyms and antonyms. Or consider these examples described by Taylor:

> Just as our colour concepts are given their meaning by the field of contrast they set up together, so that the introduction of new concepts will alter the boundaries of others, so the various meanings that a subordinate's de-meanour can have for us, as deferential, respectful, cringing, mildly mocking, ironical, insolent, provoking, downright rude, are established by a field of contrast; and as with finer discrimination on our part, or a more sophisticated culture, new possibilities are born, so other terms of this range are altered. And as the meaning of our terms 'red', 'blue', 'green' is fixed by the definition of a field of contrast through the determinable term 'colour', so all these alternative demeanours are only available in a society which has, among other types, hierarchical relations of power and command. . . [and] the set of social practices which sustain these hierarchical structures and are fulfilled in them. (1985b: 22–23)

3.1.1. Mechanistic understanding

Having seen that social science functions as an interpretive practice – that is to say, a way of understanding things in our world – more generally, we can distinguish four types of understanding that play roles in the explanation and illumination of our experience. The first is *mechanistic* in terms of efficient causation (e.g., the instrumental picture of action). This mode of understanding is most closely associated with natural-scientific modes of explanation where an event or process is understood if the appropriate relationship between the cause of the event or process and its effects are clarified. The stories told to illuminate the happenings of events or processes are cause–effect stories where the latter relation is understood in the sense of efficient (mechanistic) causation.

For instance, the reason why the eight ball rolled into the corner pocket was because it was struck by the cue ball at a particular angle with a particular force. Furthermore there are at least some psycho-physical relationships exhibiting efficient cause–effect chains. An instance would be the photons emanating from the computer screen impinging upon my retinas causing an image of what I am typing to appear before me (in contrast to the wall behind me which I cannot see because those photons reflecting off it are not reaching my retinas). A simple example of a social-science explanation would be: 'His belief that the generals should be stopped led him to poison their food'. Here, the belief that the generals should be stopped is viewed as an efficient cause of the poisoning of the food. Other modes of understanding might become involved in probing the belief and its formation.

Maximum abstraction in the first mode (physical context) often enables a scientist to focus on a small number of relevant causes in highly controlled situations. The success of this approach in the natural sciences, however, should not be taken as licensing the strong metaphysical claim that all events and processes in this world (in both the physical and social realms) are only efficient cause–effect chains (i.e., weak world-shaping: Chapter 1, sec. 4).

3.1.2. Historical understanding

A second mode of understanding is *historical* (origins and development). This mode is most closely associated with the work of historians and various interpretive modes of explanation, where an event or process is understood if its origin is specified and its development traced. The stories told to illuminate the happenings of events or processes are in terms of a series of decisive events – which may or may not be viewed causally – by which the event or process to be understood came into existence and proceeded to develop. The relationship between human beings and the effects of these relationships on others, as well as people's motives and actions, along with the social, economic, geographic and political conditions in which these relationships and actions take place all figure into historical understanding. Examples would be the origins story of a particular culture or the birth and development of modern science. Such accounts typically do not make much use of abstraction in either mode.

One might argue, for instance, that a description in terms of the motives and decisions of the North's leaders during the American Civil War would not be sufficiently deep for understanding how their victory came about. The North would have won anyway given their superiority in resources such as population, industry and transport, greater international support as well as the presence of tens of thousands of slaves in the South. Many variations on the motives and decisions of the North's leaders would have led to victory over the South, though our best accounts of those motives and decisions, in combination with the other advantages possessed by the North might clarify why the North won at the particular time that they did. This would be a form of historical understanding in terms of economic, geopolitical and other factors that played important roles in determining the outcome of the war.

3.1.3. Practical understanding

The third mode of understanding to be distinguished is *practical* or *embodied* (how to do things, sense things). This mode, sometimes referred to as en-acted, first-person or situated, is most closely associated with postmodern and hermeneutic modes of explanation where an event or process is understood if the sense the event or process has for a situated agent is clarified. It is ba-sically the perspective described as strong world-shaping (Chapter 1, sec. 4). The stories told to illuminate the happenings of events or processes are point-of-view stories of embodied agents engaging things in the world in concrete ways. Consider a basic example of situatedness by Taylor:

> As I sit here and take in the scene before me, this has a complex structure. It is oriented vertically, some things are 'up,' others are 'down'; and also in depth, some are 'near', others 'far.' Some objects 'lie to hand,' others are 'out of reach'; some constitute 'unsurmountable obstacles' to movement, others are 'easily displaced.' My present position doesn't give me a 'good purchase' on the scene; for that I would have to shift farther to the left. And so on. (Taylor 1993: 318)

To say that we are engaging something in the world as an embodied agent means that the story describing the experience necessarily uses terms that only make sense against the background of the particular type of bodies we have. All the terms in quotes in the Taylor passage are understood only from the perspective of an agent having the same body as us. To understand what it is to 'lie to hand' requires being an agent with the bodily capacities of a human being. Hence the very nature of experiencing things in the world as human beings is constituted by our particular form of embodiment and the terms describing this experience make sense only in relation to our embodiment. Eugene Gendlin puts it this way:

> Let us begin with the body, rather than the five senses. Your body senses what is behind your back right now, without seeing, hearing, or smelling it. You sense not just the things there, but your situation, what would happen if you suddenly turned around, or if you pounded on the wall where your neighbours live.

> The body senses the situation more encompassingly than cognition. If an experienced pilot says 'I don't know why, but I'm not comfortable about the weather', don't go.
>
> For example, a researcher pursues 'an idea'. It's not really an idea. It's a pregnant bodily sense acquired in the lab. If it is new, the bodily sense is at first inarticulate. 'It' will be *carried forward* by many odd thoughts and moves in the lab, until 'it' develops into a feasible project. 'It' stays stable only when nothing comes to carry 'it' forward. '*Carrying forward*' is a useful concept, because so many processes are neither predictable from pre-existing units, nor arbitrary. Einstein's autobiography reports that for fifteen years he was 'guided by a feeling for the answer'. Obviously the feeling didn't contain the finished theory. No wise scientist or programmer ignores such a 'sense'. (1999: 236)

Maximum abstraction along the second axis (embodied context) yields an objectified view that is totally disembodied – that is to say, leaves the practical stance producing a purely theoretical stance. Although appropriate in natural-science contexts, such abstraction is wholly inappropriate to contexts where we are trying to understand embodied experience (e.g., discerning meanings in people's body language).

3.1.4. Moral understanding

The final mode of understanding is *moral* (broadly construed as moral, religious, cultural, etc.). It is more closely associated with interpretive explanations and particularly tied to practical/embodied forms of understanding, where an event or process is understood within the context of embodied agents in a historical flow of moral and cultural meanings and values. Both historical and practical modes of understanding are typically involved here as the existent larger geographic, social, political and economic conditions – of which people may not be aware – guide, though do not determine, actions. As well, the larger cultural surroundings are experienced as embodied beings making practical decisions about how best to get about in the world. An example would be understanding the concept of deference. Deference is an attitude I adopt in the presence of those wiser than myself as an acknowledgment of my estimation of their status in my eyes and as a reflection of the value I place on wisdom as well as an estimation of the status particular people have within my community or society. This deferential stance is played out in conversation with various cues such as my being hesitant to speak up or standing a step further back from my wiser conversation partner or my suggesting that the wiser person be the first to address or comment upon something in a public forum. It is an embodied stance that I – body and all – live in the context of a set of meanings or values that are crucial to understanding the act and its context.

3.2. Philosophical meaning

The natural-scientific approach to social science appears to assume that all 'real' questions about social reality can be answered on the basis of empirical or formal methods. This is likely a legacy of positivism, which emphasized empirical experiment and formal languages as crucial to science, as well as the influence of the natural sciences (see Chapter 1, sec 2.1; Chapter 2, sec. 2). As Berlin (1962) and Bernstein (1976) point out, the Enlightenment viewed experiment and formalization as ways to distinguish between mere opinion, superstition and bias, on the one hand, and fact and warranted knowledge, on the other. Positivism picked up this general thread, but appears to have ontologized its epistemology. That is, it moved from emphasizing these empirical and formal ways of knowing to the view that the only kinds of objective or genuine knowledge were those amenable to such approaches. All else was meaningless or relegated to being purely subjective (manifestations of the subject-object ontology and epistemology and the fact/value distinction).

Berlin saw this as a turn from 'liberating ideas' to a 'suffocating straightjacket' (1962: 1). The meanings that constitute social and political reality can neither be comprehended nor addressed adequately through only empirical and formal means. That is to say, if the only mode of understanding is mechanical, then the only genuine knowledge and understanding is what this mode delivers. If the only objectively real or warranted knowledge is that which is empirical or formalizable, then whither meanings?

Instead, Berlin (1962) argued there was a third legitimate route to genuine knowledge, one that he called *philosophical*. It is philosophical in that it is normative knowledge and theory that results, and because it views humans as self-interpreting beings. The ways of seeing things and understandings humans have of themselves is constitutive of the actions, practices and institutions composing social and political life. Thus, ways of seeing things and understandings cannot be the mere subjective, meaningless items that empirical and formalist perspectives take them to be. In other words, relying on mechanistic understanding alone will leave out a number of crucially important features of social and political behaviour. Historical, practical and moral modes are needed as well.

So Berlin was actually challenging the possibility of value-neutral social sciences that empirical and formal approaches assumed: 'The idea of a completely

Wertfrei [value-free] theory (or model) of human action...rests on a naïve misconception of what objectivity or neutrality in the social studies is' (Berlin 1962: 17). The idea of being able to correlate private, subjective beliefs with public, objective behaviour – as mainstream social scientists tend to try to do following empirical and formal methodologies – is mistaken, Berlin argues, because there is no tidy public/private, objective/subjective dichotomy possible. Human action in social and political life is constituted by interpretations involving individual and shared norms, values and meanings, where public and private run together so to speak, and everything ultimately is evaluative. If the mechanistic understanding of regularities in the social realm leaves out the interpretations of people, then the results will be misleading because the regularities in question may only be due to the interpretations of the people involved (e.g., an uncritical acceptance of a dominant political ideology, or unrealistic ideals of human health or beauty).

3.3. Bringing understandings together

In actual practice, natural-scientific modes of social inquiry draw on our ordinary understandings of human activity life in society, moral convictions, aspirations for happiness and so forth for their intelligibility in contrast to pure mechanistic explanations which generally lack explicit appeals to such understandings. And even natural science cannot get along without a wider context of values and meanings informing its practice and is heavily dependent on human judgement. To put the matter differently: mechanistic understanding can only find meaning within the context of historical, practical and moral understandings.

In contrast to purely mechanistic kinds of explanation, like the instrumental picture of action, we always engage the world from a practical perspective of an actor/experiencer, whether we are a scientist or not. But this does not undermine the possibility of different modes of social inquiry giving us useful and illuminating accounts of human life.[10] However, we need to recognize that many accounts by their very nature *abstract away* more or less from the myriad entangling factors of our environment and our socially situated humanity. The caution, then, is to be aware that many accounts of social behaviour abstract away from social reality for particular purposes. To treat social reality as if it *is* these abstractions commits a version of what William James calls the *psychologist's fallacy* (1950: 196–98):[11] inferring that social reality is identical with or very similar to our abstracted picture.

From the limited perspective of the theoretical stance, however, human action is reduced to mere behaviour in a way that largely erases intentionality and agency from the scene. To be sure, some thinkers have striven mightily to reinterpret intentionality within the theoretical stance (e.g., Dennett 1987). But at best this approach can resurrect a narrowly instrumental conception of action that is, as we have seen, full of paradoxes, hard to maintain, tends to undermine its own best values, and may inadvertently reinforce some of our most troubling social trends. In the end, the theoretical stance largely treats people as just one object among many other objects. We can restore the reality and integrity of human action, as well as take advantage of scientific investigation of the human realm, by at least insisting on equal priority for the engaged or practical stance, treating people in fully personal terms and viewing them in meaningful, dynamic relationships with other persons, their history, and their physical and social worlds. In other words, treat humans as we *actually are*, not as we are *idealized to be* by the package deal of the instrumental picture of agency and a subject-object ontology and epistemology (i.e., avoid committing the psychologist's fallacy).

To be sure, knowledge of the human realm derived from the theoretical stance can illumine some of the necessary conditions of human activity, while not providing sufficient conditions for such activity (Vogel 1998; Williams 2001). While we cannot violate the constraints imposed by the physical world in our undertakings (e.g., humans do not have the unassisted power of flight overcoming gravity), limiting human action and creativity to simply exemplifying those constraints is entirely unnecessary. To do so makes little sense in light of the fact that such scientific accounts themselves have been fashioned by human actors in a holistic lifeworld – a lifeworld rendering creative scientific endeavour possible in the first place.

For the most part, mainstream social science has tried to set aside the practical stance and striven instead for a 'neutral', disengaged description and explanation of human behaviour. The astonishing successes of the natural sciences along with the wide degree of unanimity of agreement among the practitioners of the various branches of the natural sciences has apparently influenced social scientists to think that natural-science practices are the only credible approaches for reaching genuine knowledge. To adopt this approach, however, is to fall into what may be called 'physics envy', obscuring much of the context making human activity what it is. We end up ignoring how value judgements are part of the process of inquiry even in the natural sciences (Polanyi 1962; Kitcher 1993), let alone the extent to which meanings and values imbue the everyday lifeworld that is the proper focus of most social-science inquiry (Berlin 1962; Bernstein 1976; Taylor 1985a; 1985b; Richardson, Fowers and Guignon 1999).

Another influence leading social scientists to imitate the natural sciences is the normative drive to have a value-neutral form of social inquiry. However, we have also seen that in many respects this is a false norm: we cannot be truly value-neutral as this is merely one more value-laden point of view. The normative question – should social science inquiry be value-neutral? – looks to receive a negative answer. Of course, if the answer to this normative question were 'yes', then there would clearly be a genuine need for social inquiry to be as value-free as possible. But with the answer of 'no', is there still a need to pursue the goal of value-free inquiry? The answer seems to be 'depends' in the sense I described earlier in the conversational model. If we discern that particular values colouring social inquiry are objectionable (e.g., racism or sexism), then yes there is a genuine need to expunge those. On the other hand, if we discern the values to be unobjectionable, there may be no real need to expunge them, but we should be careful to remain ever aware of their presence and effects as we evaluate and seek to make use of social inquiry.

If clarifying what social science is all about is as philosophically taxing and, in a deeply human way, as confusing as suggested here, then a real resolution to the problems and paradoxes of value-neutrality will be hard to accomplish and only come slowly. As one fruitful first step, it seems to me, we must make a concerted effort to close the distance between theoretical and practical stances in social inquiry. This gulf is assured when social scientists rely heavily on methodological approaches grounded in the kinds of abstraction and objectification described in previous chapters. To close this gulf we will have to treat the 'all too human' purposes, meanings and values animating our lives and imbuing the everyday lifeworld – including our profoundly influential interactions with other people, near and far, present and past, who are likewise animated by such meanings and goals – as essential *means* for understanding human action, not as mere irrelevancies or epiphenomena to be excluded from view. Moreover, we will have to engage these meanings in our theorizing as well as begin to view theorizing as another practice in which human agents engage because of particular meanings and purposes. After all, these 'all too human' meanings and interpretations inform the theoretical stances social scientists take.

Secondly, it appears that it will be impossible to do justice to the interrelatedness of human phenomena within a framework of strict efficient causation as the instrumental picture of action requires. Instead, we will have to expand our notions of cause and agency to accommodate everyday realities of human life. Social scientists, need to seek out additional types and avenues of influence. Psychology and sociology often appeal to past events as crucial for understanding present behaviour. They largely assume that current circumstances form a context in which past influences can come to expression, but most theories in psychology and sociology are strictly past-oriented. It may be impossible to make sense of these influences, however, unless we view the context of present circumstances, as well as our present interpretation of those past events, as formal causes. Our current interpretations of past events shape how those events now influence us. As such, these interpretations constrain or activate past influences as well as shape our responses to the current situation (Bishop 2002; see below).

3.4. Narrative accounts

If we take seriously the ideas that there is no outsider's perspective available to us – hence there is no genuine subject-object ontology or epistemology – and that conceiving human activity as purely or largely instrumental is too distorting of the lifeworld we wish to study, here is one possible alternative for reconceiving social inquiry. My suggestion weaves together three strands: conversation, narrative accounts (due to the narrative structure of the lifeworld) and multiple modes of social inquiry (recall the conversational model discussed in Chapter 3, sec. 5 and above).

I need to say a bit more about narrative accounts of human action.[12] Narrative approaches do not characterize human action exclusively or mainly in terms of context-free laws of behaviour, or strictly in terms of efficient causes as do natural-scientific modes of explanation. Instead, various types of formal modes of causation as well as ends (i.e., goal-directed activity or motivation from a vision of who I want to be in the future), in part, give narrative accounts their structure and flow. The central premise of the narrative approach is that humans live and act in a cultural and historical context spanning the past to the present and into the future, a context that, to a large degree, constitutes our present selves and relationships (e.g., sets the way we see things). Early on in our lives our identities are shaped – one could use the word *determined* – but not mainly in the sense of efficient causation; rather, they are shaped by the cultural and social traditions in which we grow up. Also, however, from the beginning of our life history, we are existentially and morally engaged in these traditions and, at some level, are reinterpreting them.

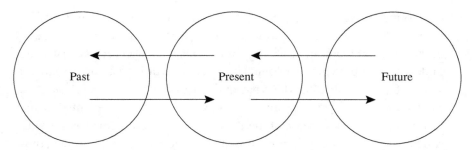

Figure 6.1 The Lifeworld
In the narrative picture of the lifeworld, our past affects how we see our present and future, while our present shapes how we see our past and future, while our vision of our future influences how we see our past and present. These three views of ourselves mutually shape each other like three conversation partners engaged in meaningful give and take.

Your past experiences, traditions and involvements shape your present view of yourself. As well, your current understanding of yourself sheds light and new understanding on your past experiences, traditions and involvements which in turn further illuminate your current view of your self (see Fig. 6.1). Likewise, your view of your future – your goals, the kind of person you imagine you want to become, etc. – gives shape to your current view of your self (which also changes how you view your past). And your current view of yourself also colours your view of the future, which then further clarifies and illumines your current view of your self. The unforseen surprises and disappointments of life as well as the books we read, movies we watch and the friends we keep play into this ongoing interpretive enterprise. After all, our lives are intertwined with the lives of others through literature as well as the relationships and involvements we have with other people in the course of daily life. These relationships and involvements are never fully under our control and are always full of surprises, both pleasant and disturbing or hurtful, that further shape how we see our present, past and future self.

Human action and social life have a narrative structure taking place in time. In the human realm, the shape of our lives individually and collectively takes the form of rough stories that are told and retold over time, sustained and modified through dialogue with others and other forms of mutual influence. According to a narrative picture, humans are thoroughly embedded in history and culture, and are self-interpreting beings where 'our own life-stories only make sense against the backdrop of possible story-lines opened by our historical culture' (Guignon 1989: 109). Our lives are a kind of unfolding, where our past lives as well as present activities gain their meaning from a rough, often implicit, sense of where our lives are going as a whole similar to how events in a novel gain their meaning from what they seem to be pointing to over the course of the novel. We are what Dunne (1996) calls 'storied' selves, a kind of becoming in time that has the rough, changing unity of a narrative whose last chapter has not yet been written. Many narrativist thinkers stress that our being existentially and morally engaged in this process means that we come to appreciate the meaning of the stories we inhabit primarily by actually *living* them. We move forward by hammering out our convictions in risky and uncertain circumstances, including the unpredictable emotional adventures of human relationships – not, in the main, through more distanced or detached rational analysis, or through the relatively more bloodless business of calculating what are more or less efficient or effective instrumental actions and adjusting our behaviour accordingly. On the narrative picture, we are much more intimately involved with the various influences and struggles of life than the instrumental picture and the subject-object ontology indicates.

The kind of understanding achieved in social inquiry, in a view more attuned to this narrative structure, is simply a more reflective and systematic version of the sorts of insights or understandings, be they illuminating or distorting, oc-curring in ordinary life (i.e., as in the activity conception). The understandings or accounts we develop rely only partially on efficient causation, and char-acterize the human activities involved only peripherally in terms of more or less successful instrumental behaviours. This view, as well, is committed to a metaphysics of the human realm in terms of which it simply makes no sense to base narratives solely on genetic and neurophysiological mechanisms. From this perspective, it is entirely implausible that coherent psychological and so-cial narratives of this type could arise from mere genetics and neurophysiology. The meaningfulness and coherence of these narratives are found only at the social level or the level of a dynamic, holistic lifeworld. Your understanding of your own life as a whole within your social context shapes the meaning par-ticular experiences have for you, not your genes. In turn, the meaning of these experiences change the understanding of your life as a whole and your social surroundings for ever.

Finally, to press the idea of our lives as yet unfinished narratives means a fundamental shift in our view of human action, no longer explicated solely or mainly in terms of context-free laws and efficient causation (i.e., via a mechanis-tic form of understanding of human agency as mainly instrumental). Instead, we will want to find new ways to explicate activity in terms of enacted narratives, conversation and other forms of interdependence and mutual influence among people.

Recall the example of the conversation with a friend I gave earlier. One of the upshots was that every participant in conversations comes away somehow changed by the event and the steady accumulation of such encounters over time makes up much of the reality of human life. But it is not just conversations with friends, families, colleagues and so forth that have this life-changing influence. As well, we are in conversation, so to speak, with our culture and traditions as we are constantly engaged in deepening our understandings of these meanings and reinterpreting them. This includes our 'conversations' with the books we read, music we hear, TV and movies we watch and other elements of culture.[13] All of these sources of meanings and interpretations alter how we see ourselves, which in turn shapes our vision and understandings of our past and future.

Another of the upshots was that conversation as a model for how different modes of social inquiry can influence and interact with each other gives us increasing purchase on the biases of our own approach to understanding human and social action as well as the biases of other approaches – a more realistic picture of what objectivity can be than the 'view from nowhere' connected with an outsider's perspective. But a further upshot is that genuine conversation involves a willingness to listen to and wrestle with differing points of view. It requires courage and humility to open yourself up to differing perspectives and how they may inform or change your own. And it involves a kind of commitment to yourself and your conversation partners that goes beyond simply respecting them or tolerating their values and perspectives.

The approach I have outlined certainly does not mean that efficient causation plays no role in the human realm, or that more mechanistic accounts in no way illumine the context of human agency. Our practices of abstraction, idealization, experimentation and so on give us insight into the causal workings of many processes. However, our best scientific theories and models are themselves creative, inventive interpretations of the world. Partly for that reason, mechanistic explanations both of nature and human action find their meaning ultimately in a larger story that is historical, practical and meaningful in character – after all, we are the ones who find these accounts significant and as fulfilling various purposes we have. There is much that various branches of natural science can teach us about the conditions of dyslexia, cancer or the physics of athletic and artistic performances. Correlational studies surely have a place in the study of human agency and interactions, helping us detect enduring patterns or regularities that might otherwise go unrecognized. But, the role these processes and patterns play in our lives, the way they seem to us, as well as the nature and direction of our efforts to cope with or alter them, are determined by the place they come to occupy within unfolding individual and social narratives. It seems, then, that we should resist the temptation to strongly oppose mechanistic forms of explanation with interpretive forms of understanding.

4. Taking stock

Over the course of the last few chapters, we have seen that hidden *moral* motivations as well as immaculate scientific ones have moved many capable minds in the social sciences to forge accounts of human action that ultimately fail to do full justice to the reality of their subject matter. We have also seen that the answer to the ontological question – can the social sciences be value-neutral? – is 'no', because there simply are no such viewpoints. There is no perspective completely free of values from which to conduct social inquiry. As well, the attempt to be neutral towards all values is likewise a significantly value-laden viewpoint. This situation might go some length to explaining why Weber struggled so mightily to fashion an approach to social inquiry that combined objectivity and value-neutrality with a moral immediacy and relevance for human living. He was chasing a kind of unobtainable dream influenced by the natural sciences, never realizing how inherently value-laden his own approach was. Squaring the circle in Weber's way cannot work because there is no circle to square!

Further, we have seen that the answer to the normative question – should the social sciences strive to be value-neutral? – in a genuine sense also is 'no', because we are really just pretending to strive for some unobtainable value-free outsider's perspective all the while running serious risk of our social inquiry being unduly influenced by disguised ideologies. Finally, there is a practical question that arises – is there a genuine need for social inquiry to be value-free? Here, the answer depends on the nature of the values and ideals in question. If social inquiry is enmeshed in sexism, racism or hyper-individualism; yes, these are things ripe for rooting out of our social science. On the other hand, if respect, tolerance, fairness and other liberal values are present; no, we do not necessarily want to root these out, but we do want to be aware of their presence and their effects on our inquiry. Authentic objectivity has little to do with value-neutrality, with the supposed refusal to take any position, or editorially splitting the difference between two sides of a question irrespective of their perceived merits. These are the wooden attempts to achieve an outsider's perspective, a viewpoint completely above the fray that does not exist. Instead, authentic objectivity has everything to do with our getting clearer on our own values, purposes and projects, those of our interlocutors and what, if anything, we should do about these.

If all we have available to us are various possible insiders' perspectives, then we really do need to find viable alternatives to the objectifying theoretical stance – the package deal of the instrumental picture of action along with a subject-object ontology and epistemology – for social inquiry. My sketch of an alternative is meant to point in such a direction, but philosophers and social scientists have only just begun to pursue such alternatives.

One thing to keep in mind is that all of our scientific descriptions are partial, limited and inexact due to the limitations on our intellectual abilities in the face of the complexity of the world we are seeking to describe. This is one of the reasons that both aspects of abstraction described in the previous chapter have proven to be so useful for particular purposes. They offer us limited, focused, yet serviceable ways of coping with bits and pieces of the multifarious world of our experience. Obviously if our theories and models are partial, values will enter into determining which things to ignore or describe inaccurately in order to achieve what limited understanding can be had. Hence, both natural and human sciences inevitably incorporate value judgements about what phenomena on which to focus and how best to interpret them.

More deeply, I have argued over the last three chapters that substantial ethical commitments play a crucial role in the value judgements of social scientists regarding how to investigate and interpret human behaviour. There is a deep connection between distinctly modern (and often worthwhile) values and the adoption of objectifying approaches that assume strictly efficient causation and instrumental analyses of action. And I have discussed the limitations these approaches face regarding their choices of how to understand the psychic and social worlds. The interpretations and meanings we carry with us – hopes, fears, opinions, ideas, language, culture, etc. – constitute crucial parts of who we are, forming the framework for the narrative character of our lives, yet are often left out of mainstream social-science mappings of human activities. Such interpretations and meanings constrain and move us; that is, they are reasons or grounds for why we are who we are and do what we do. Our narrative accounts must draw on influences capable of appropriately distinguishing gestures of flattery from gestures of respect, false humility from genuine humility, pyrrhic victory from noble defeat and so forth. If we are not able to make such distinctions or to discern the meaning of an act for an individual, a community or a society within our explanatory scheme, then we are either overlooking the appropriate sources of influence or operating with an impoverished view of causation (Berkowitz 2000). Mainstream approaches to human behaviour are limited in just these sorts of ways, so to understand human activity requires that we move beyond such models.

For further study

1. How are the views of Weber and Nagel on value-neutrality similar? How are they different?
2. Is it possible to have a value-neutral social science? Why or why not?
3. Contrast and compare the natural-scientific view of objectivity with the dialogical view sketched in this chapter.
4. Contrast and compare the four modes of understanding. Come up with an example of each not mentioned in this chapter.
5. What is the lifeworld? How does it provide a basis for social inquiry?

Recommended reading

C. Guignon, 'Truth as Disclosure: Art, Language, History', *The Southern Journal of Philosophy* 28 (1989): 105–21.

E. Nagel, 'The Value-Oriented Bias of Social Inquiry', in *The Structure of Science: Problems in the Logic of Scientific Explanation* (New York: Harcourt, Brace & World, 1961), pp. 485–502.

C. Taylor, 'Interpretation and the Sciences of Man', in *Philosophical Papers'* vol. 2: *Philosophy and the Human Sciences* (Cambridge: Cambridge University Press, 1985b), pp. 15–57.

Methodological Holism and Methodological Individualism

In Chapter 2, we saw that some social scientists, such as Weber, thought the appropriate way to analyse and explain social phenomena was to start with individuals and their properties and work up to societies and institutions. This is a position known as *methodological individualism*: that explanations for social phenomena ultimately must be given in terms of the intentions and actions of individual social actors. On the other hand, others like Durkheim thought the appropriate starting point for social inquiry was to start with society and social forces and work down to individuals and their behaviour. This is a position known as *methodological holism*: that social-science explanations should be given in terms of the social facts and forces which, in turn, make individual actions intelligible. The question of whether human action should be analysed and explained in terms of individuals or in terms of groups and societies has received extensive discussion in social-science and philosophical literature.

Given the prevalence of liberal individualism (Chapter 5) – at least in Western societies – one might think that this issue has actually been resolved in terms of methodological individualism. After all, a component of the liberal individualist view is ontological individualism – that the basic unit of human reality is individual persons, pictured as autonomous, distinct units having determinate characteristics somehow prior to and independent of their social existence. 'We're all individuals now', so to speak. On the other hand, liberal individualism is a cultural ideal that looks to play the role of one of Durkheim's irreducible social forces. The reason why 'we're all individuals now' is because the social matrix shapes and moulds each of us from birth to think of our selves and to function as individuals in societies geared for individuals.

So it seems there is room for debate about methodological individualism to continue. But perhaps the terms of this debate set up a false dichotomy, presuming that we have to ultimately make an all-or-nothing choice of one viewpoint or the other. Instead, it looks more likely that an appropriate framework for analysing human action must draw upon both individualist and holist elements to form an adequate picture.

1. Traditional holism/individualism debates

One way to frame the debate is the following: do social forces largely shape and guide who people are and how they behave or do the actions and beliefs of people largely determine the characteristics of institutions and societies? As mentioned in Chapter 2, Durkheim (1950) distinguished what he called social facts as irreducible to individual psychology. Examples of such facts would be the customs of my society channelling or coercing my obligations and feelings of obligation towards my parents and siblings, or the beliefs and traditions of a religion to which a believer conforms. Another example might be the practices and standards of a profession (engineering, say) into which one is apprenticed through university education. Durkheim views these kinds of social facts or forces as channels of thought, feeling and behaviour that are not only external to the person, but also have coercive force to impose upon and shape her behaviours and ways of seeing things. These social forces are neither ultimately biological nor psychological in nature because they represent ways of thinking and affordances for action that only exist at the level of societies.

It is important to understand that methodological holism does not presuppose that there is no individuality; that is that there is no individual response to such social forces. Rather, the point is that these social forces shape the attitudes towards and possibilities for actions. People are still free to move along various contours of possibility for action – so they are not determined by social forces to act only in particular ways – but the contours themselves are generated or governed by social forces. So normally the picture is not one of social determinism of individual actions (though extreme versions of holism do take social forces to be deterministic).

Another important thing to understand is that although these debates are really about the appropriate frameworks for understanding or explaining human action, very few social scientists would explicitly label themselves as methodological holists. In this sense, there are a number of sociologists who practice forms of explanation in social science that are inconsistent with methodological individualism (e.g., many forms of sociobiological or evolutionary explanations of culture).[1]

In contrast, methodological individualism maintains an adequate understanding of human action places emphasis on individual psychology and actions (Weber 1968: ch. 1), and sees Durkheim's social forces as somehow arising out of individual interactions in various social situations. The social forces, then, are not genuinely external to human behaviour, but somehow result from the aggregation of individual attitudes and actions, producing a kind of collective effect at the social level we call traditions, practices and so forth. John Watkins puts the distinction as follows:

> There may be unfinished or half-way explanations of large-scale social phenomena (say, inflation) in terms of other large-scale phenomena (say, full employment); but we shall not have arrived at rock-bottom explanations of such large-scale phenomena until we have deduced an account of them from statements about the dispositions, beliefs, resources and interrelations of individuals. (1957: 106)

The half-way explanations only invoke social phenomena to explain other social phenomena (e.g., explaining inflation in terms of full employment, a social concept from macroeconomics). Rock-bottom explanations invoke individual factors to explain social phenomena (e.g., explaining inflation in terms of the buying habits of individuals).

The key reason why this framework for analysing social phenomena is called methodological individualism is that, although the actions of individuals are taken to underlie such phenomena, the actions of people are due to their individual motives and intentions. So to understand social phenomena requires understanding these individual motives and intentions, but only individuals are capable of possessing motives or intentions (e.g., corporations do not possess motives or intentions except as aggregated from the individuals composing them). Hence, by privileging motives and intentions as ultimate springs of action, this framework entails privileging individuals as the methodological unit for understanding the social arena.

From the standpoint of methodological individualism, we might seek an explanation for political actions (e.g., voting or joining an anti-government demonstration) as the actions of individuals. The causes of these latter actions would be the attitudes or beliefs of the individual actors. Or we might seek to explain the development of a banking system and a centralized economy in terms of individual actions (conceiving economic structures, passing laws, setting up structure, etc.). The aim or goal of these actions, however, would be ultimately due to the self-interest of individuals. More generally, microeconomics (Chapter 12) has traditionally been taken to exemplify methodological individualism with its explanations rooted in the interests and rationality of individual economic actors.

As Steven Lukes (1968: 123–27) points out, however, the aim of grounding such explanation solely in individual actions and their motivations runs into problems. To identify actions as political makes inescapable reference to social institutions and rules defining voting contexts, government institutions and the like. These latter features are not properties of individuals in any sense (neither individual actions nor motivations). Similarly to classify actions as economic makes inescapable reference to social institutions like banks and money. No matter what your motivations are, they will be informed by, and the range of your actions will be constrained by, these institutions (e.g., try withdrawing more money from your bank than you have in your account without taking out a loan to cover the difference). In the absence of a substantial argument demonstrating that all social phenomena are reducible to individual motivations and actions, to restrict explanations to only those solely in terms of individual factors arbitrarily rules out any other kinds of explanations.

So it looks, one might argue, that to allow references to such social features as givens and then proceed in terms of individual factors would no longer be a methodologically individualist framework for explanation. These would not qualify as rock-bottom explanations if references to social phenomena were allowed, so it could be claimed. It is sometimes maintained, however, that methodological individualism does not restrict explanation to a vocabulary devoid of terms referring to social phenomena. As Miller puts the point:

> Very likely, no individualistic *definition* of 'marriage', for example, can be given. But if a marriage custom can be explained as due to participants' beliefs about marriage, the individualistic constraint on explanation is still satisfied. (1978)

One problem with this response is that if institutions like marriage and the banking system are irreducibly social, vocabulary referring to such institutions is not so innocent. Miller's response presupposes that such vocabulary only plays a descriptive role regarding the social institutions to which it refers. This is usually not the case, however, as such social institutions are inextricably bound up with social practices that ground our social vocabulary. In other words, the vocabulary of marriage or the banking system only makes sense in light of the social practices constituting marriage and banking. But these social practices also cannot exist apart from this or some related vocabulary (Taylor 1985b: 32–37). Social practices and their associated vocabulary are co-constituting (Chapter 11, sec. 2). So marriage customs and banking practices cannot be explained solely in terms of participants' beliefs about these institutions without invoking the very elements of social reality that are supposed to be ruled out on methodological individualist grounds.

One of Miller's arguments against methodological individualism is that it is an invalid constraint on social-science explanations because many of the explanations social scientists want to give of human behaviour are, in fact, inconsistent with methodological individualism's explanatory framework (1978: 396). He uses Marxist sociology as a counter-example because a number of such explanations cannot be given in strictly individualist terms (1978: 397–409). Another kind of explanation for individual and social behaviour inconsistent with methodological individualism's constraint would be mimetic explanations, where the behaviour of individuals is largely motivated by imitating the example or desire of others in their families, communities and societies (Girard 1966; Bourdieu 1977). My imitation of some example or desire may be triggered by another individual, but might also be triggered by a group (e.g., the chivalry of mediaeval knights) or a culture (e.g., Italian attitudes towards work and leisure).

A simpler example might be that of participation in social institutions like marriage or banking. Since the beliefs and actions of the participants are deeply imbedded in and informed by the social practices and vocabularies constituting the arena of participation, explanations of such participation cannot be given solely in individualist terms. However, these kinds of explanations are not allowed by methodological individualism, so either these explanations are simply invalid or the constraint on explanations represented by methodological individualism is invalid. But the behaviour of participants in marriage and banking are inexplicable apart from these social practices and vocabularies, making the constraint look suspicious. Furthermore, many social scientists find such constraint-violating explanations plausible, making methodological individualism look implausible as a framework for all social science explanations.

Watkins' distinction between 'unfinished or half-way explanations' of social phenomena in terms of other social phenomena and 'rock-bottom explanations' in terms of individual beliefs, motives and actions also appears to undercut the need for such a methodological-individualist constraint. He maintains that while 'half-way' explanations may not tell us everything we would like to know, they are not necessarily meaningless or false. So explanations ignoring the constraint are not invalid after all.

There is also the possibility they actually might tell us everything meaningful there is to know about a particular social phenomena whereas continuing down to the level of the actual beliefs and thinking of individuals adds nothing. During the 1990s, for example, the United States experienced a steep decline in violent crime. Among the different hypotheses offered as explanations for this social phenomena were:

- Changes in community policing practices.
- Hiring of more police.
- More stringent gun laws.
- Increased severity of sentencing guidelines for offenders.
- A general rise in religiosity.
- Changes in the demographic profile of the population.

Many of these hypotheses can be evaluated statistically. For instance, since the decline in crime happened in different jurisdictions where a number of different policing strategies were tried (including doing nothing particularly different than in the past), it is possible to show that changes in policing practices and numbers of police on the streets likely had minimal effect.

Most of the hypotheses on offer here are 'half-way' explanations, whereas a 'rock-bottom' explanation would explain the decline in crime solely in terms of individual attitudes and intentions. But suppose we discovered that the decline was largely due to changing demographics (e.g., as the population ages, there are fewer young men). This is an informative discovery, but what would be added by proceeding to look for an explanation satisfying methodological individualism? Even if we understood precisely what criminals were thinking and feeling in this period of decline, that would not add anything to the explanation of the decline itself since the demographic shift implies there are fewer criminals in the overall population.[2]

One defence given for methodological individualism as an explanatory framework is that it allows social scientists to avoid fallacies associated with attributing group interests to individuals. For example, the traditional 'interest group' theory of democratic politics typically assumes that groups sharing a common interest also have an incentive to promote that interest, by actions such as lobbying politicians, contributing to campaigns, funding research and voting. But a number of individuals who might be identified with such interest groups do little or nothing in this regard (many of them might not even vote for a candidate championing their interests!). Or, as another example, in many respects national economies and financial markets operate with a kind of group rationality resembling rational pursuit of self-interests. But this situation in no sense implies that individual participants in economies and markets are motivated largely by self-interest and act rationally to maximize these self-interests. A wide variety of motives and intentions as well as divergence of reasoning among individual participants can aggregate to yield such a 'group' rationality. Methodological individualism counters such fallacious inferences by forcing social scientists to seek the participant's perspective as a guide to his or her actions.

On the other hand, this individualist constraint also can generate fallacies. Objectifying individual attitudes and behaviours, and aggregating these into social behaviour using large-scale data collection and analysis techniques can lead to illegitimate generalizations about the characteristics of these attitudes in groups. As Arthur Stinchcombe observed (1968: 68), the stability of a belief in a population very rarely depends upon its stability in individuals. There can be considerable volatility at the individual level, but so long as changes in belief run equally in both directions, the prevalence of a belief in the population will remain unchanged. As an example, suppose 10 per cent of the population lost their faith in God every year, while 10 per cent experienced a religious conversion. There will be no change in the overall level of religiosity though, as Stinchcombe points out, it is 'intuitively difficult for many people' to avoid falling into fallacious sociological thinking in such a situation (1968: 67). Inferring the stability or instability of belief based upon individuals is often misleading.

2. Methodological individualism, social atomism and reductionism

It is important to emphasize that methodological individualism and social atomism in the form of ontological individualism (Chapter 5, sec. 2.1) are distinct. Recall that ontological individualism is the concept that individuals are the only or main form of social reality, the basic units of human reality with determinate characteristics that are assumed to exist even if there were no social reality enveloping them. Or, as British Prime Minister Margaret Thatcher reportedly once declared, 'There's no such thing as society. There are individual men and women and there are families.' Ontological individualism is a metaphysical thesis about the reality of the social world. Methodological individualism, on the other hand, is a constraint on the appropriate methodological form social-science explanations should take: namely that explanations be in terms of the motives, intentions and actions of individuals.

Jon Elster draws the distinction between methodological individualism – 'To explain social institutions and social change is to show how they arise as the result of the actions and interaction of individuals' (Elster 1989: 13) – and ontological individualism – 'The elementary unit of social life is the individual human action' (Elster 1982: 463). The former is a methodological claim, while the latter is an ontological one. In contrast, Watkins appears to run the two concepts together when he reformulates methodological individualism as the claim that the 'ultimate constituents of the social world are individual people' (1957: 105).

Some trace the origin of methodological individualism back to Hobbes and the 'resolutive–compositive' method elaborated in the opening sections of the *Leviathan* (e.g., Lukes 1968: 119). But what Hobbes has in mind is social atomism and offers one of the earliest expressions of *ontological* individualism. People are pictured 'as if but even now sprung out of the earth, and suddainly (like Mushromes)' and are considered fully mature, but having had no involvements with each other contributing to that maturity. In other words, individuals are completely characterized psychologically in a way that is asocial. Then Hobbes proceeds to deduce what will happen when a group of such individuals enter into interaction with one another (1998: ch. 8). These are all ontological rather than methodological claims.

2.1. Psychological reductionism

Elster goes on to claim at various points that maintaining methodological individualism commits him to *psychological reductionism* with respect to sociology (1989). This is roughly the view that all social phenomena ultimately are reducible to individual psychological phenomena. Popper attempted to introduce a contrast between methodological individualism and psychological reductionism (1945: 89). Nevertheless, it is arguable that his formulation of methodological individualism is equivalent to some form of psychological reductionism.

Recall that Durkheim held social facts and forces were not reducible to psychology. Methodological holists have largely followed this line of thinking. One motivation for this lies in the intuition that groups of individuals are more than the sum of their individual members in some sense. Another reason for this holist line is the motivation to demonstrate that social factors and forces studied by sociology, history and other disciplines are autonomous from psychological features of individuals. If this is so, then these disciplines would also be autonomous from psychology (i.e., ultimately not reducible to psychology). So there is a fear of reductionism lurking in the background here, one that, no doubt, is driven in part by ontological individualism. After all, if the ontological units of social reality are individuals and their psychological states, then it seems that social features of reality must be reducible to these individual features even if we are not able to describe how the reductions go (presumably God could describe the reductions even if they are intractable for us). In other words, psychological reductionism is an ontological thesis, not a thesis about our limitations in fully working out such a reduction.[3]

In general, the reductionist challenge to sociology (or other social-level disciplines) runs as follows. Suppose there is some social phenomenon, like suicide, that is considered to be explainable only at the social level, as Durkheim thought. The psychological reductionist can argue that individual cases of suicide are always caused by the psychological facts of the individual involved. If this is so, then it may be possible to generalize over these individual factors, finding relations among them that serve to explain the social phenomenon of suicide (e.g., the number of suicides per 100,000 in the general population, or why some sub-populations experience higher incidences than the general population). In other words, it is the individual psychological factors that explain why the social facts of suicide obtain. Further, if there are psychological regularities and patterns relating these factors, then they would help explain sociological regularities and patterns, for example those linking social integration with suicide rates. Social facts about suicide would then be reducible to psychological facts about individuals and the regularities relating these facts. Hence, sociology ultimately would be reducible to psychology.

This general line of reductionist argument receives much of its support from a distorted history of reductionism in science, a kind of philosophical urban legend if you will. According to this legend, much of physiology has been reduced to biology, and much of biology has been reduced to chemistry. In turn, much, perhaps even the whole, of chemistry has been reduced to physics. Psychology is – or the correctly formulated psychology will be – reducible to biology and, by extension, sociology is – or the correctly formulated sociology will be – reducible to psychology. But like most urban legends, this philosophical reductionist legend is oversimplified at best and false at worst. For instance, the most crucial feature of chemistry – the structure of molecules – is not reducible to physics (Bishop 2005b). Neither are the behaviours of genes or of natural selection reducible in any reasonable sense to chemistry. The upshot is that the philosophical urban legend of reductionism does not lend support to the argument that sociology is reducible to psychology. And suppose this philosophical urban legend was largely correct for the natural sciences. It still would not follow that reduction holds for any of the social sciences, unless we can already demonstrate that the latter are sufficiently similar to the natural sciences.

It is at this point that the in-principle (God could do it)/in-practice (we are unable to do it) distinction bites. The psychological reductionist maintains that just because we cannot work out the reduction of social facts to psychological facts, this is no evidence against the ontological thesis – namely, that sociology in principle is reducible to psychology. But without the philosophical urban legend of reduction and without sufficient warrant that social sciences are reducible in the ways some have thought natural sciences are, the psychological reductionist is merely standing on an intuition. And an intuition is insufficient proof of the reductionist thesis in the absence of some credible evidence that social facts are reducible to psychological facts.

Methodological individualism, on the other hand, does not necessarily involve a commitment to particulars about the individual psychological features of individuals. So in principle, as a constraint on explanations it remains open to the possibility that human psychology may have an irreducibly social dimension. Or so its advocates have maintained. While this admission of an irreducibly social dimension may cause problems for the constraint as discussed above, one potential way of accentuating the difference between ontological individualism and methodological individualism is to note that the former entails a complete reduction of sociology, say, to psychology, whereas the latter does not.

There are various problems with ontological individualism and reductionism. A key problem is the presupposition that the beliefs and motives individuals hold in fact are internally generated by those individuals (recall Hobbes' picture of agents as fully formed as if hermetically sealed off from social influences). Otherwise the integrity and autonomy of individuals looks to be violated as their beliefs and motives are at least partly (perhaps largely) shaped by social forces leading to worries about domination and oppression (see Chapter 4, sec. 2). But the latter features are ruled out by ontological individualism. However, as we have previously seen, the ideal of individuals getting their beliefs and motives 'wholly on their own', so to speak, is an unrealistic idealization or exaggeration of people's experience. Our beliefs, motives and ways of seeing things are always significantly shaped by our families, friends, co-workers, communities, the books we read, the movies we watch and so forth. Desires, beliefs, motives and our ways of seeing the world simply are not held so individualistically as ontological individualism requires (though this situation need not imply people are being oppressed or dominated).

As an example of how individuals do not develop as asocially as ontological individualism pictures them, consider explanations of much typical teenage behaviour in terms of peer pressure. At least some amount of teen drinking, smoking, drug use, sexual activity and so forth is driven not by individually or asocially formed desires and beliefs. Rather, many of these behaviours are driven by the expectations and example of peer groups playing crucial roles in shaping the desires and beliefs of individual teens – wanting to be accepted as part of the 'in crowd' or desiring to look cool to friends. Many social scientists find such peer explanations for behaviours plausible and even offer evidence from various kinds of studies to substantiate the reality of these social pressures. Methodological individualism may not be committed to treating peer pressure as reducible to individual psychological factors, whereas ontological individualism is – the behaviours in question all must ultimately derive from the psychology of the individual self with no influence from peers on the ontological view.

Ontological individualism is a component of liberal individualism (Chapter 5, sec. 2). Hence, the worries about people's autonomy and individuality being threatened if their beliefs, desires and purposes are not wholly self-formed in an asocial way comes straight from the value commitments and ideals of liberal individualism. One way to see that ontological individualism is as much a moral ideal as it is an ontological one, is to note that in pre-modern societies, individuals were not the basic elements of social reality – the very concept of ontological individualism makes no sense in such societies. A substantial ethical ideal has to come into being for ontological individualism to be intelligible and plausible. One has to have a conceptual framework where people identify themselves as individuals first rather than as members of a group. Reductionism of social features to individual features drinks deeply from the well of liberal individualism

3. Methodological individualism and liberal individualism

Advocates of methodological individualism usually deny that this constraint on explanation is morally motivated. Methodological individualism appears to be a neutral constraint on the accuracy or appropriateness of explanations in social inquiry. In this sense, defenders of this explanatory framework maintain that it is not motivated by political or ideological commitments; rather the framework is motivated by motives and intentions as sources of individual actions. This defence is not so convincing as it might first appear. What is the sources of an individual's motives and intentions? If the sources are the kinds of social forces and bonds Durkheim indicated, then methodological individualism's emphasis on individuals looks misplaced if these social forces are ultimately irreducible. We then also need methodological holist explanations to complement or illumine our individualist explanations, so the constraint does not really do the job its advocates claim. The alternative of embracing reductionism regarding these social factors lands the methodological individualist in ontological individualism and, hence, the ethical ideal of liberal individualism.

On the other hand, if the source of individual motives and intentions is ideally supposed to originate within the individual, then the ideals of liberal individualism and autonomy are supporting the methodological framework for explanation. The worries animating the explanatory framework are the same as those found in liberal individualism – the integrity and autonomy of the individual is at stake. Then methodological individualism and liberal individualism would be mutually reinforcing (similar to the way we saw earlier that an instrumental picture of action and liberal individualism are mutually reinforcing).

This dilemma leaves no easy way out for the methodological individualist. She can admit that irreducible social features play important roles in the motivations of individuals, thus admitting her criterion for social explanations is no real criterion. Or she can admit that her criterion for explanation is largely a morally motivated criterion. If methodological individualism really is an important criterion for explanation, she should grasp the second horn of this dilemma.

Grasping the second horn comes at a price, however. Although liberal individualism contains a number of worthwhile values, this ideal, as we have seen, has a tendency to undermine its own best values (Chapter 5, sec. 2.5). More pointedly, the tendency toward an idealized, hyper-individualism – the punctual or asocial self that chooses its own values hermetically sealed off from any surrounding social reality – reinforces some of the most troubling tendencies that social scientists and social theorists have identified in modern Western societies.

3.1. Individualism and the personality market

Erich Fromm (1969), for instance, graphically portrayed the kind of personal disorientation that accompanies a hyper-individualized, instrumental way of life in modern society. He argued this way of life was a major source of emotional problems in daily living. One feature of this way of life he called the 'ambiguity of freedom'. In modern times, Fromm argued, we have developed a sense of 'freedom from' arbitrary authority and from dogmatic or irrational obstacles to freedom, learning to exercise greater control over nature and ourselves. This is very much the Enlightenment ideal of protecting individual integrity that we see in the ideals of liberal individualism and autonomy. 'Freedom from' emphasizes things like freedom from constraint, or obstacles prohibiting us from doing what we want. However, Fromm continued, we sorely lack a corresponding sense of 'freedom to' or 'freedom for' – a positive account that would give context and direction, or supply deeper purpose to our increased freedom and opportunity – a sense of what our freedom is 'good for'. After the constraints or obstacles are removed, what is worthwhile to do with our freedom? Simply what we want?

As a result, Fromm (1969) argued, we tend to become interchangeable cogs in the social machinery (somewhat akin to the worries of Weber about *zweckrational* and Durkheim about individualism). In his view, in a hyper-individualized, instrumental way of life, people tend to become directionless and empty, and to be led by the nose, as it were, by whatever 'sells' in the marketplace. In a market economy and consumer-oriented society, hyper-individualism's over-emphasis on 'freedom from' leads people to increasingly see their identities deriving from the possessions they own.

More troubling, for Fromm, this includes a widespread 'personality market', where even our personal qualities must be revised or manipulated to accommodate the impulses or preferences of others. In essence, we as individuals become interchangeable with other individuals like commodities depending only on the qualities we take on or discard (one sees examples of this behaviour in politicians and entertainers 'reinventing' themselves, but also in our attempts to remake ourselves so that others will like and accept us). Commenting on the success of the *Oprah Winfrey Show*, Lee Siegel captures this sense of interchangeability that had Fromm's attention:

> Oprah has said, 'If there's a thread running through each show we do, it is the message that "you are not alone" '. . . We are not alone because we can blur into another person or become another person at any moment. We can make over our appearance, achieve our 'wildest dreams', or be heartened by the evidence of charity or by the revelations that the rich and famous are creatures of feeling, too, which makes their lives possibly habitable phases in the spectrum of exchangeability. (2006: 21)

Given this interchangeability, we tend to treat others and ourselves as depersonalized objects, manipulating these qualities that we can 'take off and put on' like changing clothing fashions (recall the punctual self discussed in Chapter 4, sec. 2). Increasingly, a person experiences himself as both the commodity to be sold and the seller, leading to a 'shaky self-esteem' that depends largely on the acceptance and affirmation of others (Fromm 1975: 76–80). But as commodities, people find themselves becoming more superficial. Hungry for substance but unable to find it, in Fromm's view, we tend to sell out our freedom to fascism, fanaticism, the illusion of total fulfilment in romantic love, craving and seeking the approval of others at all costs, numerous forms of escapism or just going shopping. We tend to throw ourselves into these things, rather than seeing ourselves as meaningfully connected to others, our communities and traditions (the latter running contrary to a hyper-individualism in many ways). Seeing ourselves as increasingly interchangeable does provide possibilities for personal change and growth. But it also represents a capacity to conform, accommodating ourselves to the wishes and expectations of others around us. We end up stretching and moulding ourselves in any direction that seems rewarding or affirming, unconstrained by truth, consistency or character.

Along with the effects of the personality market, hyper-individualism also generates a number of psychological and social problems. As Schumaker notes, many recent studies show that cultures that largely focused on individuals and their material interests and satisfactions tend to promote self-centredness, lack of generosity towards others, lower the value of self-respect and have less happiness and satisfaction with 'life as a whole' (2001: 37–39).

A problematic hyper-individualism shows up at the heart of psychotherapy theories and practices or of various theories of social organizations as well as management techniques, for instance. Approaches coloured by utilitarian individualism (Chapter 5, sec. 2.2) clearly give prominence to a calculating, means–end rationality that expands our mastery in important ways (e.g., new techniques for curtailing obsessive thoughts, assertiveness training). But, as critical theorists have argued, this kind of *zweckrational* mastery undermines our ability to evaluate the worth of our ends, to set priorities and needed limits in personal and social life, and to achieve integrity as well as mastery in living.

Expressive individualism (Chapter 5, sec. 2.3) tends to view the world and others largely as aids for or impediments to our projects and self-actualization. This is clearly in tension with our common-sense notion of moral commitment as something, in part, that sets a limit to the exercise of our freedom and the kinds of projects we pursue. Therapies or management systems promoting self-actualization of this sort by itself seem insufficient for overcoming egoism, resolving conflict, or achieving lasting social ties among mature individuals, particularly if the model for maturity is the hyper-individualized punctual or asocial self.

Existential individualism (Chapter 5, sec. 2.4) admirably includes the need for a more substantial kind of authenticity and integrity in an increasingly impersonal, highly bureaucratized society. However, in line with Fromm's critique, existential thinkers seem much clearer about what they are against than what they are for. Existentialists oppose arbitrary authority and copping out on one's responsibilities, but largely come up short of articulating the superiority of one way of life over another. Radical choice of our ultimate values boils down to simply registering brute preferences, or just arbitrarily settling on one option over others (Guignon 1986). Why, on the existentialist view, should we choose a life of authenticity or integrity at all, or why should we nurture our own or others' existential freedom? In the absence of a positive account of why these are worthwhile aims, there are no good reasons. Such wide-open options tend to undermine meaningful choice, not enhance it. This is a recipe for eroding genuine autonomy in the face of the tyranny of desire over the long run.

Fortunately, more often than not, what happens on the therapist's couch or in the boardroom is that common sense tempers these internal contradictions at the heart of the theoretical frameworks lying behind our approaches and techniques. So things are not nearly as bad as they could be, but this does not mean that hyper-individualism and instrumentalism are somehow mitigated and remain harmless. Rather, the effects of these tendencies make their way through our theorizing and explanations into the concrete business of living and back to our theorizing and explanations (the double hermeneutic!) We will see examples of this in the next chapter.

4. Taking stock

There is a more theoretical problem for the debates about social explanations discussed in this chapter that is also connected with cultural ideals. Formulating these debates in terms of methodological individualism versus methodological holism tends to foster a picture of an either/or choice when there really is no such choice. Instead, we face something more like a both/and choice. To see this, consider that the principle of rooting explanations in individual motives and actions presupposes the modern Western ideals of liberal individualism and autonomy. Pre-modern societies are not analysable in terms of solely individualist explanations – group identities, spiritual and moral traditions, social customs and so forth are far more important to understanding individual and social behaviour than supposed individual motives. In other words, a major influence on the motives of modern individuals is liberal individualism which cannot be reduced to the motives and actions of individuals because the cultural ideal is required for individual motives to be intelligible. A methodological individualist cannot have her cake and eat it, too.

So the methodological individualism/methodological holism debate is not really as value-neutral as it appears to be on the surface. In an interesting sense, the debate is not really well-formulated in pitting a choice between explanations ultimately in terms of individual motives and actions versus explanations involving irreducible cultural and social factors. The very idea of rooting explanations in individual motives and actions does not make sense apart from substantial cultural ideals of individualism and autonomy at work.

We really need forms of social explanation that incorporate both individual and social features to get purchase on individual and social reality (e.g., the narrative picture sketched in Chapter 6, sec. 3). But this situation leads to what, at first, may appear to be an odd predicament. To illuminate the motives and actions of individuals, we need to invoke various cultural and historical features; individual motives and actions receive their meaning, in the main, from these larger meanings. On the other hand, the motives and actions of individuals shed light on these larger cultural meanings, their nuances, the degree of their plasticity, and, as interpretations of these latter meanings, individual motives and actions further clarify as well as rework these meanings. These larger meanings and traditions change for us in the business of living, meaning they are evolving with us. This almost looks like a chicken-or-egg problem.

In reality, this interplay between the individual and the social is more like a chicken-*and*-egg situation. The individual and the social are partially constituting of each other and shed light on each other. Consider the following example: individual words receive their meanings largely from the sentences in which they occur. But these very sentences also receive their meaning from the individual and groups of words composing them. Similarly with individuals and societies. What we really have here is a kind of hermeneutic spiral:[4] holist features of our explanations shed light on individualist features while individualist features further illumine holist features.

As we have seen, cultural ideals like liberal individualism and autonomy play important roles in explanations of individual and social realities. They feature in our modes of analysis, albeit as disguised ideologies, as well as in methodological individualist and holist approaches to explanation. But as disguised ideologies, these ideals can perpetuate and amplify themselves in our social inquiry, perhaps explaining why the results of social science do not always have the effects intended. We will look at some examples of this next.

For further study

1. Contrast and compare methodological individualism and holism.
2. Do you think social-science explanations must be methodologically individualist, holist or a combination of the two? Why?
3. What is the difference between ontological individualism and methodological individualism? How is liberal individualism related to the latter?
4. Explain hyper-individualism and the personality market. How do you see these showing up in ordinary life?

Recommended reading

E. Fromm, *Escape from Freedom* (New York: Avon, 1969).

S. Lukes, 'Methodological Individualism Reconsidered', *British Journal of Sociology* 19 (1968): 119–29.

R. Miller, 'Methodological Individualism and Social Explanation', *Philosophy of Science* 45 (1978): 387–414.

Garbage in – Garbage out: Passing Values off as Scientific Research

In Chapter 6, we saw that research correlating voting attitudes and behaviour, or correlating self-esteem with student test performances were not value-neutral. The kinds of questionnaires used in such studies have the ideals of autonomy and liberal individualism built into them, presupposing a significant moral point of view. We also saw in Chapter 7 that the methodological-individualist constraint on explanations ultimately places emphasis on the values, ideals and attitudes of individuals as social actors as well as reinforcing our cultural ideals of autonomy and liberal individualism.

While many of the values at work in modern conceptions of the good life are not necessarily bad in themselves (e.g., tolerance, respect, fairness), natural-scientific and descriptivist modes of social science operate under the pretence that social inquiry is value-neutral and objective (outsider's perspective). This pretence is not as innocent as one might hope because these cultural ideals have their own internal inconsistencies and tend to contribute to many of the problems of modern life. If social inquiry remains oblivious to the presence of disguised ideologies, then our research results and recommendations are likely to simply pass on or exacerbate these problems. I have chosen three examples of social inquiry – hardiness and health, population problems and the good marriage – which illustrate how the social-science 'cure' is more likely to perpetuate our problems than help.

1. Correlations and values: hardiness research

Hardiness is touted as a personality construct or personal stance that 'facilitates coping effectively with stressful circumstances, be they acute or chronic, by accepting them as a natural part of living and working actively to transform them so that they become less stressful' (Maddi 1997: 294). As a personality feature, hardiness is identified as having three components (Kobasa 1979; Maddi 1997):[1]

(1) *Control*: hardy persons have a belief that they can influence or manage the events they experience.
(2) *Commitment*: hardy persons feel deeply involved with the activities of their lives.
(3) *Challenge*: hardy persons see change as an exciting opportunity to further personal development.

Persons exhibiting a strong sense of control are characterized as believing that with effort they can usually influence or manage outcomes of what occurs in their lives. Such persons see themselves as having the 'capability of autonomously choosing among various courses of action', the ability to 'incorporate various sorts of stressful events into an ongoing life plan', and 'a greater repertory of suitable responses to stress developed through a characteristic motivation to achieve across all situations' (Kobasa 1979: 3).

Persons exhibiting a strong sense of commitment are characterized as believing that 'by involving themselves actively in whatever is going on, they have the best chance of finding what is interesting or worthwhile for them' (Maddi 1997: 294). They are strongly interested in their activities and, although they do have involvements with others, apparently, 'staying healthy under stress is critically dependent upon a strong sense of commitment to self' (Kobasa 1979: 4).

Persons exhibiting a strong sense of challenge are characterized as believing that 'what is ultimately most fulfilling is to continue to grow in wisdom through what they learn from experience' (Maddi 1997: 294). They 'value a life filled with interesting experiences' and a 'basic motivation for endurance'. For such people, 'at the core of the search for novelty and challenge are fundamental life goals that have become, in adulthood, increasingly integrated in a widening diversity of situations' (Kobasa 1979: 4).

Much of the study on hardiness has explored the correlation between individuals with high hardiness and health (e.g., Kobasa 1979; Maddi 1999). There appears to be a strong correlation between stress and illness. Many individuals undergoing high or sustained stress due to personal, work and other kinds of events in their lives show higher incidences of serious illnesses. But there are other individuals who, while undergoing similar stressful life events, do not show any signs of increased susceptibility to serious illnesses. Hardiness has been hypothesized as an important personality component or stance mitigating the supposed unhealthy effects of stress.

First, a word about correlational studies. Uncovering a correlation between stressful life events and higher incidences of illness, though intriguing, does not indicate that a causal relationship exists between stress and health. This is because correlations never indicate which way (if any) a possible causal connection points. For instance, the correlations uncovered between stress and health do not tell us if stress is a contributing causal factor to increased health problems, or if increased health problems are a contributing causal factor to stress, or if there is a third factor that is causing both stress and health problems. Note that correlational studies on stress and health are not controlled for effects of disguised ideologies. So it could very well be the case that a number of features of modern society play causal roles in both stress and health problems leading to the measurement of persistent correlations between stress and health. If this is the case, then the correlation is spurious in that it indicates no connection between stress and health.

This inability to indicate causation is a generic feature of correlational studies. So, as Suzanne Kobasa notes, 'one usually finds some caution urged about too quickly concluding a causal relationship between stress and illness on the basis of correlational and methodologically weak studies'. She goes on to say, however, that 'this warning is mitigated, however, by a sense of optimism that there is something to this stress and illness connection and a wish for studies that are more sophisticated in design and methods of analysis' (1979: 2). How, exactly, optimism and wishes are supposed to overcome this particular weakness of correlation studies is never made clear.

The basic methodology for discerning correlations between hardiness and health in the presence of stressful life events is to use questionnaires. In this way, information can be gathered from the group under study regarding the kinds of illnesses they have been and are suffering, the kinds of stressful events they have been experiencing, and the three components of the hardy personality. The initial studies as well as many longitudinal studies were carried out on middle and upper level managers at a Midwestern utility company. The compiled information was statistically analysed to produce two sub-populations – high stress/low illness and high stress/high illness. The hypothesis to be tested was that hardy individuals would predominantly be found in the former sub-population. Various correlations supporting the hypothesis were found, though some of them were, by statistical measures, quite weak.

One objection to these correlational studies has been that the kinds of questionnaires pressed into use for measuring hardiness and health were actually designed for different personality features (Funk and Houston 1987). Without a questionnaire and a scale for scoring it that were verified specifically for the components of the hardiness personality construct, the correlations uncovered could not rigorously be interpreted as telling us anything about hardiness.

This objection was supposedly met by the introduction of a questionnaire and corresponding scoring scale – the Personal Views Survey II (Maddi 1997; 1999) – designed specifically to measure the three components of hardiness. Some of the kinds of items composing this questionnaire are:

Control: 'What happens to me tomorrow depends on what I do today.'
'Most of what happens in life is just meant to happen.'
Commitment: 'I really look forward to my work.'
'Ordinary work is just too boring to be worth doing.'
Challenge: 'It's exciting to learn something new about myself.'
'The tried and true ways are always the best.'

Scoring responses to such items on a numerical scale ranging from 'strongly agree' to 'strongly disagree' supposedly gives a reasonable measurement of the presence of these three components in a person's personality.

Aside from the problem that correlational studies like these do not indicate causality, there are questions about how to interpret the correlations of those managers who experienced high stress while remaining healthier than the high stress/high illness cohort. Kobasa and others interpret these results as univocally indicating that hardy personalities mitigate the unhealthy effects of stress. But perhaps the high stress/low illness managers function so well because of incentives and/or high capacities for stress. Or perhaps these managers are compensating for being exploited by their companies in ways that their high-illness cohort are not. We really cannot say based on these correlation studies, but some indications that the hardiness interpretation is not the only, nor perhaps the best, interpretation are found in that it is not always the case that all three components of the hardy personality are present in such studies (Funk and Houston 1987; Hull, van Treuren and Virnelli 1987).

The deeper problem with hardiness research, I want to suggest, is the way in which it smuggles existential individualism in as a disguised ideology. Kobasa is explicit in noting that the hardy personality construct derives from existential approaches to psychology (Kobasa 1979: 3), with their 'emphasis on how people construct the meaning in their lives through the decisions they make and the importance, therefore, of their accepting responsibility for what they become' (Maddi 1997: 294–95). What hardiness researchers do not realize is the extent to which the existentialist individualist form of liberal individualism pervades their research. There is a heavy emphasis, here, on self-creation. Control, commitment and challenge are ways we exercise ultimate responsibility as authors of ourselves and our world.

The interest of hardiness researchers is often expressed as a narrowly instrumental one. They often emphasize developing personality features that 'can aid in a productive and healthy life' (Kobasa 1979: 10) or view hardiness as something that 'enhances performance, conduct, morale, stamina, and health' (Maddi 1999: 83, see also 85). Nothing is said about whether performance, effectiveness, stamina and the rest are good or worthwhile goals, nor about how these goals fit into worthwhile conceptions of the good life. Nothing is said about the place or value of suffering in life; rather, minimizing suffering seems to be one of the goals of this line of research. No doubt these rather stark omissions are partly due to the political-liberalist impulse to not privilege any particular vision of the good life over any others, though these researchers implicitly are advocating a particular notion of the good: an effective life (whatever that is) as a meaningful, worthwhile life.

Another reason for the stunning lack of any ethical sensitivity exhibited in this research doubtless is the overemphasis on the individual so characteristic of liberal individualism. Take the control component of hardiness, for example. This appears to be a personality feature that would only be privileged in Western cultures, while seen as unsuitable, improper or even wrong-headed in other cultures. Characteristic features such as seeing oneself as 'autonomously choosing' courses of action or as motivated 'to achieve across all situations' come straight out of the liberal-individualist picture (which is not to suggest autonomy or desires to achieve are necessarily bad things – such judgements depend on the circumstances, not on the personality bent of people). The focus on autonomy and achievement leaves out any discussion about how our social involvements and obligations temper or shape our understanding of what it means to chose autonomously and what achievements really are worthwhile. This focus reinforces the instrumental emphasis and leaves us with little recourse but to conclude that effectiveness, productivity and health are key components of individual well-being. Health we might believe, but effectiveness and productivity?

Or consider the commitment component of hardiness. According to the characterization, hardy people believe their involvement in what is happening to and around them gives them 'the best chance of finding what is interesting or worthwhile for them'. The emphasis, here, is on the self and what is worthwhile for it. Given the repeated emphasis on productivity and effectiveness in hardiness research, it is hard to escape the conclusion that what is worthwhile for these individuals is productivity, effectiveness and health rather than worthwhile lives, their social involvements and obligations to others. Indeed, as Salvatore Maddi notes, 'the sense of meaning in hardiness is more a function of individual predisposition' in contrast to social connection (Maddi 1999: 92). Hardy individuals are strongly interested in their activities. And, as noted above, staying healthy under stress is crucially dependent on a 'strong sense of commitment to self'. But does this commitment to self to stay healthy come at the expense of our wider obligation to family, friends, communities? We could easily conclude this because hardy persons 'have both a reason to and an ability to turn to others for assistance in times demanding readjustment' (Kobasa 1979: 4). In the absence of any further commentary, why are these reasons and abilities not to be understood as largely instrumental – viewing others as mere means for coping with stressful situations? Maddi explicitly contrasts this with turning to family members for 'pampering' (1999: 83–84). But this makes it sound like turning to our co-workers as means for coping is more important or worthwhile than our family ties.

The characterization of the challenge component of hardiness pictures individuals as believing that 'what is ultimately most fulfilling is to continue to grow in wisdom through what they learn from experience'. The overemphasis on individual welfare makes this notion of 'ultimate fulfilment' sound indistinguishable from self-actualization or self-fulfilment in contrast to the deep satisfaction we experience in our relationships and social involvements with others that are not focused on our selves. Further, hardy people 'value a life filled with interesting experiences', like the stressful events presenting them with new opportunities for growth rather than meaningful involvements with others.[2] (Students often remark that instead of representing a mature person, this description reminds them of teenagers!) Hardy persons exhibit a 'basic motivation for endurance' rather than a basic motivation to be involved with family, friends, religious and other communities' and so on.

Not surprisingly, these disguised ideals and overemphases show up in the kinds of questions used in the Personal Views Survey II. For example, a person with a strong sense of control over the events in his or her life will strongly agree with the statement 'What happens to me tomorrow depends on what I do today', sounding very much like the kind of self-creation found in existential individualism. But what happens to me tomorrow depends at least as much on my social involvements and obligations as well as on what others decide. A person with a strong sense of challenge will strongly agree with the statement 'It's exciting to learn something new about myself'. Construed individualistically in line with the conception of hardiness, this sounds like a person who is more interested in what she can learn about herself than the involvements with people and traditions in her life.

Here is another way to see how liberal individualism pervades both the statements on such a questionnaire and its scale for scoring responses. Imagine mediaeval knights taking such a survey. They certainly would exhibit commitment, but their commitment would be to each other in their group and the king or princess they serve, not to themselves. Their ideals of chivalry and honour were deeply tied to mutual group obligations and their allegiance to their royal leaders. Similarly, the concepts of control and challenge would also be conceived quite differently. Hence, they would not be considered very hardy because their scores would not tally with our modern Western ideals shaping the items and scoring scale. Or suppose a massive Buddhist shift occurred in a modern Western society. Again, the items and scoring scale would no longer be valid as they are tied to the liberal individualism pervasive in modern Western cultures.

Although a number of things about the values and ideals of modern Western cultures are worthwhile, overemphases on individualism and instrumental reasoning also have a number of deleterious effects (e.g., Fromm's personality market fostering alienation and isolation) that a number of social scientists and commentators have argued contribute to our stressful, overextended lives and a number of mental and perhaps physical health problems. There is a complete lack of awareness of the disguised ideologies underlying hardiness research. It seeks to provide prescriptions for 'buffering' people from illnesses and increasing their effectiveness and productivity by promoting particular personality characteristics. As such, there is a very real possibility that promoting these characteristics surreptitiously contributes to and exacerbates a number of modern maladies. A greater awareness of how disguised ideologies are at work in this research and its supposed value-neutral prescriptions would enable us to better understand just what is going on with this research and how we might better deal with the challenges modernity presents to our health and well-being.

2. Ideals, science and public policy: the problem of the commons

In 1968 Garrett Hardin wrote an essay, titled 'The Tragedy of the Commons', setting off a number of public-policy debates.[3] The term *commons* designates those goods that by right belong to all and are necessary for survival and thriving (e.g., food, shelter). One of Hardin's theses, though not original to him, was that the continued unchecked growth of the population put the commons at risk, at least with regard to the availability of adequate food supplies for every person on earth. Unless food production can keep pace, the growth in the population will eventually reach a point where a (perhaps significant) portion of the population is not able to obtain the maintenance calories necessary to continue existing, much less thriving. So, Hardin reasoned, the commons is threatened by continued population growth – the carrying capacity of the earth, if you will, eventually will be strained beyond the breaking point.

Hardin casts the problem along utilitarian lines: what is it we wish to maximize? We cannot maximize population because this would lead to a potentially large number of the people suffering severe malnutrition and death. If we want to maximize the good per person, then we have to establish what is good. Suppose we decide that individual freedom is the chief good we should maximize. Consistent with this, suppose we further assume, along with Adam Smith, that an individual who 'intends only his own gain' is led, as if 'by an invisible hand to promote . . . the public interest' (1937: 423). This suggests an attitude on the part of government and society of allowing individuals to make their own decisions, particularly regarding reproduction. This attitude is justified, as Hardin points out, by a 'tendency to assume that decisions reached individually will, in fact, be the best decisions for an entire society', a tendency that lies at the heart of a tradition of rationality and self-interest that traces back to Hobbes through Smith (see Chapter 10). If this is all correct, then 'we can assume that men will control their individual fecundity so as to produce the optimum population' (Hardin 1968: 1244). However, if individually self-interested decisions do not lead to the common good, then we would be forced to reconsider individual freedoms to see which are defensible. For, as Hardin argues, we cannot maximize all freedoms for all individuals.

His argument proceeds by way of an analogy. Consider a large pasture open to all herders – the commons – fixed in size (e.g., the earth). Consistent with the above assumptions, each individual herder will keep as many cattle as possible on the commons. For a significant amount of time, this arrangement might work quite well since tribal wars, disease, poaching and whatnot will keep the numbers of herders and cattle below the carrying capacity of the pasture. After some number of centuries, suppose the society of herders stabilizes (i.e., no more war or poaching, diseases are treated, etc.). Then, consistent with our assumptions, since each herder is a rational being, they will all seek to maximize their gain by assessing the benefit of adding one more animal to their herds. A positive benefit from adding one more animal derives from the additional income a herder receives from the sale of an additional animal. If we assume such benefits are normalizable (a questionable assumption), then the positive benefit a herder can expect is close to $+1$. On the other hand, there are overgrazing costs associated with adding one more animal. These costs will be spread over all herders, so the negative impact any particular herder can expect is only some fraction of -1.

The rational herder will add the positive benefits and negative impacts and see that the reasonable course to pursue is to add one more animal to the herd. And then that another should be added, and another and so forth. But every herder sharing the pasture, being rational by our assumptions, will make the same decision. One can clearly see this situation will lead to severe overgrazing of the pasture and the eventual destruction of the commons. So if each herder rationally pursues their self-interest, disaster awaits for such a society that believes in the freedom of the commons. As Hardin concludes, 'Freedom in a commons brings ruin to all' (1968: 1244).

By analogy, allowing unfettered freedoms, one of which is the freedom of procreation, leads to disaster. As the population increases, for instance, so does pollution as the natural chemical and biological recycling processes become overloaded. This has implications for how we conceive property rights, particularly the right of each person to do as they please with their property. But this situation would also adversely affect the rights of property holders to enjoy their property as they please (e.g., to enjoy a homestead or lake front free of pollution). Similarly, allowing unfettered freedom to procreate would lead to severe degradation of the commons of the food supply – the carrying capacity of the earth – making it impossible for people to pursue other freedoms like the arts, leisure and philosophy. We cannot maximize all our freedoms without losing some in the process. Hardin's conclusion is that government, as a matter of public policy, must restrict the freedom of people to procreate.

The usual response to an analysis like Hardin's is that there will always be a technological solution to such problems. Recall that Comte envisioned society finally reaching a stage of development where science would be applied to solve all society's problems (Chapter 2, sec. 2). In Hardin's view there is a difference between policies based on technical solutions and those based on non-technical solutions. A technical solution for Hardin is 'one that requires a change only in the techniques of the natural sciences, demanding little or nothing in the way of change in human values or ideas of morality' (1968: 1243). A non-technical solution, by contrast, is one that mostly demands a change in human values or moral ideals.

Belief in scientific and technological progress can appear to reinforce a belief that all problems have technical solutions, particularly those of a technical origin, like the proliferation of nuclear weapons. But in this case, it is unclear there could be any technical solution. Suppose we develop a fool proof defence against intercontinental ballistic missiles. There are still countless ways to deliver a nuclear payload to a designated target, limited only by the creativity of nefarious minds. There seems to be no technical solution available here at least in the near term given the current status of our science and technology. This situation suggests that pursuing foreign and internal security policies based on technical solutions might prove inadequate.

But problems that are of non-technical origin, like population-driven problems, such as pollution and overpopulation, are even less likely to have technical solutions in Hardin's view. Even if they do have technical solutions, such solutions are likely to be so far in the future that the cure will not arrive in time. His recommendation, then, is that policies be set based on proscriptions – restricting the freedom of people to pursue particular goals (e.g., unrestricted procreation, unrestricted dumping of materials and chemicals) so as to enhance or preserve other freedoms that are deemed worthwhile.

Clearly Hardin calls into question the possibility of a society run solely on a technical or scientific basis (contrary to Comte's vision). If many policy decisions have to be made regarding problems where there are no technical solutions, then those policies must be decided on ethical or other non-scientific grounds. Morals, common sense, good judgement, perhaps even wisdom traditions that have long been ignored must be deployed to arrive at policy decisions. This situation runs counter to the trend of seeking to apply scientific-looking rationality schemes like game theory as paradigms for making policy decisions (Chapter 10). Hardin makes an insightful contribution here to understanding that modern predicaments are not always matters of appropriate technology or effective technique. Ironically, he did not realize that his application of a utilitarian maximization framework is exactly the kind of technical approach to analysing and solving problems he is arguing cannot work when it comes to population problems.

Hardin also – perhaps unwittingly – highlights the role that scientific developments, both theoretical and experimental, play in revealing, assessing and framing problems. Incredible improvements in medical care – prenatal, postnatal and others – along with various technological developments have increased life expectancy and lowered death rates across the board in developed countries as well as to a large degree in developing countries. Furthermore, scientific arguments play a role in assessing what kinds of impacts increases in population due to these improvements might have as well as some of the possible solutions.

It is precisely at this latter point where assumptions can play a tremendous role in shaping the terms of the arguments, the framing of problems and solutions, and so forth. Notice that Hardin's analyses and arguments regarding population problems and what he takes to be failed attempts to avert problems presuppose exactly the kind of idealized instrumental picture of action pervading the conceptual frameworks of mainstream social inquiry. That is to say, people are assumed to be agents who seek to maximize their individual welfare to the exclusion of other worthwhile goods and values. The emphasis is on means for achieving ends rather than the ends themselves. If anything, we only see that we must question our means when we see what a mess we are making of things. But then how are we going to reconsider our ends? Surely not within the same narrow framework of maximization, individual welfare and instrumental reasoning. As critical theorists have long pointed out, this framework gives us no purchase on evaluating the worth of our ends.

Hardin's discussion also presupposes the ideals of autonomy and liberal individualism – particularly utilitarian individualism (Chapter 5, sec. 2.2) – with individual freedom treated as an unquestioned good. He is right that freedom is multi-faceted – humans do not have or exercise freedom, but *freedoms*. And clearly it is the case that not all of our freedoms are consistent with each other. This much we already knew, but what is striking about Hardin's analysis is that particular freedoms are to be curtailed solely on the basis of their outcomes, not on the basis of what is worthwhile. At the same time he arrives at the conclusion that we cannot realize the ideal of autonomy for individuals – we cannot allow people to choose whatever they like regarding procreation – the instrumental/individualist framework of his analysis prevents him from thinking through and evaluating the worth of the ends we might seek and how we might address the competing conceptions of the good life that underlie these problems.

This is the way Hardin frames the problem of the tragedy of the commons. One might think that consciousness raising would avert the tragedy of the commons due to over population. But Hardin argues that any appeals to conscience share a fatal weakness: any family who, due to conscience decides to limit the number of children they have will be at risk of elimination if a significant portion of the population continues to procreate unabated. After all, the latter families will produce many more children than the conscientious ones leading to the diminution of such people and their eventual disappearance from the population. However, this argument is only plausible *if* the dominant rationality of agents engaging in procreation is that assumed in his analysis of the problems.[4] Critical-theorist, postmodernist and hermeneutic social scientists would, of course, argue that framing problems, analyses and solutions in this way is as likely to distort the nature of the problems, their analyses and proposed solutions – that is, the policies – in ways that are unlikely to get a fix on what is really going on and on what might really be helpful or worthwhile for bringing about change.

Also note that Hardin exhibits his own brand of schizophrenia. On the one hand, he argues as if rational agents are welfare maximizers, concluding that particular freedoms such maximizers seek must be restricted. On the other hand, he imagines the benefit of these restrictions as enabling a host of other freedoms and social goods that either make no sense on the view that agents are purely welfare maximizers or, best case, are seriously undermined by the self-interest-maximizer viewpoint (recall the instabilities of individual liberalism and the instrumental picture of action discussed in Chapters 4 and 5). This is the same mixture of unacknowledged cultural ideals that we have seen pervading mainstream social inquiry and that seems guaranteed to perpetuate many of the problems we seek to solve.

3. Individualism and the good marriage

To a large extent in the USA, marriage and family psychology, and to an ever increasing extent society itself, presuppose a liberal individualist conception of family of one of two types. The first is utilitarian individualism (Chapter 5, sec. 2.2). Recall that this form of individualism assumes humans have basic appetites and fears and pictures human life as an effort to attain one's desires while reducing aversive experiences through strategic action. This comes to expression, for instance, in relationships being viewed mostly in contractual terms, where relationships are formed on the basis of self-interest. This results in the tendency to view marriage as simply another means for meeting individual needs and desires. The second form is expressive individualism (Chapter 5, sec. 2.3). We saw earlier that this form of individualism advocates following the 'voice of nature', so to speak, revealed in our unspoiled feelings and the spontaneous purposes that naturally emanate from within us. This comes to expression, for example, in viewing relationships – and marriage in particular – as functioning as the primary arenas for emotional satisfaction, belonging and purpose. Both versions of individualism tend to transmute marriage into an instrument or means for the fulfilment of goals, needs and desires of the individual, as well as a source of refuge from the outside world. This contrasts with viewing marriage and family as primarily arenas for commitment, sacrifice, selfless giving and the pursuit of excellence.

The individualist conception of marriage shapes much family and marriage research. Numerous studies are carried out investigating correlations between overall personal happiness and marital satisfaction. Many marriage researchers take a key upshot of their research to be that marital satisfaction is one of the strongest indicators and sources of overall personal happiness and satisfaction, more so than friendships, jobs or money (Lee, Seccombe and Sheehan 1991). Note, however, that personal happiness is a distinctly individualist value. With the modern emphasis on inwardness and feeling, it is rather easy to see that marriage, viewed instrumentally, could be transformed into a primary means for achieving or maximizing personal happiness. The point, of course, is not that personal happiness is somehow a bad thing; rather, the key question is whether this particular value should be elevated to such primary status with respect to a host of other perhaps more worthy values and goods like self-sacrifice for the greater good of a group or commitment and obligations to others.

The usual interpretations of the strong correlation between personal happiness and marital satisfaction are the following: either (1) satisfying marital relationships are causally relevant to promoting personal happiness or (2) satisfying marital relationships and personal happiness are strongly correlated because they are brought about by some set of common causes. These are the first two interpretive possibilities that might come to mind in a natural-scientific approach to marriage research seeking objective regularities. But, as Berlin pointed out (see Chapter 6, sec. 3.2), keeping only to the level of empirical and formal-correlation studies tells us little if anything about the correlates when self-interpreting beings are involved (as in the case of correlations in hardiness studies). For example, perhaps it is the case that people experience tremendous satisfaction when they believe their lives are fulfilling a paramount cultural ideal, in this case the aspiration toward a satisfying marriage. If this ideal, which itself represents an interpretation at the social level, were to change, the correlation between satisfying marriages and personal happiness might disappear altogether.

Some other characteristic features of the individualist conception of marriage are (Bellah et al. 1985):

(1) Marriage is viewed as the primary avenue for the nurture and expression of love, but love itself is viewed primarily in terms of personal feelings and desires in contrast to a sense of obligation or commitment to someone or something larger than the self.

(2) Marriage is viewed as the primary place for getting our needs met, but if spouses do not meet each others' needs, then dissolving the marriage appears highly desirable as this may be the only way for them to pursue their individual interests.

(3) Commitment within marriage is primarily seen to be an expression of personal autonomy rather than as taking on an obligation.

To the extent that a marriage enhances personal happiness, it is considered to be a *good* marriage. This represents a vision of the good life – as conceived from the perspective of liberal individualism – and the role good marriages play in fulfilling this vision.

Understood in this light, divorce rates in the USA – among the highest in the world – take on an alarming meaning. The expectations of the number of marriages that will end in divorce has been placed at anywhere from 42 out of every 100 to 64 out of every 100! Following divorce, a very large number of people remarry, roughly half of these doing so within three years of their divorce (Cherlin 1992). Americans marry at one of the highest rates in the world, seeking happy marriages and the personal satisfaction they bring. But Americans also are quite willing to leave an unsatisfactory marriage and remarry if these needs are not met. They have developed very high expectations of what marriage should deliver, so that if spouses feel that marriages are delivering on these expectations, they tend to report very strong satisfaction with their marriages (Fowers, Lyons and Montel 1996). At the same time that they have maximized their expectations for emotional fulfilment and self-satisfaction in marriage, Americans have minimized their sense of obligation and commitment to spouses and children as well as to marriage as an institution. Paradoxically, the more important marriage has become to Americans, the more vulnerable it has become because if marriage is not yielding the expected benefits, people are more likely to divorce to pursue a more satisfying marriage.

This destructively paradoxical situation is a relatively new cultural development as marriage has not been seen primarily in terms of personal fulfilment until very recently (Hareven 1987; Mintz and Kellogg 1988; Shorter 1975). In pre-modern cultures (as well as some more traditional segments of current Indian, Asian and African cultures), marriages were most frequently arranged. There was very little in the way of expectations for romantic or other forms of personal fulfilment. Experiencing the kind of passionate love idealized in contemporary Western cultures used to be viewed as a form of madness or loss of self-possession. Recall, that in pre-modern cultures, people saw their worth primarily in terms of fulfilling a role or place in a meaningful cosmic order. In contrast, we moderns tend to focus more on the fulfilment of our inner needs and desires as primary indicators of how well we are living. As David Popenoe puts it:

> Traditionally, marriage has been understood as a social obligation – an institution designed mainly for economic security and procreation. Today marriage is understood mainly as a path to self-fulfillment. One's own self-development is seen to require a significant other, and marital partners are picked primarily to be personal companions. Put another way, marriage is being deinstitutionalized. No longer comprising a set of norms and social obligations that are widely enforced, marriage today is a voluntary relationship that individuals can make and break at will. (1993: 533)

A very important aspect of this paradoxical revaluation of marriage is the role played by our modern ideals of autonomy and liberal individualism. When individual freedom and autonomy are privileged, as they are in the USA, the kind of unconditional commitment that lasting relationships and mutual obligations require becomes impossible because autonomy and unconditional commitment are inconsistent with each other. If we really are free to live our own lives as we see fit, then we must also be free to change or end our commitments as we see fit. Mutual obligations and unconditional commitments, however, curtail the modern ideals of individual freedom and autonomy. But without unconditional commitment and a deep sense of mutual obligations ('for better or for worse, for richer, for poorer, in sickness and in health . . . til death do us part'), marriage will rarely be a lasting relationship. As long as marriage is meeting the spouses' individual needs and desires, maintaining it is consistent with the freedom and autonomy to pursue their individual aims. When it is not fulfilling, commitment and marriage represent burdens and obstacles to our freedom. Hence, our very cultural ideals tend to undermine marriage and render it vulnerable. For instance, an individual emphasis on self-fulfilment runs counter to self-sacrifice for the good of your spouse. As individualism becomes emphasized (hyper-individualism), the quality and stability of marriage is increasingly seen as resulting from the desires, decisions and skills of the individuals involved. This conceptualization of marriage, however, leaves us no ability to see how the fragility of contemporary marriage is affected by a very potent vision of the good life as personal fulfilment and individual freedom.

It perhaps is not surprising that the contemporary view of marriage in the USA would reflect the pervasive cultural ideals of liberal individualism. It also is not so surprising that the individualist conception of marriage would harbour tensions tending to undermine the very qualities taken to be of value regarding marriage. Intimacy, companionship, a sense of belonging along with the other goods marriage offers tend to be undermined when the only basis supporting them is that of personal fulfilment and self-interest. Hence, many contemporary problems within marriage as well as the instability reflected in high divorce rates have much to do with the cultural ideals guiding the contemporary vision of the good marriage.

What may be more disturbing is that contemporary research on marriage, though ostensibly aiming to be value-neutral, actually presupposes the very cultural ideals shaping the contemporary vision of marriage. The mainstream approach is coloured by the scientific ideal of discovering universal, context-free laws with the aim of applying them to therapy and education so as to effectively deal with marital problems and instabilities. Marriage is recognized as a socially important object of study and correlation studies supposedly highlight the apparent link between marital satisfaction and personal happiness. However, despite the fact that correlational studies do not indicate causation, researchers take these correlations to be important. Such correlations signal the importance of researching the causes and cures of marital dissatisfaction and divorce as well as studying features promoting satisfying, successful marriages.

The idea is that if these causes were well-understood, or if a solid theory of marriage could be produced, then perhaps causes leading to marital satisfaction and stability or dissolution and divorce could be predicted. Presumably such knowledge would enable us to establish and protect conditions enhancing marital success and reduce the frequency of divorce.

Most marital research focuses on satisfaction or stability (Karney and Bradbury 1995). One of the most widely used measures of marital quality is the ENRICH Marital Satisfaction scale (Olson, Fournier and Druckman 1987). This instrument gives a number of statements to which a person can give responses ranging from 'strongly disagree' to 'strongly agree', covering various dimensions of marriage such as communication, religious orientation, sexual relationship, financial management and equalitarian roles. Some sample items include: 'I am very happy with how we handle role responsibilities in our marriage', 'I am unhappy about our financial position and the way we make decisions and resolve conflicts', 'I am very pleased about how we express affection and relate sexually'.

Clearly the focus here is on individual satisfaction with various aspects of marriage. This reflects the popular emphasis on individual satisfaction in marriage. Of course, to carry out this line of research, one must have a definition or model for a 'good marriage', otherwise there is no target at which to aim. The consensus in marital research defines good marriages in terms of individual satisfaction, accepting uncritically the widely held individualistic perspective on what is valuable about marriage. The use of scored questionnaires and statistical techniques for data analysis certainly looks empirical, but the approach is hardly value-neutral. The supposed empirical measures look just like the contemporary cultural ideal of the individualist conception of marriage. In other words, the supposed value-neutral attempt to produce empirical measures uncritically uses the very ideals that characterize the individualist ideal of marriage, the same ideals that prove so problematic for the health of marriage!

Much marital research has focused attention on communication patterns in the hopes of devising strategies for improving communication among spouses. As a result of this research, social scientists often advocate training in particular communication skills as key to perpetuating marital satisfaction and reducing prospects for divorce (Gottman 1993; Markman et al. 1993). Almost all approaches to divorce prevention, marriage enrichment and therapy teach these skills (Gottman 1994; Markman et al. 1993; Guerney, Brock and Coufal 1987). The aim is to support marital stability through increasing understanding and personal satisfaction in marriage. Again personal satisfaction shows up as a key to strong, lasting marriages and is taken to be dependent upon improving communication, enhancing intimacy, fostering egalitarian relationships and encouraging spouses to work at improving their marriages (Fowers 1998).

Most of this research assumes personal satisfaction with marriage is the primary measure of its quality. Additionally, if one views the development of a satisfying marriage as a technical problem, as the instrumental picture of action encourages, then the acquisition of good communication skills appears to be an effective means for achieving the goal of marital satisfaction (Gottman and Silver 1994; Markman, Stanley and Blumberg 1994). This is a means–ends approach to treating the disaffection within and dissolution of marriages. But the primary goal of individual satisfaction in marriage is never challenged. It is simply assumed; hence, these researchers are actually reinforcing the popular cultural notion that feelings about the marriage are the central goal of a lasting, solid relationship as opposed to commitment and mutual obligations.

This is exactly the mark of the instrumentalization of moral dimensions of human living, turning these dimensions into technical knowhow, that critical theorists analyse and warn against.[5] The goal of personal satisfaction in marriage is treated as a given and not questioned while the focus is almost exclusively on the best means for achieving this goal. An instrumental framework (*zweckrational*) does not make provision for probing the ends and evaluating their worth (*wertrational*). Hence, marital research tends to advocate and reinforce a particular vision of the good marriage and discourage or shut out others. This is not to say that the links between communication, satisfaction and stability within marriage are not real. There are communication patterns that exacerbate marital distress, promote disaffection, even, in some cases, lead to physical abuse. Identification of these patterns is an important achievement. But the nearly exclusive focus on means of communication skills and the unquestioning acceptance of the goal of personal marital satisfaction diminishes marriage as an institution at the same time that it further endangers that vulnerable institution.

So contemporary approaches to marriage research are not value-neutral. Rather, they take the individualist conception of marriage as given, meaning that these research efforts perpetuate the very ideals of contemporary culture rather than challenging such ideals or exploring alternatives.[6] Furthermore, if it is indeed the case that current ideals shaping the concept of the good marriage are actually undermining marriage, contributing to the modern stress and instability of that institution (Bellah et al. 1985; Furstenberg and Cherlin 1991), current research approaches are simply perpetuating these damaging cultural ideals. This means that the cures on offer from such research are just as likely to maintain or exacerbate or pass on the very problems with which we are concerned.

4. Taking stock

In modern Western culture, a great deal of emphasis is placed on technical solutions to problems: a *zweckrational* approach to life. For instance, if improved communication is identified as a key component to a satisfying marriage, then many marital problems are treated by discovering and teaching good communication techniques to enhance openness and intimacy. In other words, much of a good marriage is taken to be a matter of right or good technique that has been scientifically validated. Similarly, with hardiness research the components of a hardy personality are treated as the means to improved coping with stress, improved health and increased productivity.

Whether we are worrying about social institutions like marriage or other social goods like justice or clean air, it is clear from the examples in this chapter that strictly natural-scientific approaches do not have the resources to deal with the disguised ideologies underlying the problems. Nor does mainstream social science adequately address these problems, or its own role as part of the problems in its attempts to offer solutions. Rather, such approaches are likely to simply reinforce or reify the current cultural ideals by simply carrying them along in the supposed value-neutral methods. Furthermore, if our moral categories for going beyond mere empirical and formal methods are similarly limited or coloured by current cultural ideals, as in Hardin's (1987) analysis of population problems and freedom, then even our attempts at broader analyses of social and political problems and policies are likely to simply perpetuate the very injustices and obstacles we are seeking to overcome.

This is the power of disguised ideology: hidden, yet ever present. Mainstream social science cannot extract itself from being involved in the very values and ideals driving many of the maladies it seeks to treat. Like the addict in denial, becoming aware of our disguised ideologies is a first important step to helping social scientists make genuine distinctions between problems and solutions. And this is one area where philosophers can make a rich and socially beneficial contribution by raising awareness of supposed value-neutral social science's unacknowledged advocacy of cultural ideals that stand in need of challenge and reinterpretation.

For further study

1. Explain the three components of a hardy personality. How is this personality construct coloured by disguised ideologies?
2. Why are correlation studies unable to determine any causal relations?
3. How does liberal individualism show up in Hardin's analysis of population problems?
4. What cultural ideals show up in contemporary conceptions of marriage and in marriage research? In what ways are these ideals harmful to marriage?

Recommended reading

B. Fowers, 'Psychology and the Good Marriage: Social Theory as Practice', *American Behavioral Scientist* 41(1998): 516–41.

G. Hardin, 'The Tragedy of the Commons', *Science* 162(1968): 1243–48.

B. Karney and T. Bradbury, 'The Longitudinal Course of Marital Quality and Stability: A Review of Theory, Method, and Research' *Psychological Bulletin*, 18 (1993): 3–34.

S. Maddi, 'The Personality Construct of Hardiness: I. Effects on Experiencing, Coping, and Strain', *Consulting Psychology Journal: Practice and Research* 51(1999): 83–94.

Part Three

Psychology and the Behavioural Sciences

9

Chapter Outline

As was noted in Chapter 1, many commentators have observed how striking it is that, as compared with the natural sciences, there is very little in the way of widely endorsed systematic theory in the behavioural sciences (e.g., Taylor 1985b; Slife and Williams 1995; Richardson, Fowers and Guignon 1999). Perhaps the closest thing to such systematic accounts are familiar and influential personality theories like Freud's and its many successors, and particular broad orientations toward human behaviour such as behaviourism, existentialism and cognitive psychology. Thus, I will focus much of my attention on a limited number of these theories or orientations so as to clarify and illustrate various issues.

Concentrating on how these issues arise in psychology is particularly useful because psychology's dilemmas are representative of the problems facing all behavioural-science disciplines (e.g., social psychology, management science, organizational behaviour, ethology). Furthermore, psychology most richly illustrates a core concern many critics have about twentieth-century social science, namely that it seeks to understand and treat some of our most intimate or personal struggles with what seem to many to be starkly detached, depersonalizing methods. For instance, whereas family, friends, communities, religious and moral perspectives all provide resources and support for people dealing with their grief, psychology as a discipline offers . . . adjustment.

I will briefly sketch behaviourist, psychodynamic, cognitive and humanistic pictures of human behaviour, all of which have been very influential in twentieth-century psychology. Each of these approaches, their differences notwithstanding, exemplify the issues facing behavioural-science inquiry.

1. Theories and perspective on human behaviour

1.1. Behaviourism

A fundamental assumption of behaviourist approaches is that behaviour is strictly determined in various ways by environmental stimuli and reinforcing events. Stimuli and reinforcements impinge upon us as efficient causes and our various patterns of thought and action in the world are the lawful effects of these causes. Consider the reflex response of touching a hot stove, where the hand immediately pulls away in a purely automatic reaction (the impulse to withdraw the hand going no higher than the spinal cord). For the behaviourist *all* human behaviours – including theorizing about behaviour! – are of this basic type. Of course people are conscious thinking beings, but even consciousness and thought should be understood and investigated as behaviours learned in an automatic way, following just such a stimulus–response–reinforcement pattern. For example, a behaviourist would explain a jogger's 'desire' to run daily by noting how the 'runner's high' acts as a positive reinforcement to run while skipping a day leads to a negative reinforcement in the form of her body feeling relatively lousy.

B. F. Skinner emphasized that most behaviours result from conditioning because no matter why behaviours first occur, they are almost always followed by either positive or negative reinforcements. Behaviours are controlled by their consequences, so on this view all 'learning' really amounts to conditioning (albeit of a very complicated sort: Skinner 1965; 1974). Therefore, on the behaviourist analysis, human behaviours are the product of the causal nexus of stimuli and reinforcements acting upon us. Particular stimuli and reinforcements become associated with particular behaviours in lawful ways. Our behaviours are controlled in a law-like way by environmental events and not by our 'will' ('will' being just another conditioned response). In this way, behaviourism exemplifies the universal-laws conception with its emphasis on laws and the methodological conception with its emphasis on methodologies focused on external stimuli and overt behaviour.

The goal of behaviourism is to uncover laws governing human behaviour by studying observable aspects of the environment (e.g., stimuli, responses and reinforcements) rather than unobservable mental constructs (e.g., intentions, motives and desires) leading to precise prediction and control of human behaviour. Supposedly behaviourism would then be able to responsibly guide behaviour-change activities. Behaviourist literature is suffused both with constant claims that all behaviour is strictly determined and the repeated expression of extravagant hopes for extensive mastery and control over the environment and behaviour that behaviourist knowledge can make possible. The sharp tension between belief in determinism – all behaviour governed by impinging stimuli and reinforcement – and such ideals of mastery and control, which themselves must also be behaviours governed strictly by the deterministic interplay of stimuli and reinforcements reflects the freedom–determinism dilemma I will examine in more detail in Chapter 14.

Behaviourism's demise as a serious psychological explanation of behaviour after the 1960s is somewhat complex. A large contributing factor was the rise of cognitive views (below) which promised purchase on the internal workings of the mind. The decline of logical positivism (Chapter 1, sec. 2.1) also played a role.

1.2. Freud and psychodynamics

Interestingly, Freudian psychoanalytic theory, which behaviourists typically view as heinously unscientific, shares a very similar commitment to determinism in the human realm. For Freud mental events, and human behaviour generally, result from interacting and counteracting 'forces' within a psychic 'apparatus' or mechanism that engages in particular functions and can be understood by applying the same principles used in explaining other sorts of mechanisms investigated by natural science (Yankelovich and Barrett 1970;

Wachtel 1997). The workings of the mind are made intelligible by character-izing the 'economy' of forces or energies shifting through the system. In his tripartite scheme, the ego – self-conscious desires and willings – the super-ego – roughly culture: for example, social expectations and rules, peer pressure of friends and family – and the id – unconscious desires and drives – are the sources of these forces and energies. Freud assumed that nothing in the mind occurs by chance. Hence, loose talk about the 'association of ideas' found in older approaches to psychology, in his view, should be replaced by precise efficient-causal explanations.[1]

Freud departs radically from traditional Cartesian notions of a mind imme-diately intelligible to itself (i.e., having access to its entire contents of beliefs, desires, ideas, etc.). In his view the unconscious is the true psychic reality. We cannot know it directly and must infer the action of deep psychic forces on the basis of our knowledge of the apparatus' inputs and outputs. But determinism still reigns and, thus, Freud characterizes the ego as a 'poor creature' buffeted about by id forces and painful reality constraints of the super-ego on gratifying our fundamental sexual and aggressive drives (1964: 40–56). For Freud these sexual and aggressive drives are pervasive influences on our behaviour and must be accounted for in any list of efficient causes or forces explaining behaviour. He argued, for instance, that the sexual instinct lies at the source of virtually all our behaviours, implying that almost all aspects of our relationships with others are driven by the need for libidinal gratification.

Fixation is another key feature in Freud's unconscious taxonomy. Freud believed that as people mature they pass through stages characterized by grati-fication demands and different routes to these gratifications at these different stages. If we receive either too much or too little of the right sort of gratification at a given stage, we become fixated; that is to say, unconsciously we continue to have the same desire for this appropriate amount of gratification we should have had earlier in life. On Freud's view, fixation never goes away, always remaining outside our conscious awareness, influencing our every move.

It is also true that Freud, while a strict determinist, is not a complete reduc-tionist. Psychic 'forces' are at the same time 'meanings' or feelings and motives. They and many of their convoluted dynamics in the psyche can be described in meaningful, ordinary language terms like 'love' and 'fear'. Rather than be eliminated in favour of a pure natural-science vocabulary, such meaningful or intentional terms can and should be employed for many valid theoretical and therapeutic purposes. So there is a blend of deterministic and purposive vocabulary in terms of 'forces' and 'meanings' in an attempt to be scientifically rigorous while simultaneously capturing some sense of meaningful experience and personal agency.

But there is a tension here. For Freud, accurate and useful explanations of human events formulated by theorists or therapists are possible only on the assumption that a rigid determinism holds sway in the psychic realm. As Rieff (1959; 1966) makes clear, Freud took the consequences of determinism quashing any possibility for meaningful action very seriously, to the point of arguing that it was quite inappropriate even to try to offer consolation aimed at mitigating determinism's impact on a person's self-conception. Rieff characterizes Freud as 'a moralist [who] derives lessons on the right conduct of life from the misery of living it', facing up as squarely as possible, among other things, to the truth of determinism (Rieff 1959: ix). Indeed, the core of Freud's recommended outlook in a world devoid of larger purposes and traditional meanings is unbending realism about these losses and adoption of a stringent 'doctrine of maturity . . . with its acceptance of meaninglessness as the end product of analytic wisdom' (Rieff 1966: 43).

To be sure, as Rieff points out (1966: 63), Freud himself never completely abandoned the idea of somewhat liberating individuals from undue repression (e.g., unconscious drives or an overweening reliance on family or others). He also wanted to at least marginally increase their satisfaction in living. It is hard to imagine psychoanalysis or any other form of therapy continuing to exist and being utilized without some such ideal in force. However, that does not necessarily mean that Freud should have despaired utterly or that therapeutic activities should cease. It might mean that an almost ineradicable sense of life's meaningfulness in humans should prompt us to reconsider the presumed truth of strict determinism (Chapter 14).

Friendly critics of Freudian theory (e.g., Habermas 1971; Schafer 1980) point out a deep incoherence: a fundamental goal for Freudian theory is to understand and nurture the kinds of self-reflection that lead to rational self-transformation in therapy and even perhaps in society generally. But Freud's mechanistic storyline leaves it unclear how such rational self-transformation could be achieved. Freud's mechanistic picture rules out choice and responsibility.

Freud's ideas were foundational for a range of personality theories classified as *psychodynamic*, as well as being influential in almost all modern developments in psychology. Even recent versions of psychodynamic theory suffer similar difficulties. Kohut's self psychology (1977) attempts to humanize and enrich the psychodynamic approach by viewing the self as a dynamic continuum of ideas, ambitions and skills striving to realize its built-in potential (expressive individualism; see Chapter 5, sec. 2.3). In this view, parental involvement plays a primary role in the development of the self. If our parents (or other parental figures) fail to provide the appropriate nurturing at various stages of growth, we will suffer from various kinds of 'structural defects' that will be with us for our entire lives. Yet, the idea of deep forces at work in the psyche beyond our sphere of awareness and control remains. Furthermore, Kohut views the self as unfolding in drive-like fashion on the basis of some pre-given blueprint; hence, a strong form of determinism is at work in this popular and influential revisionist psychodynamic theory.

1.3. Cognitive approaches

Psychology and other behavioural sciences today have been greatly influenced by what has become known as the 'cognitive revolution' of the 1960s. The perspectives and research spawned by this movement usually centre on notions of information and information processing. According to Jerome Bruner, these approaches adopt computability as a necessary criterion of a good theoretical model (1990: 4). Bruner describes how many originators of the cognitive revolution (himself included) intended to bring 'mind' back into the human sciences after a long cold winter of behaviourism (1990: 1–4). Unfortunately, as many critics have pointed out, the 'new cognitive science' that emerged gained 'its technical successes at the price of dehumanizing the very concept of mind it had sought to reestablish' (Bruner 1990: 1) by reducing the making and remaking of important human meanings and ideals to a much narrower kind of 'information processing'.

These possible limitations of a cognitive approach to understanding humans is closely linked to its retaining a rigid deterministic viewpoint on human action. Most cognitive approaches in psychology subscribe to an input–processing–output model of cognitive functioning that, at bottom, still characterizes human activity as a flow, albeit at the level of cognition or mental events, of law-governed efficient causes and their effects (Taylor 1985a; Bishop 2005a). Behaviours may not be seen as necessarily determined by the environmental stimuli or reinforcements or by the underlying physical or chemical 'hardware' of the body or brain. Nevertheless, such behaviours are taken to be determined primarily by inputs and innate or acquired 'software'. However complicated and subtle the information processing determining resulting performances, this processing is portrayed as determined by prior environmental input (e.g., memory) and innate propensities or capacities. The whole validity and usefulness of a science of cognition depends on this deterministic premise (Bandura 1977; 1986). A simple way to see this deterministic commitment is the following. Suppose you are typing an essay on your computer. If the computer is not deterministic, then from time to time random words, phrases or sentences might be added to or deleted from your essay. When you try to go back and correct these problems, perhaps some other words, phrases or sentences might be randomly added or deleted and so forth. The computational paradigm requires the processing of input be deterministic for the output (e.g., behaviour) to be ordered and effective at achieving its goal.

Motives, intentions, desires, thoughts and so on are reduced to information input and cognitive processing units on this view (Sternberg and Ben-Zeev 2001). Consider a father who never expresses love or praise thereby causing his son to grow up with a set of perfectionist behaviour patterns always striving to win the approval of potential father or authority figures. These early childhood dynamics can be viewed as 'programming' or 'software' providing instructions for how various cognitive units such as memory or recognition ('hardware') are to process new information derived from the son's social interactions with peers and authority figures along with information stored in memory. In this way, cognitive psychology seeks to make such behaviours understandable, quantifiable and measurable.

Some cognitivists might argue that we can exert a great deal of influence over the information entering our information-processing apparatus. For instance, we might close our eyes to focus on isolating a sound we are trying to hear. This influence, however, is often thought to be dependent upon attentional processes over which we can exercise very little conscious control (Williams 1987). Moreover, information called up from long-term-memory storage (a process over which we exercise no conscious control) also influences present stimuli. The information (present stimuli and memory) and its properties determine how it is processed by the cognitive system. So it seems that we can exercise very little if any influence over the input–processing–output scheme on the cognitive analysis.

Some more refined theories have cognitive processes working at all stages of the input–processing–output scheme, so that incoming information is mediated and filtered by these cognitive processes before central processing takes place. These mediation processes along with the cognitive system are usually taken as inborn and, therefore, they determine what information we process, how we process it and, ultimately, our behaviour. On this picture, it is unclear how a person could 'intervene' in the cognitive apparatus to somehow influence or soften the deterministic processes at work.

1.4. Humanist approaches

Historically, humanist approaches developed in response to behaviourist and psychodynamic approaches. Although there are a broad range of theories in this category, the unifying theme running throughout humanist approaches is their explicit rejection of the hard determinism characterizing the mainstream theories just surveyed (Slife and Williams 1995: 32). In place of deterministic forces and influences, a number of humanist theories substitute a unique potential within each person that constitutes an inborn sense of identity, a guide for what we can become and a source of direction for our decisions. To develop ourselves along the lines of this inner potential is to become 'self-actualized' in Abraham Maslow's terms (1998), clearly articulating expressive individualism. In order to develop this unique potential, according to humanist approaches, we need (1) the freedom to pursue our own developmental path, (2) the ability to meet our needs and (3) the capacity to understand our needs.

However, it is not clear that humanist approaches have avoided determinism, although the rejection of determinism seems to be the one thing that otherwise quite varied humanistic theories have in common. The unique potential within each person exerts a very strong influence over our sense of identity, our behaviour, our needs, as well as over our psychological health. If this inner potential is rooted in biology (Maslow 1998), then it is a dominating factor over which we have no control. The presence of such influences outside our control is not all that different from psychodynamics or behaviourism. Furthermore, the capacity to understand our needs is not pictured as a conscious capacity; rather, it is a special kind of instinctual knowledge or feeling lying below the surface playing a role somewhat like that of the unconscious in psychodynamics. Although these forms of determinism can be understood in ways that soften their impact relative to the forms at work in psychodynamics and behaviourism, the account of agency and freedom needed to act effectively in a causally ordered world is typically left unaddressed in humanist theories.

2. Efficient causation and instrumentalism

Almost all of these theoretical perspectives embody the natural-scientific mode of social inquiry – for the most part humanist approaches are simply too vague to make clear judgements, but they often appear to take the form of natural-scientific or descriptivist modes. Furthermore, their significant differences notwithstanding, all these perspectives appear to fully embrace efficient causation and an instrumental conception of action (see Chapter 4).[2] The same is true throughout the behavioural sciences. Further, the perspectives surveyed here share in common – along with much of the rest of behavioural science – a belief that the past is causally sufficient to explain present behaviour, although the account of how the past is causally sufficient differs. There are two different models of efficient causation and determinism, one or the other of which shape the core of many, if not most, theories in the behavioural sciences.

2.1. The physics model

The first model I will call the *physics model*. Just as a full accounting of the appropriate physical forces enables us to understand the dynamics of some physical process (Fig. 9.1), a full accounting of the psychic and social forces involved enables us to understand the human behavior in question (Fig. 9.2). Both psychodynamics and behaviourism exemplify this model with their reliance on forces as efficient causes of behaviour, as do humanist approaches to a large degree. Human behaviours are explained in terms of the forces producing them (drives and so forth in psychodynamics – see Fig. 9.2; stimuli and reinforcement in behaviourism; inbuilt inclinations in humanist approaches). Instead of viewing people as creators of meanings and values, this model views them more like electrons responding to forces in law-like ways.

For example, behaviourist theory reduces loving to a set of behaviours brought about by environmental forces. Agents exhibit loving behaviours because ultimately they have been shaped or conditioned by brute environmental

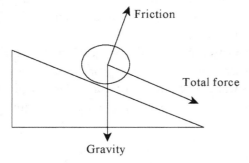

Figure 9.1 Physical Forces on a Rolling Ball
The total force on a ball rolling down an inclined plane is the sum of the force of gravity pulling down on the ball plus the force of friction applied by the plane against the ball.

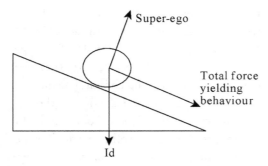

Figure 9.2 Psychological Forces on the Ego
Imagine the ball on the inclined plane represents the ego. On Freud's view the id and super-ego forces sum to produce a person's behaviour.

forces and contingencies. Like electrons, agents respond to these external forces in law-like ways and engage in behaviours determined by these forces. So on this analysis, each partner in a marriage will be attracted to each other due to the effects of stimuli and reinforcements impinging upon them. The couple constantly receives such stimuli and reinforcements from each other through various behaviours as well as other elements of their environment (e.g., family and friends, Hollywood movies). Learning something new about a partner's interests is an example of this kind of stimulus–response–reinforcement cycle. Or perhaps a conflict arises with one partner building up resentment as a response to the frequent negative stimuli received from a particular annoying habit exhibited by the other. Too many such negative reinforcements and the forces may lead to one partner dissolving the relationship.

Loving appears, then, to be constituted by stimuli and reinforcements modifying behaviour, looking very much like the behaviour of electrons being modified by electromagnetic fields and other forces in their environment. Loving, in this picture, is not constituted by the meanings we often take it to have. In this sense, theorizing about the marriage relationship actually changes the meaning this form of committed relationship has from our everyday perspective. This is an example of how theorizing in the social sciences is not about an independent realm but actually tends to transform the very objects and practices that are the subjects of theorizing (see Chapters 10–13).

2.2. The computer model

The second model is the computer model. Here the causal role is played by the rules and structures governing the input–processing–output scheme of cognition and by the nature of the information put into the system. Cognitive psychology exemplifies this model by relying on the crucial role information input and processing play in explaining behaviour, relying on various modes of memory storage and retrieval, multi- or parallel-processing, feedback loops among various levels of processing, mediation – where cognitive processes select and modify information at each stage of processing – and so forth. All human behaviours including motives, intentions, desires and such are reduced to information input and the processing of the cognitive apparatus. This model pictures agents as machine-like, operating according to logical or rational information-processing rules. Instead of viewing people as creators of meanings and values, this model reduces all behaviour to the structure of the cognitive system and the nature of the information put into that system.

In the computer picture, for instance, a spouse's loving behaviour is reduced to information input, representation and cognitive computation. Each partner in a marriage will have a mental representation of the other, including not just physical form, but personality traits, desires and so forth. The couple constantly receives information from each other through conversations and actions. Cognitive units process this input and generate responses. Perhaps the representation undergoes a change such as learning something new about a partner's interests. Or perhaps a conflict arises with one partner building up resentment as a response to frequent arguments. At some level pros and cons of staying in the relationship are weighted based on the information received, the processing performed and the outputs generated that compose the relationship.

Loving then appears to be constituted by information input and processing, taking on a machine-like or computational character rather than being constituted by the meanings we often take it to have. This information-processing characterization of loving contrasts strongly with our experience of loving and the meanings it has. So again, our theorizing about marriage transforms the meaning marriage has from our everyday perspective. Worse, to the extent that we change our everyday perspective to conform more to this 'scientific' image of marriage, we transform marriage into an instrumental relationship that is actually detrimental to this social institution (see Chapter 8, sec. 3).

Looked at in this light, it is easy to see why some thinkers consider cognitive approaches to simply be warmed-over behaviourism (e.g., Bruner 1990). Instead of stimulus–response–reinforcement cycles, cognitive approaches have information input, innate software/hardware and output (behaviour) generation. The only significant difference appears to be that cognitive approaches allow for the mind to have internal mechanisms and states, with the same emphases on efficient causation and determinism as behaviourism.

2.3. Efficient causation and the lifeworld

In the physics model, everything is pictured as various forms of efficient causation. Behaviourism, for instance, relies on stimuli, response and reinforcement to account for behaviour, while psychoanalytic theories rely on internal and external forces to account for behaviour. In the computer model, brute reliance on sequential information input and mechanistic models of information processing are the efficient causal explanations of behaviour. These pictures of human behaviour contrast strongly with the more holistic, narrative character of everyday living described in Chapter 6.

In the narrative picture, human activity always takes place against a backdrop of explicit or implicit assumptions, values, commitments and practices deriving from our cultural–historical situation – cultural traditions, family upbringing, past experiences and so forth – which cannot always be articulated and often remain unclarified (Polanyi 1962; Taylor, 1985a; 1985b; 1993). This background operates somewhat like disguised ideologies in that they often remain below the surface of our conscious awareness. Our actions are always simultaneously channelled by this background (formal causation) as well as simultaneously shaped by our vision and understanding of our own future (final causation). Recall as well that this narrative structure is also dynamic: as we engage in the daily activities of life, the meanings this background and our vision of the future have for us are always changing, shedding new light on our present view of ourselves and the world around us.

From this holistic perspective, the past (memory) and the future (as presently envisioned by us) are simultaneous with our present influencing our interpretation of the present, while the present colours our interpretation of our past and future. The story of our lives has the character of an unfinished novel, but it is also reinterpreted and adapted in the light of new, often surprising realities. And while it is true that these events occur sequentially (just as they do in a novel), the narrative structure constituted by the simultaneous presence of past, present and future acts as a context (formal causation) for interpretations of and responses to these new events.

For example, a student's understanding of her past and future typically changes markedly from entering college to graduation, due in part to the friends she meets, courses she takes (including those not her first choice!) and the new community to which she moves during her studies. She starts out with a set of expectations about her future (to become a nurse, say) and an understanding of her past (as someone always quick to aid others in need). But through the unpredictable twists and turns of college life she emerges with new expectations (to become an inner-city school teacher, say) and a changed vision of her past (as someone who has always wanted to make a difference in the lives of those who are less fortunate than her). In this holistic sense, the present changes the past as much as the past – from the efficient-causal perspective – changes the present.[3]

Many would claim that our lived experience is more holistic in character with a past, present and future that co-constitute a current context in this formal causal sense (Chapter 6). They would argue that a strict reliance on efficient causation leaves out crucial features of human interactions and behaviours – such as how our current vision of the future reshapes our interpretations of the past – about which we surely want to understand more.

Many behavioural scientists, particularly cognitivists, might object that they do take formal causation into account, in terms of scheme and cognitive structure, as well as final causation, in terms of goals and wishes. Unfortunately, the cognitivist understanding of scheme and cognitive structures is in terms of information stored in memory and the coordination of processing units (Izawa 1989: ch. 10; Sternberg and Ben-Zeev 2001: chs. 3–4). The latter coordination arises from 'software' (previously learned instructions) and 'hardware' (neurophysiology). So whatever cognitivists take to stand in for formal causation is deeply coloured by the computer metaphor and is driven entirely by the efficient-causal effects of past input. In other words, they are simply calling efficient-causal mechanisms formal causes, which is a category mistake. Similarly the goals and desires taken to stand for final causation are also viewed as the products of past information input and processing. Hence, what passes for formal and final causation in the information processing view really amounts to efficient causation. Formal and final causation as found in the lifeworld are missing from almost all mainstream approaches to psychology and other behavioural sciences.

2.4. Instrumental picture of action

As we have seen in previous examples (e.g., Chapter 8, sec. 1, 3), psychology largely presupposes an instrumental picture of human action. And its reliance upon efficient causation and mechanism derives much of its plausibility from this instrumental picture of action and supporting disguised ideologies (Chapters 4–5). On the instrumental picture, agents are fully immersed in the efficient causal flow of events and processes, while, at the same time, are somehow able to turn onto this causal flow and manipulate it to fulfil their preferences or achieve their goals. On the physics model, these preferences are formed by stimuli and reinforcement, say, while on the computer model, they are formed by information input and processing and, in turn, play an important role in that processing forming a basis on which 'computations' might be carried out determining how to steer the course of events.

The instrumental picture of action appears to fit well within a physical world of efficient causal interactions and this, in part, explains why psychologists, along with most other behavioural scientists, feel so comfortable with their mechanistic/deterministic pictures of the world and action. So comfortable, in fact, that they do not even notice it is a picture and that the picture is in tension with our everyday conceptions and actions. Agents operating through efficient causation acting on a world conceived of as an interconnected web of efficient causes present a strongly compelling picture of action in the world amenable to scientific study. However, at the same time agents are manipulating the causal flow of the world around them, we saw above that they are simultaneously subject to a rather hard determinism due to the very same channels of efficient causation flowing through them. In other words, there is an implicit assumption of some kind of freedom *and* a picture of agents that leaves no room for such freedom. This tension will be explored later (Chapter 14).

As we have seen (Chapter 4, sec. 3), this overemphasis on instrumental action, technical knowhow and control at the expense of culturally meaningful activity and shared meanings leads to a progressive loss of our ability to evaluate the worth of ends on any basis other than personal preference or sheer desire (e.g., choosing a career solely because it will make me a lot of money or because I merely want to help people). Think again of the computer-model view of loving in a marriage. Positive and negative stimuli are supposedly being received by both partners. The benefits of staying in the marriage are weighed against each spouse's preferences and goals. Are the latter being met adequately? At what cost? This is, essentially, a model treating marriage partners as strategic calculators seeking to maximize their self-gratification focused almost exclusively on the individual (Chapter 8, sec. 3). From this perspective, intentions, thoughts, wishes, meanings all turn out to be the results of information input, representation and cognitive computation. Each partner is constantly processing the information input from the relationship relative to the stored goals and objectives for the relationship, weighing the merits of various options (maintain the status quo, make minor or major adjustments, divorce). Marriage then becomes a means toward maximizing gratification or toward self-actualization. However, this view turns marriage into an instrument, focusing on what is considered best or beneficial for the spouse rather than on any deeper meaning of love or sacrifice.[4]

Do therapists and organizational-management consultants literally treat their clients in the mechanical, depersonalized way pictured by their theoretical schemes? Usually not because in the course of their dealing with clients, they often (thankfully) operate at a human, personal level to the extent they can while not violating what they take to be obligations of objectivity and neutrality. Unfortunately, therapists and organizational-management consultants do not always see how such theoretical commitments shape their personal interactions with clients.

We see here an example of a disconnection between theory and practice. On the one hand, the explicit commitments to determinism, efficient causation and instrumental agency in the theoretical perspectives are not explicitly part of the practice of many practitioners in their treatment of clients. On the other hand, these commitments and the tensions they bear can often show up implicitly in practitioners' dealings with clients. Imagine what an existentialist therapist who takes the hardiness conception of personality (Chapter 8, sec. 2) seriously might do with her clients without even realizing the underlying disguised ideologies at work in her theoretical conception.

3. Atomism

The strong notion of individualism colouring psychology and other behavioural sciences also lends support to another key assumption, namely an atomistic view of agents. In general, atomism is the idea that the fundamental elements – the atoms – are independent of each other though they may be combined in complicated ways. The atomistic view of agents in psychology takes the form of *social atomism*, the idea that society is composed of self-contained individuals, each seeking their own purposes (Taylor 1985a: ch. 8). It flows directly out of the punctual or asocial self and the fact/value split, and is reinforced by the general emphasis on autonomy, liberation and individualism so pervasive in Western cultures. It is really a straightforward implication of the commitment to ontological individualism. This form of atomism might be one reason psychology does not tend to view persons as at least partially constituted by the social–historical context in which they are embedded (as in the lifeworld). Social atomism assumes that people are basically hermetically sealed agents interacting within the world. This picture of agents fits nicely with assumptions such as strict adherence to efficient causation, instrumental action and liberal individualism, and colours much of mainstream psychology.

Atomism finds a very congenial home in psychology's typical pictures of agents, though it is quite problematic. At the social level, it certainly presupposes an individualist picture of agents as punctual or asocial, contrasting sharply with the more holistic lifeworld, which is rich with meanings, values, hopes, fears, interdependencies and struggles, all of which take shape for us against the backdrop of our view of our past and future. For instance, apart from the religious community, significant persons and other social experiences within her culture forming such a backdrop, our student would not have formed the desires and vision of herself leading to her becoming a teacher. Moreover, such qualities also take shape for us against the social–cultural–historical matrix in which we live, move and have our being.

To consider the psychological subject as somehow standing apart from these constitutive influences, as the punctual self implies, is to literally view the subject as disengaged in the weak sense of world-shaping (Chapter 1, sec. 4). No doubt psychologists see themselves as attempting to understand agents as acting in the everyday world so that to attribute a disengaged flavour to their approach seems terribly unfair. But here there is a confusion between the two senses of world-shaping distinguished in Chapter 1. Recall that weak world-shaping is characterized by how our surroundings – physical and social – are externally related to agents in terms of efficient causation. In contrast, strong world-shaping is characterized by the possibilities open to us given the kinds of bodies we have, our form of life and our history. Psychologists would be right to object that they do not treat subjects as completely disengaged, but, unfortunately, mainstream theoretical commitments only have room for agents to be conceived in the weak world-shaping sense, a picture dominated by channels of efficient causation. On the cognitive picture, for instance, historical and cultural realities have to be represented somehow in stored memory as the results of efficient-causal inputs from our past. But viewed in this way, it is very problematic to understand how the historical and cultural influences constituting something like deference can be meaningful.

Many would argue, however, it is the strong sense of world-shaping that is characteristic of humans, setting them apart from other things like rocks, amoebas and computers, which all 'engage' their surroundings only through efficient-causal relations. Psychology's picture of the subject is a largely disengaged one, restricted to probing those channels of efficient causation deemed relevant. In contrast, the strong sense of engagement requires formal and final notions of causation as well as a more holistic conception of the lifeworld inhabited by human beings in order to make sense of human activity in all its involvements.

Assuming social atomism does allow psychologists to study subjects in an isolated fashion, attempting to imitate the kinds of controlled, reproducible experiments that are the hallmark of natural science. However, when psychologists adopt this narrow perspective, they effectively settle for studying a subject limited with respect to the full range of social connections and human capacities with which we are interested.

Social atomism also has implications for the theoretical picture of groups and social interactions as in families, group therapy, the management of organizations or the activities of political parties. In the social-atomist picture, groups are simply aggregates of asocial selves interacting with each other via efficient-causal connections rather than via meaningful involvements, mutual obligations, camaraderie and the like. In our theoretical pictures, these latter involvements are transformed into external forces (physics model) or information input (computer model). Again, most psychologists and behavioural scientists are not likely to treat people in their lives as atoms with which they interact through channels of efficient causation. But the theoretical picture at the core of their inquiry does so treat people, reinforcing the instrumentalism and liberal individualism driving this atomist picture. Both the physics and computer models picture agents as asocial centres of causal power able to interact with and manipulate other selves for their own purposes. Such theoretical constructs tend to undermine social cohesion and mutual bonds leading to a growing sense of isolation and alienation, exactly the opposite of what we usually want to foster.

4. Intentionality and reducibility

Most often, the issues raised in literature on the philosophy of psychology are practically indistinguishable from those raised in the philosophy of mind. What is a mind? How is it related to the brain? What is the nature of conscious experience? What is intentionality? Are there representations of external reality in the mind and if so how does this happen? Is psychology reducible to neurobiology? Most of these issues lie far beyond the scope of this book. But the question of psychology's relationship to neurobiology is a topic that can be introduced in a compact way and has a connection with reductionism (see Chapter 7, sec. 2.1).

Much of the subject matter of psychology deals with things like emotions, desires, beliefs, motivations, attitudes and the like. This is the kind of subject matter that we might categorize as *intentional*. Our ordinary meaning of this word is captured in 'purposive', but philosophers have a special meaning of intentional that includes our ordinary sense. Philosophers will say that beliefs or desires are intentional in that they have propositional content – that is, they somehow contain propositions or statements about things: a belief is about a proposition that is believed. On this view, a belief is a relation between a sentient being and some statement: in philosophers' speak, 'X believes that p'. The statement 'I believe that there is Belgian beer in my fridge' is an example. I am the agent (X) and my belief is about the statement: 'There is Belgian beer in my fridge' (p). The latter statement represents a state of affairs in the external world, namely Belgian beer being in my fridge. I believe this state of affairs as expressed in the statement is true or false. Attributing this belief to me, then, contains this statement as its contents in some sense. My desire to drink a Belgian beer is similar: 'I desire that I drink a Belgian beer'. The content of my desire is the statement 'I drink a Belgian beer'. That is what I wish to become true if I desire it. In this way, philosophers talk about desires, beliefs, hopes and other cognitive states as being intentional in that they have propositional content or are about such content.[5] Philosophers sometimes say that these are *psychological attitudes* about or towards the contents expressed in statements or propositions.

We do not pretend to know how cognitive states in our brains can 'contain' such contents. Perhaps the ideas of 'containing' and 'contents' ultimately are metaphorical. This gets to a central problem in philosophy: how brains (or minds, if they are different from brains) represent the way the world is, our desires about the world and so forth. For brains to 'contain' statements means that brains have to somehow represent the content of such statements in some way other than written scripts in the grey matter. Not only do we not know how this feat might be accomplished, we face a problem with the representation itself.

Consider a book, say a history of the New York Stock Exchange. The book contains many pages of sentences and we recognize these sentences as a mode of representation of that history. But the words on the pages themselves do not represent anything. After all, a book is just some combination of ink, pulp and other products combined in a particular way. Imagine by chance our history book simply came together. It would not represent anything just as a shrub that happened to grow into the shape of the Disney character Goofy's face would not represent Goofy. For the book or the shrub to represent requires being capable of taking the marks in the book or the shape of the shrub to have meaning. This is what gives them their representational character.

One might respond to this by arguing that meaning just is something like correct representation. So when the brain correctly represents the shape of the shrub as Goofy from the cartoons, we have all that is needed to make meaning. The real difficulty, however, is that meaning is not a matter of correct representation of an external object or reality. Concepts such as freedom, equality, dignity and the like are not external conditions that give substance to our words 'freedom', 'equality', 'dignity', and the like. Rather, such concepts are constitutive of a way of life for a particular society – ways of being with each other requiring people to understand, interpret and live out in thought and action. Any theory of meaning focused purely on representation will be inadequate to capture the social relational/constitutive quality of such concepts and how they constitute people's relations with one another as they arise in particular societies. The same goes for such emotions as shame or embarrassment, or for social stances such as deference. Such concepts, emotions and social stances are part and parcel of who we are as persons involved with other persons in particular societies (e.g., shame, embarrassment and showing deference differ from society to society), not matters of correct representation of an external reality. In these cases, which are legion, there is no external reality to represent.

Furthermore, to even attempt representations for such concepts, emotions and social stances, they must first be understood in their social relational/constitutive nature, or else there is no way to satisfy the conditions that the representation captures the thing to be represented. This is to say that representation is not primary to meaning. Put another way, the very idea of a representational approach to meaning presupposes a prior interpretive, everyday approach to meaning, for to even try to identify the criteria guaranteeing an accurate representation requires prior understanding of these relational/constitutive features along with their articulations. Put simply, grasping an interpretive, everyday approach to meaning is a necessary condition or foundation for a possible representational approach to meaning.

Suppose I am reading the history of the New York Stock Exchange and the content of the book is being represented in some part of the brain. Who is the interpreter who recognizes the meaning, say by 'reading' the configurations of neural firings? Who grasps the criteria by which to judge whether the configuration of neural firings accurately represent the history told in the book? We are tempted at this point to say that the mind possesses the meaning and criteria necessary to do the trick. But now we face a dilemma. If the mind is distinct from the brain, we have to solve the problem of how something distinct from the brain can actually interact with the brain. On the other hand, if we say that the mind is identified with some other part of the brain, the problem of 'reading' the configurations recurs. It has simply been put off by one step with no seeming possibility of any final 'reader' – in other words, the 'reading' buck never stops.[6]

For these reasons, some psychologists and philosophers maintain that the human powers of thought, meaning, representation and the like cannot be explained in terms of neural processes alone. If correct, then psychology, which deals with such powers, is not reducible to neurobiology alone. And as we saw earlier (Chapter 7, sec. 2.1), since the philosophical urban legend about reductionism is false, the burden is on the neural-reductionist to produce some good evidence that psychological states are reducible to neurobiology if he wants the reductionist claim to go through.

5. Taking stock

Thinking about psychology provides another window or analogy for seeing the role disguised ideologies play in the behavioural and other social sciences. Recall Freud's picture: The id – the unconscious – harbours various desires and drives that remain hidden below the surface of conscious awareness. Nonetheless, such hidden desires and drives colour and shape our every thought, feeling and act. Similarly, disguised ideologies remain hidden below the surface, in the id behind the scenes if you will, of our behavioural and social inquiry. Nevertheless, these disguised ideologies colour and shape all aspects of our human inquiry. Like unconscious drives and desires, the effects of liberal individualism, autonomy and the instrumental picture of action are manifest in social and psychological research (Chapter 8). And like Freudian drives and desires, such disguised ideologies need to be recognized before we can unmask their power and evaluate how to best deal with them.

The role of disguised ideologies in psychology and other behavioural sciences is a problem that remains largely unaddressed in the behavioural-science literature just as in the social sciences in general. This is one reason I have discussed the issue in such detail. But disguised ideologies may hold the key to a problem mentioned in Chapter 1. Recall that in discussing the various conceptions of science, we noted that the behavioural sciences exhibit a great deal of theoretical and methodological disunity. Many commentators have noted how striking this contrast is with the natural sciences. There is very little in the way of widely endorsed systematic theory in the behavioural sciences. Taking the major personality theories and perspectives like cognitivism, one sees that there are large disagreements among the adherents of these differing views. Even within these views there is much disunity.

Another disturbing feature of the behavioural sciences, noted in Chapter 1, is their enormous fragmentation. The major disciplinary branches are greatly isolated from one another and within each there are at least hundreds of tiny, relatively isolated islands of theory and/or research. Inquiry within them is being pursued independently, often with quite different methodologies. This lack of unity within the behavioural-science disciplines contributes directly to another deep problem: namely, the wide gulf existing between theory and practice (Bernstein 1976; Taylor 1985a; 1985b; Slife and Williams 1995; Richardson, Fowers and Guignon 1999). The practice of physicists is deeply informed by the theories of their domain. One looks far and wide in psychology and other behavioural sciences, however, to find such a pervasive influence of generally accepted theories on researchers and therapists. To an amazing extent, researchers and professionals are on their own when it comes to selecting, devising or applying maps or models of human activity.

One possible explanation for this stark contrast between the behavioural sciences and the natural sciences is the following: from the founding of the social sciences, there has been a strong drive to apply natural-scientific methods to them. The success of these methods in social inquiry, of course, presupposes that the latter is highly similar to natural-science inquiry. Although we have seen arguments both for and against the similarity of these two kinds of inquiry, if the natural and social domains really have fundamental differences, then we should expect that the application of largely natural-scientific approaches to social inquiry would lead not only to little progress, but perhaps to the fragmentation we see. One reason to think this is that the search for universal laws to ground empirical theory (universal-laws conception) is tied to particular forms of explanation that sometimes work well in the natural sciences, but may be inconsistent when applied to the social sciences. We will investigate explanation later (Chapter 15), but if natural-scientific modes of explanation turn out to be inapplicable in the social sciences, then there is a huge philosophical problem needing serious attention: what alternatives for explanation are appropriate for psychology and the rest of the social sciences?

Given that liberal individualism, autonomy, the instrumental picture of action and political liberalism all support natural-scientific modes of inquiry in the social sciences, could it be that these disguised ideologies actually contribute significantly to the tremendous disciplinary fragmentation in the behavioural sciences?

For further study

1. Describe how cultural ideals come to expression in two of the psychological theories and perspectives described in sec. 1.
2. What are the physics and computer models of causation? How do they show up in psychological theories and perspectives?
3. Define and illustrate social atomism.

Recommended reading

B. Slife and R. Williams, *What's Behind the Research? Discovering Hidden Assumptions in the Behavioral Sciences* (Thousand Oaks: SAGE, 1995).
C. Taylor, 'Engaged Agency and Background in Heidegger', in C. Guignon (ed.), *The Cambridge Companion to Heidegger* (Cambridge: Cambridge University Press, 1993), pp. 317–36.

Rational-Choice Theory 10

An increasingly influential viewpoint in the social sciences focuses on the rationality of agents as a means for explaining individual and social behaviour. *Rational-choice theory* and *game theory* are two names given to this kind of theorizing. This viewpoint adopts a particular picture of rationality and makes rational beliefs central to explaining behaviour. The goal is to develop theories of practical reasoning that are descriptively accurate, predictively successful and explanatorily powerful. In short, rational-choice theory is another version of empirical theory in the natural-scientific mode (Chapter 3, sec. 1). Its advocates argue that rational-choice theory's universality, simplicity and explanatory power make it an ideal unifying framework for the social sciences.

1. Brief history of the rational-actors picture

While some advocates of rational-choice trace its roots to Plato and Aristotle, more likely neither of these philosophers would recognize themselves as advocates of this picture of rationality. One can more clearly trace the rational-choice picture to the highly mechanical view of life advocated by Hobbes (see Chapter 2, sec. 1). He argued that our actions are driven by our desires (e.g., for food or rest) and aversions (e.g., to avoid work or pain). When these desires and aversions come into conflict, we are pulled in mutually exclusive directions of action. Reason, or deliberation, then renders a judgement on how best to satisfy a given set of desires via some kind of calculation (Hobbes 1994: chs V–VI). For Hobbes, reason does not appraise the desires and aversions appearing before it, but merely weighs up or calculates factors dealing with the means for satisfying desires and avoiding aversions. The upshot is that there are particular rules of action common to all agents that can be recommended as means for satisfying desires and avoiding aversions. Many of these desires are also common to all agents, like the desire to preserve one's own life. So a general rule of action, such as one needs to eat regularly to live, would also be applicable to everybody. This clearly puts reason and at least some actions in an instrumental light (Chapter 4).

The next addition to the picture comes with Jeremy Bentham's (1748–1832) development of utilitarian ethics. For Bentham, every action is to be approved or disapproved depending on whether it promotes the interest or utility of the agent. Utility, here, is to be understood as the property anything has that tends to produce benefit, advantage, pleasure, good, satisfaction or happiness – Bentham took these as largely synonymous – for the agent (Bentham 1970: ch. 1). For example, the enjoyable taste of a soft drink or the runner's high of jogging would be viewed as utilities. Bentham also shifts the emphasis toward mental states resulting from actions, giving reason a more active role in choice and action. He argues it is rational to do what maximizes happiness (utility) over the rest of an agent's life even if current desires point in a different direction. This is because every action possesses some utility, which by hypothesis is a measurable quantity, so that utilities can be added and subtracted. So every problem in rational choice becomes a problem of maximization of utility. Rationality, then, is not the slave of passions, as David Hume (1711–76) maintained, but the calculator of their utility (more accurately, the utility of the actions resulting from passions). The most rational choice is the one that maximizes an agent's utility. Or more precisely, agents seek to maximize their expected utility because there is always some uncertainty as to whether an action will lead to the utility envisioned. Suppose an agent expects that going to the local shop and purchasing some items will maximize her happiness. On her way to the shop, it is struck by lightning and burns to the ground. She would not receive the increase in happiness she was expecting.

If the utilities associated with particular things are measurable, some way of describing the units is needed. Economists and others often assume that utilities are real units corresponding to a *cardinal utility*.[1] This means that utility can be measured as 0 units of utility, 1 unit of utility, 2 units of utility, and so forth. In this way, we can say whether an agent prefers one thing to another twice as much, half as much, 20 per cent more and so forth. Within the rational-actors picture (see below) this assumption allows various theorems to be proven regarding agents' behaviours given assignments of various units of utility to various commodities, services and courses of action among other things. Moreover, it has been generally assumed that interpersonal comparisons of utility can be made, though no procedure for making such comparisons exist. Still, the assumption is that such comparisons among agents can be made in principle so that one can describe varying degrees of strength of desire among different agents.

In the twentieth century, rational-choice theorists largely dropped the hedonistic language of happiness, pleasures and desires, focusing more on preferences of agents. They have also tended to focus more on agent's rankings of preferences. The key assumption, here, is that agents are able to consistently rank the alternatives facing them. Spelling this assumption out, it has two basic features:[2]

1 Rankings are complete. That is, for any two alternatives x and y, either the agent prefers x above y, or the agent prefers y above x, or the agent is indifferent.[3]
2 Rankings of alternatives (preferences) are transitive. This means that if the agent prefers x above y and y above z, then the agent prefers x above z.

On this view, a rational agent possesses complete and transitive preferences and chooses among the feasible alternatives whatever is most preferred. And whatever is most preferred is what maximizes an agent's expected utility. An irrational choice, on this view, would be a case where an agent with complete and transitive preferences chooses some feasible alternative that is not most preferred (e.g., preferring Coca Cola to Pepsi, but choosing Pepsi anyway when both are available). Although this is a general picture of rationality for agents, one can distinguish economic rationality from political rationality from others by the content of the motives or preferences of the agents concerned (e.g., economic gain, political causes).

So an agent is, by definition, an entity with preferences. In the case of people, rational-choice theorists evaluate their relative utility by reference to a person's own implicit or explicit judgements of it. Suppose a person loves the taste of dark chocolate but dislikes other kinds of chocolate. This person would be said to associate higher utility with states of the world in which, all else being equal, she consumes more dark chocolate and fewer other kinds of chocolate than with states in which consumption is reversed. Many theorists take utility to denote a measure of subjective psychological fulfilment (this is indeed how the concept was generally interpreted by Bentham and others into the 1930s).

Partly due to the rising influence of behaviourism (Chapter 9, sec. 1.1), some objected to the theoretical use of 'unobservable' entities like psychological states and their fulfilment. The economist Paul Samuelson (1938) set out to give an alternative definition of utility in such a way that it becomes a purely technical concept. No direct appeal to psychological states would then be needed. On Samuelson's proposal, an agent's utility is simply whatever it is that the agent's behaviour suggests she consistently desires. This is a circular definition, but theorists who follow Samuelson intend the statement 'agents act so as to maximize their expected utility' as a tautology. Though the tautology is not useful in itself, it does serve a role in fixing the context of inquiry. It also serves another important function. Many rational-choice theorists think the concept of utility – and rational-choice theory in general – should apply to any kind of agent: persons, bears, ants, companies or even countries. They do not want a theory restricted simply to agents with human minds and psychological states. So when these theorists say that agents act so as to maximize their expected utility, this is to be part of the definition of what it is to be an agent, not an empirical claim about possible inner states or motivations.

A further piece to the picture was added by psychologists. During the 1950s, psychologists adopted various tools for statistical inference and data analysis. Once entrenched, these tools came to be viewed as models for cognitive processes once behaviourism's prohibition on cognitive processes began to loose its grip (Gigerenzer and Murray 1987). Various kinds of statistical methods became models for how the mind made causal attributions or how the mind detected and discriminated among stimuli. Further, these statistically based cognitive mechanisms came to be associated with the calculation of utilities and the maximization of expected utilities.

2. Rational-actors picture

We are now in a position to more fully characterize the *rational-actors picture*. On this picture, as mentioned above, rational actors possess a complete, transitive ordering of preferences. Additionally, this picture of rational agents assumes that preferences are largely strategic – that is, preferences are aimed at goals or objectives important to the agent. This is also a *zweckrational* picture of reasoning – rational agents focus on the best or most effective means for achieving these goals (recall the kind of means–ends reasoning Hardin cites as leading to population problems discussed in Chapter 8, sec. 2). Furthermore, rational agents, in this picture, have complete information about their preferences and all possible courses of action, as well as about other agents' preferences and courses of action. Reasoning always follows strictly logical or some other law-like or algorithmic form and agents are completely devoid of cognitive limitations (e.g., they have perfect memory, think infinitely quickly, etc.). Crucially, the rational-actors picture – consistent with an emphasis on strategic rationality – assumes that rational agents always act so as to maximize their expected utilities. In other words, agents are fundamentally self-interested rather than others-interested. Finally, utilities are assumed to have cardinal measurability – they come in discrete units – and can be compared between people.

Given all these assumptions, this picture of agents purports to explain behaviour. Presumably, if agents act rationally according to this picture, we can understand why they behave as they do in a given set of circumstances. Equally, if not more important from a practical standpoint, the rational-actors picture in principle enables precise predictions of their choices and actions. All we need to know are agents' preferences and utilities. Assume an agent knows all the possible pizza combinations available. Given this information and knowledge of his favourite pizza, we could accurately predict which one he will order. This predictive power would enable economists, for example, to make judgements and recommendations about welfare so that governments can appropriately distribute goods and benefits to those in need. If a government is committed to maximizing total expected utility, and can see that welfare resources have more impact on the poor than the rich, then it is rationally justified in distributing these resources to the former. Or the rational-actors picture could allow political scientists to forecast election outcomes for candidates and issues. Such ability might be crucial for a potential candidate's decision whether to run for elective office, or for helping a political group determine whether to invest in a particular ballot initiative.

Consistent with this emphasis on prediction, a large part of rational-choice theory focuses on the formalization of conditions of rationality and their implications. In addition to being a complete and transitive set, suppose an agent's preferences also satisfy a continuity condition. Then these preferences can be represented by an ordinal-utility function, U. This means that it is possible to define a function representing the agent's preferences so that:

U(X) > U(Y) if and only if the agent prefers X to Y

and

U(X) = U(Y) if and only if the agent prefers X and Y equally.

So the function U formally represents the preference ranking, but does not contain any information over and above this ranking.[4]

By adding a further independence condition on an agent's preferences, along with some other technical conditions, they can be represented by an expected-utility function. There are various forms an independence condition might take, but they all roughly assert that preferences between alternatives are somehow independent of the features the alternatives have in common. Suppose you are offered a choice between two bets involving flipping a fair coin. In both cases you lose $1 if the coin lands tails, but the prizes you would win if the coin lands heads differ. The independence condition says that if you are rational, your preference for one bet over the other turns on your preference for the prizes when the coin lands heads and not on the outcomes when the coins land tails.

2.1. Further developments: Savage's theory

Going back to Bentham, the rational-actors picture assumes that agents' desires, beliefs, hopes, fears – that is, their preferences – are all commensurable.

That is, the utility of every preference is measurable on the same scale so that comparisons among preferences and across agents can be made. This assumption does not follow from any picture of rationality; instead, it is a psychological hypothesis about preferences. Without this cardinal measurability assumption, the rational-actors picture would not work – there would be no way for reason to add up or weigh utilities.

We have no genuine evidence for this cardinality assumption about agents' preferences. Further, as previously mentioned, many have thought that an ideal conception of rationality ought to be independent of such psychological assumptions. Work by Vilfredo Pareto, Samuelson and Leonard Savage sought to set rationality on a firm, non-psychological foundation. Savage's (1954) theory of rationality is still considered by many to be the most satisfactory treatment of rational choice.

Fundamentally for Savage, rationality is to be understood in terms of the consistency of decisions with one another. There are three fundamental notions in his theory. The first is the concept of states of the world, which can be taken to be events like a coin toss turning up heads, two dice landing snake eyes or the local baker being sold out of bagels by 10 in the morning. The second fundamental concept is an act, by which Savage means a list of conceivable consequences. There is one consequence for each event and agents choose among consequences. An act might be the payoff for a coin landing heads or having to buy something more expensive from the baker if he has run out of bagels. The third fundamental concept is preference and an agent's preference is taken to be *revealed* by the choice she makes among acts. In this way, Savage does not directly invoke assumptions about what preferences are; he only needs agents to reveal their preferences through their behaviours.

Given these fundamental concepts, Savage makes a number of postulates (some of which are technical). Roughly, the four main postulates are: (1) that rational actors have a complete, transitive ordering of preferences over all conceivable acts, (2) that an actor's preferences can be defined between any given pair of acts given that the corresponding events can conceivably occur, (3) that such preferences only depend on the consequences of those acts in that event and are independent of the description of the event itself and (4) that one event is subjectively more probable than another if the actor would prefer to bet on the first rather than the second. From the postulates, Savage derived a theorem to the effect that an actor whose preferences satisfy all the postulates will choose as if she is maximizing her expected utility. Moreover, it is possible to assign a number or weight to each consequence so that the ranking of consequences by number or weight is identical to the actor's ranking. These numbers play the role of utilities of the corresponding consequences. And it turns out that these numbers can be chosen so that for every pair of acts, the ranking of acts in terms of expected utility will correspond to their ranking in the actor's preference ordering.

So on Savage's theory, no explicit psychological assumptions about desires or beliefs are made. Agents can be pictured as if they are making utilitarian calculations involving measures of utility and probability to arrive at the expected utility of each act among their possibilities for choice. The utilities and probabilities as well as their meaning are supposed to be revealed by the choices agents make. So the mathematical framework is similar to the one used in the rational-actors picture previously described, but the psychological assumptions about preferences and utilities supposedly are gone.

Savage's theory, for all its elegance, is far from problem free however. For instance, it still assumes all of the perfect or idealized rationality assumptions mentioned above (e.g., that choice is made in some algorithmic fashion, that people have complete information available to them and are free from cognitive deficits). Moreover, it is plagued with paradoxical explanations for people's behaviour like coordination among many persons, commitment, self-sacrifice, suffering, reflection and hesitation (see Hollis and Sugden 1993; Jaeger et al. 2001). There are a number of attempted resolutions of these paradoxes within the theory, but given the assumption that agents are fundamentally self-regarding, these attempted resolutions all look very counter-intuitive and seem to be constructed merely to save the theory as opposed to being soundly motivated within the theory.

Second, all reasons or motivations for action are always forward-looking and never backward-looking. In other words, choices are always motivated by strategic reasons about future expectations and never by feelings of guilt, remorse or shame over past actions. On the face of things, this looks to leave out a number of powerful emotional reasons motivating some people's actions like giving to charities to assuage a guilty conscience or out of a sense of shame or embarrassment over one's wealth. Or the history of dealings or agreements between two parties is completely wiped out by the description of consequences simply in terms of utilities and forward-looking reasons. Defenders of Savage's view usually respond to this problem by reinterpreting such backward-looking motivations as utility numbers representing a future restored reputation, say. But there are at least two problems with this move. One is that it removes all trace or grounds of the reasons for someone's actions and turns all motivations into numbers or weights – the utilities. Second, this move simply misdescribes our everyday motives and behaviour. Hardly any choice we make is purely forward-looking, but is always coloured by our past. To say otherwise is to try to theorize real behaviours into something other than what they are; this is no innocent objective, accurate description but a reinterpretation of people's actions!

A third difficulty for Savage's theory is the assumption that preferences are independent of the description of events. This assumption is needed for technical reasons, but if it is not the case that people's desires, beliefs, feelings about things and so forth are independent of the description of events, then the theory is unworkable. But recall, as we saw in Chapter 6, sec. 3, that events admit of multiple descriptions and furthermore, that these differing descriptions need not be identical in meaning. In fact, different descriptions will typically carry different shades of meaning or interpretation of events. Why, then, should we expect a person's preferences to be insensitive to these different descriptions? Beliefs, desires, feelings and the way people see things vary in reaction to differences in description or meaning (e.g., the glass half-empty vs. the glass half-full, in general a description emphasizing negatives rather than positives). So Savage's theory must actually assume not only that multiple descriptions of events are equivalent in meaning, but that this equivalence is readily apparent to people – rather unrealistic assumptions to say the least. Or, if Savage's theory is not making these kinds of assumptions about transparent, univocal meaning among multiple descriptions, then it is making an equally unrealistic assumption about people's ways of seeing things being completely independent of the descriptions of things.

A final problem is that, contrary to the claim that it is independent of any psychological assumptions, Savage's theory is actually shot through with such assumptions. The absence of mental states like beliefs, desires, feelings and so forth is the assumption of psychological behaviourism (Chapter 9, sec. 1.1). And the operations of choice and preference ranking must take place along lines similar to stimulus–response–reinforcement cycles. What other possibilities are there for the agents pictured in the theory? These are hardly innocent psychological assumptions. In addition, the account of forward-looking reasons as motivation *is* a psychological analysis of motivation, so Savage has not given us a theory that is free of psychological assumptions. Furthermore, his account makes substantial metaphysical assumptions about agents just like the rational-actors picture generally (see below). There are serious commitments to cultural ideas of liberal individualism, in the form of ontological and utilitarian individualism (Chapter 5) as well as an instrumental picture of action (Chapter 4). So this theory of rationality harbours serious moral commitments as well (see below).

3. Methodological individualism and the rational-actors picture

Historically, both Friedrich von Hayek and Popper, among others, were strongly motivated to pursue methodological individualism (Chapter 7) so as to avoid grand theories in the style of Marx. This motivation had more to do with worries that such grand theorizing promoted 'collectivism', 'rationalism' or 'historicism'. Von Hayek and Popper thought these casts of mind were conducive to totalitarianism. As time wore on, and the dangers of creeping totalitarianism in Western societies seemingly became increasingly remote, this fear of collectivism motivating many debates over methodological individualism progressively weakened.

Serious discussion of methodological individualism might have disappeared completely had it not been for the sudden explosion of interest in rational-choice theory among social scientists beginning in the early 1980s. A key reason for this interest was the prisoner's dilemma and the development of game theory or game-theoretic analyses of individual and collective action. The game-theoretic framework provided a simple yet powerful model that could be used to represent the structure of individual interactions. This in turn gave new life to methodological individualism. Theorists could diagnose more precisely the errors that social theorists could be (and often were) making when they ignored the motivations and actions of individuals. Methodological individualism became important, not as a way of avoiding the political thought-crime of 'collectivism', but rather as a way of avoiding demonstrably fallacious inferences about the dynamics of collective action. While the existence of a common interest might seem motivation enough for explaining the actions of agents, it appears to generate a free-rider incentive. Individuals benefit from acting to promote the common interest, but they would benefit even more by sitting back while other members of the group acted to promote it. But if each individual benefits more by free-riding, then no one has motivation to act to promote the common interest.

The prisoner's dilemma takes a very simple form and illustrates the kind of game-like structures occupying much rational-choice theorizing. Suppose

Table 10.1 Simple Prisoner's Dilemma

	Confess	Do not Confess
Prisoner 1	3,3	1,5
Prisoner 2	5,1	2,2

two suspects are taken into custody and separated. Although the authorities believe that the suspects are guilty of a robbery, say, they do not have adequate evidence to gain a conviction in court. The authorities sit down with each prisoner individually and go over the following alternatives. If both do not confess, they will be charged with some lesser crime like illegal possession of a weapon. Consequently, the prisoners will both receive minor punishment. If they both confess, they will be prosecuted. But in return for confessing, the authorities will recommend a penalty less than the maximum sentence. However, if one prisoner confesses while the other does not, then the confessor will receive lenient treatment for turning state's evidence while the latter will get the maximum sentence. The problem for each prisoner, then, is to decide to confess or not.

The decision is converted into the rational-actors picture in the following way. Suppose the consequences of each decision are represented by their pay-offs, the number of years in prison to be converted into expected utilities (in Table 10.1, the first number in the ordered pair refers to the sentence prisoner 1 would receive, the second number refers to the sentence prisoner 2 would receive based on their individual decisions).

If neither prisoner confesses, they would each get a lighter sentence of 2 years. If they both confess, then they would each get 3 years. Finally, if the first prisoner confesses, while the second prisoner does not, then the first prisoner gets 1 year while the second gets 5. If the second prisoner confesses while the first does not, then the second prisoner gets 1 year while the first gets 5. The task then is to deploy the rational-actors picture to determine what is the rational choice for each prisoner to make while emphasizing the individual nature of the choices.

The distinction between methodological individualism and the rational-actors picture progressively blurred in the latter half of the twentieth century. For instance, Elster (1989) assumes that commitment to methodological individualism leads to a commitment to rational-choice theory. Elster's picture of rational choice explicitly endorses the instrumental picture of action: 'actions are valued and chosen not for themselves, but as more or less efficient means to a further end' (1989: 22). He further argues that instrumental rationality is implied by the fact that rational-choice theorists are able to represent the rational actions of any agent possessing a well-behaved preference ordering as the maximization of a utility function (e.g., via Savage's theorem). Not everyone who endorses the rational-actors picture agrees with Elster's arguments on this instrumental connection. Nevertheless, Elster's arguments played a crucial role in methodological individualism becoming widely identified with the rational-actors picture.[5] The problem with this identification, however, is that it implies that individualist explanations must be in terms of the rational-actors picture. Although this picture of rationality is normative – prescribing when an agent acts rationally – methodological individualism is presumably independent of the kinds of rationality in which agents engage (including acting irrationally in various ways).

4. Criticisms of the rational-actors picture

The rational-actors picture is quite elegant in many respects. And it appears to give a very clear standard for what rationality is that can be widely applied across the social sciences (examples are discussed in Chapters 11 and 12). On the other hand, it is a deeply problematic picture of human rationality and action.

A simple difficulty with the rational-actors picture concerns the individuation of the objects of preference or choice. Consider what is called a multistage ultimatum game. Smith can propose any division of $100 between herself and Jones (an ultimatum). Jones can accept or reject Smith's proposal. If Jones rejects the proposal, then the amount of money drops to $50, and he gets to offer a division of the $50 which Smith can accept or reject (a second ultimatum). If Smith rejects Jones' offer, then both get nothing. Suppose that Smith proposes to divide the money with $70 for herself and $30 for Jones. He declines and offers to split the $50 evenly ($25 for each). Assuming that Jones prefers more money to less, this choice appears to be a violation of the transitivity condition on preferences. Jones prefers $30 to $25, yet he declines a sure $30 for the possibility of $25 (there is a slight chance Smith will decline Jones' ultimatum resulting in both getting nothing).

This behaviour looks irrational under the rational-actors picture, but, in fact, is common (Ochs and Roth 1989: 362). Under the rational-actors picture, the objects of choice are quantities of money. Actually, there is more going on in the choice situation than just money and preferences for potential economic gain. Jones is turning down $30 as part of 'a raw deal' – the unfair division of the $100 Smith originally proposed. So Jones actually favours getting $25 as part of a fair arrangement to getting $5 more as part of an unfair arrangement. So long as the objects of choice are defined as money, then transitivity fails. However, if the objects of choice include matters of fairness, there is no failure of transitivity because fairness is preferred by Jones to any possible amount of money he might get in the game.

This is a very plausible observation, but it raises a serious problem. Without some constraints on how the objects of choice are individuated, conditions of rationality such as transitivity are empty. Fairness is not the same kind of object as money. Jones' choice of X over Y, Y over Z and Z over X does not violate transitivity if 'X is preferable to alternative Y' is not the same object of choice as 'X is preferable to alternative Z'. At the very least, additional substantive conditions have to be imposed on how to individuate choices. But the nature of choices like preferring justice or fairness over receiving more money are morally laden and have much to do with how people see their situations, not some quantification of utilities. So it is unlikely that some kind of objective or non-interest-relative constraints could be imposed.

A second problem arises from the basic idea that agents maximize their expected utilities. This presupposes some notion of expectation. However, there are several possible mathematical definitions of expectation: arithmetic mean (i.e., the average of a set of numbers), geometric mean (i.e., the nth root of a set of numbers), median (i.e., the middle of a distribution of numbers). And if we want to take uncertainties in expected utilities into account, then there are numerous measures of variability about some expected value. But there is nothing about the world – or that we know about reasoning – that picks out any one of these definitions or measures as being uniquely true. Without that uniqueness, there is ambiguity in the mathematical formalization of the rational-actors picture.

The rational-actors picture is a normative picture of rationality, meaning that it sets the standard for what rationality ought to be. If an agent fulfils all the conditions specified in this picture, but makes a choice contrary to what this picture identifies as rational, she has acted irrationally. Or if an agent does not meet all the requirements, then she is judged as being deficient or limited in the respects where she falls short. But this standard of rationality is problematic as it assumes so many unrealistic idealizations rendering it poorly suited as a guide to human rationality. The unsuitability of the rational-actors picture is witnessed by its stunning failures in explanatory and predictive power in laboratory as well as everyday situations (Tversky and Kahneman 1981; Rayner 1986; Ochs and Roth 1989; Tversky and Thaler 1990; Hollis and Sugden 1993; Jaeger et al. 2001). Some of these difficulties will be discussed in Chapters 11 and 12.

4.1. The rational actors picture and plausibility

Given its problems, and its rather implausible assumptions (e.g., complete preference rankings, complete knowledge of all outcomes, no cognitive deficits, perfect algorithmic reasoning), why is the rational-actors picture considered so plausible by so many? Part of its plausibility derives from the use of everyday stories to dress up and hide the gross idealizations of the picture, as well as to provide an interpretation of the elements of the framework. Otherwise, the assumptions only provide a mathematical framework for proving theorems, but no connection with real-world phenomena. As such, without everyday stories to provide an interpretation of the mathematical elements of the framework, the rational-actors picture would not have any empirical content and, hence, would not be testable.

Consider the prisoner's dilemma story told above. It depicts a scene with which we are all familiar from books and TV, a scene where strategic decisions would clearly be expected to be in play. Such a scene matches the abstract structure of a strategic game under an appropriate interpretation. All the actors in the scene are clearly identified as well as all the alternatives and consequences. The story, then, functions as an interpretation of the rational-actors picture of rationality as well as the 'consequence matrix' depicted in Table 10.1 earlier. Technically, all we need are the assumptions of the rational-actors picture, the actors' preferences and this consequence matrix, and the rational decisions on the part of the actors are completely determined. But the story allows us to match up elements of the rational-actors picture and the consequence matrix with concrete features of the scenario. One can argue that only to the extent that the story and interpretive matching are highly plausible would the rational-actors picture have explanatory and possibly predictive power (Grüne-Yanoff and Schweinzer 2005).

One thing to note about the interpretive work such stories accomplish is that they transmute a decision situation into cases of strategic rationality. This may be fine when describing a situation where strategic decisions are being made. But if every decision in everyday situations is supposed to be translated into the rational-actors picture, then such stories serve to distort decisions rather than merely connect situations with the rational-actors picture. Suppose you are trying to decide whether to buy a car and the primary factor is whether to purchase a hybrid, flexible-fuel or high-fuel-mileage, conventional-fuel car. These are clearly components of a strategic decision situation, where economics over the lifetime of the car are the main factors. On the other hand, suppose you are only interested in which car is more fun for you to drive no matter what the economics. Then it is much less plausible that you are engaged in strategic rationality, so deploying a story to reinterpret this choice as a case of strategic rationality in the rational-actors picture looks to distort your choice into something it is not.[6]

There are other ways to manipulate the story so as to make the rational-actors picture look more plausible. If we stipulate that neither prisoner has any qualms about turning state's evidence against the other prisoner, then the situation resembles one of strategic rationality more. However, if we were to stipulate that both prisoners felt duty bound by the 'criminal's code of honour' to not rat on a fellow criminal, then the idea that strategic rationality is the crucial feature of the scenario looks much less plausible. This raises two additional problems for the scenarios that are being shunted into the rational-actors picture. First, every scenario is capable of indefinite redescription and each description can be indefinitely refined. But this feature seriously impacts on just how a given scenario 'fits' with the rational-actors picture because as the descriptions are refined or the situations redescribed, the meanings change (see Chapter 6, sec. 3). Unless one is purposely describing a situation, or refining a given description, so as to fit the rational-actors picture as closely as possible, there is no guarantee that either the new or more refined description will plausibly bear much relationship to the picture. In turn, this means that there really is no objective description of a given situation demonstrating that the situation really is one of strategic rationality suited for the rational-actors picture.

As another example, consider the rational-actors picture applied to explaining addiction – so-called rational-addicts theories (Becker and Murphy 1988; Elster and Skog 1999). On these kinds of theories, addicts are pictured as forming rational plans regarding optimal consumption and as having stable preferences. In other words, the utility-maximization picture is applied to addicts seeking their highs. Considering addicts as rational actors – applying instrumental reasoning to determine the most effective means for maximizing their utility – is a stretch to say the least. Typically, we take addicts to be paradigm examples of people behaving irrationally to their harm (but that is because we draw on a different action of rationality in such judgements). The very idea that addicts are operating without any cognitive deficits, are really taking their long-term interests into account, and are applying flawless logic or some other decision algorithm to their choices seems absurd. But storytelling can do much to cover up the implausibility of the rational-actors picture of addiction (see Rogeberg 2004).

Various things might be addictive to a person such as cigarettes, cocaine, jogging, religion or gambling. On rational-addiction theories, we usually tell stories about addictions along the lines of the following. The more an addict smokes or injects something today, for instance, the worse off she will be to-morrow regarding her health. But the more she smokes or injects today, the more rewarding her experienced high will be (the higher her marginal utility[7] in the addictive commodity). Moreover, participating in her addiction may also bring status and acceptance she desires with a particular social crowd, making her addiction beneficial to her for more than just the high it brings (achieving other preferences she has). So the perceived benefits and her preferences lead her to continue her addiction and to form rational plans to optimize her pay-offs through the addiction. To quit her addiction today – for example, going cold turkey – brings more suffering today (lowering her marginal utility in the addictive commodity). But quitting her addiction can bring her improvements in health, not to mention easing the significant drain on her bank account the addiction represents (raising the marginal utility of other goods she might pur-sue). Or perhaps she meets the man of her dreams and he is drug-free. This change in her circumstances might make her addiction seem of much less value to her now (decreasing the marginal utility of the addictive commodity). By adding up the utilities of these other preferences, the addict may come to see that kicking the habit is the way to go for her life. If so, rational-addiction theory says that the marginal utility of her addiction now is very low relative to the other utilities. Rationally it is now impossible for her to continue in her addiction be-cause these preferences now outweigh her preference for smoking or injecting.

Such storytelling connects alternative preferences to utility values so that the machinery of the rational-actors picture operates to both explain the addiction and predict under what conditions the addict will quit (when the marginal utility of the addictive commodity is lower than other utilities in her other preferences). Again, these scenarios are capable of indefinite refinement in their descriptions as well as redescriptions. And any given refinement or re-description is not guaranteed to preserve the rational-actors picture unless the storyteller *explicitly strives* to keep to interpretations and refinements that continue to connect the scenario with the elements of that framework. So there is no objective description of a situation such as addiction demonstrating that the rational-actors picture of addiction is somehow true. But it is easily possible for the advocate of the rational-actors picture to fool himself into thinking that it plausibly applies to any given situation by interpreting and describing it to fit his preferred picture as do advocates of rational-addiction theories.

A second, and related, problem is that as self-interpreting beings, people's views of situations are deeply coloured by the meanings and interpretations that animate them. As discussed earlier (Parts One and Two), the actions and decisions of self-interpreting beings are largely constituted by their self-understandings. One thing this implies is that no situation is one of strategic rationality unless the persons involved see it as such. To describe a situation involving choice as one where the rational-actors picture is applicable is to arbitrarily impose a particular theoretical perspective on the actors themselves whenever they actually see their situation differently from that of the theoretical description. This is another example of how theoretical description can actually change the meanings of people and the practices in which they are engaged. Unless there is some non-interest-relative, objective evidence or reasons for giving a description suited for the rational-actors picture, then the description ends up making substantial assumptions about people that stand in need of serious justification; otherwise, the assumptions are purely arbitrary.

4.2. The rational-actors picture and cultural ideals

This last point leads to a second reason so many find the rational-actors picture so plausible: the role of cultural ideals as disguised ideologies (Part Two). A good deal of the supposed plausibility of the rational-actors picture derives from cultural ideals like the instrumental picture of action, autonomy and liberal individualism.

For example, the rational-actors picture presupposes social atomism (Chapter 9, sec. 3) in that it assumes all social actions are simply aggregations of individual choices. It also assumes rationality is a property of individuals (i.e., that there is no such thing as an independent larger social or collective rationality). But this is the ontological individualism that underlies liberal individualism (Chapter 5, sec. 2.1). Furthermore, with its emphasis on agents as being largely expected-utility maximizers, the rational-actors picture clearly exemplifies utilitarian individualism (Chapter 5, sec. 2.2). Even when the rational-actors picture is applied to social action, groups, institutions and even governments are interpreted as utility-maximizing individual agents to fit them into the picture. But this can be very problematic from the standpoint of understanding collective action and forming social and economic policy. For instance, urban sprawl creates numerous sustainability challenges: for example, jobs–housing imbalances, concentrated poverty, fiscal disparities, socio-economic polarization, pollution and health risks, habitat loss, species endangerment. The rational-actors picture addresses such difficulties by modelling individual people, families, businesses and governments as individual agents seeking to maximize their utility. However, the challenges presented by urban sprawl call for concerted collective action, the kind of action that the rational-actors picture is ill-suited to address (Jaeger et al. 2001).

Moreover, this framework clearly exemplifies an instrumental picture of action. It transmutes all decision situations into cases of strategic decision-making, as well as turning all decisions into problems of maximizing expected utility. Although we sometimes face exactly these kinds of situations in life, not all decisions we face are of this nature – perhaps the majority are not. The rational-actors picture does not discriminate between kinds of choices, but views them all as instrumental matters of maximizing expected utility, illustrating exactly the kind of confusion between technical knowhow and moral knowhow critical theorists have identified (Chapter 4, sec. 3).

Cultural ideals such as liberal individualism and the instrumental picture of action, operating as disguised ideologies, do much to cover up the implausibility of the rational-actors picture. Such ideals reinforce the rational-actors picture as a credible – some might even say true – view of human rationality. After all, if everyone is a utilitarian individualist, then the rational-actors picture is the right one to use for characterizing individual choices. In actuality, the rational-actors picture represents a substantially morally animated picture of action, one that also tends to reinforce the cultural ideals animating it. After all, if the rational-actors picture is true, then everyone should be a utilitarian individualist. To the extent that social scientists, policy-makers and others trumpet the rational-actors picture as a scientific view of human rationality and action, they surreptitiously endorse and reinforce the very cultural ideals that underlie so many problems with modern Western ways of life.

Sometimes these cultural ideals can be quite damaging in their effects (as in transmuting all action into cases of instrumental action). The extreme picture of self-interested individuals as mostly pursuing their own utility maximization is a case in point. As noted above (sec. 2.1), this particular feature of the rational-actors picture causes serious problems for explaining social cooperation, self-sacrifice and suffering, high marks of spiritual and ethical development on almost all religious and moral perspectives. But the adherence to the view of all agents as self-interested paints a very dark picture of humanity, one that encourages us to go further in our hyper-individualism to get all our needs met. Fortunately, our spiritual and moral traditions stand squarely opposed to this self-interested feature of the rational-actors picture. But being told by scientists who still carry much weight as authority figures in our culture that we are fundamentally driven by concern to maximize our individual utility tends to break down the spiritual and moral barriers to self-serving behaviour. These restraints act to rein in what many would call our worst behaviour, not our fundamentally scientific behaviour. So once again we see that the supposed objective, scientific picture – in this case the rational-actors picture – is anything but objective or value-neutral. It actually reinforces a particular ethical picture of people as self-interested agents whether the advocates of the rational-actors picture wish to do this or not.

4.3. Wordy elaborations of the obvious

Those blinded to the implausibility of the rational-actors picture by the considerations just elaborated, often hail this framework as delivering important insights into various social phenomena like the emergence of cooperative behaviour among self-interested agents. Consider the following recent summary of work within the rational-actors picture, some of it focused on game theory:

> Recent models have demonstrated how evolutionary processes (genetic or cultural) can maintain cooperation in large groups or without repeated interactions. Costly signaling models have shown how cooperation by 'high-quality individuals' (those who are potentially desirable as allies or mates) can be sustained if such individuals can accurately signal their quality by making substantial cooperative contributions to public goods . . . For example, great hunters might supply all the meat for a public feast, or millionaires might donate a recreational center to their community. Similarly, reputation-based models have shown how cooperation can be sustained if individuals' reputations for not contributing to public goods reduce their own payoffs (or fitness) by altering how others treat them in certain dyadic social interactions. . . Finally, models that allow individuals to both contribute to the public good and to [punish] noncontributors have revealed stable cooperative solutions, especially when the strategies for cooperation and punishment are influenced by social learning. . . Thus, a number of possible stable solutions to the puzzle of cooperation in large groups, or cooperation without repeated interaction, have now emerged. (Henrich 2006)

Notice that stories play a role in making these results more plausible to the reader as well as the emphasis on strategic and instrumental features. However, it is simply false that insights or solutions to the 'puzzle of cooperation . . . have now emerged'. We have known about what makes cooperative behaviour tick at least since the times of ancient Greece (Aristotle anyone?). What has emerged in recent times is a mathematical framework to model such behaviours, but it does not provide any new insights into cooperative behaviour. In fact, the rational-actors picture is much less deep in what meagre insights it can deliver than our great spiritual and moral traditions (gruel compared to a four-course Italian dinner). Moreover, the rational-actors picture actually obscures what goes on in social behaviour due to its wildly implausible assumptions about what constitutes rational agents, particularly its emphasis on strictly self-regarding behaviour.

Many might argue that the cultural and social developments represented in our religious and moral traditions are really due to biological evolution (hinted in Henrich's quote). But that response presupposes that cultural and social phenomena are reducible to biological phenomena. And this presupposition depends on the philosophical urban legend that reductionism is true, an urban legend distinctly lacking evidence (see Chapter 7, sec. 2.1).

4.4. The rational-actors picture and falsifiability

Also as noted above, the rational-actors picture rarely fares well in terms of its predictions versus empirical evidence (Tversky and Kahneman 1981; Rayner 1986; Ochs and Roth 1989; Tversky and Thaler 1990; Hollis and Sugden 1993; Jaeger et al. 2001). There are ways to try and cope with this problem. One is to bite the bullet, admit that the rational-actors picture falls short empirically and abandon the framework for a more suitable one (e.g., Gigerenzer and Selten 2001). Another possibility is to treat the rational-actors picture as an analytic reconstruction of the factors used to make decisions. Whether or not people actually choose in the way the framework pictures them is beside the point. All that matters is whether the outcomes of decision processes are close to what the framework predicts. In other words, treat human beings *as if* they are idealized rational actors. This response does not really go very far in addressing the stark predictive failures of the rational-actors picture.

Another response is to recognize the serious inadequacies of the framework and attempt to modify it to meet the evidence. Unfortunately, most of these latter attempts are either very ad hoc and counter-intuitive, or they actually render the framework unfalsifiable. Popper defended what he called a falsificationist methodology, where scientists should formulate theories and hypotheses that are 'logically falsifiable'. That is, theories or hypotheses must be possibly inconsistent with some possible observations. A standard example of a logically falsifiable statement is 'All swans are white'. All that is needed to prove it false is one instance of a non-white swan (e.g., a black one). Should a theory or hypothesis fail under testing, Popper maintained that scientists should be willing to reject it, provided there were alternative theories or hypotheses that had yet to fail any tests (Popper 1992: 87). However, passing a test for Popper does not confirm a theory or hypothesis or even provide positive evidence to believe it. It only justifies scientists in continuing to employ it since it has not yet been falsified. Furthermore, scientists should continue attempting to falsify theories and hypotheses until they fail such testing.

Falsificationism has severe drawbacks as a comprehensive analysis of scientific method, but the idea that theories and hypotheses must be at risk of being proven wrong is generally taken to be a crucial feature of science. Indeed, if a theory or hypothesis is unfalsifiable, it is generally believed to be unscientific.[8] On this score, the highly idealized rational-actors picture fares very poorly. It looks to have been falsified because of its failures in the face of empirical evidence. On the other hand, the framework looks to be unfalsifiable. If we examine the assumptions of the rational-actors picture, we see that it only holds under perfect conditions – conditions that are never actualized in our world. Hence, strictly speaking, the framework is not testable in our world because we can never implement the conditions necessary to test it. Often proponents of the rational-actors picture blame its failings on the imperfections of our world, but this renders the framework unfalsifiable as fault is always located outside the theory.

Even if proponents do not blame imperfect people in an imperfect world for the failures of the rational-actors picture, the framework is still easy to render unfalsifiable. A standard response to objections made earlier regarding cultural ideals and other values and meanings is to argue that these are simply influences playing a role in the formation of agents' preferences. The rationality picture, after all, does not presuppose anything about how people's preferences are formed, so the claim goes. However, this response renders the rational-actors picture unfalsifiable because any expression of behaviour can always be reconstructed in this fashion. This means that any deviation from the rational-actors picture supposedly can be saved by redescribing the preferences of agents suitably along the lines of these ideals and values influencing preferences. Hence, supposing such redescription is possible, clearly this simply means that if a defender is clever enough, she can recast the agent's preferences in such a way as to make the predictions of the rational-actors picture come out right. But this is the mark of a pseudo-science rather than a scientific approach to human action.[9]

Increasingly, effort is being focused on changing some of the assumptions in the rational-actors picture. For example, by relaxing the assumption that agents have perfect knowledge and, instead, allowing agents to learn as they go along, modelling comes closer to actual human behaviour. Or allowing agents to actually reflect and introspect on what they are doing seems to help as well. Although, these developments tend to create a picture with better predictive success, they also tend to drive home the point about wordy elaborations of the obvious even more as the picture of agents approaches our everyday picture of our selves and others.

5. Taking stock

There is another way in which the rational-actors picture is value-laden rather than value-neutral. Particularly in Western societies, we are greatly influenced by expert opinions. So if economists, political scientists and other social scientists trumpeting the rational-actors picture tell us we are utility maximizers or that we are mostly self-interested, we tend to believe them and behave accordingly. This is the double hermeneutic at work, where the theorizing of social scientists can actually change the way people see themselves which, in turn, shapes their behaviour (Chapter 3, sec. 2). This is also part of what Foucault means when he argues that social-science categories shape and reorient human living (Chapter 3, sec. 4.2). The rational-actors picture describes people as utility maximizers and as self-interested, two deeply moral qualities that are generally considered negative moral qualities.

One might respond to this by invoking Nagel's distinction between appraising and characterizing value judgements (see Chapter 6, sec. 1). What the rational-actors picture does, its advocates may claim, is characterize the extent to which people are utility maximizers and are self-interested.[10] The framework, and its advocates, do not appraise whether these are morally good or bad qualities. Rather, social scientists are trying to work out the consequences of these characterizations. But if the social scientist's conceptual picture of agents actually changes people's moral pictures of themselves and their behaviour, she is actually advocating the moral qualities of the conceptual picture as the picture of the good life whether she means to or not. In this sense, the rational-actors picture is not neutral towards the moral characterizations it contains; rather, it is decidedly partisan in favour of these moral qualities. After all, this is a *normative* picture of rationality! And the advocate of the rational-actors picture is also decidedly partisan in favour of these moral qualities as well to the extent that she argues the framework accurately describes people. She may personally detest self-interested people and behaviour, but in her pretence to be value-neutral, she leaves these appraisals out of her research. Ironically, by not being explicitly critical of these moral qualities of the framework, her advocacy of the rational-actors picture reinforces the very self-interested and utilitarian moral qualities she personally detests.

Once again we see that social science cannot avoid advocating values and a conception of the good life for everyone. The sooner social scientists and philosophers recognize and come to grips with this situation, the sooner we might make progress towards unravelling the deleterious effects of values and cultural ideals in the social sciences.

For further study

1. Pick three assumptions of the rational-actors picture and evaluate their plausibility.
2. Describe what you take to be the strongest objection to the rational-actors picture and say why.
3. How are disguised ideologies involved in the rational-actors picture?

Recommended reading

J. Henrich, 'Cooperation, Punishment, and the Evolution of Human Institutions', *Science* 312 (2006): 60–61.

C. C. Jaeger, O. Renn, E. A. Rosa and T. Webler, *Risk, Uncertainty, and Rational Action* (London: Earthscan 2001).

O. Rogeberg, 'Taking Absurd Theories Seriously: Economics and the Case of Rational Addiction Theories', *Philosophy of Science* 71 (2004): 263–85.

11 Political Science

Political science grew out of the discipline of political philosophy, leaving behind, so it was thought, various theoretical and value prejudices found in the latter. As the name suggests, political science adopted 'scientific methods', that is, natural-scientific modes of investigation, further distinguishing itself from political philosophy. Hence, political science is typically conceived as being a dispassionate scientific study of the facts of politics and political systems, among other things, free of metaphysical and value commitments. Along with this natural scientific turn comes the fact/value distinction. Political philosophy – going back at least to Plato and Aristotle – is the normative study of political structures and theories, where one can evaluate and argue about what ought to be the case. Ideally, political scientists strive to uncover and examine political facts independent of any evaluations.

Sheldon Wolin puts the difference between political science and more traditional political philosophy – political wisdom, if you will – this way:

> The antithesis between political wisdom and political science basically concerns two different forms of knowledge. The scientific form represents the search for rigorous formulations which are logically consistent and empirically testable. As a form, it has the qualities of compactness, manipulability, and relative independence of context. Political wisdom . . . [is found in]

history, knowledge of institutions, and legal analysis . . . knowledge of past political theories might also be added. Taken as a whole, this composite type of knowledge presents a contrast with the scientific type. Its mode of activity is not so much the style of the search as of reflection. It is mindful of logic, but more so of the incoherence and contradictoriness of experience. And for the same reason, it is distrustful of rigor. Political life does not yield its significance to terse hypotheses . . . Context becomes supremely important, for actions and events occur in no other setting. Knowledge of this type tends, therefore, to be suggestive and illuminative rather than explicit and determinate. (1972: 44–45)

For instance, imagine a political scientist is responding to the question 'Should social security be privatized?' This is a normative question, asking for what we ought to do as an answer. Ideally, the political scientist's response would be along the lines of citing how much support there is in Congress for passing such legislation or how proposed legislation would 'play among the voters'. In other words, her answer would be a descriptive one in terms of causes and effects, not moral reflection on what is the best way to address a social-insurance programme. However, this descriptive move is not so innocent as it might seem because it actually transforms the initial moral question into a political one. Whether the political scientist realizes it or not, she has implied that there is no distinction between normative and political questions. But this is no insignificant move because it opens the door wide open for disguised ideologies to masquerade as political facts in supposedly objective descriptions.

Another example would be studying correlations between voter attitudes and voting. This is taken to be a value-neutral way of uncovering political facts regarding voting behaviour, where statistical techniques might be used to enable political scientists to make inferences and predictions about further political facts (e.g., likely winners in the next election). But as we saw in Part Two, such inquiries are anything but value-neutral or objective. And it is no surprise that political science is no more value-free than any other social-science discipline: like others, it drinks deeply from disguised ideologies of political liberalism, liberal individualism and autonomy and tends to deploy the package deal of instrumental action and a subject-object ontology and epistemology.

1. Sketch of political science

As an academic discipline, political science emerged in the late 1800s.[1] The discipline exhibits largely natural-scientific and descriptivist forms of inquiry organized, in part, around topics of differing scale and character:

- Attitude/preference formation of citizens, voters and leaders; for example, how these various actors think about political outcomes, make voting choices, form their views of the political world.
- Social organizations, groups and classes; for example, organizational design, reform, community power.
- Institutions up to the size of nation-states and their constituent elements; for example, executives and legislatures, political parties, interest groups.
- International relations among nation-states; for example, interstate cooperation, national interests, trade.
- History of social and political organizations.

The methods employed by political scientists are quite varied, ranging from the study of texts, both historical and contemporary, to in-depth case studies of particular events or political figures and movements, to questionnaires and survey instruments. Though there is a wide variety of methods of inquiry, and the meaning of government and politics as subject matter can be quite broad, there is a strong emphasis on studying 'outcomes deemed important by participants or observers' (Polsby 2001: 11698).[2]

Early twentieth-century political science was dominated by an approach known as *institutional realism*. As the name suggests, there was an emphasis on the study of institutions like branches of government, political parties and interest groups. Realism comes from a focus on studying the actual relationships between these institutions in contrast to their legal relationships. The aim was to uncover the facts of the political realm, and explanations or descriptions were given at the level of institutions, consistent with a methodological holist approach (Chapter 7).

In response, a very influential movement known as *political behaviouralism* arose, advocating the application of the epistemology and methodology of the natural sciences to the study of political phenomena. Behaviouralism combined strands from behavioural psychology (Chapter 9, sec. 1.1), empirical sociology and economics (Chapter 12) and had as its goal the description, explanation and prediction of political phenomena based on quantitative data. Such data could be collected and analysed by borrowing techniques such as random sampling, questionnaires and statistical analysis from other social-science disciplines. This approach enshrines the fact/value distinction as a key feature of inquiry and, not surprisingly, emphasized explanation and prediction of the political realm in place of evaluating or changing that realm.

From the behaviouralist standpoint, the rest of political science was seen as lacking explanatory and predictive power as well as sophistication. Institutional realism, for example, failed to give an adequate explanation of the rise of European fascism through an analysis of institutions and their relations alone. Behaviouralists generally advocated methodological individualism as a proper approach to explanations (Chapter 7), Weber's aspiration for value-neutral judgements of political facts and the framework of logical positivism (Chapter 1, sec. 2.1). This was viewed as a rigorous, scientific approach to the study of political phenomena (Simon 1947).

Political behaviouralism was perhaps the dominant approach to political science in the 1960s and 1970s. After this time, the term behaviouralism fell out of favour (much as behaviourism did in psychology), but the empirical and methodological emphases of the movement continue to shape much contemporary political-science inquiry. In the shift away from realism to behaviouralism, the analysis of day-to-day politics receded into the background and was replaced by the analysis of theoretical concepts like political decisions, political roles, political systems, political power and interest groups.

It is through behaviouralism that political science picked up its strong orientation towards empirical theory (Chapter 3, sec. 1) as the basis for explaining and predicting political phenomena. Along with this orientation comes an emphasis on understanding the causes of political behaviour, both psychological and social.

Political theorizing under behaviouralism maintained that all theoretical terms and statements must be translatable into observable language (an affinity with logical positivism). That is to say, all theoretical statements somehow must be attributable to public, observable behaviour to be empirically confirmable or verifiable. Even attitudes and beliefs must be objectifiable, hence the widespread reliance on surveys that express such attitudes and beliefs as propositions with which people can agree or disagree. The demand for univocality of theoretical concepts and empirical data is also widespread throughout political science. This picture of theorizing contrasts sharply with that of classical political theory, which is largely based on philosophical or ethical norms – hence not value-neutral – or of Marxist theorizing.

The contemporary picture of theorizing in political science relaxes some of behaviouralism's constraints. Empirical demands are no longer seen as requiring every theoretical statement be translatable into some statement about observable behaviour. Instead, along with much of the rest of science and philosophy of science, the only demand is that theoretical statements be at least indirectly capable of confirmation or falsification. Nevertheless, the emphases on objectification and univocality remain.[3]

2. Methodological issues

So the conventional approach in political science is to pursue empirical theory with a view towards producing explanatory and predictive hypotheses and testing these hypotheses (see Geddes 2003). Mapping the law-like causal relations governing the political realm is one of the main goals of mainstream political science (universal-laws conception). Recalling the distinction between the contexts of discovery and justification (Chapter 2, sec. 5), there are a number of ways one might approach formulating theory in political science. One might take particular metaphysical and value commitments derived from political theory and/or other sources to fashion theory. One might start with careful observations of various sorts of regularities in political behaviour and generalize these to produce theory. Or one might focus on particular case studies, presidential elections, say, using these as a base to formulate theory. However one comes up with theory in the context of discovery, the proof of the pudding is only found in the confirmation of theory within the context of justification. It is this latter activity where the explanatory and predictive hypotheses derived from theory may be put to the test against the realities of the political realm (Elman and Elman 2001).

Whether the emphasis is on statistical methods or more qualitative approaches like case studies, political scientists largely focus on causal inference – deducing the causes underlying or bringing about the political phenomena of interest (Thomas 2005: 855–58). While there is much debate about the appropriate methodology for uncovering cause–effect relations (methodological conception), mainstream political inquiry clearly takes place in a natural-scientific mode with descriptive modes offered as qualitative alternatives or complements.

The example of using voter surveys to uncover correlations between voter attitudes and voting behaviour illustrates a typical quantitative methodology (Chapter 6, sec. 1). One much discussed qualitative approach is that of *case studies* (Thomas 2005). A case study is generally conceived as a detailed examination of a particular example from a class of phenomena (e.g, the 2000

US presidential election from among the class of presidential elections). A traditional use of case studies has been in the preliminary design of some larger research project (perhaps to be carried out with a quantitative methodology). On the traditional view, single cases, no matter how detailed, cannot yield reliable information about the class as a whole, and, hence, cannot be used to produce the kinds of generalizations needed for genuine empirical theory. But single cases can be useful for formulating hypotheses that might be tested systematically against several cases from the same class. Various sorts of correlational methods and statistical measures might then be employed to test the hypotheses and produce genuine generalizations.

There are other uses of case studies than the traditional one. A case study might be used to sharpen the definition of key concepts involved in aspects of the political arena. And comparison of individual cases can help produce and sharpen classifications and categorizations relevant to political theorizing. It is increasingly acknowledged that there is a link between the study of cases and the development of theories. As we refine and deepen our study of cases, we refine theories. The idea is that as we achieve a better understanding of cases and the concepts involved, we are enabled to build better theories (Ragin 2004). Additionally, the in-depth study of one or a few cases may shed light on the underlying causes at work in a class of phenomena as well as the context-sensitivity of these causes, that is, how the causes work together to produce their effects (Thomas 2005: 859–63). This kind of detailed causal knowledge is particularly difficult to divine from data sets and statistical methods. And if purchase can be gained on causal mechanisms by in-depth case study, then genuine generalizations may be possible based on such studies and cases may serve well for testing causal hypotheses (Eckstein 1975).

In a recent review essay aimed at showing that quantitative methods have qualitative foundations – indeed, that qualitative and quantitative methods are converging in some sense – George Thomas summarizes an important role of qualitative methods and judgements in political-science theorizing:

> Before we can elaborate our theoretical arguments, we need to conceptualize what we are talking about. This begins from our understanding of the world, and it is an essentially qualitative project. Indeed, the first step in concept formation is picking words to describe what we are talking about. Even if we go with accepted definitions, we are relying on past qualitative judgments. Assigning cases to our conceptual definition also requires qualitative judgments. As we examine cases, compare and contrast them, we refine their boundaries and gain important conceptual distinctions. This will

give us both more homogeneous cases for proper comparison and a sharper conceptual understanding of what we are talking about . . . This qualitative work is foundational to quantitative or statistical tests of theory. It requires that we specify concrete criteria by which to measure concepts, so that our measurements will allow for the assignment of cases to particular categories based upon the operationalized concepts . . . This is all central to carrying out rigorous testing of theory that other researchers can replicate . . . Even when scholars take off-the-shelf indicators to measure a concept, or apply a well-defined concept to new cases, such judgments are unavoidably qualitative. In fact, relying on off-the-shelf indicators and extending concepts to a greater number of cases so they may be properly tested raises concerns about conceptual stretching and measurement validity. Picking up concepts and allying them to new empirical situations may lead to invalid causal inference. (2005: 858)

There are a number of things to note about this passage. First, beginning with our 'understanding of the world' means beginning with social and political reality as we conceive it. In Western democracies, this means starting with the cultural ideals of political liberalism, liberal individualism and autonomy that largely shape social and political reality (whether we are aware of them or not). To the extent that political scientists are unaware of how these ideals are at work in societies they study – and they are largely unaware – is the extent to which disguised ideologies shape their theorizing and research. One of the consequences of there being only insiders' perspectives is that there are no culture-free understandings of the political and social worlds. Many political scientists acknowledge that values are involved in problem selection and definition, selection of methodology, concept formation and the like, but believe, like Weber, that the results of their research are value-neutral if appropriate attention has been paid to proper methodology. But this misses the point of disguised ideologies (Part Two).

Clearly the fact/value distinction is at work here. That liberal Christians tend to vote Democratic may be judged either encouraging or deplorable, but the fact of this tendency is taken to be neutral with respect to such judgements. Simply describing such political facts is not very illuminating – no science is just a collection of facts. Political science, if it is to deliver on its promises of explanation and insight must go beyond mere accumulation of facts. This, of course, is what empirical theory is supposed to do for political science, to make plain and systematic the features of political and social reality explaining such facts as the above, or that sitting vice-presidents, running on peace, prosperity and a sound economy associated with the policies of their administration, usually win in a landslide. On the natural-scientific model, mapping the causal relations of politics would reveal all we wish to know in a value-free way, giving us 'just the facts' (e.g., clarifying how economic relations affect social structures and how political processes affect economic relations).

We have previously discussed a number of problems with this naive view of social inquiry. Political inquiry drinks just as deeply from the myth of value-neutrality as all other social sciences. Natural-scientific and descriptivist modes of inquiry attempt to avoid value judgements, but this hampers political scientists from giving penetrating analyses of political phenomena (see Chapter 3, sec. 3). Worse, the pretence to value-neutrality and objectivity represents subtle advocacy of political liberalism and its notion of neutrality as the chief good (see Chapter 5, sec. 1). Or, as was noted in our discussion of correlations between voter attitudes and voting behaviours (Chapter 6, sec. 1), the methods of data collection and analysis presuppose ideals of liberal individualism and autonomy. Furthermore, picking up 'off-the-shelf indicators' and applying 'well-defined concepts' to new situations also means passing on disguised ideologies if care and awareness are not exercised. Political science, like its social-science kin, often passes on disguised ideologies in its research and results (see Chapter 8).

Second, note that Thomas's summary makes clear the role of descriptivism as a qualitative approach in political science. Here, it is deployed in the service of clarifying concepts and definitions in preparation for the appropriate application of natural-scientific modes of inquiry (this is one sense in which Thomas sees a convergence or cooperation between quantitative – natural scientific – and qualitative – descriptivist – methods). It is assumed that political scientists can make sound judgements about descriptive vocabulary and conceptual definitions that pick out what is 'really going on' in an objective way. Given that both natural-scientific and descriptivist modes of inquiry share the package deal, their being used in cooperative fashion is perhaps not too surprising. Getting clear on concepts and categorizations, discerning which cases fall under these, refining the boundaries of categorizations and cases, improving conceptual distinctions and the like are all quintessential descriptivist tasks.

Doubtless such work will improve theorizing as Thomas and others suggest, but this also presupposes that the definition and boundaries of our concepts and categorizations are somehow objective. Examples of such concepts and definitions would be class (e.g., middle class, political class, socio-economic class), government, interest group, community and activist. However, there are no concepts or categorizations of social or political phenomena that are objective – they are all *interest-relative* (Chapter 13). That is, such phenomena like voting behaviours are not univocal – they admit of multiple interpretations and can be indefinitely categorized and refined depending on our purposes. The very concept of class, along with nebulous class boundaries, are drawn in numerous ways depending on what goals we have for analysis. In other words, the ways in which we cut up the political and social worlds for analysis are inseparable from the value commitments and purposes we have. Political and social classes do not exist apart from our conceptions and practices in the way that atomic particle masses do. This is a point descriptivist approaches overlook. To the extent political scientists engage in these kinds of qualitative activities, their categorizations and concept definitions will reflect whatever purposes and ideals are animating their research design and goals.[4] For instance, someone committed to a liberal-individualist view will catagorize political actions and institutions quite differently from how a committed Marxist would.

A related but more subtle point, is that Thomas's account presupposes the vocabulary used is purely descriptive and not, at least partially, constitutive of the practices and institutions being described. To be partially constituitive, means the vocabulary we use partly establishes what the practices and institutions are. But as we saw earlier (Chapter 7, sec 1), our political practices cannot be identified in abstraction from the language we use to describe them or to carry them out. That is to say the vocabulary used to describe the practices is shaped by the practices themselves – without the practices, the vocabulary could not be sensibly applied. And the practices cannot exist apart from the vocabulary which, in turn, illuminates and refines the practices.

Take voting as an example, something crucial to Western democracies and their institutions. For there to be such practices of voting, we need various distinctions. So there must be verdicts or outcomes such as some person being placed in office, or some measure being either passed or defeated. And there must be some criterion for determining the outcomes such as simple majority in the case of an election, or 60 votes out of 100 to shut off a filibuster in the US Senate. Further, there must be some specification of who is allowed to vote such as citizens in a presidential election, or the stockholders of a particular company at their annual meeting. These distinctions give meaning to the various actions we call voting (e.g., marking a sheet of paper, raising a hand at the appropriate time) as well as to counting the votes, determining eligible votes, declaring when someone has been elected or a measure passed and so forth. Crucially, there must be a distinction between free and sham elections, between genuine and forced choices, if the practice of voting is to be like our practices in Western democracies. Citizens must be able to distinguish in their self-interpretations between autonomy and forced choice when it comes to the options on their ballots.

All these activities like marking pieces of paper, tabulating results and declaring winners are inseparable from intentional descriptions if they are to be counted as voting practices. This vocabulary specifies a range where we can come to agreement about what voting is, what results are and so forth. That is, whether some practice is voting rather than harassment or entertainment is partly determined by the vocabulary a society establishes as appropriate for engaging in or describing it (Taylor 1985b: 35). Practices of voting in Western democracies contain an implicit vision of people and their relation to society, a vision made explicit in our descriptions of the practices by means of terms like 'autonomy', 'forced choice', 'free election', 'majority rule' and the like. The vocabulary describing voting practices also articulates norms defining appropriate actions, fair elections and so forth, which are essential to liberal-democratic traditions. In other words, change the vocabulary and you change the norms of liberal-democratic tradition. In turn, the practices of voting change from something recognizable as found in Western democracies (e.g., the practice of having only candidates from one party on ballots in 'elections' in many communist countries).

This is to say, the norms articulated in our voting vocabulary play a role in establishing our practices of voting. As well, the practices partly establish the vocabulary deployed to describe and engage in voting. Hence, the vocabulary – used to describe cases and in theorizing, to formulate concepts, to give definition and to categorize – on which Thomas relies is not merely descriptive, but is partially constitutive of those activities and practices. Indeed, mainstream political science, whether qualitative or quantitative, misses out the fact that political theorizing – like all social-science theorizing – shapes the very practices they are about (see below). Since practices are the very objects of such theorizing, political theorizing tends to transform practices like voting in an intimate and immediate way. In contrast, natural-science theorizing does not transform its objects of study (e.g, electrons). So political inquiry hardly has the value-neutral, objectivist air that Thomas's picture – typical of political scientists – suggests.

3. Theoretical issues

In the wake of political behaviouralism, theorizing in political science proceeds in a natural-scientific mode. Political theory is taken to be a conceptual picture of an independent political reality just like theories in natural sciences such as physics and chemistry are taken to be pictures of an independent physical reality. In this sense, theory developed in political science is seen as yielding an account of the underlying mechanisms or causes of political activity which would then provide the basis for more effective social planning and political action. Not surprisingly, political science is heavily coloured by an instrumental picture: given that outcomes are a crucial focus of political inquiry, a precise knowledge of the causal determinants of political activity and outcomes would be beneficial for discovering the most effective or efficient means for bringing about desired outcomes (e.g., increasing voter turnout or achieving an election victory).

It is at this point, however, that the double hermeneutic (Chapter 3, sec. 2) has a particularly interesting effect largely ignored in political theorizing. In physics, for instance, theorizing about atoms and molecules changes nothing about the atoms and molecules themselves nor the factors constituting their behaviour. This is because the objects of theorizing – the atoms and molecules – are independent of the theories and theorizers. The only significant interpretive questions appear to involve the framework for theorizing itself because atoms and molecules are not self-interpreting beings. Natural-science theorizing only involves a single hermeneutic. In contrast, human beings are self-interpreting, as we have seen, so theorizing in political science is not an activity that is independent of the agents and factors constitutive of political reality. That is to say political theorizing introduces a change in our conception of what is going on in political activity, which can also affect that very activity of theorizing.

Take elections where we decide political offices and referenda by majority vote as an example (see Taylor 1985b: 93–104). In Western democracy, for a vote to be legitimate, it must be uncoerced; that is, we cast our ballots freely and independently. These are features that are constituitive of voting practices in Western societies. We are aware of these features when we cast our votes and can make judgements accordingly about whether there is foul-play or manipulation involved.

Theorizing about such practices and activities aims to make explicit 'what really is going on' in elections. But in the process of theorizing about elections, the practices become reconceived or reinterpreted from a different standpoint, and are thus changed. Put another way, our practices are largely established or constituted by our understandings or interpretations of them. Change these understandings and interpretations and the practices necessarily also must change.

Consider Marxist theorizing about such elections. Such a theorist sees a capitalist economic system as seriously restricting the choices open to citizens of countries maintaining such systems. Options which threaten to reduce profitability are generally foreclosed in such societies because economic decline and mass unemployment are effects capitalist societies will not tolerate (or at least the owners of capital will not tolerate). So on the Marxist analysis, the options offered to voters in capitalist societies will be severely restricted to only those that are consistent with continued smooth operation of the economy. In this way many of the outcomes of supposedly free elections are actually structurally determined. The independence and freedom we think we are experiencing when we vote in elections turns out to be largely illusory according to Marxist theorizing. The practices of elections turn out to be something utterly different than we took them to be. If we take such theories seriously, citizens of capitalist societies are wrong about both their self-understandings of what they are doing when they cast votes as well as their interpretations of elections.

Or consider a more widely endorsed – if only implicitly – picture of social and political reality, the liberal-individualist picture, where social atomism (see Chapter 9, sec. 3) colours political theorizing. Elections then produce the outcomes of the votes cast by individuals out of their own self-interested goals. The interactions of individual agents casting their votes produce goods for society as a result of the aggregation of these interests. On many of these theories, citizens who go to the polls to cast their ballots for what they take to be an expression of the greater good of their country or society as they understand it would also be mistaken. What they are really doing, perhaps largely unbeknownst to them, is simply acting out of their own sense of their personal best interests. There are no larger or greater goods to inform their actions except those that are aggregated out of all the individual self-interests that get pooled together in elections. To the extent that citizens in Western democracies take such theories seriously, we would see our voting more as expressions of our self-interests rather than as an exercise of our civic duties and privileges or as expressions of our vision of the greater good. The draining away of these larger meanings of voting in exchange for narrow self-interest may go a long way towards explaining the decline in participation among eligible voters in US elections in the second half of the twentieth century.

Purely self-interested motivations appear insufficient to sustain the very voting practices required by liberal democracy.

These are two examples of how theorizing about elections is actually theorizing about a set of practices that literally reshapes those practices by the theoretical conceptions imposed by the theories. The practices of voting are transformed into something other than what citizens took them to be. Because social and political practices are at least partially constituted by our self-understandings of them, theorizing about such practices reshapes those practices. In other words, altering our theory about such practices changes our understanding of those practices, which, in turn, changes those practices. This is the two-way interpretive street at work, a feature that appears to be largely absent in theorizing in the natural sciences. To the extent that the general voting population comes to believe one or another theory about electoral practices, their own self-understandings of those practices and what they personally are doing when engaging in them will change. This is a consequence of there being only insiders' perspectives available for social inquiry and the fact that changes in these perspective lead to changes in how we take social reality to operate which transforms the workings of social reality itself. Changes in theories in physics, by contrast, never transform atoms and molecules or their properties in any way like this.

Theorizing in political science can reshape our understandings of political practices more or less radically. Likewise, theorizing can reinforce as well as be reinforced by cultural ideals. To the extent that political scientists take on the liberal-individualist bent of Western cultures unawares, their theorizing will be coloured in numerous ways by such ideals (another example of the double hermeneutic). Their theorizing can then act to reinforce these ideals. Or consider another example. Suppose we lived in a culture that had a great deal of social and economic stratification driven by some metaphysical hierarchy of being. Suppose further that political theorizing simply 'soaked up' this metaphysical hierarchy unawares. Such theorizing would reinforce this hierarchy by making explicit and plausible (at least by the lights of the metaphysical commitments) criteria for who can legitimately cast votes in such a society (e.g., necessary levels of intelligence, wealth, mental constitution). Such theorizing could easily justify restricting the vote to educated males, for instance, or denying the vote to women. Our drive to be value-neutral would undermine our ability to detect and address such moral evils as well as their metaphysical underpinnings.

4. Rational choice in politics

A very common conception of how to explain behaviour in the social sciences is via propositions of the form (Chapter 3, sec. 1):

> If an agent desires *a* and believes that *b* is a means to attain *a* under the circumstances, then the agent will attempt *b*.

Explanation in political behaviouralism, and through it in much political science, takes this form, where beliefs, desires or other drives of political actors are viewed as key determinants of their behaviour. In addition, depending on one's view about methodological individualism (Chapter 7), organizational norms or other social factors might need to be invoked in explanations as well.

An alternative movement within political science that has gained in prominence since the late 1970s has emphasized deploying the rational-actors picture (Chapter 10) for the explanation of political activities. The rational-choice picture includes beliefs, desires and social norms. It emphasizes that these influences shape individuals' strategic preferences, while maintaining that individuals pursue their preferences as rationally or strategically as their knowledge, resources and context permit.[5] Rationality is taken to be independent of individuals' preferences: simply feed in a strategic preference and means–ends reasoning will yield the course of action best suited for achieving the desired outcome. So, under the behaviouralist picture, one would analyse and explain the behaviour of members of Congress by appealing to the norms and expectations established by members of government and their constituents. Under the rational-actors picture, one might analyse the behaviour of members of Congress by noting that their primary preference is re-election. Consequently, they behave strategically to maximize the likelihood of that outcome.

As another example, in the 1960s behaviouralist analyses of presidential elections had largely concluded that the chief determinant of voter choice was party identification. In turn, party identification was thought to be mostly apolitical, the result of socialization (i.e., if your parents voted Democrat, you grew up to follow them in voting Democrat as well). Party identifications were viewed as being almost immutable the way some other forms of socialized behaviour were thought to stick with people for life. In contrast, the rational-actors picture sought to demonstrate that voting behaviour was also strategic, reflecting instrumental reasoning. Under this picture, issues like education, the economy and tax cuts as well as government performance would be important as they matched up with voters' preferences. The social upheavals and protests of the late 1960s and early 1970s were also marked by people who had been long-time Democrat voters switching parties or voting independent. Under rational-choice analysis, this behaviour was explained by identifying a political component to party affiliation, a component that matched up with people's strategic preferences.

Along with the criticisms discussed in Chapter 10 (e.g., that the rational-actors picture can too easily be rendered unfalsifiable, that it often fails to make sense of actual behaviour, or that it represents a form of idealized rationality unsuited to human beings), there are some that are specific to its application in political science. One problem is that rational-choice theory has some fairly strict limits in its explanatory power. For instance, it appears to be much more applicable to political elites (e.g., presidents or presidential candidates) than average citizens. Decisions of the former are typically highly significant, such as changing the course of national policy, prosecuting wars and so forth. Under such circumstances, it is more likely that elite actors would resort to strategic reasoning. In contrast, the vote of ordinary citizens in presidential elections are mixed in with millions of others. The consequences of such decisions are likely to be viewed as trivial or as not contributing to the election outcome at all under the rational-actors picture. Hence, rational-choice theory has no compelling explanation as to why millions of ordinary citizens bother to vote in presidential elections.[6]

A second problem for the rational-actors picture is its narrow focus on strategic preferences and means for achieving them. Motivations such as civic duty, patriotism or the exercise of a privilege are not strategic (*wertrational* versus *zweckrational*), hence do not figure prominently in rational-choice theorizing about voting behaviour. Nor do the unique cultural–historical matrix shaping the operations of political institutions, processes and practices play any consequential role in such theorizing. Therefore, many would argue, crucial constituitive features of political practices are either left out of the rational-choice picture of political reality or that these features are drastically reinterpreted by rational-choice theory (see above and Chapter 10, sec. 4.1).

Finally, the rational-actors picture inherits all the problems of disguised ideology that is associated with the instrumental picture of action. This is because rational-choice theories are basically sophisticated applications of instrumental reasoning to choices. Moreover, the rational-actors picture is explicitly normative in its core notion of what constitutes rationality (see Chapter 10, sec. 1). Hence, it represents advocacy of a particular vision of the good life – in this instance the political good – namely, a particular form of rationality and means–ends reasoning as the hallmark of consummate political actors. At the same time, it has no means for defending this vision of the good life within its narrow confines. Nor does it have the resources to diffuse quandaries such as: 'What if we discovered the best way to achieve our strategic ends was to deny the privilege of voting to particular minority groups or to those with too low a level of education?' This, of course is where many of our best liberal values are supposed to come to the rescue, but this mix of strategic reasoning and liberal values is unstable (as we saw in Chapter 5). There is nothing preventing those pursuing strictly strategic rationality from deciding that the most effective means for achieving their political aims is to ignore liberal values. Many of the problems American democracy is facing in terms of the dominance of special-interest politics is actually due to this kind of illiberal pursuit of strategic self-interests on the parts of various groups and industries. So the rational-actors picture and the attendant disguised ideologies are hardly objective and innocent; rather, they have a number of pernicious effects on modern democratic politics and society.

5. Taking stock

Unlike psychology and economics, there currently is no established literature or subdiscipline for philosophy of political science. What I have tried to do here is indicate how some of the themes from earlier chapters play out in theoretical and methodological practices in political science. Mainstream approaches in political science tend to presuppose that there is a determinate structure to the political arena (similar to mainstream approaches toward social reality in the social sciences more generally). The approach is analogous with natural sciences, such as astronomy taking the galaxy to have a determinate structure. Moreover, the political realm is viewed conceptually as being distinct from the political scientist as observer (again in analogy with the natural sciences). In other words, natural-scientific and descriptivist modes of political inquiry presuppose the package deal of an instrumental picture of action and a subject-object ontology and epistemology.

But, as we have seen, political theorizing about political reality is not inquiry into an objectively structured, independent realm. Rather, such theorizing is about practices and changes those practices as it reconceives them. Another way to put the point is that the political realm is not objectively determinate, but, like social reality in general, is an arena of cooperative action. Cultural influences shape this arena of action as do the ways people engage in political practices. This is not to deny that there are any efficient causal features at work in political action. Rather, it is to emphasize that the political realm is largely symbolically structured by cultural and individual meanings. This is another way of seeing why the concepts and definitions Thomas (2005) refers to above cannot be universal or objective features of scientific analysis. They will be infused with meanings that also stand in need of examination. There are only insiders' perspectives, but this does not mean that we cannot carry on inquiry into these perspectives and the insights they deliver (Chapters 6; 17).

One upshot of this predicament is that political science – like all social sciences – is not able to deliver the kind of objective, value-free results that one might expect to take as input for the construction and analysis of public or social policy. If public officials and policy analysts are treating the pronouncements of political scientists as objective results from the outsider's perspective, then there is every likelihood that disguised ideologies will simply be enshrined in public and social policy at governmental levels (similar to the examples in Chapter 8). So not only is political liberalism being surreptitiously advocated as a conception of the good life (see Chapter 5), but other cultural ideals such as liberal individualism and the instrumental picture of action are also likely being advocated and promulgated as public and social policy. Given that there has been an increasing interest in orienting political science towards public and social policy (e.g., Portis, Levy and Landau 1988), the role of hidden assumptions and disguised ideologies looms large as deserving of more attention.

For further study

1. How do institutional realism, political behaviouralism and the rational-actors picture applied to political reality differ from each other?
2. In what ways does theorizing in political science differ from theorizing in the natural sciences?
3. How are disguised ideologies involved in political science?

Recommended reading

C. Taylor, 'Social Theory as Practice', in *Philosophical Papers'* Vol. 2: *Philosophy and the Human Sciences* (Cambridge: Cambridge University Press, 1985b), pp. 91–115.

G. Thomas, 'The Qualitative Foundations of Political Science Methodology', *Perspectives on Politics* 3(2005): 855–66.

12 Philosophy of Economics

Philosophy of economics is a very active field of research with a large literature. It focuses on such issues as the appraisal of economic outcomes, institutions and processes, rational choice, and the ontology of economic phenomena as well as the possibilities of acquiring knowledge about these phenomena. Philosophical reflection on economics is ancient. Aristotle, for example, addresses some problems we would recognize as at least partly falling under economics, such as how to manage a household. But the conception of the economy as a distinct object of study dates back only to the eighteenth century.

Getting a precise picture of what economics is about is difficult and controversial, however. While it is obvious that economics is concerned with aspects of the production, exchange, distribution and consumption of commodities, these terms are somewhat vague. And arguably economics is relevant to a great deal more. For instance, economists are mainly concerned with the consequences of individual pursuit of wealth, though it takes some account of less significant motives such as aversion to labour. These pursuits perhaps touch on most areas of individual and social life.

Many have questioned whether thinking in terms of individual pursuit of wealth and aversion to labour is sufficient for understanding the economic behaviour of people. Sometimes people seek happiness through asceticism. In other instances, people rationally prefer sacrificing all their worldly possessions for a spiritual or political cause. But economists largely have supposed that such preferences are rare and unimportant to economics. Instead, economists are primarily concerned with phenomena deriving from rationality coupled with a desire for wealth and consumption.

Most economic analyses are based on key simplifying assumptions. Two important ones are (1) that individuals are rational decision makers as in the rational-actors picture (Chapter 10) and (2) that individuals act on purely self-interested motives. These assumptions turn out to be problematic in a number of ways, however.

1. The rise of economics

With the increasing importance of trade and of nation-states in the early modern period, came an increasing recognition of the importance and complexities of the financial management of the state, of trade balances and the regulation of currencies. It became increasingly recognized that sources of wealth such as the quantities of manufactured goods, annual harvests, the products of mines and so forth depended on facts about nature, individual labour and enterprise, as well as state and social regulations. So, while people discovered that there were a number of interrelationships among various economic factors, it was only in the eighteenth century that the idea of an economy with regularities that can be investigated came into prominence. This can be seen, for instance, in the writings of Richard Cantillon (c.1680–1734), who many acknowledge as the first major economic theorist, Hume and, in particular, Adam Smith. The latter is famous for, among other things, his account of the 'invisible hand': the idea that economic agents, by pursuing their own self-interests end up promoting socially beneficial ends they never intended. This is an example of social atomism (Chapter 9, sec. 3), where the intentions and actions of individuals sum up to a social outcome that, Smith maintained, was often to the benefit of all. The existence of such unobvious regularities, the unintended consequences of individual choices for social goods, presents an object suitable for scientific investigation.

In the nineteenth century, philosophers, such as Mill, emphasized that individuals act rationally in their pursuit of wealth and goods as well as in the avoidance of labour. Although a step in the development of economics, they had no explicit theory of rational economic choice. That required the additional developments like a theory of consumption and marginal utility, linking choice (and price) of some object of consumption to its marginal utility rather than its total utility. The total utility of some product or service is, roughly, the satisfaction associated with the consumption or acquisition of that good or service (Chapter 10, sec. 1). Marginal utility is the amount of benefit an agent derives from consuming or acquiring an additional unit of a product or service. For example, if you are thirsty you will get lots of satisfaction out of drinking a glass of water. As your thirst is quenched, the satisfaction you derive from drinking a second glass of water correspondingly diminishes. Similarly the third glass would deliver even less satisfaction and you might not even finish drinking it.

So-called neoclassical theories maintain that agents make consumption choices so as to maximize their own happiness or economic welfare (which amount to the same thing for most economists). Assuming only utility, agents would spend their money on water or beef or clothing with all consumable goods making the same contribution to their happiness no matter how many units of each they obtained. The utility of a dollar's worth of each consumable good was considered the same in contrast with the concept of marginal utility. For instance, water is useful, but in much of the world water is so plentiful that another glass more or less matters little to an agent. Hence, water is cheap – its marginal utility is very low and you are unwilling to pay much for it. In contrast, total utility does not take the relative availability/unavailability of a commodity into account in terms of its value to an agent.

1.1. Classical versus neoclassical economics

The theorizing of Cantillon and Smith represents what is called *classical* economic theory. Classical economic theorists tended to argue that governments should not intervene in the economy to cause economic growth or cure economic ills. Rather, classical theorists believed economies were better left to the dynamics of free trade and free markets ('laissez-faire' economics). They also thought that the value of a bushel of corn, say, depended only on the costs involved in producing the bushel. So the value of some consumable good was considered to be a property inherent in the item itself represented by the costs of production. Moreover, the output or product of an economy was thought to be distributed among different social groups in accordance with the costs born by those groups in producing the output.

One of the problems with classical economic theory was that prices in the market place did not usually reflect the value defined by the theory. People often proved willing to pay more for a consumable item than its worth determined by the theory. This and other problems, along with new conceptual developments, led to *neoclassical* economic theory. On the neoclassical view, the value of a consumable item was determined by the relationship between that item and the consumer. So the value, hence the price, of goods was a function of both production costs and subjective desires of consumers. The relationship of price to production costs and subjective preferences was later called 'supply' and 'demand'. This was known as the *marginal revolution* in economics (which played an important role in the development of instrumental reasoning; see Chapter 4, sec. 1).

Neoclassical economic theory can be summarized as follows. Consumers attempt to maximize their gains from obtaining various goods and services. In general, they prefer more commodities to fewer, and will increase their purchases of a particular consumable item until what they gain from an extra unit is just balanced by what they have to pay to obtain it. Consumers also are pictured as having *diminishing marginal rates of substitution*, roughly meaning they will pay less for units of a commodity when they already have lots of it and more when they have little of it. In this way they maximize their utility. Similarly, individuals provide labour to firms wishing to pay to employ them. Individuals are pictured as balancing the gains from offering the marginal unit of their services (wages received) with the disutility of labour itself (loss of leisure).

Moreover, employers attempt to produce units of some item or service so that the cost of producing the incremental or marginal unit is just balanced by the revenue it generates. Firms attempt to maximize profits in the face of diminishing returns (e.g., increasing production of an item when the increased availability to consumers will cause its price to fall, another instance of marginal utility). In this way they maximize profits. Firms also hire employees up to the point that the cost of the additional hire is just balanced by the value of output that the additional employee would produce. Supply and demand then can be considered in terms of the unlimited desires and wants of consumers colliding with the scarcity of goods and services due to production constraints.

Markets are the vehicles that solve the decision problems faced by consumers and producers, while prices signal to consumers and producers whether their conflicting desires can be reconciled.

Take the price of cars as an example. Suppose you want to buy a new car. There may very well be others who want to buy cars at the same price you are considering. But car makers may not want to produce as many cars as everyone wants due to various constraints they face or because that may not be their most profitable strategy. You and other consumers may feel frustrated at the availability of the cars you want to purchase and this may lead to everyone 'bidding up' car prices, so to speak. Increased car prices will eliminate some potential buyers while encouraging some marginal car makers to produce more. As the price changes, the imbalance between buy orders and sell orders is reduced, headed towards an equilibrium. This is an example of what economists call *optimization under constraint*, and the upshot is supposed to be that this kind of market interdependence will lead to an economic equilibrium, according to the neoclassical picture.

Neoclassical economics can be thought of as a *metatheory*. This is to say it is an understanding of fundamental assumptions defining satisfactory economic theories. But it does not constrain economic theorizing so much that the options are very limited; rather, there are about as many neoclassical theories of economics as there are economists! Instead, it is a set of shared understandings among a large number of economists. Some of these fundamental assumptions are:

1 Agents have rational preferences among outcomes.
2 Agents act to maximize utility.
3 Agents act independently on the basis of full and relevant information (i.e., social atomism).

Economic agents can be individuals, households or firms (e.g., firms seek to maximize their utility by maximizing profits). Agents' preferences are considered to be largely self-interested. That is, individuals are pictured as not necessarily caring about the outcomes and behaviours of other individuals except as they affect their own economic interests positively or negatively. Most economists interpret this self-interested stance as agents being morally neutral towards other agents: agents neither like nor dislike others' outcomes or behaviours so long as there is no effect on their own economic well-being. Theories guided by these assumptions are classified as neoclassical theories.

Neoclassical economics looks at the social and economic complex of a society or nation as an economic system, having interacting components, variables, parameters and constraints. However, this is the same language as that of physics in the middle of the nineteenth century. Indeed, mechanics was the model for the neoclassical framework: agents were like atoms or point particles; utility analogous with energy; utility maximization had parallels with the minimization of potential energy (compare with the physics model in psychology: Chapter 9, sec. 2.1). In this way, economics became rhetorically linked to successful science. The importance of this linkage was that any challenge or criticism of neoclassical economics looked like a challenge to or criticism of science and progress.

1.2. Microeconomics versus macroeconomics

Contemporary economics is extremely diverse even within the neoclassical picture. While most approaches only rely on rather rudimentary theory, some approaches in economics are highly theoretical. Whether more or less theoretically sophisticated, almost all approaches in economics are focused on concrete applied questions. The diversity of theoretical and applied work can be divided into two categories: microeconomics or macroeconomics.

Microeconomics focuses on relations among individual agents (which can include households and firms as well). Consumer demand typically is treated as an aggregation of individual demands (an example of social atomism). Individual agents are considered to be rational, that is, they possess complete and transitive preferences governing their choices (Chapter 10, sec. 1). This is the rational-actors picture and is a common idealization economists make. In accordance with the rational-actors picture, microeconomic explanations of consumer choice attribute to consumers perfect information about available alternative choices and complete information about constraints on the consumer. These assumptions, along with the above rationality conditions, lead to consumer's choices being uniquely specified and, it is hoped, their economic actions being predictable.[1] As mentioned above, economists conceive of the outcome of the profit-maximizing activities of firms and the attempts of consumers to best satisfy their preferences as an equilibrium. In an equilibrium, ideally there would be no excess demand for goods or services in any market. In other words, anyone who wants to buy anything at the going market price is able to do so, hence, there is no excess demand (unless some commodity is free, there also is no excess supply).

In contrast, *macroeconomics* focuses on relations among economic aggregates, paying particular attention to problems concerning the business cycle and the influence of monetary and fiscal policy on economic outcomes. Other questions macroeconomics treats concern growth, finance, employment, agriculture, natural resources, international trade and so forth. While explanations in microeconomics largely follow methodological individualism, macroeconomic explanations are methodologically holistic (see Chapter 7). There has been much interest in unifying macroeconomics and microeconomics, but few economists have thought the attempts to do so have been satisfactory.

In addition to the division between micro- and macroeconomics, *econometrics* represents a third branch of economics. It is devoted to the empirical estimation, elaboration and, to some extent, testing of specific microeconomic and macroeconomic models and predictions.

2. Methodological issues

Given the sheer diversity of approaches in economics, one would expect that an enormous number of methodological issues are constantly in debate. In this section, I will focus on some methodological problems that have proven to have an enduring presence in philosophical reflection concerning economics.

2.1. Positive versus normative economics: the fact/value distinction

The fact/value distinction shows up in economics in a number of ways, but it crucially appears in the distinction between positive and normative approaches to economics. A 'positive science' concerns itself exclusively with facts in accordance with the natural-scientific model of inquiry. On the other hand, normative inquiry of any form focuses on what ought or should be the case. Most economists believe that there is a reasonably clear distinction between facts and values, and conceive of economics as a science of facts. Under this guise, economics is thought to provide policy-makers and others with unbiased information and guidance for choosing appropriate means to accomplish their chosen ends. Economics, since it ostensibly only deals with facts, ideally has no bearing on the choice of ends.

The first extended reflections on economic methodology appeared in the 1830s, with Mill's essays on political economy and methodology published in the 1830s and 1840s proving extremely influential. Mill focused on inductive methods. He recognized that some of his inductive methodologies were only workable when there were few causal factors operating or in which experimental controls are possible. His *method of difference*, for instance, involves holding fixed every causal factor except one and then checking to see whether the effect ceases to obtain when that one factor is removed. Such methods parallel the kinds of methods used in controlled experiments in the natural sciences of his time.

Mill was working within the classical picture of economics, and theoretical predictions were often far afield of the actual economic outcomes. But the classical theories continued to hold sway for more than half a century. The consistently unfavourable data usually were explained away as due to various kinds of uncontrollable or disturbing causes. Mill defended this mismatch between theory and data by arguing that economic theory only includes the most important causes while necessarily ignoring minor causes. Methodologies like the method of difference would be expected to fail in such situations. For economics, Mill recommended a kind of indirect inductive method. One first determines the laws governing individual causal factors in situations where his more direct methods would be applicable (universal laws conception). With these laws of individual causes in hand, one could then investigate their combined consequences deductively. By deducing the effects of these combined causes, one could make predictions that could be confirmed or disconfirmed by observation. In this sense, at least, Mill is taking economics to be an arena for the application of natural science methods (methodological conception). However, because there are so many causes involved in an economy, this kind of testing would have comparatively little weight compared to the direct methods of controlling causes mentioned earlier. More often than not, the most one could find out using indirect methods was that there were causes or disturbances left out of one's theory. It is impossible, by means of this indirect approach, to get positive evidence in favour of economic laws from the phenomena of the economic realm.

The predictive claims of such theories, then, would be expected to be imprecise, and perhaps sometimes way off the mark. Mill's view was that the principles or laws of economics only hold in the absence of unaccounted interventions or disturbances. Nowadays philosophers call this view *ceteris paribus*, meaning that such principles, laws or theories only hold in the absence of outside causes. In other words, a *ceteris paribus* law tell us what will happen in a particular situation provided only the influences it covers are in play. Mill provided an account of how the principles of economics can be true *ceteris paribus* even though they usually failed in their predictions.

Mill's vision of theory and methodology survived the neoclassical revolution in economics and continued to exert influence in important methodological treatises concerning neoclassical economics into the first third of the twentieth century. Economists then began to propose ways to replace or move beyond Mill's picture of theory and methodology, but the most influential proposal was Milton Friedman's 1953 essay, 'The Methodology of Positive Economics'. Friedman begins by distinguishing between positive and normative economics, as described above. He conjectures that policy disputes are typically really disputes about the consequences of alternatives; hence, such disputes should be capable of resolution by progress in positive economics. Friedman takes it that the goal of all positive sciences is empirical theory (Chapter 3, sec. 1) yielding correct predictions concerning phenomena. This clearly represents a natural-scientific approach to economic inquiry. Not surprisingly, Friedman's conception of theories is heavily instrumentalist: theories are means to the end of useful predictions, which can then serve as the means for other goals. With such theory and predictions in hand, economics could then provide accurate, value-neutral guidance to policy-makers.

There are a number of questions that can be raised against this positive science/empirical theory emphasis pushed by Friedman and others. One of the most important problems is that economics is trying to be a positive science about human activity, but all human activities – including economic ones – are infused with values. As I have discussed before, almost all aspects of an economy (e.g., banking and currency systems, markets) are based on values and ideals that individuals and societies hold. If these values and ideals change, then the economy and its systems and institutions will also change. This means that the regularities that empirical economic theories are describing as laws or principles only hold as long as a particular constellation of values and ideals holds (more precarious than *ceteris paribus* conditions on unknown causes). In other words, an economy, like most other aspects of society, is symbolically structured by meanings rather than context-free laws (Chapter 3, sec. 1; Chapter 4, sec. 4). This situation dims the prospects for a value-neutral economics as a positive science of an independent realm of economic facts considerably. The distinction between facts and values largely vanishes in many situations.

Moreover, it is questionable whether the values and ideals colouring the activity of economists are sharply distinguishable from those guiding policy-makers. The purported independence of economic information and theorizing from policy formation needs serious clarification if economics is to play its supposed role of providing neutral guidance for policy-makers. To the extent that policy-makers and economists are guided by disguised ideologies like political liberalism and liberal individualism (Chapter 5), the advice economists give to policy-makers would simply reinforce those cultural ideals. This situation has the potential to produce policies exacerbating rather than relieving various social and economic problems (cf. Chapter 8).

To take another example, much of economics is built around a normative theory of rationality, the rational-actors picture (Chapter 10). The disguised ideologies of liberal individualism and the instrumental picture of action are inherent in the rational-actors picture used by economists. But these ideals are imbedded in methodologies of policy formation and assessment because policy-makers increasingly use the same rational-actors picture for their work. If both economics and public policy are largely coloured by a maximizing view of individual rationality (tied to utilitarian individualism: Chapter 5, sec. 2.2) and social atomism, then it becomes increasingly likely that social policy will view maximizing growth, wealth or welfare as means for maximizing freedom, rights or equality. But this would be to confuse means with ends in just the fashion critical theorists argue (Chapter 4). Furthermore, as we noted in Part Two, this situation leaves us no basis from which to discern which freedoms, rights or values are worthwhile.

Has positive economics produced genuinely successful empirical theory? Not really. Does it need to? According to Friedman, not really. In his argument for this conclusion, he starts with a point similar to Mill's: it is difficult or impossible to carry out controlled experiments and there are far too many phenomena left unaccounted for in economists' observations. This situation makes it difficult to interpret and judge whether particular economic theories provide good bases for predictions or not. Consequently, Friedman argues, economists most often 'test' theories by the realism of their assumptions, not by the accuracy of their predictions. Friedman thinks this is seriously mistaken because theories may be of great predictive value even when their assumptions are extremely unrealistic. He argues at length that the realism of a theory's assumptions simply is irrelevant to its predictive value. For example, many economic theories assume as a principle that firms seek to maximize their profits. From the standpoint of empirical theory, however, whether this assumption is realistic does not matter. All that matters is the predictive success of such theories. Hence, theories should be appraised exclusively in terms of the accuracy of their predictions. Notice this is a normative judgement privileging the value of predictive accuracy over the accuracy or realism of assumptions being offered by a leading exponent of value-free positive economics!

Critics (e.g., Brunner 1969) have pointed out that Friedman equivocates on the meaning of 'assumptions' – that is, he takes assumptions of theories to be several different things in different places within his writings. But Friedman aims his criticism at the empirical investigation whether firms in fact attempt to maximize profits. So he must have in mind central explanatory generalizations like 'Firms attempt to maximize profits' as an assumption many economic theories make. What would it mean for such a generalization to be unrealistic? Surely, Friedman must, among other things, mean that this generalization is false (or at least more or less false). So if it is a mistake to judge theories in terms of the realism of assumptions, he is arguing that it is a mistake to judge theories by investigating whether their central explanatory generalizations are true or false.

Moreover, the falsity of the principle that firms attempt to maximize profits looks like it should bear directly on the cogency of the empirical theory pre-supposing such a generalization. Since such a generalization plays the role of a prediction of the theory, one might argue that by his own lights, the falsity of this prediction is sufficient to judge any theory making such a prediction as defective in some way. But Friedman is not concerned with every prediction of economic theories. Rather, he contends that economists are interested in only some of the implications of economic theories, namely those which the theory was designed to explain (1953: 8). Other predictions, such as that firms maximize their profits, are irrelevant to policy since those are not what such theories are trying to explain. In other words, Friedman believes that economic theories should be judged in terms of their predictions concerning things like prices and quantities exchanged in markets. So it is a rather narrow predictive success that Friedman defends, not overall predictive adequacy.

If he is right, economists can simply ignore observations showing that firms do not always seek to maximize their profits (Lester 1946; 1947). Apparently they need not be troubled if their theoretical picture unrealistically idealizes agents as knowing the prices of all present and future commodities in all markets. For Friedman, what counts is whether the predictions concerning market phenomena turn out to be correct. But here is one problem for anyone taking Friedman's narrow 'predictive success only' line. Any market outcomes deviating from a theory's predictions can be explained as being due to any number of uncontrolled causal factors. Part of Friedman's argument is that experiments are difficult or impossible to carry out in the economic domain because there are far too many causal factors to take into consideration. So there would never be any evidence that could potentially disconfirm an economist's theory on Friedman's view. However, this renders economic theories unfalsifiable, hence, unscientific (see Chapter 10, sec. 4.4).[2]

I should point out that towards the end of the twentieth century, there was a rise in experimentation in economics. So Friedman's methodological views, though still very influential, have lost some ground in the economics community. But the positivist picture of economics as a value-neutral field of inquiry is still very much alive.

2.2. Idealizations and cultural ideals

From what has been said so far, it is clear that economics utilizes a number of severe idealizations. For instance, when economic theories assume the rational-actors picture, they are stipulating that economic actors are perfectly rational, have perfect information and no cognitive deficits whatsoever, among other idealizations. Another such idealization often made in economic theorizing is that commodities are infinitely divisible. Obviously, such assumptions are false, but sometimes idealizations are required to make a situation tractable enough to carry out modelling or calculations. Other times, such idealizations arise because of commitments to a conceptual ideal of rationality. Or, as discussed in Part Two, sometimes idealizations, like the instrumental picture of action, reflect hidden cultural ideals. These idealizations certainly go a long way towards explaining why economics as a discipline has so little in the way of successful empirical theory after literally decades of sustained effort and hundreds of millions of dollars of investment in research.

The presence of such idealizations also partly reflects the pragmatic residue of Friedman's emphasis on prediction as the only criterion of theory appraisal. If one devalues explanation in favour of predictive success, one can afford to engage in an 'anything goes' attitude as far as what goes into economic theories and models if they result in accurate predictions. This attitude also reflects an instrumental approach to theorizing: theories and models are viewed as means towards achieving the end of obtaining accurate predictions. Questions of truth or 'getting it right' tend to fall by the wayside at the expense of usefulness. Unfortunately, this push for instrumental usefulness reflects the disguised ideology of instrumental rationality at the same time that it reinforces that cultural ideal.

Another aspect of idealization comes out in the *ceteris paribus* nature of economic theorizing briefly described earlier. Because economists only can study a limited number of causes, every theoretical claim and prediction must be treated as *ceteris paribus* – that is, they can only hold true if there are no other causes or other factors present. But, as explained previously, this *ceteris paribus* understanding of theories and their predictions opens the door to such theories being unfalsifiable and, hence, unscientific. So when, if ever, can this approach be justified in a scientific discipline? This is very much an open question in the philosophy of science.

2.3. Causation

Economics seeks to uncover the causes at work in the economic realm just as other social sciences seek to in their domains. Economists adopt the same picture of theorizing as other social scientists influenced by the natural sciences: inquiry and theorizing are about an independent realm of economic facts and principles (as physics studies matter and its laws). Given the situations described in the previous two sections, the task of discovering causal laws and principles is difficult, to say the least. The law of demand, for instance, maintains that a price increase will diminish the quantity being demanded. There is supposed to be a causal relation here between desires of consumers (demand) and prices, but such a relation can only hold *ceteris paribus*. How can we really identify and study the key causes of economic behaviour without already knowing all the relevant causes at work in the economic realm?

Before the heyday of logical positivism (Chapter 1, sec. 2.1) in the 1930s and 1940s, economists generally used explicitly causal concepts and language. Under the general anti-metaphysical influence of positivism and a drive to emulate the natural sciences as closely as possible, economists tended to avoid causal concepts or language.[3] So, instead of formulating the law of demand in causal terms (demand, consequences of price changes), many tried to focus on possible mathematical functions relating price to quantity demanded. One consequence of this move was to shut off careful analysis of causal concepts while such concepts were tacitly invoked (Hausman 1983). Talk of a mathematical function relating price change and quantity demanded implicitly draws upon the very causal concepts being shunned (e.g., demand as the desires of agents). Another consequence of this move to avoid causal concepts and language is to open the door even further to the unacknowledged presence of various values and disguised ideologies. Suppose economists focused exclusively on the functional relation between the low-wage labour market in the USA and the supply of immigrant and migrant labour. Such a focus would both reflect and tend to reinforce an instrumental picture of such labour as well as paper over potent value-laden issues surrounding illegal immigration needing serious and sober reflection.

In the last two decades of the twentieth century, economists have warmed towards explicitly invoking and reflecting on causation in their theorizing. Much of the renewed interest in causal analysis has been inspired by work in econometrics (Cartwright 1989; Hoover 2001).

2.4. Methodological individualism

Theorizing in microeconomics typically presupposes methodological individualism (Chapter 7), the idea that economic behaviour finds its ultimate explanation in the preferences and actions of individual agents. But many economists in the first half of the twentieth century, as pointed out above, avoided appealing to individual psychological factors like beliefs and desires as causes in favour of functional relations and statistical correlations between economic variables (this parallels the behaviourist movement in psychology eschewing beliefs and desires as causes: Chapter 9, sec. 1.1). One of the critics of this trend, von Hayek, argued that this focus left economic phenomena unintelligible. Suppose, in studying the movement of prices, one noticed a constant correlation between the date of the first frost and fluctuations in the price of wheat. Such correlations do not explain very much, in particular, they do not explain the behaviour of individual agents. If one thinks that methodological individualism is an important constraint on explanations, then economic understanding can only be found in the rational actions of individual agents. For instance, the correlations between early frost and reduced yields would lead to less intense price competition among individual suppliers, but more competition among individual consumers for a scarcer commodity. In this way, von Hayek argued, macroeconomic analysis of such a situation would be incomplete without the individual dynamics found in microeconomics.

Von Hayek also thought that emphasizing a microeconomic point of view shed light on various ways in which economic phenomena emerge as the unintended consequences of rational actions of individual actors (harking back to Adam Smith). The outcomes people achieve might bear no resemblance to the ones they intended. But, von Hayek argued, it was still important to know what people thought they were doing. One reason is that it is important to know why people persist in pursuing such courses of action when in fact they are not producing the intended consequences.

Part of von Hayek's motivation for endorsing methodological individualism was his belief that the individual actor's perspective provided needed limitations on theorizing and economic understanding. Take a macroeconomic variable like the rate of inflation. Although inflation rates play particular roles in economies, individual actors usually do not respond directly to information about such variables. (When was the last time you ran out to buy a computer because you heard that inflation was going up?) Consumers largely only see changes in the immediate prices they must pay for production inputs or consumable items, so this is what more directly affects their purchases. The large-scale consequences of consumers' choices made in response to price changes are largely unintended; that is, they are not intentionally responding to or trying to affect inflation rates. So any regularity in these consequences constitutes a spontaneous order based on the views of consumers. This order is structured by the meanings of agents and not some independent economic reality governed by context-free laws. Von Hayek largely ignored the self-interpreting nature of people. But he maintained that only when we see operations of the economy through individuals' eyes we can begin to understand things like the advantages of decentralized markets and their self-coordination.

Von Hayek illustrated the importance of individual perspectives through an example of the process leading to the development of a path in the woods. Suppose someone works his way through, choosing a route offering the least local resistance. This act of passage reduces, even if slightly, the resistance offered along that route to the next person who walks though the woods. The next person, then, is more likely to choose to follow the same route than any others. But that increases the chances that the next person will do so, and so forth. A path through the woods is the net effect of all these people passing through even though no one intended to create a particular path. Conscious decisions of numerous people spontaneously produce order. As Hayek describes it, 'human movements through the district come to conform to a definite pattern which, although the result of deliberate decisions of many people, has yet not been consciously designed by anyone' (von Hayek 1942: 289).

So by ignoring the agent's perspective, von Hayek argued, we can easily be mislead to overestimate our powers of rational planning and control. So methodological individualism is useful for helping us see the limitations of our own reasoning. From a purely macroeconomic perspective, we can easily be misled into thinking that we can successfully manipulate interest rates, unemployment rates, inflationary pressures or other variables to intervene in the economy. Von Hayek points out that these concepts are abstractions that we create. Abstractions that are not used to guide individual action, but are our descriptions of the net effect of millions of individual decisions (i.e., social atomism). Hence, von Hayek maintained, methodological individualism encourages greater modesty with respect to social and economic planning.

After the 1950s, von Hayek stopped mentioning methodological individualism. He seems to have come to the conclusion that one needed more than just the viewpoints of individual actors to satisfactorily explain economic and social phenomena. Indeed, his later writings emphasize evolutionary explanations which violate the methodological individualist constraint. As well, we have discussed other reasons why a purely individualist form of explanation is unlikely to yield satisfactory explanations of social and economic reality (e.g., that some references to large-scale social and economic facts are irreducible to the views and actions of individuals: Chapter 7).

3. Rational-choice theory in economics

Nevertheless, many economists think that the proper explanation of economic as well as many other social phenomena should be in terms of individual choices (e.g., microeconomics). These choices are usually explained in terms of reasons (e.g., she bought a new computer because she desired or needed it), so economics must picture agents as rational to some extent. For most economists, this means invoking the rational-actors picture (Chapter 10) as a framework for understanding economic agents. Whether this picture of agents obeys the strictures of methodological individualism, however, depends on precise details of how individual agents form their preferences.[4]

Recall that the rational-actors picture assumes agents have a complete ordering of their preferences, and that this ordering is transitive, as well as that agents have complete information, no cognitive deficits and so forth. As formulated, this picture of rationality is incomplete because it says nothing about what is rational when agents have uncertainty in their knowledge relevant to their choices. After all, in most situations people do not have complete information about all their possible choices. Much economic analysis needs to deal with such situations where uncertainty exists (e.g., situations involving unknown risks). Moreover, one can argue that the rational-actors picture as formulated may also be too strong. There is nothing particularly irrational about having incomplete preferences in situations involving uncertainty (Levi 1986). Many times we think someone is rational to suspend judgement in situations where some or all of the alternatives are not well understood. But the rational-actors picture seems to imply that such agents are acting irrationally, a judgement that cuts against some very strong intuitions about what we think is rational to do in such situations.

One response to these worries has been to point out that transitivity of preferences is a plausible condition for rationality (transitivity implies an agent knows all his possible choices). In particular, the *money pump* argument supposedly demonstrates that unless preferences are transitive, an agent can be exploited. Suppose Smith prefers apples to oranges, oranges to bananas and bananas to apples. Then his preferences are intransitive. Suppose further that Smith is willing to pay some small amount of money, x, to exchange oranges for apples, bananas for oranges, and apples for bananas. This would mean that Smith could be exploited by some nefarious vendor at a market: starting with bananas, Smith will fork over x for oranges, then x again for apples, then x again for bananas and so forth. The intransitivity of Smith's preferences provide no rational stopping point for his economic exchanges with the nefarious vendor.

It is obvious that people normally are not this stupid. So either people are able to adjust their preferences to eliminate intransitivity, or the rational-actors picture is not a good framework for analysing the behaviour of people. There is considerable experimental evidence that people's preferences are not transitive (Tversky and Thaler 1990). If one insists on maintaining the rational-actors picture, then the judgement that people largely make irrational choices is unavoidable. On the other hand, it seems quite reasonable to take this evidence as counting against the rational-actors picture.

The rational-actors picture has a number of other problems as discussed earlier in Chapter 10 (e.g., the rational-actors picture can too easily be rendered unfalsifiable, it often fails to make sense of actual behaviour, it represents a form of idealized rationality unsuited to human beings). But its applicability to economics in particular can be questioned. The conception of individuals as perfect strategic-rationality calculators seems more plausible when applied to people with tight budgets than those who have comfortable or great wealth. After all, if you are 'pinching pennies', then almost all of your economic decisions must be made with the goal of staying within your budget while meeting your purchasing objectives. Every economic decision has significant consequences for tight budgets. On the other hand, for those with comfortable or great wealth, many economic decisions may have few or no consequences at all (e.g., purchases made on a whim, investing some amount of money just for fun). Rational-choice theory loses plausibility for such cases as many of these decisions would be judged as strategically irrational when intuitively they might appear quite reasonable under the circumstances.

Moreover, as mentioned in the introduction to this chapter, many people give all kinds of reasons for avoiding wealth, or sacrificing by donating to charities and what have you. Moreover, a number of poor people do not make strategic choices to save money or only spend on needs, but also spend money on entertainment and other desires that do not contribute to the financial health of their households let alone lead to wealth accumulation (Banfield 1990; Mayer 1998). These are not the wealth-maximizing choices that economists believe are the major sources of economic reality, but they are far from insignificant. So-called *homo economicus* – the rational wealth maximizer – would not make these kinds of decisions as his preferences and means are all strategically economically related. At best, the rational-actors picture needs major supplementation to handle such cases plausibly. At worst, the framework is simply not well suited to analysing the everyday behaviour of human beings.

Finally, the rational-actors picture inherits all the problems of disguised ideology associated with the instrumental picture of action. Since the rational-actors picture is explicitly normative in its core notion of what constitutes rationality, it represents advocacy of a particular vision of the good life. In this instance, it represents the economic (and some would claim social) good life – namely, a particular form of rationality and means–ends reasoning as the hallmark of consummate economic agents and practices. Moreover, the double hermeneutic (Chapter 3, sec. 2) clearly can be seen at work here. If members of a society begin to conceive of themselves as economists (and policy-makers) picture them – as individualistic utility calculators engaging in strictly strategic reasoning about wealth – they certainly could transform their behaviour to conform to various elements of this picture. As a matter of fact, people's views of what is right and wrong are influenced by their beliefs about how people in fact behave. And there is evidence that learning about theories depicting individuals as self-interested leads people to regard self-interested behaviour more favourably and to become more self-interested (Marwell and Ames 1981; Frank, Gilovich and Regan 1993).

4. Taking stock

For all its faults, economists sometimes offer the following defence of their commitment to the rational-actors picture: while it may not be true of individual economic agents, economies as a whole function *as if* individual agents were such idealized rational actors. In other words, even though people display a wide variety of reasoning, motivations and choices, their actions aggregate in such a way that the large-scale outcomes are the same as if economic agents were predominantly idealized rational actors. This defence obviously presupposes ontological individualism (Chapter 5, sec. 2.1) in the form of social atomism, where any social phenomena are simply the sum of many individual behaviours. But it also tends to allow economists to slip into the habit of conceiving of people as if they really are these idealized actors. Nor does the defence answer any of the problems plaguing economic theories discussed above.

Deploying the rational-actors picture to restructure economies and markets is far from innocent. Indeed, such actions have serious consequences as Jaeger et al. (2001: 254) make clear:

> The normative bias towards a world in which reality should be modified so that it behaves in accordance with the analytical models of perfect markets has tremendous political and social power – and considerable danger. Economic advisory boards on the national and international level often advocate social and economic measures that facilitate structures and policies in which RAP [rational-actors picture]-based behavior is either assumed or mandated. RAP analysts tend to see and structure the world in accordance with the RAP model, rather than coping with the real world, including its tensions between normative orientations and practical behavior. They also tend to offer normative advice that neither matches the imperfect world, nor helps to make the imperfect world a better place in which to live.

Although economists conceive of self-interested agents as being morally neutral towards others, this clearly is not an amoral stance: agents neither liking nor disliking others' outcomes or behaviours so long as there is no affect on their own economic well-being. This self-interested picture of agents is indistinguishable from the instrumental picture of agents. Furthermore, economists clearly treat agents along the lines of utilitarian individualism (Chapter 5, sec. 2.2). So the disguised ideologies of the instrumental picture of action (Chapter 4) and liberal individualism (Chapter 5) are clearly involved in economics as a discipline.[5] Economics is far from being a value-neutral discipline no matter how much the field strives, via natural-scientific modes of inquiry, to be value-neutral and objective. Economists largely adopt a particular morally laden standpoint along with the package deal of instrumental action and a subject-object ontology and epistemology discussed in Part Two.

Moreover, people do not actually behave in accordance with this picture of *homo economicus* (Jaeger et al. 2001). Many people do want to be treated fairly and resist unfair outcomes even when they will suffer economic loss as a consequence. A number of the values in the liberal-individualist picture, along with others like mercy, compassion and kindness, are always in play in people's choices and actions, but these are largely ignored in mainstream economic analyses. Furthermore, we do care about how our actions affect others. People do not generally adopt an attitude that whatever happens to others around them does not matter so long as their own economic well-being is not harmed. We often care about our friends, neighbours and co-workers even if it is not the most economically sensible thing to do. And we worry about our reputations. We do not want other people viewing us as crass, uncaring, self-interested individuals, but other people would view us this way if we acted like the economic picture of agents!

So either the rational-actors picture of economic agents needs drastic modification, or it needs to be discarded altogether. Economists usually resist these conclusions by putting the blame on human beings rather than their theorizing. Humans, it turns out, do not have complete information, do not always think rationally, often make less than optimal decisions and so forth. But this reaction indicates that, more often than not, economists are more interested in their conceptual picture of economic agents than in everyday human beings, the very beings producing economic phenomena! The general attitude of positive economics – that it does not have to be realistic, only predictive – still holds sway even if most economists have shifted their empirical theorizing in a rational-choice direction. And given that there has been very little predictive success in economics, perhaps it is time to re-examine the foundations of the framework. Some economists are exploring different pictures of rationality, where agents do not always choose according to the rational-actors picture or have some cognitive deficits (e.g., incomplete information, finite memories). But this still is a long way from the everyday human beings who inhabit the lifeworld (Chapter 6).

For further study

1. What are the key differences between classical and neoclassical theories of economics? Is there any sense in which you think neoclassical theories are clear improvements over classical ones or not?

2. Can the *ceteris paribus* view of theories advocated by Mill and Friedman be made consistent with the natural-scientific emphasis on empirical theory (Chapter 3, sec. 1)? Why or why not?

3. How have cultural ideals influenced both economics and public policy? Do you think that economics really can give independent advice to policy-makers? Why or why not?

Recommended reading

M. Friedman, 'The Methodology of Positive Economics', in *Essays in Positive Economics* (Chicago: University of Chicago Press, 1953) pp. 3–43.

F. A. von Hayek, 'Scientism and the Study of Man I', *Economica* 9 (1942): 267–91.

Part Four

Handling Data 13

Recall the correlators introduced in Chapter 1. One of the distinguishing features of correlators is their focus on univocal or brute data – interpretation-free data having only one meaning – and on univocal methods for collecting and processing that data. In Part Three, we have examined a number of methodological and theoretical problems in various fields within social science. All these discussions presupposed such fields had reams of data while largely remaining silent about the kinds of data, their collection and analysis.

There are a number of standardized techniques social scientists use to obtain data: observations, field experiments, interviews, questionnaires, archival searches and archeological digs among others. These techniques as well as the data obtained through them are supposed to be value-neutral, producing a set of facts that can serve as the target for theorizing as well as for confirmation of theories. However, we have seen in Part Two that questionnaires are not value-neutral nor are the data obtained through them value-neutral or even interpretation-free. Are the other kinds of standard techniques for gathering data value-free? Are the techniques used to analyze such data value-free? It turns out that values and cultural ideals also deeply colour our data-collection protocols and techniques.

1. Protocols for handling data

The various standard methods for collecting data in the social sciences all have protocols for the proper application of their techniques. Protocols are guidelines for proper conduct by the scientist as well as the application of the method. For instance, protocols specify the proper ways to construct and administer questionnaires, or the proper ways to observe a tribe, or to search for and deal with archival records. Additionally, there are protocols for how to sort data once it is collected. For example, data collected from questionnaires and interviews will be sorted according to age, marital status, gender, ethnicity, education, salary, political affiliation and so forth depending on the kind of study being performed. Decisions must be made, based on accepted guidelines, for sorting the subjects of study into various categories or kinds. A researcher will make a decision to classify subjects by sex rather than by race, or by class rather than by sex, say. To perform this kind of sorting, there must also be established definitions of race, class, sex and so forth.

Ideally, such protocols ensure the value-free collection of data as well as eliminate differences in how scientists observe, interview or describe their subjects. Unless researchers abide by such guidelines, the data they collect are treated as suspicious (e.g., not being suitably value-free, not being considered as reliable facts). Moreover, such guidelines ideally ensure that scientists handle and sort their data in standardized ways. This supposedly protects the integrity of the data by preventing arbitrary or value-laden judgements from affecting the categorization and analysis of data.

Moreover, protocols are designed to ensure repeatability and consistency of the data obtained. To formulate and test empirical theories, the data must be reliable at least in the sense that any scientist following the protocols would obtain the same or highly similar data. Only if the data are stable in this sense – only if results are reproducible – is it possible to detect persistent regularities or patterns, to generalize about the phenomena in question and to produce theories containing potential universal laws. After all, in the natural sciences, if other scientists cannot reproduce the experimental results of some researcher, the judgement is that something is wrong with her results (e.g., cold fusion, where Stanley Ponds and Martin Fleischman claimed they had produced nuclear fusion through chemical rather than nuclear reactions). Part of this consistency is that multiple researchers would agree on what the data are, what the data mean and so forth. In other words, there should be intersubjective agreement among scientists about what counts as data and their meaning. Hence, standard protocols are ideally supposed to yield facts about which all observers can agree. So if protocols are not followed strictly, the possibility for moral, political or other biases infecting the gathering and handling of data increases. Or if the protocols have such biases built into them, then value-laden data might be passed off as value-neutral facts about the social realm.

Finally, protocols ideally guarantee that social-science data are valid. There are two aspects to data validity. To be *internally valid*, data must be true of the subjects from whom they are collected. So questionnaires or anthropological observations are supposed to record how research subjects really are, what they genuinely think or believe rather than how the observer thinks subjects should be. To be *externally valid*, data must not only be true of the subjects tested, surveyed or observed, but must also be true of all other relevantly similar subjects who were not tested, surveyed or observed. If the data collected are only true of the subjects in the reference sample – the subjects tested, surveyed or observed – then social scientists cannot draw general conclusions about the whole population. Suppose for some reason, exit surveys were accurate only for the small number of persons sampled leaving voting stations. Then it would be impossible to project winners of elections based on those small samples and it would be impossible to generalize from those surveys as to why the voting population as a whole voted as they did. As another example, Gideon Sjoberg and Ted Vaughan (1993: 74–75, 90) point out how the research of William Sewell and the Wisconsin School of Sociology has presupposed a Middle American profile. As such, no matter how much internal validity this body of data and research has, it lacks external validity in that no generalizations to the whole of American society can be made.

The various guidelines for gathering and handling data clearly represent values, but are usually considered only to represent *scientific values* like integrity, purity and coherence of data. These are values crucial to the proper activity of data collection and analysis and work to counteract distortions due to deception, secrecy and passing off wishful thinking as scientific fact. These represent what are sometimes called scientific best practices. But what about moral and social values and cultural ideals like the instrumental picture of action, political liberalism, liberal individualism and the like? Ideally, protocols should counteract distortions due to these influences as well. But do they?

1.1. Standards and value-neutrality

The protocols for gathering and handling of social-science data are not meant to be descriptive statements about what researchers actually do. Rather, protocols provide standards for what social scientists *should do*. In other words, these are prescriptive guidelines or rules determining how researchers are to go about collecting and handling data. Protocols are normative: if social scientists ignore such protocols in their research, their research methods and results are considered tainted and unscientific. Such standards are used in judgements about what is good and bad science.

But note that these judgements are about scientific practices and whether they conform to appropriate standards or not. These are not judgements about the moral or value character of scientific activities. Judgements about whether scientific activities are ethical or are morally worthwhile are supposed to be completely separate matters from standards ensuring good scientific practices. This distinction between scientific values and ethical values can be traced back at least to Weber:

> Now one cannot demonstrate scientifically what the duty of an academic teacher is. One can only demand of the teacher that he have the intellectual integrity to see that it is one thing to state facts, to determine mathematical or logical relations or the internal structure of cultural values, while it is another thing to answer questions of the value of culture and its individual contents and the question of how one should act in the cultural community and in political associations. These are quite heterogeneous problems. (quoted in Root 1993: 131)

Note that in this passage moral concerns are set on one side (e.g., the duty of an academic, considering the value of culture, how one should act) while scientific concerns are set on the other (e.g., intellectual integrity, focus on facts, mathematical relations and structures). Weber considers these two sets of concerns to be heterogeneous – different in kind from each other. Scientific best practice involves the latter, not the former concerns. Put differently, valid data is not a moral good, it is a scientific good.

This is the fact/value split manifesting itself in social-science standards for practice. One consequence of this version of the split is that the validity or integrity of social-science data is completely independent of the moral rightness or wrongness of the methods used to obtain it. So, as long as the scientific protocols are followed the data will be valid, whether the data was obtained with or without informed consent.

Earlier, in Part Two, we saw a number of reasons why there often is no clear distinction between facts and values in social-science inquiry. So an important presupposition underlying standards for data collection and analysis is highly questionable. In addition, we have also seen that striving for value-neutrality in the social sciences is actually a deeply moral aim. This aim, among other things, represents a particular vision of the moral good – privilege no particular ends or conceptions of the good life (i.e., political liberalism: Chapter 5, sec. 1). So to the extent that standards for the treatment of data are designed to promote value-neutrality, they actually promote a particular moral good, namely neutrality.

Worse, by focusing exclusively on scientific values aimed at data integrity and validity, such standards make no provision for detecting and dealing with cultural ideals that may be smuggled in through the research process. For instance, the typical kinds of surveys used in exit polling conform to strict standards for their construction and administration. However, none of these standards flag the liberal-individualist ideals permeating the questions. As another example, the surveys and methods of data collection involved in hardiness research (Chapter 8, sec. 1) conform to appropriate standards for their design and administration. Nevertheless, ideals of existential individualism (Chapter 5, sec. 2.4) and the instrumental picture of action (Chapter 4) permeate the entire hardiness programme. Having clear standards for gathering and handling data actually do nothing to free social-science research from the influence of values and cultural ideals.

1.2. Standards and ethics

This separation of ethics from best scientific practices is disturbingly reflected in some professional scientific 'codes of ethics' officially sanctioning ethical violations for the furtherance of science. Consider the codes adopted by the American Psychological Association (§8) and the American Sociological Association (§12). Under some circumstances, these codes permit deception and concealment as well as possibly ignoring informed consent if the harm or the risk for harm to the subject is judged to be minor with respect to the expected significant benefits of the research results.[1] This is a strictly utilitarian and instrumental approach to research ethics, where some kind of cost–benefit analysis is the only justification for *possibly not* violating the rights and autonomy of test subjects. This is an example of where the moral good and scientific best practices part ways when they are disconnected. Of course, the judgement about whether harm or risk for harm to the subject is minor is not made by test subjects. Rather, it is made by the scientists designing the research project with respect to the scientific or educational benefits of the project's results.[2] Supposedly any harms incurred by subjects is mitigated by debriefing after the experiment, interview or other means of obtaining data. At such debriefings, the violations of autonomy and rights are explained as the curtain is lifted on what research is really taking place. But such debriefings do not undo the crass instrumental treatment of research subjects as mere means to the researcher's ends. Moreover, there is evidence that such debriefings do not mitigate harms done by concealment and deception (Ross, Lepper and Hubbard 1975), as in Milgram's experiments discussed below.

The approach to research ethics sanctioned by such professional codes actually provides very little protection for test subjects. Potential harms or risks for harms will always be judged against researchers' purposes and interests. Social scientists will not render dispassionate judgements in such circumstances when their scientific interests as well as the pressures of research grants, the lures of prestige and the stress of tenure and promotion decisions hang in the balance, colouring their appraisal of potential harms (institutional review boards are supposed to help spot these biases).

Surprisingly, the standards of protection set forth by these professional societies are much lower than the Nuremberg code governing permissible medical experiments. This is illustrated by the much discussed experiments by social psychologist Stanley Milgram (1974). He designed an experiment to discover the degree to which people would obey authority, even when their actions in obedience to authority would cause pain nearing death for others. The experimental design involves a stark degree of deception and concealment. Test subjects were misled into believing they were assisting researchers in an experiment on the effects of painful stimuli on learning tasks. The test subjects controlled a device that was attached to the supposed learning subjects. Researchers falsely told the test subjects that this device would administer electric shocks of varying voltages to the learner. Unbeknownst to the test subjects, the learners were actors who would pretend to fail to accomplish the learning task. Upon failure, the experimenter would order the test subject to use the device to give the learner an electric shock. The learner would then pretend to receive a shock, displaying signs of discomfort appropriate to the supposed level of shock received (e.g., wincing, crying out). Successive failures would be followed by the experimenter's instructions to increase the voltage, leading to more intense displays of discomfort.

Milgram found that most people were willing to administer shocks they were led to believe were near lethal. It did not matter what expressions of pain or even apparent loss of consciousness exhibited by the pretending learners. As long as test subjects were encouraged or ordered to do so by an experimenter willing to take responsibility, they would generally administer the shocks.

These experiments illustrate how scientific values trump moral or spiritual values in the name of scientific best practices. For Milgram's experiments on authority and obedience to succeed at producing data meeting scientific standards, test subjects must be systematically misled about what is really happening. Test subjects would respond very differently if they were told in advance that everything was pretence except their responses to the authority of the experimenter. So deception and concealment is required if researchers are to obtain the data they seek: to what lengths will people go in their obedience to authority? Professional 'codes of ethics' sanction these experimental violations of people's rights and autonomy. These codes also allow harm to test subjects by coercing them to intentionally inflict harm on another person in the name of collecting some supposed pure, objective data about human behaviour conforming to standards.[3] This sanctioning clearly subordinates the values and worth of people to scientific values regarding data. In other words, these 'codes of ethics' encourage treating research subjects instrumentally as means to the ends of scientific goals. One of the things informed consent is supposed to protect research subjects from is this kind of instrumental situation and the violations of rights and autonomy associated with it. There are two important points here. First, when informed consent can be ignored, or undercut by systematic deception and concealment, in the name of 'higher' scientific values and goals, then the ethical protections are non-existent.

Second, the choice to privilege scientific values over the rights and autonomy of people is a moral choice, not a value-neutral one. Consider a standard example from ethics: suppose the government has captured a terrorist who is the only person possessing knowledge of how to disarm a nuclear bomb hidden somewhere downtown in a major city (New York or London, say). Any harm caused to the terrorist by torture to extract this information would appear minor in comparison with the benefit of avoiding tens of thousands of deaths, hundreds of thousands of injuries, tens perhaps hundreds of thousands of cases of radiation poisoning and cancer in the surrounding regions where radioactive fallout disperses, incalculable disruption to the national economy and so forth.

My point in raising this example is not that strict utilitarian and instrumental considerations are wrong in the case of the terrorist. Rather, the point is that such considerations are *insufficient* to guide the social scientist when she is weighing potential harm to her research subjects against her scientific and personal interests. Nothing in such a crass instrumental framework gives her purchase on evaluating whether violations of research subjects is worthwhile (compare with Chapter 8, sec. 2). These professional codes are drawn up with the express purpose of privileging obtaining valid, useful data over the ethical worth of the people serving as research subjects. But this amounts to treating people as means in a *zweckrational* framework for scientific practice.

1.3. Validity and value-neutrality

Protocols or standards for ensuring the internal and external validity of data also do not guarantee value-neutrality. They focus on things like the validity of questionnaires to accurately measure respondents' attitudes or beliefs, or assess the representativeness of the respondents surveyed. In other words, such techniques assure intersubjective agreement on the data and the validity of the data, but tell us nothing about what kinds of values or cultural ideals might be lurking in the survey instruments themselves. Exit-poll surveys are coloured by liberal individualism or an instrumental picture of action, so these cultural ideals are never detected by tests for validity. Or, as another example, recall the developmental theories briefly discussed in Chapter 5, sec. 1. Protocols for validity will insure that the data derived from observations of children's behaviours at different ages cohere with similar observational data. But such validity completely ignores the values and ideals of the researcher that go into constructing the behavioural and maturity characteristics of the different life-stages and the picture of the good life represented by the highest stage. Children and young adults are sorted based on observations and these life-stage categories, not the other way around. So the observations of developmental psychologists, valid as they might be, are sorted into value-laden categories. Validity does not equate to value-neutrality.

Although social scientists generally do strive to avoid value commitments in their work, as Root (1993: 128–29) points out, validity also has an unintended consequence of leading to value-partiality. In brief the problem is this: while social scientists often root out overt biases like racism, the goal of validity for their data requires them to have to 'soak up' and pass on any institutional or larger kinds of ideals. So, in developmental psychology, psychologists must work with cultural notions of perfection and maturity that distinguish children from adults. To observe adults would not produce valid data about childhood stages of life. But concepts like childhood and stages of life are not natural facts like the mass of an electron or the number of protons in a carbon nucleus. Rather, such concepts represent social and institutional notions or categorizations of human life (see below).[4] Such categories and concepts are not value-neutral. Hence, in deploying these categories, developmental psychologists 'are unable to live up to their own ideal of value-neutral data' (Root 1993: 129). So if they want valid data, developmental psychologists must use and pass on these categorizations and notions of perfection in their research. The pursuit of validity requires adopting particular biases. All social scientists face this same situation regarding obtaining valid data. For instance, political scientists in surveying voters in Western societies must presuppose some forms of individualism in the construction of their surveys to insure validity. At the same time, individualism is anything but a value-neutral feature of social reality.

Sometimes internal and external validity can be at odds with each other. Suppose a group of interviewers remain equally impassive and blank-faced while interviewing people. Supposedly the responses of interviewees will not vary from one interviewer to the other. This situation would insure that the data collected by an impassive, blank-faced interviewer was internally valid, hence reliable. On the other hand, if all interviewers are impassive and blank-faced, such interviews would only reveal how people responded to such interviewers. Interviewees would not be responding as they actually are because people do not normally talk to each other in such impassive, blank-faced ways. Hence, the results of the interviews would only hold for people responding to such impassive, blank-faced interviewers and not be externally valid – that is, would not be true of the population at large in their ordinary everyday circumstances (Root 1993: 147 n. 29).

2. Classification and sorting of data

Once data have been collected according to standard protocols, they must then be sorted or organized in terms of various categories like age, gender, occupation, education history, sexual preference and marital status. If social scientists really are collecting data on an independent, law-like realm (in analogy with the natural sciences), then their categories should be something like natural kinds having an independent existence as well. Furthermore, the sorting of data into these categories should be mostly a matter of putting facts into their appropriate boxes, so to speak. Unfortunately for the natural-scientific ideal, the social realm is not like this at all.

2.1. Natural and social kinds

There is a wide-spread belief that the natural sciences deal with categories or kinds that are discovered to be 'out there' in nature. Such kinds as electrons, molecules, volcanoes, hurricanes, stars, galaxies and so forth are thought to be discovered rather than constructed.[5] As such, they would be natural objects, suitable for natural-science investigation. In the social sciences, the parallel in the natural-scientific approach (and some descriptivist approaches) is to treat social kinds – for example, adolescents, homosexuals, Hispanics, divorcees, rich, poor – as discovered rather than created. In other words, just as there were molecules, water and viruses before they were discovered, there were adolescents, upper-middle class and Caucasians before they were discovered. Social kinds are pictured as being independent of social-science theorizing as natural kinds are independent of natural-science theorizing.

For the universal-laws conception of science, natural kinds are important. Only if there are such kinds already existing in nature independent of our investigations can there be anything like universal laws. Such laws are supposed to be independent of context and if all the kinds in natural-science inquiry were merely constructed by us, they would be context-dependent. In particular, they would be dependent on our purposes and ways of seeing the world. Such constructed, dependent objects would not be appropriate targets for universal laws. So, one of the characteristic tasks of natural science is the determination of what natural kinds there are and the distinguishing of these from artificial or constructed kinds.

The distinction between natural and artificial kinds, however, does not appear very useful in the social sciences. There are two primary reasons for this. First, many, if not all, of the kinds or categories that social scientists use are artificial in the sense that they are constructed by communities of people who have chosen to organize their everyday lives in particular ways. Many of these kinds or classifications – like occupation, marital status, childhood, political affiliation, education – are tied to practical interests and social conventions of the communities who devise them. In other words, many social kinds are not independent, already existing categories or objects that are awaiting the social scientist's discovery. They arise out of human needs and ways of seeing things and can change as our needs and ways of seeing things change. As such, social kinds are not the sorts of things that would be governed by universal, context-free laws. After all, in the absence of any social, political and legal order there would not be any marital status, criminal status, class status or political affiliations, to name a few. Or take the social kind 'child' mentioned earlier. After the Middle Ages, those in the age group between 4 and 12 were distinguished from other age groups and treated differently. And in being distinguished and treated differently, they conformed their behaviours to these expectations. So, by treating children as those in need of special care and protection, it then became possible for children to become those needing special care and protection.

Second, others of these categories or kinds are constructed by social scientists to sort their subjects of inquiry and data. Races, kinds of sexualities, socio-economic classes, among others, described in social inquiry would not be what they are – might not even exist at all – had the practices of collecting, recording, comparing, organizing and analysing psychological, economic, anthropological and other forms of data not come into existence. One does not have to follow all of Foucault's postmodernist critique of social science (Chapter 3, sec. 4.2) to see that a number of social categories or kinds are constructed by social scientists for the classification, tracking and management of human activity according to various norms and purposes. As such, social kinds constructed for the purposes of social inquiry and management would also not be governed by universal, context-free laws.

Urban sprawl is an example of an artificial kind constructed for our social purposes. If this were like a natural kind, urban sprawl would be up and operating with the advent of cities as something 'natural' (indeed, this is the view of Bruegmann 2005). But the expansion of mediaeval cities beyond their walls was driven by different factors than the phenomenon of suburbanization in post-World War II America. Cities are structurally different in these two periods as well as being of vastly different scales. The reasons for growth are different: for example, external threats, technologies, economic and social structures, institutions of governance, land-use patterns, proximity of resources, not to mention starkly differing ideals of individualism, autonomy, freedom and the like. Moreover, many modern cities in America are no longer organized around a single city centre, but are composed of multiple subcentres. So whatever urban sprawl is as a constructed kind, it certainly is not a timeless, changeless category or kind.

The purpose or interest-relative nature of social kinds is one reason why the social realm is not an independent, law-like realm that can be the target of social-science theorizing in strict analogy with how natural-science theorizing treats the natural world. In Part Three, we saw examples of how social-science theorizing is not independent of the social realm (Chapters 11–12). Social-science theorizing has the power to transform or reinterpret the target of its theorizing; as well, the social realm has the power to influence and colour social-science theorizing (recall the two-way interpretive street: Chapter 3, sec. 2).

One response to this situation is to readjust the notion of natural kind in social science in the following way. If social kinds were constructed by communities of people, religious orders, the legal system or other social and political institutions before social science trained its eyes upon them, then there is a sense in which such social kinds can be discovered by social scientists. Suppose a religious order creates a distinction between believers and unbelievers, or a legal system creates a distinction between singles, marrieds, divorcees and widows. Then sociologists and other social scientists can discover these social kinds as being already existing in the social order. Such kinds do not depend on social science for their existence because their existence is created and sustained by other social or legal institutions.

Distinguishing social kinds by whether they were created or discovered by social science does not change the fact that the latter still are not appropriate targets for context-free natural laws. Nor does it change the fact that these social kinds reflect and are sustained by values, ideals and purposes. Moreover, this distinction fails to undermine the fact that social-science theorizing about the social kinds it discovers tends to reshape or change those kinds. It merely means that these are kinds the social scientist can discover rather than invent. So this distinction does not really restore the analogy with natural kinds in the natural sciences. Nor does it alleviate a pressing problem with social kinds and social theorizing. Namely, natural scientific and descriptivist modes of inquiry tend to take any 'discovered' social kinds from the existing social order to analyse that same order. So those approaches tend to accept the reigning power structure's definition of existing social reality as objective reality. This means social scientists will pass the reigning power structure's point of view on in their research as well as surreptitiously endorsing that point of view.

Furthermore, if Foucault (1979; 1980a) is right, there are very few social kinds that social scientists did not play some role in creating or shaping. Psychiatrists' creation and description of various abnormal sexual behaviours in the nineteenth century would be examples of social kinds that were constructed by social scientists, then picked up and applied by legal systems and cultures. As well, Foucault maintains, many if not most of our categories of deviant behaviour found in legal codes were first constructed and shaped by social scientists before becoming embedded in legal systems.

2.2. Sorting and judgements

Foucault's claims for the pervasive influence of social science on social kinds is controversial. Nevertheless, social kinds are constructions of social scientists, policy-makers and others based on their interests, purposes and needs. This is one reason why sorting research subjects and data into categories is not merely a shuffling of facts into appropriate boxes. The boxes – kinds – are created and sustained by values, ideals and purposes.

Another reason sorting is not merely shuffling and organizing facts is that such sorting requires judgements about who and what the subjects of study are and how they should be represented. As mentioned earlier, social scientists have to make decisions to classify subjects by sex rather than by race, or by class rather than by sex, and so forth. But the choice of viewing a person by their sex rather than their race, or their class rather than their sex, is a judgement about how that person should be viewed. Put another way, for the purposes of research, a social scientist must make a judgement about what the subjects of study are – persons characterized by sex, or by race, or by class and so on.

Social kinds like juvenile delinquent, homosexual, child abuser, drug user, upper-middle class, highly educated, intelligent and the like are not simply boxes for organizing research subjects. They are, in Ian Hacking's term (1991), *normalizing concepts*: they are concepts that prescribe what ought to be, what is normative for the category or kind in question. To be upper-middle class, one has to have a level of affluence falling in a particular range. To be highly educated, one has to have completed a particular education level. To be homosexual, one has to have particular sexual preferences. Sorting a black female subject by her race, rather than her sex, or by her sexual preference normalizes her to the characteristics essential to that social kind. This categorization then fixes or defines what is relevant about the research subject, labelling her so that other social scientists can collect and interpret data to confirm the label, creating and perpetuating stereotypes based on the essential characteristics of the label and so forth. An example of the power of such social kinds can be found in the general belief among political scientists, opinion researchers and others that there are very few Republican Party members who are black and conservative. Typically, according to the normative characteristics of the social kind, blacks are politically liberal and affiliate themselves with the Democratic Party. Exceptions are considered to fall outside the norm – that is, to be abnormal – or, in some political circles, to be traitors to their race. Under a different social kind – conservative Republican Party member – they are considered heroes and roll models! There is nothing value-neutral about these classifications and judgements.

The 'normalizing power' or influence of social kinds is evident in other ways. As Root points out:

> Housing, clothing, entertainment, employment, education, social work, law enforcement, publishing, broadcasting, art, medical care, religion, and politics are tailored, pitched, shaped, adjusted, or developed to respond to the subjects of the [social] sciences as if they were completely and accurately described as child-abusers, psychotics, co-dependents, prostitutes, rational economic men, homosexuals, alcoholics, underachievers, overachievers, or handicapped – that is, by the idealized language [social kinds] of the sciences. (1993: 165)

Just think of political campaigns, attitudes towards welfare programmes, trends in Hollywood movies, and advertising as examples of these kinds of pitching and adjustment. Social science's sorting of people into myriad social kinds often simply reproduces the labels found in society (i.e., created by government, business or the media). But social kinds created by religion, law and business clearly are not value-neutral as they are created for the purposes and needs of religious officials, courts of law, business executives and marketers to name just a few interested parties. These social kinds carry with them all the moral characteristics defining these norms. So when social scientists employ these categories in their research, they are employing the values defining and sustaining these categories. And when they make judgements about which of these categories to use and which subjects to sort into which categories, those same values are carried along in social-science research and passed on and reinforced in supposed value-neutral results.

Consider a much discussed example, the social kind marriage. It is the only kind of domestic partnership recognized by US law (although this is slowly changing to some degree). Adults sharing households are sorted into two categories by governments at all levels in the USA – married and unmarried. But these social kinds are not value-neutral. Rather, they represent both moral and political values or preferences. Public policy in the USA favours marriage over all other forms of domestic partnership by according married couples a number of benefits unavailable to unmarried couples. As long as there are legal prohibitions against same-sex marriages, a life-long homosexual couple will be sorted into the unmarried category and, hence, will be denied the benefits reserved exclusively for married couples. When social scientists employ these social kinds, the political and moral values that created and sustain these kinds enter into their research. Even if they do not recognize these values, or remain silent about them, when social scientists use these categories they are unwittingly helping to perpetuate not only the distinctions, but the values animating them as well.[6]

Furthermore, the usage of social kinds by social science lends a scientific air to their existence, thus reinforcing the kinds and their place in society. This is the two-way interpretive street at work (Chapter 3, sec. 2). Social scientists often uncritically absorb the values and ideals of the community they are studying (e.g., as in marriage research: Chapter 8, sec. 3) in their use of social kinds and their sorting of data. As well, social scientists, by employing these constructed categories to study people, can pass values and ideals back to the community through popularizations of their work, news reporting using the categories, serving as expert witnesses and commentators, or even by training research subjects into the categories.[7]

In this sense, social kinds serve a kind of dual role. They guide the social scientist in how she should treat or view her research subjects, as fitting or conforming to the norms making up the kind. For instance:

> Psychiatry, until recently, defined homosexuality as a mental illness, and, given the aims of psychiatry – namely, to treat the mentally ill and adjust the psychologically maladjusted – a judgement made in a psychiatric clinic that a patient was homosexual was a recommendation for treatment. For the psychiatrist, homosexuals were not only a kind of person, they were a kind of ill or maladjusted person – one in need of a cure. (Root 1993: 166)

Social kinds also serve to guide research subjects, as well as the rest of the general population, as to how they should picture themselves. Social kinds encode norms by which people can see how they should appraise their behaviour as to whether they are abnormal – not only themselves, but how they should see and appraise others as well. So as long as homosexuality was considered a psychiatric pathology, many homosexuals believed there was something wrong with themselves. As well, most members of North American societies also pictured homosexuals as ill, often treating them as second-class citizens. The social kind homosexuals does not simply categorize a psychological condition, but also includes an endorsement of normality/abnormality and a possible diagnosis as well as a treatment.

Finally, as pointed out in Parts One and Two, some of the most basic social kinds or categories social scientists deploy – individuals and groups – are only available given individualist ideals. Without these ideals, the very idea of an individual apart from the group makes little sense. Virtually all social-science protocols for gathering and sorting data make use of these basic social kinds. Likewise, the judgements to treat people as individuals, or as members of groups, or even to treat groups as mere aggregates of individuals presupposes or makes use of cultural ideals like liberal individualism. So even standards for collecting and sorting social-science data reflect disguised ideologies.

3. Data analysis

If values and cultural ideals are already firmly ensconced in our social-science data, statistical or other methods of data analysis will do nothing to detect and remove such influences. Rather, they will just ensure that such values and ideals are passed on unnoticed. The values and ideals informing the construction of voter surveys, for instance, will show up in the data collected from administering the surveys. This data will be sorted based upon the categories chosen by the researcher, but the categories and judgements involved will not remove nor necessarily even detect the values and ideals reflected in the survey and the data. Hence, the statistical or other methods deployed to analyse the data – since they are designed to discover correlations or other possible relationships among the data – will neither detect nor remove these values or ideals from the data while 'crunching the numbers'. So even if it is true that data-analysis methods are themselves value-neutral, they are of no help to the social scientist regarding avoiding values and cultural ideals.

4. Taking stock

In the natural sciences, our theorizing appears to be about an independent realm. The social sciences, in contrast, theorize about social constructions devised by social scientists or other social actors for their purposes and needs.

There are no social kinds that are independent in the same sense as natural kinds. This does not imply, however, that social kinds have no reality whatsoever. On the contrary, they are quite real and have potent impact on us for good or for ill.

The constructed nature of social kinds has a number of implications for social inquiry. Any approach that takes concepts and categories like class as objects that have always existed, as Marx's class-conflict analysis does, ends up treating socially constructed kinds as if they are stable, always existing natural kinds. In reality, 'class' is a socially constructed concept whose definitions and boundaries are defined and delineated by us for our purposes. Classes have not always existed, but the Marxist analysis presupposes otherwise, treating classes as eternally valid categories independent of our purposes in classification and management. To treat classes in this manner in our analysis of societies or our reading of history is to apply a modern concept like class anachronistically to earlier time periods and societies lacking these categories. One has to be extremely careful to note what kinds of distortions these categories and concepts introduce as a result of the modern purposes and ideals lying behind our construction of these categories.

The socially conditioned nature of social kinds also implies problems for constructing predictive theories in the social sciences. Prediction presupposes a stable realm of phenomena that can be reliably reproduced. But any theory taking social kinds and patterns as determinate and fixed, in analogy with natural kinds, will not produce reliable predictions. Social kinds and patterns change as we change our purposes and values. The social realm lacks the kind of stability characterizing the natural realm, rendering prediction in social inquiry suspect (see Chapter 16).

Setting standards for data collection and handling, distinguishing scientific from ethical and other values, and treating social kinds as if they were natural kinds, are ways in which social scientists attempt to parallel the natural sciences. However, social science cannot escape the ethical issues its research practices and standards for data raise because we – human beings – are the subjects of its inquiry, social scientists included. There is no parallel for this situation in the natural sciences because it is impossible to fashion research practices and standards for data that mistreat or harm electrons and molecules.[8] In the natural sciences, ethical problems might be raised by research developments like the discovery of nuclear energy or the development of methods for modifying DNA. But these ethical concerns are external to the scientific practices, dealing with the implications or applications of such developments. In contrast, social science deals directly with human beings – persons who are moral beings, who are worthy of respect and dignity, who are self-interpreting beings with their own views about themselves and their world. Social-science practices directly touch all these aspects of humanity in ways natural-science practices largely cannot.[9] Physics, for instance, does not offer guidance as to how we are to use nuclear energy nor does biology tell us what is worthwhile about DNA modifications. The social sciences, on the other hand, because they are pervaded by cultural ideals acting as disguised ideologies are always advocating what we should do and what is worthwhile.

For further study

1. What is internal validity? External validity? Explain how protocols ensuring valid data can actually force social scientists to be value-partisan.
2. Describe the difference between natural kinds and social kinds. What are the implications of this difference for natural-scientific modes of investigation?
3. Find three examples of social kinds or categories from newspaper or magazine stories. Analyse the ideals and values involved in these kinds and how the stories end up endorsing these values.

Recommended reading

M. Root, 'Collecting Data in the Social Sciences,' and 'Sorting Data into Kinds', in *Philosophy of Social Science* (Oxford: Blackwell, 1993), chs 6, 7.

Determinism and Free Will ▉14

Many commentators both inside and outside of the social sciences wonder if such sciences only amount to some kind of frighteningly manipulative behavioural technology. The very ideal of pursuing a context-free science of human behaviour appears to many to be thoroughly depersonalizing and in strong conflict with our everyday ideas on what makes for meaningful living. One way these worries come to expression is in terms of free will–determinism dilemmas. A great many theories and perspectives in current behavioural sciences, for instance, incorporate determinism as one of their key theoretical assumptions (Rychlak 1988; Slife and Williams 1995). Here, determinism is the rigid determination of all events in the spheres of human action, mental life, emotional dynamics, or the social realm by causes beyond human control. As a result, mainstream psychologists face a severe dilemma concerning determinism and freedom. On the one hand, they are dedicated to finding context-free laws of human behaviour permitting someone who possessed knowledge of them to *freely* engineer desired effects in psychic or social realms. On the other hand, paradoxically, the rigid picture of the social realm presupposed by psychologists actually rules out the very sort of freedom and ingenuity they themselves exercise in devising experiments and formulating laws and theories of human behaviour.

Other social sciences face versions of free will–determinism dilemmas. For example, if individuals' preferences as well as their decisions are determined by economic factors beyond their control, this would result in a form of economic determinism. At the same time, suppose we also have a theory of consumer choice depicting economic agents as somehow having the power to form their own preferences and choices. This is a free will–determinism dilemma: agents are pictured as being able to form their own preferences and to make choices based upon these preferences at the same time as they are pictured as being completely determined by forces beyond their control.[1] Similarly for political science or any other social sciences that presuppose both some form of social determination of all individual thought and action while simultaneously assuming individuals have freedom of thought and action.[2]

In this chapter, I will largely focus on free will–determinism dilemmas in psychology as they are the clearest examples and strike closest to home, so to speak. We will see that cultural ideals play an important role in creating and sustaining these dilemmas.

1. Determinism and freedom in psychology

Here is a very basic form of the dilemma, applicable to all social inquiry. On the one hand, there would seem to be no viable notion of freedom without some form of determination or ordered realm of causes and influences in which to act and make a difference. After all, if there is no such order to the world, how would you be able to act so as to achieve your aims? On the other hand, that freedom has to be real and meaningful and cannot just amount to simply another effect of causes that play upon the human agent (Richardson and Bishop 2002).

Mainstream psychology's picture of the world is that of a deterministic realm composed of efficient causal chains, providing both a target for scientific inquiry and an arena for effective action (Chapter 9). Psychologists strive to devise explanations in terms of context-free universal laws governing human behaviour. These explanations show how current attitudes and actions are largely the inevitable product of genetic make-up, culture, an individual's life history, current circumstances or some combination of these factors. At the same time, psychologists see themselves as mapping the determining factors of human behaviour to lay a basis for liberating individuals from unwanted influences. That way individuals might live freer lives, or actively foster more fulfilling and creative forms of social living. By assuming this picture, however, psychologists commit themselves to a doctrine of determinism that threatens to undermine many of their own cherished aims, such as freeing people from ineffective and unfulfilling lives. This threat derives from a contorted view of people as both thoroughly enmeshed in a deterministic world while simultaneously somehow having the power to transcend and freely manipulate efficient causes to produce desired outcomes – the same basic structure as found in the instrumental picture of action (see Fig. 4.1).

This obvious tension between determinism and freedom is rarely noticed, seldom analysed, and almost never viewed as something that calls the reigning conceptions of psychology into question. This is a serious, interesting and puzzling phenomenon in its own right. There seem to be two broad traditions attempting to cope with this tension in twentieth-century psychology. By far the dominant approach has been to assume or affirm a fairly strict determinist viewpoint while ignoring or sidestepping the ways in which this approach presupposes an implicit doctrine of freedom of some sort, undermines some of its own important aims, and seems belied by the free, responsible, creative activity of psychologists themselves. A smaller, diverse, relatively marginal group of humanist, existentialist and phenomenological thinkers in psychology have explicitly defended ideals of freedom of choice and self-actualization. But they usually fail to note that realization of these ideals depends upon some reliable connectedness among the events of human experience. Partly for this reason, they rarely develop any plausible alternative account of this connectedness, and so must still rely on, and are haunted by, the very sort of efficient causal deterministic viewpoint which they reject.

In Chapter 9, sec. 1, I sketched behaviourist, psychodynamic, cognitive and humanistic portrayals of the realm of human action in psychology. The physics and computer models for efficient causation in psychology were also introduced in secs. 2.1 and 2.2. Here, I only want to recall briefly how free will–determinism dilemmas arise in each of these theoretical perspectives

1.1. Behaviourism

The goal of behaviourism is to uncover laws governing human behaviour by studying observable aspects of the environment (e.g., stimuli, responses and reinforcements) rather than unobservable mental constructs (e.g., intentions, motives and desires). Achieving this goal would lead to precise prediction and control of human behaviour and, therefore, to responsible guidance for behaviour-change activities. Behaviourist psychologists claim both that all behaviour is strictly determined and that extensive mastery and control over the environment and behaviour are possible. There is a sharp tension here between belief in determinism and personal or social control over behaviour. All behaviour is governed by impinging stimuli and reinforcements while we somehow have the ability to fulfil these ideals of mastery and control (which themselves must also be behaviours governed strictly by the deterministic interplay of stimuli and reinforcements.

1.2. Psychodynamics

Rigid determinism holds sway in the psychic realm on psychodynamic views. But a fundamental goal for all these theories is to understand and nurture the kinds of self-reflection that lead to rational self-transformation in therapy and even perhaps in society generally. The mechanistic picture underlying psychodynamics leaves it unclear how such rational self-transformation could be achieved. The rigid determinism holding sway largely at unconscious levels beyond our notice rules out choice and responsibility.

1.3. Cognitive approaches

The cognitivist picture of the mind is based on the deterministic operations of a computer. At the same time, individuals are assumed to be able to intervene in or mediate these computational processes to change thinking patterns, self-defeating behaviours and other psychological forms of maladjustment. Yet if the 'computational architecture' and 'software' of the brain plus the information input into that system determine all of our behaviour, it is unclear how a person could 'intervene' to somehow influence or soften the deterministic processes at work.

1.4. Humanist approaches

If humanist approaches are unified in anything, it is the rejection of determinism reigning in human behaviour. Otherwise, self-actualization or pursuing our inborn sense of identity would be impossible. However, it is difficult to see that humanist approaches have avoided determinism. If, for instance, the unique potential within each person exerts too strong an influence over our sense of identity, our behaviour and needs, as well as over our psychological health, everything looks to be determined by something beyond our control. If this inner potential is rooted in biology (Maslow 1968), then it is a dominating factor over which we have no control. The presence of such influences outside our control would not be all that different from psychodynamics or behaviourism. Although these forms of determinism can be understood in ways that soften their impact relative to the forms at work in psychodynamics and behaviourism, the account of agency and freedom needed to act effectively in a causally ordered world is typically left unaddressed in humanist theories. Without a positive account of such agency, humanist approaches have no compelling case that they have escaped the confines of determinism.

2. Determinism

Determinism in psychology is described in the language of efficient causation, largely patterned after physics. In contrast to the latter, however, conceptions of determinism in psychology are not particularly well developed. To see that determinism as conceived in physics actually is problematic for psychology, I will first sketch the physics conception of determinism.

2.1. Determinism as unique evolution

Suppose that the physical state of a system is characterized by some key properties, say the values of positions and momenta of all the particles composing the system at some time t. A crucial feature of physical determinism is the following: given a specification of the initial state of a system and the laws governing its states, then the entire history of the system is uniquely fixed. Consider a pendulum. Each time the pendulum is raised to the same height and released, it executes the same oscillations. We can formulate this condition as follows:

> *Unique Evolution*: a given state is always followed (and preceded) by the same history of state transitions.

Roughly speaking, the idea is that every time one returns the system to the same initial state (or any state in the history of state transitions), it will undergo the same history of transitions from state to state.

Unique evolution is a strong but important requirement if determinism is to be meaningfully applied to physical systems. Imagine a typical physical system *s* as a film. Satisfying unique evolution means that if the film is started over and over at the same frame (returning the system to the same initial state), then *s* will repeat every detail of its total history over and over again and identical copies of the film would produce the same sequence of pictures. So if one always starts *Jurassic Park* at the beginning frame, it plays the same. The tyrannosaurus as anti-hero always saves the day. No new frames are added to the movie. Furthermore, if one were to start with a different frame, say a frame at the middle of the movie, the ensuing sequence of frames would still uniquely 'play'.

By way of contrast, suppose that returning *s* to the same initial state produced a different sequence of state transitions on some of the runs. Consider a system *s* to be like a device that spontaneously generates a different sequence of pictures on some occasions when starting from the same initial picture. Sometimes simply by choosing to start with any picture normally appearing in the sequence, the chosen picture is not followed by the usual sequence of pictures. Or on occasion some pictures often do not appear in the sequence, or new ones are added from time to time. Such a system would fail to satisfy unique evolution and would not qualify as deterministic.

Although some think that unique evolution is a requirement for the scientific study of physical systems, this is not the case if there are precise enough versions of indeterminism available. Moreover, there are some reasons to think that unique evolution is not as generally applicable to physical systems as is typically thought (Bishop 2006a).

2.2. 'Unique evolution' in psychology

Psychology lacks anything nearly as precise as the physical conception of determinism. Nevertheless, it is possible to formulate something like this conception in psychology. Starting with unique evolution in physical determinism as the pattern, we can try to develop a 'storyline' for the analogous property in the physics and computer models in psychology (see Chapter 9, secs. 2.1–2.2). In the physics model, given the identical psychical and social forces along with the identical biological–neurological system ('multiple runs' with 'identical initial conditions'), a person would presumably repeat her same behaviours in terms of her life history. That is, if we insert the identical person into the identical world with the identical circumstances, they will live an identical life. In the computer model, given the identical cognitive processing apparatus and identical information input, a person would presumably repeat her same behaviours in terms of her life history as well.

Formulated in terms of life histories, we have to worry about robustness. For instance, are worlds physically identical in their totality required for generating identical life histories for an individual on 'multiple runs'? How much physical difference in a given world can be tolerated before that introduces some relevant difference in the psychical/social forces (in the physics model) or the information input and processing (in the computer model) producing behaviour changes with respect to a person's behaviour in a given control or baseline world? Or suppose that two worlds are identical in every detail except that a girl, say, is born with red hair in one world and blond hair in another. What kinds of changes will result in the social forces or information inputs leading to differences in her behaviour?

These robustness questions are difficult (perhaps impossible) to answer for entire life histories, so perhaps we should look at a weaker demand. After all, requiring psychological explanations of present behaviour be found in the past does not necessarily require determinism in the sense of identical life histories. Robustness in psychological determinants – in a typical clinical situation say – can be understood along the lines of finding significant historical/relational events or patterns that serve as the cause for someone's behaviour. Consider a son who grew up with an unaffirming father. The childhood interactions with his unaffirming father form the crucial events serving to determine his behaviour in all other circumstances. Suppose these crucial events cause perfectionist behaviour patterns and a never-ending drive for approval. On the physics model, this is a set of psychical/social forces that are robust in the sense that changes in other circumstances or configurations of other psychical/social forces have little or no effect on the son's behaviour patterns. Upon his leaving home (at age 18, say), if he faced an identical set of psychical/social forces, he would conceivably exhibit the identical life history of behaviours, though such a requirement is not necessary. All that is required for a deterministic psychological description is that the forces of his past interactions with his father be strong enough to dominate all other psychical/social forces in determining his subsequent behaviours.

This property of psychological determinism can be captured in the following 'principle':

> *Principle of Psychological Determinism* (PPD): some fixed set of (at least partially) identifiable crucial factors in a person's past governs their response to present events.

For therapeutic practice, as well as other purposes, the determining factors should be at least partially identifiable if psychologists are going to be able to help or guide clients. As formulated, PPD leaves open the possibility that, in the identical circumstances, the person would behave identically or merely very similarly. I take it that similarity of response is a strong enough requirement to sufficiently clarify the sense in which the determining set of past factors governs responses. This has the effect of limiting the range of behavioural responses down to one or some small set of similar responses. So each time the son's quest for approval is denied, he gets angry, but perhaps there is some slight variation to what he does with his anger.

Though PPD is suggestive, we can already see a problem in comparison with unique evolution in physics. Strictly speaking, the fixed set of crucial factors from the son's past really determine unique behavioural responses in identical current circumstances. Otherwise, it does not sound like we have the right form of determinism. The son's possible responses sound more like the indeterministic device that sometimes displays different sequences of pictures mentioned previously. So in response to his anger, sometimes the son sits on his couch and sulks, sometimes he goes to the gym to 'work it off', sometimes he explodes in a rage at the person who did not give the approval he was seeking, and so forth. What accounts for these behavioural differences?

Another worry arises with the requirement that the set of past crucial factors be fixed. Although we can only loosely define the boundaries of this set, it should be such that the collection of factors composing it are by far the strongest determinants of a person's behaviour. What if, as surely might be the case, this set is constantly expanding and contracting? If the members of this set are constantly changing, then there would be no consistent factors that are determining or shaping the son's behaviour. That would call into question the idea of trying to pattern a principle of determinism after uniqueness as in PPD. But just because the set of determining factors is changing does not mean that a person's behaviours are not governed by *some* set of factors from the past. These considerations suggest we try a weaker 'principle':

Principle of Psychological Determinism* (PPD*): some (possibly fixed) set of (at least partially) identifiable crucial factors in a person's past governs their response to present events.

Now the crucial question for determinism boils down to the concept of governance in PPD*. The sense of the word 'govern' carries with it the idea of limiting the range of something. Think of the governor on a carburettor limiting the speed of a bus, say. I have already suggested the weaker notion of similar responses as more realistic for psychology. But this leads to the question of how much similarity is required before a response would be judged 'dissimilar'. Not surprisingly, we find ourselves in the middle of thorny free will questions (see below). Obviously if the range of possible responses is wide enough, the sense in which any past factors are 'governing' responses to present events becomes trivial. Likewise it becomes difficult to understand how the responses come about.

On the other hand, suppose some of the elements in the set of determining past factors were contributed to that set by us. Perhaps these contributions were not fixed by some prior factors earlier in history. Then the sense of 'govern' in PPD* sounds less and less like determinism and more and more like incompatibilist free will (see below). That kind of free will is thought to be inconsistent with determinism in the sense that we are the originators at an earlier point of some of the values and purposes guiding our actions in the present. In this case, our past history is consistent with, but underdetermines, this origination (Kane 1996). Perhaps, then, it should be no surprise that some thoughtful critics within psychology (e.g., Slife and Williams 1995; Richardson, Fowers and Guignon 1999) argue that psychology needs to look beyond familiar debates concerning whether or not we are entirely subject to efficient causal influences stemming from the past. In terms of our discussions in Parts One and Two, perhaps notions of final and formal causation might make better sense of how meanings and values guide our activities and projects in the human realm than determinism.

3. Philosophical accounts of free will

Another possible source of guidance might be found in philosophy since questions about determinism and free will in psychology are directly related to similar philosophical debates. But, there are problems with philosophical accounts of free will as well. A relatively small number of philosophers hold to a strict determinist view, concluding that free will is an illusion. Some might feel that this position is rendered less plausible given difficulties in maintaining determinism in physics (e.g., Bishop 2006a).

Most philosophers are not strict determinists and divide into incompatibilists and compatibilists. *Incompatibilists* contend that free will is crucially incompatible with determinism reigning in the sphere of human thought and action (e.g., Kane 1996). One of the core intuitions of incompatibilists is that we must have some form of ultimate responsibility for our purposes, decisions and actions. Otherwise, notions like praise, blame, desert, creativity and individuality do not make any sense. From this perspective, if there is no sense in which our purposes and ideals are up to us, then we cannot make any legitimate claims to dignity or moral responsibility. One might also argue that it is not merely desirable that we be able to make such claims and judgements, but that we seem quite unable not to make them in earnest and thoughtful ways in everyday life.

In contrast, *compatibilists* see meaningful free will as compatible with determinism in the human realm. The key intuition for compatibilists is that all of the ordinary freedoms we desire and experience – freedom from coercion, compulsion, oppression, physical restraint – are not only compatible with determinism but actually require it. The sort of constraint that prevents us from doing what we want may be objectionable, but it is not the only category of causation or determination. Compatibilists argue there is a kind of determination without constraint – indeed, it is self-determination – that does not impede, but actualizes our will. As long as we are free to do as we want – that is to say, act in the absence of anybody or anything constraining, restraining or coercing us – our will is not impeded. Determinism does not prevent our being the source of our deliberations or destroy our causal efficacy, rather it is obstacles and restraints that threaten our causal efficacy. We want to be free to do as we please and, compatibilist philosophers maintain, this is compatible with determinism.

Incompatibilists reply that although freedom from constraint, coercion and restraint are important, these are insufficient to guarantee a person is the ultimate source of her values and purposes. After all, if our desires and hopes are all determined by factors outside our control, in what sense are we free to choose our values and desires. Moreover, incompatibilists note, even our choices are the product of strict determinism on the compatibilist view, so where is the freedom? Compatibilists find these worries bewildering and believe the search for any further freedoms over and above these 'ordinary everyday freedoms' to be misguided or a form of mystification.

Most of this debate is framed in terms of physical determinism (see above). But the concept of psychological determinism, which is directly related to the internal conditions for autonomy, also plays an important role. Psychological determinism is often understood as the determination of our decisions and actions by prior character and motives, which in turn are determined by a chain of events tracing back through our upbringing to our birth and, perhaps, beyond. Certainly such determinism appears to undermine free will. Compatibilists attempt to diffuse this threat by clarifying how agents can have a robust freedom from compulsion, constraint and restraint in such a deterministic world. They attempt to articulate meaningful notions of responsibility, praiseworthiness, blameworthiness and the like in terms of self-determination as they understand it. Unconvinced by these arguments, incompatibilists either try to show that human agents can contravene the influences of one's history and previously formed psychological make-up or that such determining factors are not so rigid after all.

Compatibilists criticize incompatibilist freedom as at best an impossible dream and at worst incoherent. Incompatibilists argue that compatibilist freedom is an illusion and does not capture the notion of freedom we most deeply desire. Common sense suggests that there might be important truths on both sides of this debate. On the one hand, there would seem to be no viable sense of freedom without some form of determination or ordered realm of causes and influences in which to act and make a difference. On the other hand, meaningful freedom cannot just amount to simply another chain of causes and effects playing out through us. Common sense notwithstanding, it has turned out to be maddeningly difficult to blend these insights in a coherent picture of human freedom.

4. Free will, determinism and cultural ideals

These free will debates among philosophers express a tension between sharply contrasting images of our place and possibilities in a world of ordered causes. Their differences aside, compatibilist and incompatibilist theorists share a belief that efficient causation plays a key role in explaining present behaviour (not unlike psychology), although their accounts differ widely. These competing perspectives on free will picture individuals as able to rise above and freely manipulate the flow of efficient causes and their effects in both the natural and social realms. In other words, they also share a commitment to an instrumental picture of action (Chapter 4). Likewise, both sides of the free will debates articulate similar conceptions of autonomy (Chapter 4). Furthermore, both sides share the ideals of liberal individualism (Chapter 5). So, while it might look reasonable to turn to philosophy to help sort out free will–determinism dilemmas in psychology and other social sciences, we see the same cultural ideals acting as disguised ideology at work in the philosophical debates.

4.1. Psychology's reconciliation of free will–determinism dilemmas

With the possible exception of humanist approaches,[3] the psychological perspectives surveyed here share in common a rather hard form of psychological determinism. Processes and forces outside the conscious control of agents determine their choices and actions. One could boil down the determinism presupposed in these perspectives as

> (D) Human thoughts and actions are constituted entirely by the efficient causal order.

In the cognitive perspective, say, the deterministic computer – which presupposes D – has contributed to many scientific advances in areas such as learning and memory. In this sense, many cognitivists believe that any denial of this deterministic picture so as to endorse some capacities for human freedom implies stepping outside of the domain of science altogether (e.g., Bandura 1977; 1986). On the other hand, these same approaches presuppose the freedom of agents to make responsible choices to improve their lives when presented with appropriate therapeutic interventions. However, a deterministic picture of the world such as D simply leaves no room for the presupposed freedom and responsibility imputed to agents. Our psychological theorizing, then, appears to undermine the very presupposed capacities agents need in order to responsibly act on any guidance or insight for living they might receive.

How does psychology – and other behavioural sciences – reconcile free will–determinism dilemmas? It appears to have achieved at least a tenuous reconciliation through a commitment to the instrumental picture of human action: agents somehow turn back on the impinging causal flow using the knowledge of such causal chains to intervene in and alter the future course of events to suit their purposes. One could boil down this conception of agency as:

(A) Humans have the power to transcend the efficient causal order and manipulate it.

However, D and A are manifestly inconsistent, so in what sense can we speak of reconciling free will and determinism? These two pictures of agents are treated as meshing plausibly primarily for two reasons, both having to do with ideals discussed in Part Two.

First, the scientific ideal: the instrumental picture of action appears to fit well within a physical world of efficient causal interactions. Hence, it rests comfortably with psychologists' mechanistic/deterministic pictures of the world and action. Agents are pictured as operating through efficient causation acting on a world conceived of as an interconnected web of efficient causes and effects. This presents a strongly compelling picture of action in the world amenable to scientific study. Under this picture, the agent is somehow part of the deterministic flow of causes in the natural and social worlds *and* somehow able to manipulate this flow for their own purposes. This split between self and world (see Chapter 4) appears to allow psychologists to maintain a robustly humanistic sense of agency and autonomy in the midst of deep, though often implicit, commitments to determinism and efficient causation. The flow of events as sequences of efficient causes and their effects appears to mesh well with the conception of human agency as mainly concerned with an individual's manipulation of those causes to produce desired outcomes. The abstract free will–determinism dilemma, then, appears resolved by a concrete fit between the way the world seems to work and the conditions needed for successful instrumental action (i.e., weak world-shaping: Chapter 1, sec. 4).

The instrumental picture does afford us a plausible image of fit between our activity and the world in at least some areas of practical life (e.g., determining the most efficient route for a trip). This image of things also has the advantage of being much in harmony with a modern scientific outlook on the world, including its emphasis on technological solutions to human problems. The instrumental picture of action appears to be consonant with our best science and appears to provide a means for the physics and computer models (Chapter 9, sec. 2) to be applied to human behaviour in an unproblematic fashion. However, as we saw in Chapter 4, when generalized to cover the entire realm of human activity, this picture is anything but plausible and is deeply problematic.

The congruence between instrumental action and efficient causation in natural science is not the only reason why scientists enshrine such a picture of action in their models and theories of human behaviour. A potent ethical ideal is at work as well: the profound aspiration to individuality represented in liberal individualism (Chapter 5). This cultural ideal also contributes to the belief that the instrumental picture of action ultimately reconciles D and A. Recall that the self-determination and personal choice of the individual are crucial to this ideal and reinforce the instrumental picture of action while the latter picture also reinforces liberal individualism. However, we also saw in Part Two that this ideal in combination with the instrumental picture was unstable in that it tended to undermine its own best values as well as being problematic in other ways.

Because of these ideals, I want to suggest, psychologists rest comfortably with free will-determinism dilemmas. In their theoretical conceptions, there is both an implicit assumption of some kind of freedom and a picture of agents that leaves no room for such freedom. And the combination of the cultural ideals of efficient causation, the instrumental picture of action and liberal individualism tends to mask this internal tension. Hence, given the instrumental picture of action, an agent looks to simply be another link in the causal chain, but additionally is able to manipulate the causal chain. With this assumed ability to manipulate causes, why would psychologists (or compatibilist philosophers for that matter) ever feel the threat determinism raises for free will?

These rather blatant and troubling free will-determinism dilemmas in psychology have been rendered tolerable and even plausibly reconciled by means of the instrumental picture of human action. The image it provides of congruence between the flow of events and human agency makes determinism palatable, even attractive to many. Why? Because we feel we can understand how efficient causes give rise to their effects, and by grasping the chains of efficient causes and effects, we feel an agent's choices can be fully explained. This feeling, however, comes at the expense of the limited view of human activity the instrumental picture perpetuates. And irrespective of the fact that the kind of determinism it entails – agents constituted and dominated by chains of efficient causes – ultimately undermines its own conception of human freedom. If there are only chains of efficient causes and effects, there are no agents, just causes and effects – agents and agency are just some among many of the effects of efficient causes. This is why the surreptitiously presupposed ability to turn back on and manipulate these causal chains plays such a crucial role in relieving the clear tensions between determinism and free will. Moreover, as we have seen, this instrumental picture is attractive because it supports and is supported by some of our more cherished cultural and moral ideals. The support and lustre given to the instrumental picture by these ideals strongly motivates psychologists (and philosophers) to concentrate on its limited plausibility within particular spheres of activity. Furthermore, these ideals make it much easier to ignore the instrumental picture's deeper philosophical inadequacy and distortions of meaningful human activity.

While most approaches in psychology either implicitly or explicitly reconcile free will–determinism dilemmas through these ideals, this does not look like much of a reconciliation at all. The bite of determinism is typically left untouched by simply focusing on the instrumental prowess of agents; hence, determinism is still bound to crowd the presupposed freedom out of the picture. One might try to remedy this by importing a compatibilist view of free will into the picture whereby human freedom would be cashed out as something consistent with determinism. But compatibilist accounts of freedom (and most incompatibilist accounts as well) also presuppose efficient causation and the instrumental picture of action, autonomy and liberal individualism. There is essentially no new clarity to be gained by trying to enrich mainstream psychology with compatibilist philosophical approaches to free will.

4.2. Moving beyond the dilemmas

Resolving the problem of free will and determinism in both philosophy and psychology will likely only come about by rethinking these cherished modern ideals. Conceiving human activity as largely instrumental is crucial to the modern ideal of autonomy, which paradoxically requires the kind of determinism that ends up undermining that very ideal.

Is there any credible alternative conception of how freedom and an ordered realm of causes might interweave in the human realm, so that freedom is neither quashed by its context nor deprived of one? Here, I can only sketch what an alternative might look like based on the lifeworld picture (see Chapters 5–6). Taylor (1975) advocates developing a notion of 'situated freedom'. He maintains that the modern understanding of freedom focuses on 'negative liberty'. This is largely Fromm's 'freedom from' (Chapter 7, sec. 3.1), which focuses exclusively on freedom from constraints, restraints' compulsions and the like (e.g., compatibilist conceptions of free will). But as we saw, this one-sided emphasis on freeing ourselves from obstacles can lead to a destructive, 'anything-goes' attitude of 'doing whatever feels good'. Instead, Taylor (like Fromm) recommends developing a conception of 'positive liberty' like Fromm's 'freedom to': a positive sense of freedom to do things deemed worthwhile by one's community and oneself. On this picture of freedom, people are always situated in a cultural and historical context. This context provides meaningful objectives and guidelines in terms of which we can deliberate meaningfully about possible courses of action. In Taylor's view, the modern individualism's precious values of respect for human rights and dignity can best (and perhaps only) be preserved if they are embedded in a more profound and affirmative conception of human freedom.

As we saw earlier (Chapter 5, sec. 3.1), the enormous successes of the natural sciences in modern times depend heavily on the capacity to ignore or abstract away from 'subject-related qualities'. This objectifying stance is part of the subject-object ontology and epistemology that separates the self from the world as it is independent of the meanings it might have for human beings. But we also saw that this kind of detached theoretical stance presupposes a more fundamental and practical stance of our engagement with the lifeworld (Chapter 5, sec. 3.3). One of the consequences of this theoretical stance is that it tends to ignore or abstract away from the kind of creative human agency that alone would be capable of the intellectual achievement of the theoretical stance. More importantly, it tends to reduce or denude all human agency down to the instrumental picture. Given this theoretical stance, if all we have at our disposal are efficient causation, instrumental action, social atomism and determinism, it is not too surprising that we cannot do much better than free will–determinism dilemmas and their tepid reconciliation.

In the lifeworld, human existence and understanding have a fundamentally narrative character and so are not fundamentally just matters of efficient causation. The shape of our practices and quality of our experience results from the interplay and mutual influence among our understandings of our past, present and future, other people and events in our lives, the books we read, movies we watch, music we hear and so forth (Chapter 6, sec. 3). This process can be distorted by dishonesty, defensiveness or force, but done poorly or well, it remains basic in an ontological sense to everyday realities (i.e., strong world-shaping: Chapter 1, sec. 4).

Streams of efficient causes and their effects play a subordinate role in the lifeworld. Law-governed processes in the natural world, including the human body and brain, clearly cannot be revoked or directly violated by an act of will. They impose unalterable constraints or limitations on human activity (Vogel 1998; Williams 2001). In a manner of speaking, we may to some extent cooperate with these processes and instrumentally manipulate states of affairs in some desired way. But the purposes that guide both that sort of means–ends reasoning as well as other culturally meaningful pursuits are hammered out through mutual influence and conversation among the participants in an intersubjective lifeworld. Hence, efficient causation and the kind of determinism which are the focus of the free will debates in psychology (and philosophy) are not necessarily the most important aspects governing human action.

In the lifeworld, 'determinism' can be understood as referring to forms of influence and constraint that shape human personality and activity. These shapings are much more profound and intimate than the efficient causal forces of the theoretical stance. From birth, for instance, we find ourselves in a historical culture that prescribes outward practices and institutions to which one must conform in order to survive and flourish. This culture also shapes many of our most inward beliefs and feelings, indeed our very identity as a person. 'Freedom' in the lifeworld can be understood in terms of an ongoing, creative reinterpretation of these practices and norms. The direction of this reinterpretation, including the changing shape of our norms and ethical convictions, is underdetermined by our past, partly because it occurs in response to unanticipated failures or challenges and partly because it must be carried out in close concert with perspectives and values of others. We find that we need others to make adequate sense of our own predicament and options, even though their influence may transform our self-defining aims in living. In this world, being 'determined' or shaped by history and culture and being 'free' or capable of individual creativity and responsibility do not exclude or deny one another. Historical and cultural embeddedness is a condition of this kind of creativity. And a high degree of creativity and responsibility are essential to maintaining a decent and vital cultural enterprise. Indeed, in the view sketched here, 'autonomy' is de-emphasized while more demanding and perhaps also more fulfilling exercises of freedom and responsibility are brought to the fore.

On this sketch, a person is always in conversation with her family and friends, colleagues, community and culture about values, meanings, traditions and so forth. She is also in conversation with herself in terms of values and purposes within her which clash and/or cooperate with one another in the search for genuine understanding and ethical insight, in an immensely practical way in everyday life. The rough, changing unity of this 'conversational self' consists in an attitudinal or open stance toward diverse meanings and perspectives, not one single standpoint or another.

For example, most personality theories focus on how personality is formed through internalizing the perspectives or evaluations of others as part of the self. Such theories then are faced with the problem of making sense of how a central 'I' relates to these introjected elements. This central 'I', however, usually is the modern punctual or asocial self, which can only relate to these internalized representations or evaluations by either arbitrarily submitting to their influence or by treating them merely instrumentally. In contrast, the conversational self never exists apart from the natural and cultural surroundings in the first place. One becomes a self at the outset or acquires an identity by gradually coming to occupy a place in the wider community and cultural conversations. The only 'internalization' that takes place is not one of adopting this or that belief or value but of internalizing all the conversations, so to speak, and becoming a part of them. This latter view opens up the possibility of an alternative to the stark dichotomy between dominating or being dominated in the affairs of the inner life. This radically culturally embedded self is profoundly 'determined' by history and culture. But at the same time it is always engaged in interpreting and reinterpreting history and culture as well as its place in these conversations. Far from diluting freedom and responsibility, one must exercise a more strenuous kind of freedom and responsibility in carrying on the conversation as it appears in the unique place one occupies in the natural and social worlds. This is a more demanding exercise of creativity and duty (strong world-shaping) than that of disengaging from the world to identify individual wants and preferences – the mainstream view in the social sciences – and then returning to the world to instrumentally pursue these wants (weak world-shaping).

5. Taking stock

Natural-scientific modes of inquiry dominate psychology and the rest of the social sciences. And as the pre-eminent natural science, physics is often taken to be the pattern for how psychology and other social sciences should be done. But in reflecting on free will–determinism dilemmas, we can see that the pattern of physics, and natural-scientific modes more generally, give us little if any purchase on the problem of human action in the world. This lack of insight can be diagnosed as an effect of the theoretical stance with its package deal of a subject-object ontology and epistemology and an instrumental picture of action. Since the theoretical stance presupposes that chains of efficient causes and effects are exhaustive of reality, there simply is not much in the way of resources to grapple with or understand free will and determinism.

The practical stance of the lifeworld is at a clear advantage here. Although only a sketch, perhaps it is enough of one to indicate avenues whereby social inquiry might be enriched by weaning itself from such a strict adherence to natural-scientific modes of inquiry by seating them within a broader hermeneutical perspective on inquiry (Chapter 3, sec. 5; Chapter 6, sec. 3). Social scientists do not have to give up on natural-scientific modes completely. Rather, the wise approach may be to follow a more hermeneutical path in order to discern how to make wise use of such approaches to inquiry, as well as their limits.

So rethinking free will–determinism dilemmas in the social sciences is anything but a narrowly intellectual undertaking. Both the substance of deterministic doctrine and our motivations for embracing or rejecting it are intimately entangled with basic ideals of our way of life, our very conception of the good or fulfilling life, and our fundamental sense of our own identity as worthy people or a decent society. Thus, thinking through these dilemmas in social science is inseparable, in part, from rethinking and presumably revising some of our most cherished cultural ideals. In other words, working on these problems is, in part, positive ethical and social theory. No doubt many social scientists would like to keep such sensitive and conviction-laden matters at arm's length while doing their work. But as we have seen in Parts Two and Three, this simply is not possible nor is it necessarily desirable because such detached, objectifying approaches simply pass cultural ideals on as disguised ideologies.

For further study

1. Describe an example of a free will–determinism dilemma in psychology. How does the instrumental picture of action seem to make this dilemma disappear?
2. Explain determinist, compatibilist and incompatibilist theories of free will. In what ways are they similar to views of free will in psychology?

Recommended reading

R. C. Bishop, 'Deterministic and Indeterministic Descriptions', in H. Atmanspacher and R. Bishop (eds.), *Between Chance and Choice: Interdisciplinary Perspectives on Determinism* (Thorverton: Academic Imprint, 2002), pp. 5–31.

—Determinism and Indeterminism', in D. Borchert (ed.), *The Encyclopedia of Philosophy* (Vol. 3; Farmington Hills, MI: Thomson Gale, 2nd edn, 2006a), pp. 29–35.

F. C. Richardson and R. Bishop, 'Rethinking Determinism in Social Science', in H. Atmanspacher and R. Bishop (eds.), *Between Chance and Choice: Interdisciplinary Perspectives on Determinism* (Thorverton: Imprint Academic, 2002), pp. 425–45.

B. Slife and R. Williams, 'Determinism', in *What's Behind the Research? Discovering Hidden Assumptions in the Behavioral Sciences* (Thousand Oaks: SAGE, 1995), pp. 94–126.

Explanations in Social Science

15

Chapter Outline

One of the aims of scientific activity is to give explanations for why things happened or why they are the way they are (Steuer 2002). However, giving explanations is not specific to science, but is an everyday activity. We give explanations for why the colour scheme of a room does not work or why we prefer dark chocolate over milk chocolate or why we acted that way last night. We give explanations for why we did not do very well on yesterday's exam or why we ended up with our current job. In courts of law, explanations are given for how and why a criminal pulled off their crime, or why the accused is innocent of the charges.

Although the practice of giving explanations does not distinguish science from many other human activities, there have been long-standing debates about what makes scientific explanations distinct from other kinds of explanations.

I will sketch some of the main candidates for distinctly scientific forms of explanation, but will not attempt to settle philosophical debates about explanation here. Rather, given that most of the discussions about scientific explanation focus on the natural sciences, I want to explore the relevance of some of the main candidates for the social sciences.

In particular, I want to examine the value-neutrality of explanations in the social sciences. One way in which such explanations might be thought value-neutral is by being merely descriptive of the laws, causes or other key features characterizing the social phenomena to be explained. Suppose economists were giving explanations of a society's distribution of goods and services in terms of the self-interests of the social actors (see Chapter 12). Such explanations indicate that the conditions for justice and fairness do not obtain even though the explanations never invoke these moral concepts. Furthermore, the economists' explanations also make no judgements about which distributions of goods and services in a society are just or unjust. The explanations highlight the roles of taxes, employment policies, welfare distribution and the like, but remain utterly neutral with respect to the justice of taxes, employment policies and welfare distribution. Yet, such explanations are not as value-neutral as they appear: they clearly take the position that such features of society are not matters of justice at all and this is a substantially value-laden position. And when people argue that unfettered markets will most efficiently distribute goods throughout society, they mirror this same lack of concern with justice.

To what extent, then, is it possible for explanations in the social sciences to achieve genuine value-neutrality?

1. Scientific explanation

To say much concretely about the nature of explanation in the sciences is to land quickly in debate and controversy. But we can say some initial things about what scientific explanations are not, and something general about what such explanations are.

First, explanation should be separated from confirmation. A scientific explanation, on most views, is composed of a set of statements or reasons yielding an analysis or account of the occurrence of some event, say (e.g., why it is raining or what causes insomnia). *Confirmation* is the process of supporting those statements or reasons with evidence such that we believe those statements or reasons. If there is good evidence in support of a given statement, we say that statement is well-confirmed (this is weaker than saying the statement is conclusively verified or absolutely true). If there is counter-evidence for the statement, then we say that it is disconfirmed.

Second, scientific explanation should be differentiated from other forms of explanation, all legitimate for various purposes: for example, how to dance the samba, where to find Main Street, what is wrong with a colour scheme for a room. We might want explanations for the meaning of a word or poem, or why the movie ended the way it did. But the explanations for these things are not regarded as scientific explanations.

A general characterization of scientific explanation is, to quote Wesley Salmon, 'an attempt to render understandable or intelligible some particular event (such as the 1986 accident at the Chernobyl nuclear facility) or some general fact (such as the copper color of the moon during total eclipse) by appealing to other particular and/or general facts drawn from one or more branches of empirical science' (Salmon et al. 1992: 8). Although far from a precise definition, this characterization does indicate what a scientific explanation seeks to accomplish and that such explanation draws explicitly upon science.

The event or general fact to be explained is often called the *explanandum*, while the explanation of the event or general fact is called the *explanans*. Scientific explanations do not try to capture or explain every feature of the *explanandum*; rather, such explanations focus on the factors considered most relevant or crucial to the event or general fact to be explained. So the *explanans* is not intended to be exhaustive of all factors possibly connected with the *explanandum*.

It is also possible to equate scientific explanations with scientific theories. If the goal of a particular theory is to explain the phenomena within its domain, then this identification is rather obvious. However, if the goal of a particular theory is to summarize and organize data, then it is not clear the theory will be explanatory. (One can expand this division into a more general debate about whether science explains phenomena or merely summarizes and organizes phenomena. Many of the logical positivists, following Ernst Mach, took the latter view, while others, like Carl Hempel, took the explanatory view.)

2. Varieties of explanation

Contemporary philosophers of science have proposed and argued about a number of different approaches to scientific explanations. Some of the most discussed models will be briefly surveyed here. Keep in mind that these models of explanation have primarily been developed with examples from natural science as their primary background.

2.1. Covering-law model

One of the earliest formulations of scientific explanations was the covering-law model first articulated by Hempel. On this model of explanation, an event or general fact is taken to be explained if it is subsumed under or covered by a universal law (universal-laws conception). Hempel understands a universal law to be 'a statement of universal conditional form which is capable of being confirmed or disconfirmed by suitable empirical findings' (Hempel 1965: 231). This suggests that although explanation and confirmation should be distinguished, they are definitely connected to each other – only well-confirmed laws can be truly explanatory.

The covering-law model has a logical form and is part of the received view of theories described in Chapter 1, sec. 2.1 (it is known as the received view of explanation). The covering-law model is actually a family of models, the most discussed form being the deductive–nomological (D–N) model of explanation. According to this model, explanations are deductive arguments of the following form:

General Laws:	All Ps are Q
Antecedent Conditions:	f is a P
(Therefore) Conclusion:	f is Q

Put another way.

[General Laws] + [Antecedent Conditions] entail [Conclusion]

Consider the example of a figure skater increasing her rate of rotation:

The angular momentum of any body (whose rate of rotation is not being increased or decreased by external forces) remains constant. (General Law)

The skater is not interacting with any external object in such a way as to alter her angular velocity. (Antecedent Condition 1)

The skater is rotating (her angular momentum is not zero). (Antecedent Condition 2)

The skater reduces her moment of inertia by drawing her arms in close to her body. (Antecedent Condition 3)

(Therefore) The skater's rate of rotation increases. (Conclusion)

The increase in the rate of rotation (the *explanandum*) is the conclusion of the argument, while the premises constitute the *explanans*. The first premise is a universal law of nature (conservation of angular momentum) and the remaining three premises state antecedent conditions. The conclusion then follows deductively from the premises.

Clearly, the covering-law model of explanation makes a particularly strong assumption that everything within the purview of science must be law-governed – the domains of science are law-like domains. Explanation becomes a problem on this view if the domains in question are not law-like (say history or evolutionary biology as some have argued). In such cases we would only have pseudo-explanations at best and, from the received point of view, such domains would be judged pseudo-scientific at best.

One possible problem with the covering-law model for explanation is that it is sometimes very difficult to distinguish between laws and accidental generalizations. Law-statements take the form of universal statements such as 'All Ps are Q' or 'No Ps are Q'. They are universal generalizations. The law-like statement 'No signals travel faster than light' has this form. But so, too, does the statement 'No golden spheres have masses greater than 100,000 kilograms'. However, the latter appears to be an accidental generalization because it is simply a contingent feature of the universe that there is not enough gold to make such a sphere. But saying why this is an accidental generalization as opposed to being a universal law is far from straightforward.

A more serious difficulty with the covering-law model is that it is subject to counter-examples that meet the form of the explanation – citing universal laws and antecedent conditions – but which are not valid explanations. Suppose we want to explain the length of the shadow cast by a flagpole. Let the flagpole be 12 feet tall and stand on level ground. If the sun is shining brightly at 53.13°, then the flagpole will cast a 9-foot shadow. On the deductive–nomological model of explanation, universal laws of optics must be cited regarding the propagation of light along with the elevation of the sun and the height of the flagpole (antecedent conditions). This fits the deductive form for explanation and seems unproblematic. However it turns out that one can also give a deductive–nomological explanation of the height of the flagpole given the propagation of light (universal law) along with the elevation of the sun and the length of the shadow (antecedent conditions). Alternatively, we can explain the elevation of the sun from the propagation of light (universal law) along with the height of the flagpole and the length of the shadow (antecedent conditions). These last two 'explanations' seem absurd, so it appears there is something wrong with the covering-law schema in that it cannot distinguish between genuine and absurd explanations.

2.2. Causal–mechanical model

Wesley Salmon (1984) offered an account of explanation that ignores laws altogether and focuses on causal mechanisms as processes. A causal process is characterized by two fundamental concepts: production and propagation. A cue ball striking an eight ball produces or brings about the motion of the eight ball, as some of the energy and momentum belonging to the cue ball is passed on to the eight ball which propagates or carries this momentum with it. Processes for Salmon are basic entities rather than events. Events, like a baseball colliding with a window, are localized in space and time, whereas processes, like the baseball travelling from the bat to the window, have temporal duration.

But we need a way to pick out causal processes from pseudo-processes to have causal explanations. Causal processes are those processes capable of transmitting signals – features of its own structure, usually energy and momentum – in a continuous way, whereas pseudo-processes cannot. Salmon uses the criterion of transmitting a mark – a local modification in structure – to distinguish the two kinds of processes. Consider a spotlight directed at a wall. Turning the spotlight on, the light travelling to the wall is an example of a causal process since it transmits features of its own structure to the wall where it is shining. If the spotlight is rotated, the line of light travelling along the wall due to rotation is a pseudo-process, transmitting nothing. This becomes obvious if we insert a red filter between the spotlight and the wall. By inserting the filter at any point between the spotlight and wall, the light pulse, which was white, becomes red until it reaches the wall. Hence, by intervening locally, we can produce a change that is transmitted to the wall. The light pulse travelling toward the wall is capable of transmitting a mark. In the rotating case, the travelling spot will not be able to transmit a mark. Suppose we intervene at a given point between the spotlight and the wall by inserting a red filter. As the spotlight rotates, the white spot travelling along the wall briefly becomes red as the light beam intersects the filter, then turns white again as the beam continues rotating. The mark of the filter is not transmitted beyond the point on the wall where the lightbeam intersected the filter.

Causal processes, then, are self-determining in the sense that they are capable of transmitting their own structural features or changes in those structural features. Furthermore, they are uniform processes in the sense that they exhibit regularities directly connected with their structures. Pseudo-processes, by contrast, are parasitic on the regularities of external causal processes (e.g., the spot travelling along the wall is dependent upon the beam of light propagating from the spotlight). The ability to transmit a mark can distinguish between these two types of processes. However, this criterion is an empirical one as it requires experimentation to determine when interventions and marks can be transmitted.

Consider another example. The impact of a cue stick on a cue ball sets the latter in motion, which in turn strikes a stationary eight ball. The eight ball then sets off in motion and the cue ball changes direction. The impact of the cue stick marks the cue ball by leaving a bit of blue chalk on the cue ball. In turn, the cue ball transmits a bit of this blue chalk to the eight ball on impact. The cue stick, cue ball and eight ball are all causal processes capable of transmitting a mark. The various impacts among sticks and balls are causal interactions involving transfers of energy and momentum. By citing these facts about processes and explanations, we can explain the motion of the cue and eight balls. By contrast, the shadows cast by the cue stick and cue ball as they are in motion are causally and explanatorily irrelevant as they are pseudo-processes.

In summary then, causal processes (1) are self-determined and not parasitic on other causal influences and (2) transmit energy, information and causal influence. And these two features yield the capability of transmitting marks, which pseudo-processes lack. For Salmon, 'the transmission of a mark from point A in a causal process to point B in the same process *is* the fact that it appears at each point between A and B *without further interactions*' (1984: 148). A causal process is capable of transmitting or manifesting its structural features or changes to those structural features when a single local interaction at a point is introduced into the process. The causal process is the connection between the event known as 'cause' and the event known as 'effect'.

A defender of the received view initially might object to Salmon's account because causal–mechanical explanations do not cite any laws. On Salmon's view, however, causal interactions are governed by basic laws of nature. For example, the movement of an eight ball struck by a cue ball is governed by Newton's laws of motion. Once we invoke all the background conditions for the causal processes, a lawful relation between cause and effect can be established.

But there are problems with Salmon's causal account that need attention. One objection is that Salmon's mark criterion presupposes that causal processes display a degree of uniformity over a time period. But this potentially rules out very short-lived causes like short-lived subatomic particles that might play crucial roles in physical systems. More seriously, it is not clear how to apply the mark criterion in cases where there are continual interactions going on. The criterion is formulated in terms of one interaction at a localized space–time region, but realistic processes are often in continual interaction with other processes.

Another problem is that it is possible to modify pseudo-processes by a single interaction, just the sort of thing the mark criterion is supposed to rule out. Suppose there is a stationary car (a causal process) throwing its shadow (a pseudo-process) on a fence. Suddenly the fence falls over, producing a permanent modification of the shadow (changing its shape). The shadow has been marked by a single local interaction – indeed what appears to qualify as a causal interaction – namely the falling fence. Salmon does have a counterfactual requirement that the original process would remain uniform (presumably in the absence of the marking interaction, all other things being equal). This requirement is supposed to help separate out causal from pseudo-processes. But it does not help in this sort of case because the shadow would have remained uniform had the fence not fallen. Yet, the shadow surely is a pseudo-process.

2.3. Unification models

Another approach to explanation sees the kind of understanding delivered by explanation as coming through unification. This line of thinking goes back at least to William Whewell (1794–1866; see Whewell 1858). Recent exponents of such models for explanation include Michael Friedman (1974) and Philip Kitcher (1981). Though their details differ, the rough idea of a unification model for explanation is the following. A scientific explanation should seek to increase our understanding of the world by reducing the total number of independent phenomena to be accepted as given or brute. One way this might be accomplished is for a large number of independent phenomena to be explained through a small number of laws. On this view, the laws of Newtonian mechanics are explanatory because they allow us to derive the fact that planets obey Kepler's laws and that falling objects near earth obey Galileo's laws; they allow us to derive the behaviour of gases; they allow us to derive the motion of oceans and tides. The laws of Newtonian mechanics unify a number of disparate phenomena formerly treated as independent.

Another way explanatory unification might come about is that science provides a stock of explanatory argument patterns. The idea here is that a relatively small stock of such patterns can be drawn upon for the purposes of explaining a wide variety of phenomena. So a theory, for instance, unifies our beliefs about a range of phenomena when it provides the smallest number of general patterns of argument that can be used in the derivation of the largest number of beliefs we accept. As an example, consider Darwin's theory of evolution. It offered a general pattern of argument that could potentially unify a variety of biological phenomena. The pattern, as Darwin presents it, could be instantiated by a rigorous and complete derivation of some trait in a particular species. The derivation would make crucial use of the principle of natural selection as well as descriptions of ancestral forms and the nature of their environment (principles of variation and inheritance, unknown to him at the time, would also be included). Basically, the argument pattern would show how a particular trait would be advantageous to a particular species, thus explaining the trait's emergence.

Unification models are not without their drawbacks. For instance, if our explanatory stock is filled with causal mechanisms, what reason do we have to believe that this stock will be particularly small with respect to the range of phenomena to be explained? If our explanatory stock is filled with laws, then there are several questions about the relationship of these laws to the scientific beliefs we are explaining. Are laws 'outside' the set of arguments used to generate the accepted beliefs? If so, what role do laws play in these arguments? Are the laws themselves part of the set of arguments generating our beliefs? If so, then it is possible that there may be several sets of arguments that are equal in unifying power and stringency, in which event we are left unable to pick out the right explanatory stock (if there is a 'right' one).

2.4. Functional models

The basic idea behind functional models of explanation is to explain the persistence of some practice or pattern – in an individual or a group – in terms of the benefit or function or role it plays. Individual and social practices are considered to play some function in producing desirable effects. As long as the practice in question delivers desirable or beneficial effects, it fulfills a needed or desired function and is maintained. In this way, Bronislaw Malinowski (1948) explained the appearance and persistence of division of labour within groups by showing how it contributed to the well-being of the individual members. However, social scientists, who advocate functional models of explanation, do not believe that individuals or groups intentionally design their practices and institutions. Rather, practices and institutions arise and evolve unintentionally as a result of the functions they fulfil. So typically functional explanations of behaviour do not invoke the intentions or attitudes of the actors involved because these psychological features do not play a genuine causal role.

As indicated, a functional explanation can be given at the level of an individual actor as well as at the level of groups or whole societies. Functional models are thought to be equally applicable at any of these levels. So they can be deployed by methodological holists but perhaps not by individualists. Recall from Chapter 7 that methodological individualism is a constraint requiring explanations in terms of the intentions and views of agents and their individual actions. But functional explanations make no mention of the intentions and views of agents. So an individualist use of functional explanations would either have to (1) explicitly mention the intentions and view of agents as genuine determinants of behaviour, undercutting the form of functional explanation or (2) focus only on the benefits for an individual of the function being performed by the behaviour, violating the methodological-individualist constraint.

One difficulty functional models of explanation face is explaining the persistence of so many behaviours and practices that are maladaptive or harmful to agents. According to functional models, the explanation for the persistence of behaviours, practices, institutions and the like is that they serve functions yielding benefits or advantages to social actors. Maladaptive or harmful behaviours, practices and institutions do not serve such roles, but still prove very resilient (e.g., crime). One can turn to rational-choice theory to supplement functional explanations for these cases. However, this move makes it clear that functional models of explanation have definite limits. And given the problems facing the rational-actors picture (Chapter 10), this move appears to be of little help.

Another problem facing functional models of explanation is that of explaining why the particular practices or institutions arose. Presumably, several different practices or institutions could have fulfilled the same function (e.g., funeral rites, bartering practices or forms of government and administration). If the extant practices and institutions arose unintentionally, as functionalist sociologists and anthropologists, among other social scientists, maintain, we want to know how they came about. By fulfilling the function they do, such practices and institutions might be maintained, but this fact by itself does not account for their origin. Put another way, a practice or institution has a telos or goal – to fulfil a particular function or functions – according to the functional model of explanation. But these goal-directed behaviours did not arise because people specifically had those goals or functions in mind. The social scientist advocating functional explanations needs to propose some mechanism or cause that led to the practice or institution in question. A functional explanation cannot simply assume that practices or institutions arose to meet particular needs because that is to assume the very feature standing in need of explanation (and to say it arose by pure chance is not much of an explanation). This problem of explaining origins is further exacerbated if there are a number of possible functionally equivalent practices and institutions available to individuals or groups that could meet the same needs.

Suppose that a social scientist could propose a mechanism or cause for the origin of a particular practice or institution meeting particular individual or group needs. If the proposed mechanism or cause really explained why the practice or institution arose, then we no longer have a functional explanation; instead, we have a causal explanation, perhaps along the lines of the causal–mechanical model. So advocates of functional explanation face a dilemma: if they offer nothing to account for why a particular practice or institution arose, then functional explanations do not explain very much at all. On the other hand, if they offer a mechanism or cause as the explanation of the origin of the particular practice or institution, then they have switched from a functional model to some form of causal explanation.

2.5. Why the variety of models?

One way to look at the debates on scientific explanation is that the whole topic lies in shambles. There are strong advocates for taking scientific explanation to be causal or unificatory or invoke covering-laws or functions or other forms I have not surveyed here. Moreover, there are no unproblematic accounts of explanation appearing anywhere on the horizon. One of the reasons for this rather messy situation is the sheer number of strong intuitions about scientific explanation, many of which are in tension with each other. For instance, scientific explanation should be objective, be identified with logical argument forms, make references to laws (because all events are law-governed), make reference to causal factors (because all effects have their causes), deliver understanding by exhibiting a phenomenon's relationship to laws, deliver understanding by exhibiting a phenomenon's relationship to underlying mechanisms, deliver understanding based on the particular question asked, unify disparate phenomena via deriving the greatest number of phenomena from the smallest number of principles, unify disparate phenomena by connecting them with the smallest number of core causal factors, exhibit the function a particular feature plays and so forth.

There are two principled attitudes toward this situation: (1) It is a hopeless task to come up with *the* view on scientific explanation. Philosophical discussions in this area are fruitless. We have enough evidence to show that this kind of enterprise simply is not going to work, though there perhaps, have, been some payoffs in terms of philosophical developments and refinements that have proved useful for other areas of philosophy. (2) There is no *one view* of scientific explanation possible. Rather, just as science pursues a variety of approaches in its exploration of the world, we should look for a plurality of approaches to scientific explanation. Let the circumstances determine which form of explanation is best suited to the task. After all, scientists tend to be a pragmatic lot and appear to pursue a variety of models of explanation as suits their needs.

3. Explanations in the social sciences

Some of the above models for explanation have been applied to the social sciences. Durkheim, for instance, followed the covering-law model of explanation. He maintained that behaviours like suicide or marriage could only be properly explained if they are connected with social facts in a law-like way (Chapter 2, sec. 3). Others have argued that functional models are the appropriate forms of explanation in social inquiry (e.g., Kincaid 1996).

3.1. Laws and explanations in social inquiry

If one takes something like the covering-law model to be appropriate for explanation in the social sciences, then one is committed to genuine explanations always citing at least one universal law. Finding genuine candidates for universal laws of human behaviour is very difficult (some think impossible). Consider the law-like statement: 'When hungry, an agent will eat'. This has the right general form for a law of behaviour, but could never serve as an explanation for food-seeking and eating behaviour in something like a covering-law model. Why not? Because there is no universal definition of food. Food must be defined in terms of what subjects take to be eatable, but this varies not only across cultures, but across individuals as well. What is food in one context may be revolting in another. It does not help to define food as whatever agents eat in response to hunger because this renders the putative definition circular and devoid of content (e.g., if someone is so hungry he eats sawdust, we would have to say this is food on the proposed definition).

Actions of individuals and groups are what social scientists are trying to explain, but an action is identified by the purposes it aims to achieve. We read these aims from the overt action aided by our knowledge of context, particularly the person's view of the situation. Recall, the example of the chocolate box: if you are holding out a box of chocolates, it makes a clear difference to my act of reaching out my hand whether I see myself as reaching to select a chocolate or as reaching out to prevent the box from falling.

The action might be redescribed if the person credibly tells us of a different intention than the one we attribute. It is often the case that we have to understand the person's feeling or sense for things to know what she is doing. Suppose I walk into a room and my friend looks up at me with a furrowed brow. What does her action mean? Is it an expression of frustration? Of anger? Of puzzlement? If actions are characterized partly by the way people see their situation, then personal interpretation – self-understanding – enters into the very definition or conception of what an action is. This would imply that interpretation is a crucial component to social inquiry and that laws are secondary if they are even applicable at all.

Social scientists who advocate methodological holism in explanations (Chapter 7) or those who think that large-scale social features figure prominently in individual actions, do not necessarily dismiss the analysis of people's actions at the individual level. Rather, such social scientists would say that taking only an individual analysis does not go far enough in explaining the features of behaviour of interest to them. These 'larger' kinds of explanations are not inconsistent with understanding the actions of a person as being identified by his purposes or aims. Indeed, the person's purposes in acting often are significantly shaped by larger cultural factors and social forces. So an understanding of these latter features would have to be brought into the picture as well to get a fuller explanation for the person's behaviour as well as collective or social behaviour.

One response to this is to say that while a person's view of things is what defines an action, the person's views are not the causes of the action (Durkheim maintained this view). An agent's intentions might be very relevant for defining the action in which they are engaging, but the real cause of the action are the laws governing the agent's behaviour. But this response lands us back in the problems of law-like explanations in social inquiry. Most proposals for laws in the social sciences end up being so abstract as to be almost devoid of content, or unfalsifiable. Suppose a putative universal law appeals to an agent's beliefs and desires to explain behaviour. For the social scientists to deploy the law to explain actions, she first must use the law to establish that the causes – the beliefs and desires – actually obtained. However, this leads to two problems. First, no belief or desire is what it is in isolation from other beliefs and desires; that is, beliefs and desires are co-constituting or co-determining of other beliefs and desires. This means that the putative law will have to make reference to large swaths of interrelated beliefs and desires. It will have to invoke the agent's ways of seeing things, but this shifts the emphasis away from the law itself and on to the agent's self-understandings. This looks to make meanings and interpretations play the crucial role in explaining behaviour. The second problem is of a technical nature. If we have to use the putative law to first identify the beliefs and desires, then we have no independent way to confirm or disconfirm the putative law's status as a law. This implies the putative law is unfalsifiable, but one of the distinguishing features of scientific laws is that in principle they are capable of being confirmed or disconfirmed.[1]

Moreover, advocates of the covering-law model clearly must assume that universal laws lie at the heart of any scientific field (universal-laws conception). This clearly represents a natural-scientific mode of social inquiry. But if such advocates also believe that the covering-law model is the appropriate form of explanation in social science, then they are also committed to the thesis that every social-science discipline must ultimately conform to the universal-laws conception of science. However, this presumption begs the question as it merely assumes that all sciences must be aiming for universal laws or they are not genuine scientific endeavours. While there certainly are prejudices that universal laws are a distinguishing feature of any science (e.g., Comte and his followers), there are no arguments demonstrating this must be the case and there are even considerations militating against laws in science (Miller 1987: ch. 1; van Fraassen 1990; Giere 1999: ch. 5). And just because sociologists and anthropologists might be concerned with generalizations and persistent patterns does not in any way imply that they are ultimately seeking universal laws. The nature of the generalizations and persistent patterns scientists seek depends on the subject matter and sources of order in the domain under investigation, not on some preconceived ideas about universal laws.[2] It is far from clear that the covering-law model is applicable outside of a few cases in the physical sciences.

The social sciences clearly have not produced anything resembling the kinds of universal laws to which we are accustomed from physics. For instance, Gergen observes:

> A fundamental difference exists between the bulk of the phenomena of concern to the natural as opposed to the sociobehavioral scientist. There is ample reason to believe that the phenomena of focal concern to the latter are far less stable (enduring, reliable, or replicable) [than] those of interest to the former... To place the matter squarely, it may be ventured that with all its attempts to emulate natural science inquiry, the past century of sociobehavioral research and theory has failed to yield a principle as reliable as Archimedes' principle of hydrostatics or Galileo's law of uniformly accelerated motion. (1982: 12)

Those who hold the prejudice that genuine science seeks universal laws and who think that social sciences, as currently practised, are not capable of discovering universal laws tend to judge social sciences as not able to measure up to the standards of science (e.g., Gergen 1982; Rosenberg 1995). But drop the prejudice and there is no reason to think of social sciences as somehow substandard. After all, it is good scientific practice to adopt the scope of generalization suited to the nature of the persistent patterns found among the phenomena of study rather than operate with the preconception that all genuine patterns must ultimately be traceable to universal laws (for this ultimately is a metaphysical assumption).

This leads to a second problem for applying the covering-law model to the social sciences. The kinds of regularities and persistent patterns we find in individual and social behaviour – the forms of order we find in the social arena – are structured by the values, prejudices, ideals, desires and so forth of people rather than universal laws. As self-interpreting beings, our self-understandings and our interpretations of our situations and our place in them is crucial to guiding our activities. Take conformity, for example. Whether it be to a particular standard of success in business or to wearing tattered jeans, it is largely a function of how we see ourselves with respect to society's possibilities and restraints. And as people's views of themselves and their situations change, persistent patterns and regularities change or disappear completely. This kind of interpretive variability is what we should expect from a realm structured primarily by meanings. Such a realm is not well-suited for covering-law explanations.

Lastly, these considerations are related to the discussion of natural versus social kinds in Chapter 13, sec. 2.1. The very concept of a universal law depends upon there being stable kinds and enduring relations among these kinds. The natural kinds of physics (electrons, electromagnetic fields, etc.) have the right sort of invariability such that relations that figure into universal laws might be discovered. But social kinds (gender, upper-middle class, etc.) are constructed by us and change as our values, purposes and ways of seeing things change. This kind of variability is not suited for formulating or discovering universal laws because both the kinds themselves and the ways the kinds relate to one another change.

3.2. Causes and explanations in social inquiry

If a causal-mechanical model of explanation presupposes that causation is fundamentally grounded in universal laws, it will face the same problems as covering-law models. There are plenty of reasons to think that causal explanations can get along just fine without universal laws (Miller 1987; Cartwright 1989), but then the question becomes: can the causal-mechanical model of explanation succeed in social inquiry by relying solely on efficient causation?

As described in Parts Two and Three, to the extent they focus on causation, social sciences generally rely only on efficient causation. If we toss laws by the wayside, then one way to apply the causal-mechanical model of explanation is to view the economy, the political arena or any other social phenomena and institutions as kinds of causal machines. Such machines have lots of interacting parts assembled in a particular way like a car engine. However, a social realm largely structured by the meanings present in the self-understandings of self-interpreting beings and their social practices and institutions does not function like a causal machine either (D'Andrade 1986). Again, our actions – whether they be economically oriented like buying clothes or politically oriented like rallying to support a new government programme – are not primarily the results of the play of efficient causes of some social machine on us. Rather, as our views of ourselves and our situations change, the kinds of patterns and regularities that economists and sociologists are tempted to see as machine-like are altered or disappear altogether. No machine like a car engine can run if its parts change their ways of seeing things in the face of new experiences because then their behaviours will change. The very concept of a causal machine depends upon the stability of the causal actions of its parts, so purely efficient causal forms of explanation will be inadequate to understanding the social realm.

There may be some limited applicability of efficient causation in social inquiry, but the total reliance on this form of causation is inadequate to the phenomena we are trying to understand and harbours disguised ideologies (Parts One–Three). So at the very least, we need to expand our repertoire of influences in the social realm to include formal and final causes as well as taking the narrative structure of life more seriously (Chapter 6, sec. 3).[3] So causal-mechanical models of explanation might be of some use in social sciences provided they do not rely solely on efficient causation. This would mean giving up the idea that social actions and institutions have a machine-like character. As well, such expanded models of explanation would need to be brought into conversation with or significantly enriched by other modes of understanding (Chapter 6, sec. 3).[4]

3.3. Unification, functionalism and explanations in social inquiry

Applying unification models of explanation to social phenomena also looks deeply problematic. The idea of explaining the largest number of individual behaviours and social phenomena in terms of either the smallest set of laws or the smallest set of efficient causes will face all of the above problems. One might imagine trying to unify a large set of social phenomena in terms of formal and final causes, but this idea also seems to be of limited applicability. Each self-interpreting being has their own set of final causes – their own goals, purposes, dreams, visions of their future selves and roles and so forth. Classifying these final causes under broad categories like career, moral concern and suchlike does not appear to help, as these general categories do not provide much in the way of explanatory power.

One might think that resorting to functional models of explanation might help here. After all, functional explanations do have a kind of unifying characteristic. By explaining individual and social behaviours in terms of the functions they fulfil, it looks as if one could explain a much larger number of social phenomena in terms of a smaller set of functions or benefits. But, as pointed out above, functional explanations have serious difficulties. Furthermore, it is not clear that there should be a particularly small number of functions or benefits in terms of which to explain a much larger set of social phenomena.

4. Explanation and cultural ideals

Most proponents of the various models of explanation I have been canvassing would maintain that these models are value-neutral. Appealing to laws, or causes or functions, as the ultimate elements of scientific explanations of social phenomena does not bias such explanation with various values. Rather, by seeking to conform our explanations to acceptable models, social scientists are seen as more likely to avoid making value judgements appraising situations and factors as good or bad. For instance, advocates of functional models of explanation would claim that judging a particular behaviour or institution as adaptive or fulfilling a social function is only a characterizing judgement.[5] The presence of some behaviour or institution is explained in terms of the role it plays in a society, say, and this characterization involves no appraisals of right or wrong. Moreover, proponents would say, such explanations do not advocate any particular vision of the good life or any particular values.

As we have seen throughout this book, such appeals are anything but value-neutral. Focusing exclusively on laws or efficient causes as natural-scientific and descriptivists modes of social inquiry do is animated by and carries with it a number of disguised ideologies like political liberalism, liberal individualism, autonomy and the instrumental picture of action.

Consider a typical functional explanation in biology. On an adaptationist view, the behaviours of biological organisms like human beings are explained in terms of what traits contribute most to the transmission and survival of genes given a particular environment. On this model of explanation, a biologist might explain why men invest less time in child care relative to women as the result of traits adapted to maximize the transmission and survival of a male's genes. These traits were adapted to particular environments and such behaviours then continue to be passed down to offspring, thereby maximizing the fitness of males. The possibility that males might alter their environments so as to invest more time in child care without compromising fitness is ignored by such functional models of explanation. The environment is considered to be a fixed feature to which organisms adapt, given the influence of their genes.[6]

Now consider a parallel kind of functional explanation in social science, that the behaviours of individual members of a group are adapted to satisfying their needs or preferences given some set of group or society structures as their environment. In this way, one might try to explain why rituals and other practices are entrenched in particular groups or societies – the latter form a kind of fixed environment in which individual actors adapt their behaviours to increase the likelihood of satisfying their needs or interests. But this is hardly a value-free attempt at describing human behaviour. It enshrines liberal individualism (particularly, utilitarian individualism: see Chapter 5, sec 2.2) and the instrumental picture of action (Chapter 4) as crucial presuppositions of the functional scheme of explanation. In other words, this explanation takes particular cultural ideals and promotes them to elements of the natural order of things in the world when they are decidedly moral visions of how a human being *can* be. Social scientists advancing such functional explanations may not see themselves as advocating these cultural ideals – that would be to appraise them as good or bad. Nevertheless, they are surreptitiously advocating these ideals by 'naturalizing' such ideals as part of the objective reality of the social order.

This is simply to be an unwitting partisan for particular moral visions of human living while pretending to be neutral. But it is not just a phenomena that is isolated to the academic ivory tower. Makers of public policy increasingly look to social scientists for supposedly unbiased theories and guidance for creating and sustaining social and economic policies. Hence, these same cultural ideals enshrined in social-science theories and explanations can be transmitted to public policy, further reinforcing these cultural ideals. This means that public policy will also fail to be value-neutral. More importantly, one-sided ideals such as liberal individualism, autonomy and the instrumental picture of action contribute to many of the problems facing modern Western societies. Social and economic policies that simply pass on and reinforce these ideals then can hardly be expected to genuinely solve these problems. Rather, such policies are likely to perpetuate these problems or even make them worse.

Recall the example I gave in the introduction above: typical economics explanations of a society's distribution of goods and services are in terms of the self-interests of the social actors. By their very construction, such explanations leave no room for conditions of justice and fairness. So, by implication, the roles of taxes, employment policies, welfare distribution and such are not matters of justice at all. These are hardly value-neutral explanations. They have numerous disguised ideologies buried within them such as political liberalism, liberal individualism and the instrumental picture of action (see Chapter 12). Now suppose these theories are handed off to public-policy-makers to serve as guidance for crafting economic policy. The policy-makers have been given instrumental knowledge representing the wisdom of economists on the most effective means to distribute goods in a society. But the policy-makers have no further guidance about whether any given distribution of goods in a society is more worthwhile or fairer than another. Nor have they been given any guidance on what a just or worthwhile distribution of goods means or even if the economists' theoretical picture of agents and markets is just or worthwhile. This is the logical conclusion of Weber's process of the rationalization of *zweckrational* (Chapter 2, sec. 4), the instrumentalization of all aspects of life: notions of justice, fairness and the good life simply become technical problems of the most efficient means of distributing goods and services in a society. But this is to take an ethical stance on what justice, fairness and the good life are!

5. Taking stock

A curious feature of the various accounts of explanation surveyed here is that they tend to discount people's views of their own actions. An action crucially depends on the person's view of things: what she sees herself as doing. But so-called scientific explanations tend to replace her view of things with an appeal to universal laws, or efficient causes or functions – anything but the way the person sees her world and her activity in it. This is a further example of how social-science theorizing reconceives or reinterprets people's behaviours instead of understanding people's behaviour in their own terms. In other words, social scientists tend to replace people's own explanations and understandings of their behaviours with the social scientists' preferred way of explaining and understanding people's behaviours. This is the bias of the expert, the one who sits above the fray, seeing things with a clear eye. Except that, as we have seen over the course of this book, there is no such outsider's perspective, and, hence, no objective reason for the social scientists to prefer their modes of explanation.

The moral, spiritual and other kinds of reasons people have for seeing the world the way they do and acting in the world as they understand it (*wertrational*), are replaced by the social scientists' purported laws, efficient causes, functions and so forth (*zweckrational*). This carries the implication that we are all largely mistaken about the sources of our actions – and indeed misunderstand our actions, too! Consider a Christian activist who sees her crusading on behalf of environmental protection as deriving from deeply informed religious beliefs. The social scientist explains these beliefs as the products of some efficient causes in the social realm or in terms of adaptations to the social environment. The activist is interested in and engaged with her beliefs and their implications for environmental policy. The social scientist is interested in how the belief is caused or how it fulfills some function meeting her or society's needs. Clearly, the social scientist has privileged his interests over hers in the 'scientific' explanation; but on what basis? That his is somehow the truer account? Hardly, as his account replaces hers as a rival, completely redescribing – likely misdescribing – her springs of action. In his account, the social scientist makes a decided value judgement that the activist's interest in the truth of her beliefs and their implications for the environment are not important or worthwhile. What is really important or worthwhile are the causes of her beliefs or the role they play in meeting her or society's interests.

Social scientists cannot avoid such partisan judgements by hiding behind a particular explanatory scheme that they judge to be scientific.

For further study

1. Choose one of the models of explanation described in sec. 2. Explain this model and apply it to an example from social science. What problems do you see this application of the model having?

2. Explain the difference between viewing the social world as a causal machine versus the narrative structure of the lifeworld. What are the implications of these differences for explanations in social inquiry?

3. Give some examples of how social-science explanations fail to be value-neutral. How do you see these failures impacting debates about how social science is similar to natural science?

Recommended reading

M. Root, 'Functional Theories in Sociology and Biology', in *Philosophy of Social Science* (Oxford: Blackwell, 1993), pp. 78–99.

W. Salmon, 'Scientific Explanation', in M. H. Salmon et al. *Introduction to the Philosophy of Science* (Indianapolis: Hackett, 1992), pp. 7–41.

16 Natural Science and Social Science

A key question raised in Chapter 1 was: 'Are the natural and social sciences similar to each other?' Whether looking at the conceptions of science (Chapter 1, sec. 1) or at Kuhn's paradigmatic analysis of science (Chapter 1, sec. 4), we saw what appeared to be reasons for answering this question positively and negatively. On the other hand, the differences between correlators and interpreters (Chapter 1, sec. 5) suggested that there might be at least one fundamental difference between natural and social sciences. This difference has to do with the nature of the objects of study in the two branches of science. The social sciences study human beings, our actions, interactions, institutions and so forth. But in contrast to the natural sciences, people are self-interpreting beings, the kind of beings who see the world in particular ways, who are animated by values, ideals, hopes and dreams. Our actions cannot be fully understood apart from our attitudes and purposes – these establish or define what our actions are. In other words there are no human actions apart from the meanings of such actions. Apparently there is nothing analogous to this kind of self-interpreting subject in the natural sciences. Electrons, atoms, enzymes, volcanoes, hurricanes and the like are not self-interpreting – they are not bearers or makers of meaning. So their behaviours appear to be fully understandable and describable without appealing to their view of what they are doing.

How crucial is this difference in subject for the question of the similarity of natural- and social-science inquiry? Are there other relevant differences? Are these differences matters of kind or merely matters of degree?

1. Some differences between natural and social sciences

Throughout this book, we have investigated a number of issues in social science. During the course of this investigation, a number of instances of what look like differences between natural and social science inquiry have come to light. In this section, I want to summarize some of these differences.

1.1. Non-interpreting objects versus self-interpreting beings

As has been noted several times, the objects of natural-science inquiry are not constituted by meanings and values. Atoms, trees and tornadoes do not have beliefs, feelings, attitudes, aspirations or fears. They do not have points of view on themselves and the world. They do not engage in traditions and practices nor the interpretation and shaping of those traditions and practices. On the other hand, human beings do have points of view about themselves and the world. We do have a sense for how things are or ought to be. We live in the light of interpretations and meanings, engage in practices and their reinterpretation, and so forth. Our actions cannot be understood apart from this insight, implying that human action is not strictly a matter of efficient causation.

1.2. Weak versus strong world-shaping

The distinction between weak and strong world-shaping was introduced in Chapter 1, sec. 4. Weak world-shaping is characterized by a total reliance on efficient causation as the only form or channel of interaction in the natural and social worlds. In contrast, strong world-shaping also draws upon (1) our particular form of embodiment in the sense that our actions only make sense against the background of the particular type of bodies we have, (2) our particular form of life in the sense that our actions are connected with everyday practices and beliefs and (3) our particular history in the sense that our actions are significantly shaped by family upbringing, community customs and traditions. Strong world-shaping includes forms of influence like formal and final causation in addition to efficient causation. Weak world-shaping is characteristic of the natural sciences while strong world-shaping looks more appropriate for the social sciences.

1.3. Natural kinds versus constructed kinds

In Chapter 13, we saw that natural-science inquiry depends on the existence of natural kinds. These are phenomena or objects that exist in the world independent of any human observation or interpretation. Molecules, minerals and mountains are naturally occurring phenomena and would be what they are whether humans existed or not. Moreover, natural kinds are characterized as intersubjective, meaning that everyone can come to agree on what these phenomena are. In contrast, social kinds like family, lower-middle class, political party and sexual preference are created by human beings. These kinds or categories would not exist apart from our needs and purposes. The definitions and boundaries of these categories are imprecise and not intersubjective to the same degree as natural kinds. In other words, the meanings of these kinds are the source of interminable debates among social scientists and other thinkers.

1.4. Theorizing about an independent versus dependent reality

Closely related to the natural/social kind distinction is the role of theorizing in scientific inquiry. The natural world is taken to exist as an object independent of human thought and action. In this sense, theorizing in the natural sciences describes and explains an independent realm. Therefore, our theories about the natural world do not reshape that world or cause its elements to re-envision who or what they are. Our mathematical descriptions of nature, in contrast, are human constructions, so they are neither fixed in stone nor wholly arbitrary.

Social theorizing, on the other hand, has no such reality independent of human thought and activity. As we saw in Chapters 11–13, theorizing about human practices and institutions reshapes those practices, sometimes to a greater or lesser extent, sometimes for good or for ill. In other words, in the natural sciences there is a single hermeneutic at work, but in the social sciences, there is a double hermeneutic – the two-way interpretive street (Chapter 3, sec. 2).

1.5. Ethics

Another difference that arises in thinking about the natural and social sciences is the nature of ethical issues in each kind of science. We saw in Chapter 13 that ethical issues really cannot be separated from the standards for collection and handling of data in social inquiry. This means that ethics genuinely is an issue internal to social-science practices. In contrast, ethical issues arising as a result of natural-science research are largely external to the practices and results (see Chapter 13, sec. 4). Both natural and social sciences share ethical issues regarding research practices like not forging data, not plagiarizing results, giving proper credit for results and other such matters of scientific conduct, however.

1.6. Cultural ideals as disguised ideologies

Cultural ideals like political liberalism, liberal individualism, autonomy and the instrumental picture of action might characterize how natural scientists see themselves. However, these ideals do not affect their objects of study (e.g., molecules, proteins, amoebas, oceans), nor shape their research methodologies or results. In other words, cultural ideas do not shape natural-science research and practice, though they do shape judgements about and applications of such research. This contrasts strongly with social inquiry, where we have seen that such ideals work as disguised ideologies shaping all facets of social-science research and practice.

1.7. Predictability

One other difference between natural and social sciences that has only been indirectly addressed is predictability. One of the hallmarks of natural sciences like physics and chemistry is their predictive power. And one of the keys to this power is that such sciences are able to formulate theories and models in terms of variables that hold for all times – past, present and future – for the systems under study. In Newtonian mechanics, for instance, the flight of a cannon ball or the motion of a pendulum can be characterized in terms of variables like position and velocity. The nature of these variables does not change over time though their values generally do change in time. However, this feature of having a vocabulary – for example, variables and forces – where the nature and meaning of the terms does not change over time for a given system is not sufficient to guarantee predictability of the system; it is only a necessary condition (Bishop 2003).

By contrast, social reality, societies, political institutions, people's behaviour and so forth cannot be described in a vocabulary where the nature of the terms or variables taken to describe them do not change over time. This is because people are self-interpreting beings. We are who we are because of – we are constituted by – our self-definitions and self-understandings and the nature of these self-definitions and self-understandings changes over time. As a result of these changes, we change – who we are, how we see ourselves, others and society, how we behave, and so forth flow directly out of these self-definitions and self-understandings. This is why, as Berlin (1962) argued, sciences or descriptions relying only upon empirical and formal vocabularies or approaches are inadequate for the full reality of human beings. The self-definitions and self-understandings of humans today are not the same as they were in the mediaeval period nor as they will be in the distant future. The hopes for predictability as a hallmark of social inquiry are dim as a result of this situation.[1]

2. Kuhn, natural and social science

Recall that Taylor takes the main difference to be that natural science's objects of study are brute – that is, natural kinds are not self-interpreting. Therefore interpretation does not enter into the natural sciences as something integral or constitutive of their practices. Objects of natural science inquiry, like molecules, earthquakes and stars, do not make their own meanings nor do they change their meanings over time. What these objects are is discovered by intersubjective scientific investigation. As natural kinds, they are what they are independently of any human discovery about them. Interpretation, on the other hand, is central to the social sciences because its objects of study are self-interpreting beings. We are meaning-makers and we do change our meanings – our ways of seeing ourselves and our world – over time. This view of the interpretive differences in natural science versus social science comes out clearly in Taylor's characterization of correlators versus interpreters (see Chapter 1, sec. 4). For him, this is a difference in kind between the natural and social sciences.

Taylor is often interpreted as claiming the natural sciences are essentially positivist, and this characterization of his views is further reinforced by his description of these sciences. Taylor largely describes natural science in positivist terms (see Chapter 1, sec. 2.1) along with emphasizing their goal of empirical theory (see Chapter 3, sec. 1). Independently of whether he thinks that the natural sciences actually are largely positivist, many of his writings leave readers with this impression. A more plausible reading of Taylor's discussions is that he is actually characterizing a scientific ideal to which many social scientists and philosophers aspire. This ideal is largely positivist even if the model of the natural sciences inspiring it has mostly been discarded after Kuhn's influential writings. In other words, Taylor need not believe the natural sciences conform to the positivist ideal to critique social science's fascination with this ideal.

Kuhn's point of departure in his discussion of natural and social science differences starts with his disagreement regarding Taylor's way of posing the difference (Kuhn 2000). Kuhn thinks that interpretations play crucial roles in natural-science inquiry as well. The example he gives is that of ancient Greek astronomy in comparison with contemporary astronomy. The ancient Greeks placed the sun and moon in the same category as Jupiter, Mars, Mercury and the like. In other words, these were all planets and shared appropriate similarities to be classified together. And these heavenly bodies were thought to be significantly different from the ancient Greek categories of 'star' and 'meteor'. Moreover, they placed the Milky Way in the same category as rainbows and meteors. We, of course, recognize the sun as being a star, the moon as being in a category different from stars or planets, and the Milky Way as being composed of stars. So there clearly are significant differences between the ancient Greek account of the heavens and our contemporary account.

The obvious reaction to this predicament is to identify the differences in accounts as differences in beliefs about the objects populating the heavens. Whether one thinks the moon or sun are planets makes no difference to whether one could point a telescope at these objects and observe them. But Kuhn thinks that concepts about the natural and social worlds are possessed by communities of people (e.g., scientists). He argues that both types of concepts are subject to much interpretive difficulty within and across communities as well as across time. To be able to point to, identify and re-identify a planet, for instance, requires that we grasp a concept of planet. Otherwise, we cannot successfully pick out a planet from a meteor, nor can we successfully point to the planet again and again. For a conception of planet to be recognized and grasped requires a community that can point to particular instances of the concept and transmit this concept to others (e.g., to the next generation of scientists).[2] If everyone in the community each points to a different object as being a planet, we would say that no one grasps the concept 'planet'.

On Kuhn's view, the difference between the ancient Greek heavens and ours is rooted in the differences of our conceptual vocabulary. This situation in the natural sciences is supposed to be parallel to how differences between ancient Greek democratic practices and contemporary American democratic practices are rooted in differences of conceptual vocabulary. Furthermore, this conceptual difference about planets cannot be bridged from ancient Greek understandings to ours by descriptions based on brute data – the kind of data admitting one unique interpretation. Nor can the difference be bridged by appealing to purely behavioural descriptions (e.g., describing how the ancient Greeks point to some different objects than we do when asked to give an example of a planet). Moreover, if we were to describe ancient Greek astronomical practices and concepts in our own conceptual vocabulary, we would distort their ideas and practices, perhaps beyond recognition.

> No more in the natural than in the human sciences is there some neutral, culture-independent, set of categories within which the population – whether of objects or of actions – can be described. (Kuhn 2000: 220)

To get a connection between ancient Greek conceptual vocabulary and ours, requires the kind of hermeneutic interpretation and understanding many have argued for in the social sciences. In other words, interpretation is at work in such natural-science concepts and interpretation is required to understand the differences in cultural understandings of such concepts, on Kuhn's view.

What is the upshot for the natural sciences if Kuhn's characterization is plausible? First, our contemporary natural sciences – like those of any time period – are based on a set of concepts that scientists inherited from their predecessors. These concepts are historical products and, so, are matters of interpretation and understanding – they are neither univocal nor fixed for all time. Second, natural scientists put these inherited shared understandings to use in the course of what Kuhn calls normal science (Chapter 1, sec. 3), the kind of problem-solving activities that advance and deepen a particular scientific field (as opposed to the kinds of activities revolutionizing such fields). As such, these researchers are unlikely to realize they are basing much of their work on interpretations rather than univocal facts. In this later work, what Kuhn formerly called scientific revolutions (Chapter 1, sec. 3) can now be termed reinterpretations of nature (2000: 222).

According to Kuhn, there is a similarity and a difference here between the natural and social sciences. The similarity is that both kinds of scientists cannot do their work apart from concepts representing historically formed meanings and vocabulary. That is, both kinds of scientists assume a number of shared meanings and interpretations rendering their activities intelligible. The difference for Kuhn is that social scientists are constantly engaged in interpretation and reinterpretation – there is nothing like stable problem solving within a fixed framework of meanings. In contrast, natural scientists are largely unaware of the interpretive nature of their framework of meanings, but in any given field they share so much in the way of meanings that they can engage in problem solving without explicitly engaging in interpretations. A second kind of difference follows from this. According to Taylor and others, ever deeper interpretations should be the objective of the social sciences (rather than laws, say). The natural sciences, on Kuhn's view, do not consciously seek out new interpretations; rather, these happen as a by-product of the enterprise of problem solving. Indeed, these revolutions or reinterpretations often are recognized after the fact by the next generation of scientists. As Kuhn summarizes the two kinds of science:

> The natural sciences, therefore, though they may require what I have called a hermeneutic base, are not themselves hermeneutic enterprises. The human sciences, on the other hand, often are, and they may have no alternative. (2000: 222)

According to Kuhn's reinterpretation of his own work, even if the social sciences are explicitly interpretive, this does not imply that they must always be so. For, he conceives, it is possible that some social sciences over time might strike upon relatively fixed frameworks of meaning. These frameworks would serve as paradigms for these fields and support the kind of problem-solving research so characteristic of the natural sciences. In this sense, Kuhn still judges the social sciences to be pre-paradigmatic relative to the natural sciences.

Although Kuhn speculates that there may be nothing in principle preventing some of the social sciences from reaching this kind of paradigmatic status, there are reasons to think other social sciences might be prevented from ever reaching such status. In the natural sciences, natural kinds remain fixed. So in the case of the transition from the ancient Greek understanding of the heavens to the more modern view (from the Ptolemaic to the Keplerian solar systems, say), the objects in the heavens remained stable. The sun, moon, stars, meteors, planets and so on as objects 'out there' did not disappear or alter themselves sparking a transition in our understanding of them. Rather, in repeatedly encountering difficulties with the interpretive framework of the ancient Greeks during problem solving, the groundwork was laid for the Keplerian reinterpretation of these objects. Crucial to this reinterpretation, however, was the fixed, unchanging nature of the natural kinds populating the heavens.

Given the nature of social reality, this same kind of stability cannot be expected. Social reality is constituted by meanings and interpretations and these change over time. In other words, social kinds are not fixed, unchanging objects or categories existing 'out there'; rather, they are fluid, evolving with our purposes, interests and needs (see Chapter 13). There is no permanently unchanging base upon which a long-lasting framework of meanings could be built and problem solving to be established. The prospect of reinterpretation is all that might be hoped for in such social sciences. Kuhn does not clearly indicate which social sciences may be in this unstable situation, but it is possible that all of them are.

In these terms, then, the natural sciences are more interpretive than is often pictured. This appears to soften the difference between the natural and social sciences in that the former are more like the latter rather than the other way around! This way of framing the issue also suggests that the difference between the two kinds of sciences is more a matter of degree, than of kind, given that both are pictured as fundamentally interpretive. But Taylor, and others, would insist that this reading of the natural and social sciences leaves out an important feature of the latter. Namely, that while Kuhn has pressed the degree to which a one-way interpretive street exists in the natural sciences, these sciences lack a two-way interpretive street (see above). That difference looks to be a difference of kind, not merely a matter of degree. And, perhaps, Kuhn's acknowledgement of the unstable nature of social and political reality is pointing in the direction that the double hermeneutic and the instability are consequences of the self-interpreting nature of the subjects of social inquiry.

3. Social science as naturalistic

Those advocating that the natural and social sciences are similar – often called *naturalists* – maintain that a natural-scientific mode is the only appropriate framework for social inquiry. They generally maintain two theses (see Kincaid 1996):

(1) Social science is subject to the same standards as the natural-sciences and can meet these standards.
(2) Only by meeting natural-science standards can social science be good science.

Naturalists would reject both Kuhn's and Taylor's lines of thought. They might not attack the picture of natural and social science as both fundamentally involving shared frameworks of meaning. But they would deny that social science must make explicit reference to meanings and interpretations in its practices and explanations.

3.1. Social science need not appeal to meaning to be explanatory

One argument supporting this denial is that social sciences as currently practised often do not make reference to meaning, nor need they necessarily to have scientific explanations of social phenomena (see Kincaid 1996: 193–94). Macroeconomics, for example, often gives explanations in terms of inflation and interest rates, unemployment, productivity and other large-scale economic and social factors. These explanations invoke causal mechanisms and relations among various factors, but are independent of particular assumptions about the beliefs, attitudes or feelings of individual people. Yet, they are perfectly respectable explanations by natural-sciences standards. Indeed, such explanations look to be compatible with a variety of assumptions about human drives and motivations, or with no such assumptions at all. Hence, social science need not take meanings and interpretations into account to have explanatory power.

One assumption behind this line of argument is that an explicitly interpretive approach to social-science practice and explanation must be methodologically individualist. Notice that the claim is that explanations at the social or political level have a kind of independence from the individual level. But it is at the level of individual actors where meanings and interpretation become relevant, so this line of thinking goes. As long as adequate explanations of social phenomena can be given without reference to individual beliefs and actions, there is no need for social science to appeal explicitly to meanings and interpretation. However, as we saw in Chapter 7, the social and individual levels are not neatly sealed off from one another. Cultural ideals, social norms, community practices and other social forces shape individual beliefs and attitudes. Likewise, individual interpretations and reinterpretations, in turn, shape these social forces. So social features like inflation and productivity and the like do not have an existence that is somehow independent of the meanings and interpretations of individuals. Rather, such features and categories are created by us. Macro-economic explanations tacitly presuppose a fixed set of values and meanings in, for example, Western individuals and societies. If these values and meanings change, social features like banking systems, inflation and productivity that are supposedly free of interpretation and meaning on this line of argument will also change. So it is unclear that this line of argument against social science as crucially interpretive is even coherent.

Also note that this argument totally ignores the surreptitious role cultural ideals of liberal individualism, autonomy, the instrumental picture of action and political liberalism play. These disguised ideologies shape the theories and practices of macroeconomics and other social sciences dealing with large-scale social and political features in their explanations. As a result, social kinds – at both the individual and social levels – look very different now in Western societies than in other societies and other times. And many of these social kinds are only possible against the backdrop of such cultural ideals. To suppose that social-level explanations are somehow independent of meanings and interpretations is simply implausible.

3.2. The presence of meanings in social science make no difference

A naturalist might grant that both the individual and social levels of reality are shot through with meaning and interpretations, but argue that this makes no real difference to the application of natural-scientific methods (see Kincaid 1996: 205–15). If one takes Kuhn's picture of the natural sciences seriously, then interpretations and meanings play a much deeper role in these sciences. Put differently, there are no brute, univocal data in the natural sciences either. What the relevant data are, what they mean, why they are significant, how they should be described, what they imply and so forth are questions that can only be made intelligible and answered within some stable framework of shared meanings. Furthermore, if natural scientists having different frameworks of meaning approach the same data, they will answer these questions differently. Adjudication of disputes then takes place at the level of the frameworks themselves, where some form of fair comparison – both conceptual and experimental – takes place (see Miller 1987: ch. 4). According to the defender of naturalism, there is no significant difference between the natural and social sciences here.

As it stands, there are a number of responses to this line of argument. One is to note that the naturalist is ceding much ground in the sense that she is leaning much more in the direction of the interpretivist – the natural sciences are sounding more and more like the social sciences. But the naturalist reply is that even so, the natural sciences proceed with natural-scientific modes of inquiry. So the pervasive presence of interpretation and meaning does not imply that explicitly interpretive approaches are necessary in any sciences.

Another response to this line of argument is to point out that the adjudication of frameworks of meaning may be significantly different between natural and social sciences. Consider the naturalist claim that these adjudications take place through 'fair tests' (Kincaid 1996: 206) – empirical tests that are independent of any differences among the frameworks in question. If such tests only presuppose what proponents of differing frameworks share in common, then the outcomes of such tests can be used to make judgements about the viability of competing frameworks. But this response fails to account for a crucial difference between natural and social sciences; namely, that in the latter, the subjects of investigation are self-interpreting beings. Unlike objects of study in the natural sciences, where such fair experiments are possible, the very data from any kind of experiment or observation in the social sciences depend for their meaning, in part, on the ways self-interpreting beings – including social scientists – see things. This is to say that there will always be human meanings and interpretations involved in constituting what the social-science data are. The adjudication of frameworks of meaning in the social sciences will always involve invoking additional meanings and interpretations. So if the claim of the naturalist is that there are meaning-free ways to decide among different frameworks in the natural and social sciences, she is simply mischaracterizing the latter sciences. On the other hand, if she is admitting that there are no meaning-free ways to decide among frameworks even in the natural sciences, then her 'fair tests', empirical as they might be, also involve meanings and interpretations. But this suggests that natural sciences are not as value-free or objective as is usually claimed by the naturalist.

There is another problem with this 'fair test' response of the naturalist. It also presupposes that frameworks of meaning generate theories about a reality independent of the theories or frameworks. In other words, that theorizing about objects or phenomena do not alter or reshape those phenomena. This is the typical understanding of natural-science theorizing about its objects. But, as we have seen, no such theorizing possible in the social sciences – theorizing in social inquiry always changes or reconstitutes the practices about which it is theorizing (Part Three). This implies that there are no 'fair tests' in social science because the very 'social facts' constituting data for such tests are, themselves, pictured differently by different theories and frameworks of meanings. Put another way, social kinds differ from framework to framework in the social sciences, whereas natural kinds presumably do not differ from framework to framework in the natural sciences. The presence of meanings and interpretations in the social sciences do seem to lead to significant differences with the situation in the natural sciences.

3.3. Causal explanations

Sometimes the naturalist maintains that even though meanings and interpretations are part and parcel of the social realm, scientific explanations in the social sciences cite causes just like explanations in the natural sciences. Hence, the real explanatory work is carried out by causal attributions, not by considerations of meanings and interpretation. So in the macroeconomics example above, explanations in terms of inflation, interest rates and productivity are taken to be some form of causal explanation. But meanings and interpretations are not causes, so their presence does not generate a significant difference between natural-science and social-science explanations on this view.

In our survey of different conceptions of scientific explanations in the previous chapter, we saw that there are different kinds of explanations that scientists might invoke in understanding various phenomena. This objection based on causal explanation presupposes one of the key points at issue in debates over the similarities and differences between natural and social sciences: namely, that efficient causation is the only form of interaction or influence in the social realm. But we have seen numerous reasons throughout this book to cast doubt on efficient causation as the only mode of interaction or influence in the social world (e.g., formal and final forms of causation also play roles in social phenomena). So this supposed similarity between the two kinds of science is not compelling.[3]

3.4. Pressing social science into the natural-science mould

Harold Kincaid (1996) offers a recent, spirited defence of naturalism, the thesis that the social sciences are similar to the natural sciences and that methods from the latter are appropriate for the former. He invokes the arguments surveyed in this section as well as others in an attempt to show that there is largely methodological unity between these two kinds of scientific pursuit. And one of his central theses is thesis 2 above: that social sciences are only good science insofar as they conform to the standards of the natural sciences and, by implication, deploy natural-science methods.[4]

According to Kincaid, the standards of 'good science' are the following empirical virtues (1996: 50–51):

Falsifiability: hypotheses and theories must be capable of standing before the court of experience and being proven wrong.

Predictive Success: empirically adequate theories exhibit both a high quantity and high quality of predictions borne out by observation and testing.

Scope: theories should predict and explain a wide variety of phenomena.

Coherence: good theories exhibit logical consistency as well as cohering with the best information available from other sciences.

Fruitfulness: theories should lead to new insights and developments, suggest new avenues for research and guide experimental investigation among other results.

Objectivity: our best theories should reflect the way the world is, not the way we want it to be.

This list looks very much like what one would draw up as standards for good empirical theory (Chapter 3, sec. 1). There is certainly much to be said for these empirical virtues. But an important point to notice is that, as applied to the social sciences, these standards are powerless to detect and deal with cultural ideals working as disguised ideologies in social inquiry. For instance, our economic and political theories are largely surreptitiously suffused with ideals of liberal individualism and an instrumental picture of action. Suppose one of these theories exhibited a high degree of predictive success – its predictions seemed to be on the mark many more times than not. Obviously these empirical successes would not reveal to us the disguised ideologies colouring the theory. Nor does the predictive success of this theory somehow tell us that liberal individualism and the instrumental picture of action are 'true' of the social world. If, for example, the USA were to undergo a massive shift to Buddhism, these ideals would vanish and the theory would lose much if not all of its predictive power. Likely the imagined predictive success of our theory only tells us that the social scientists creating the theory unknowingly 'soaked up' the cultural ideals of the social world they were investigating and passed such ideals through as 'scientific' results of their research. That is, the imagined theory would be a successful instance of the two-way interpretive street, but what else could we conclude about the theory other than it might be instrumentally useful so long as these ideals stay relatively fixed?[5] Scope, coherence and fruitfulness are similarly powerless in the face of disguised ideologies.

Another point to note about Kincaid's list is the requirement of objectivity. As we have seen, the outsider's view associated with this requirement is, itself, a value-laden point of view. Perhaps, for the most part, in the natural sciences this point of view is harmless (though depending on how radical the interpretive basis of natural science is, it may not be so harmless after all). Additionally, in the social sciences, this drive for objectivity – understood as value-freedom – is an expression of political liberalism as well as being connected with other cultural ideals like liberal individualism and autonomy. As such, to require the social sciences to adopt this standard is to require them to be blatantly partisan with respect to such ideals. But this is exactly the opposite of what we think we mean by objectivity in the natural sciences.[6]

So there are at least two problems with the way Kincaid seeks to make his case that natural-scientific inquiry is the proper mode for the social sciences. One is that the arguments he marshals, reviewed above, either do not prove what they claim or perhaps lead in the direction of making the natural sciences radically more interpretive than he wants. Another problem is that Kincaid's picture of social science squeezed into a natural-science mould will simply perpetuate the problem of disguised ideologies. This likely means that social science, done in the natural-scientific mode only, will perpetuate and even exacerbate the pressing social problems it seeks to understand and remedy (Chapter 8).

4. Natural sciences as interpretive sciences

Recall Taylor's three characteristics of an interpretive social science (Chapter 6, sec. 3.1):

1   The categories of 'sense' or 'coherence' – meaning – must apply to the objects of study.
2   The 'sense' in question must be at least relatively distinguishable from its expression or embodiment – the same meaning is often capable of alternative expression.
3   This 'sense' must be for or by a subject.

The first characteristic obviously applies to natural-scientific inquiry as the field of questions surrounding objects of study like genes and volcanoes are what give us the ability to say if something 'makes sense' or is 'nonsense', is coherent or incoherent. Knowledge and understanding of natural objects does not exist without human knowers engaged in the activity of understanding.

Recall that an important feature of characteristic 2 is that 'scientific truths' always be capable of re-expression. This feature is not limited to the social sciences, but is found in the natural sciences as well. For instance, patterns in the data can only be seen as meaningful when we adopt a particular point of view, but not just any view. In the 1950s, particle physicists were perplexed by some odd coincidences in the decays of mesons, subatomic particles playing a role in nuclear forces. The leading idea for trying to understand this behaviour was to propose that there were two sorts of mesons that were the same in all respects except for spatial reflection. No attempts pursuing this point of view yielded an answer. Then Tsung Dao Lee and Chen Nign Yang (1956) made their simple, yet Nobel-calibre, suggestion that mesons did not have unique behaviour under such reflections. This one-particle model supplied the insight needed to understand the behaviour in question, but it only came about by adopting a different point of view for the data. This point is sometimes summed up in the slogan: 'Theory is always underdetermined by data'. As Kuhn (1996) argued, judgement has to be applied as to how to look at the data as well as for understanding where difficulties might arise in our acquisition of the data (e.g., sources for false signals or for interference). Physical theory does not always give us ideas of how to look at these questions.

The experiments that eventually confirmed Lee and Yang's ideas had been practical possibilities for experimenters for many years, but nobody considered the experiments interesting until the right questions were asked. Once the experiments had been performed, many people had to give up their explanations for meson behaviour because nature had spoken with a resounding 'No!' to their ideas. Social attitudes and beliefs influenced the practice of physics here, but did not construct its results. Yet, although it is a human activity and although nature often appears to be recalcitrant, thundering 'No!' to our best ideas, our limited mappings of the world in the natural sciences are being extended and enriched, and in the process are becoming more accurate.

A different example of such re-expression comes from fluid mechanics. The Lagrangian viewpoint pictures fluid flow as if an observer were riding along with the fluid. The Eulerian viewpoint describes properties of a volume of fluid as it moves past a stationary observer. In all cases these two descriptions agree conceptually and empirically. In this example of re-expression, the alternative descriptions bring different emphases and different insights that serve to illuminate the phenomena in question. Another example is provided by electromagnetism. Up to the mid-nineteenth century, electricity and magnetism were considered to be independent phenomena though some suspected there must be some connection between the two. It was later demonstrated that electricity and magnetism could be reinterpreted as manifestations of the same fundamental phenomenon by means of a sufficiently elegant and powerful electromagnetic theory. This reinterpretation brought clarity and unification to the separate subfields of electricity and magnetism. Another interesting case of re-expression found in quantum mechanics would be the various competing quantum theories (e.g., von Neumann, quantum stochastics, decoherence, Bohmian mechanics). In this instance the redescriptions disagree as to the fundamental ontology of the phenomena (e.g., some countenance classical particle trajectories while some do not, some are deterministic while others are not) and these differences, among others, lead to competing interpretations of the quantum world with much clarification remaining to be carried out (no univocality here!).

Characteristic 3 is obviously true of the natural sciences as it is human investigators – the scientists! – who, based on individual and consensus values and purposes within their discipline, choose which phenomena to investigate, which questions to ask, which methods of inquiry to pursue, how to apply the knowledge gained and what counts as significant in each of these choices. At a more general level, the whole notion of natural science as a practice points to the fact that it is an activity that *we* find meaningful; otherwise, we would not bother with it. More concretely, the example of different quantum theories just mentioned is a case where scientists engage in discussions and debates with each other in an attempt to clarify for themselves what some phenomena are like. Natural scientists are subjects seeking clarity, sense and coherence among themselves about the objects they are studying similar to social scientists.[7]

So whether one follows Kuhn's analysis of the natural sciences sketched above, these sciences are properly seen as a form of interpretive practice – that is to say, a way of understanding things in our world. More often than not, they focus on what I earlier called a mechanistic mode of understanding (Chapter 6, sec. 3.1.1) concentrating on efficient causation. But concentrating primarily on that mode of understanding does not make the natural sciences any less interpretive.

5. Taking stock

Some of the options on the table for conceiving of the relationship between the natural and social sciences are the following. First, the social sciences are no different than the natural sciences. Empirical standards, like those advocated by Kincaid, are equally applicable to both kinds of science, and natural-scientific modes of inquiry are appropriate for all science – period.[8] Second, the natural sciences are no different from the social sciences. The natural sciences are indelibly interpretive and, as such, the standards of empirical science are not so applicable to them as we have been led to believe. This seems to be the upshot of Kuhn's reconception of the sciences described earlier. At least, one would not expect these empirical standards to apply to any science until it had achieved a relatively fixed, long-lasting constellation of meanings and interpretations providing a suitable framework for the problem solving of normal science. Third, the natural sciences are different from the social sciences in matter of degree. The difference might be, Kuhn suggests, the fact that the natural sciences have largely achieved such long-lasting frameworks of meanings while the social sciences have yet to achieve any. This is a reworked version of the claim that the social sciences remain largely pre-paradigmatic. Fourth, the natural and social sciences are different in kind from one another. This difference would ultimately be rooted in the kinds of phenomena they study. The difference is that social science studies self-interpreting beings while natural sciences do not.

Suppose the natural and social sciences are significantly different in the ways suggested by this fourth option. Does this imply that natural-scientific methods have no role to play in social inquiry? Not at all. The lifeworld (Chapter 6) allows for a kind of conversation between naturalist and interpretive modes of inquiry, that is, between natural-scientific methods and descriptivist, critical and hermeneutical approaches. Cooperation among these different modes of social inquiry is likely a more fruitful path to pursue than trying to press social science into the natural-science mould or ignoring natural-science methods altogether. But demoting natural-scientific modes immediately raises the spectre of relativism in social inquiry, to which we will now turn.

For further study

1. Can you think of other candidates for differences between natural and social science that have cropped up throughout the book, but which have not been discussed in this chapter? Why are they possible differences?
2. Which possible difference between natural and social science inquiry do you think is the strongest and why?
3. Which of the four options for relating the natural and social sciences do you favour and why?

Recommended reading

H. Kincaid, *Philosophical Foundations of the Social Sciences: Analyzing Controversies in Social Research* (Cambridge: Cambridge University Press, 1996).

T. Kuhn, 'The Natural and the Human Sciences', in *The Road Since Structure* (Chicago: University of Chicago Press, 2000), pp. 216–23.

C. Taylor, 'Interpretation and the Sciences of Man', in *Philosophical Papers*, vol. 2: *Philosophy and the Human Sciences* (Cambridge: Cambridge University Press, 1985b), pp. 15–57.

Beyond Objectivism and Relativism 17

From reading the foregoing chapters, you may have developed the impression that social inquiry, as currently practised, is deeply troubled and unable to acknowledge its troubles. For one thing, you may have formed a picture of the social sciences as being only slightly better than worthless. Given the kinds of problems we have surveyed, how is it possible that social inquiry could ever be relevant or genuinely matter to human life? It seems that the only way social science could impact on our lives significantly is as Foucault has argued: social science is one of the main perpetrators and supporters of power regimes, creating categories and interpretations of social reality that manipulate and manage social behaviour. Although Foucault's critique is too radical, there is a very real worry that social scientists do little more than construct social realities rather than merely describe the workings of an independent social realm.

Just as troubling, we have seen that social scientists largely are trapped in a morass of ideals and values even while they strive to steer their research clear of such entrapments. Pursuing objectivity – the outsider's perspective – appears to many as the correct path to take for the social sciences. However, as I have argued over the course of this book, there is no such thing as an outsider's perspective free from all ethical commitments.

But this realization leaves us uneasy. If we cannot have the kind of objective view scientists think they are pursuing, what is the alternative? A thoroughgoing relativism, where anything goes? Surely this spells the end of science as a pursuit of truth and understanding. This represents the proverbial throwing out of the baby with the bath water as giving up on our traditional notion of objectivity looks to trap us forever in the local understanding of each person's own subjectivity.

Such worries and uneasiness have much to do with the subject-object split that has been a theme of this book (see Chapter 3). A useful way of capturing the tensions here is in the form of what at first appears to be an exhaustive dichotomy between objectivism and relativism. On the one hand, objectivism is the conviction that there is or must be some permanent, ahistorical framework to which we can ultimately appeal in determining the nature of rationality, knowledge, truth, reality, goodness or rightness. The primary task of the philosopher or scientist is to discover this standard or framework, develop sound methods and apply them to produce genuine, universal knowledge (universal-laws conception). Without such a framework and proven methods, philosophy, knowledge or language cannot be grounded in a rigorous manner, seemingly opening the door to radical scepticism and relativism. And as we have seen, natural-science approaches to social science are very much aimed at forever closing this door.

On the other hand, relativism is the conviction that all concepts of rationality, truth, reality, right, good or norms are always relative to a specific theoretical framework, conceptual scheme, form of life, society or culture. There is no substantive overarching framework by which we can rationally evaluate competing claims or alternative paradigms. Instead, there are only local understandings – the understandings and agreements of a particular society, particular community, particular family, particular individual. The kind of universal knowledge and understanding sought by scientists simply does not exist.

Neither objectivism nor relativism seem entirely convincing or even desirable. Objectivism looks to be undermined by the endlessly changing nature of our interpretations as well as being prone to dogmatism (one of the bogeymen of the Enlightenment that we are supposed to slay in modern times). Relativism contradicts our deep sense that some beliefs and values *are* better than others, that truth beyond local understandings exists, as well as undermining a sense of personal integrity and moral conviction. Is there not some 'third way' we can pursue for a meaningful, insightful social science?

1. Objectivism and relativism in social science

One of the attractions of objectivism is that it captures the Enlightenment contrasts between reason and tradition, reason and opinion, and reason and authority.[1] As such, an objectivist view looks to be just the antidote needed for freeing people from the bonds of superstitions, traditions and false authorities. But relativism also is very appealing for similar reasons (not surprisingly, because it shares so many of the same commitments). A relativist perspective also looks like an antidote to traditions and illegitimate authorities by undercutting any basis for their commanding any allegiance from us.

Objectivism and relativism also gain some attraction from their attachment to liberal individualism and autonomy. Relativism has a direct attachment in that one of its implications is that if I am freed from allegiance to superstitions, traditions and authorities, I can then make my own way in life and choose who I want to be. Objectivism has a somewhat more indirect attachment in that, as we saw in Part Two, the outsider's perspective works in the service of these cultural ideals of liberal individualism and autonomy as well as being reinforced by them. Again, as an antidote to superstitions, opinions and traditions, objectivism offers to give us the same kind of freedom from obstacles as relativism.[2]

Yet, neither objectivism nor relativism are tenable or even desirable.

Mainstream social science – natural-scientific and descriptivist modes of social inquiry – are driven by a focus on correct methodology producing universal, lasting knowledge that fulfils objectivist expectations. The approach of the correlators (Chapter 1, sec. 4) is typical of mainstream social science. Recall that correlators are characterized by three key features: (1) 'brute' data, (2) interpretation-free data operations and (3) physicalism. These three features supposedly ensure that all data and research results are univocal – admitting only one interpretation – and, consequently, are objective (free of any interpretation or bias). The foundations and methods of sound social science ideally conform to these three characteristics.

The picture of knowledge that mainstream social scientists tend to pursue has discernible Cartesian roots through the following features:

(1) Strict dichotomy between subjective and objective (subject-object ontology).
(2) Genuine knowledge as a correct representation of an external object or reality (subject-object epistemology).
(3) Conviction that reason can free itself from prejudice and tradition.
(4) Belief that self-reflection can transcend historical and cultural contexts to know things as they really are in themselves (outsider's perspective).
(5) Universal methods for securing a firm foundation for knowledge, then building upon that foundation.

Our modern emphasis on correct foundations and methods traces back to Descartes, but over the course of this book, we have seen that this focus has contributed much to distorting and obscuring the actual process of understanding human activity. The social sciences have very much succumbed to a tyranny of method in their pursuit of a pristine objectivity, a non-existent outsider's perspective. We have seen how the pursuit of correct foundations and methods in social science harbours disguised ideologies that end up deeply colouring how social scientists look at the social world.

Moreover, the subject-object split at the heart of objectivism leads social scientists to view the social actors they study as objects whose behaviours are governed by universal laws, functional relations, social structures and the like. Meanwhile, social scientists carry out their research activities somehow unconstrained by these social forces or with the instrumental power to turn back on and manipulate these forces for their own research purposes. However, this viewpoint ignores the double hermeneutic (Chapter 3, sec. 2), that social scientists are just as much a part of the reality they study as their research subjects. For instance, we have seen examples of how social science either imposes or submits to humanly created categories and understandings of the social arena rather than discovering natural kinds (Chapter 13). And we have seen examples of how theorizing in the social sciences reinterprets or recasts social reality, rather than merely describing an independent reality (Part Three). Our scientific accounts of human activity are not neutral depictions of an independent reality. These articulations of human reality define and give shape to that reality, helping to constitute it. Thus, theories in the social sciences do not simply mirror a reality independent of them, but define and form that reality, possibly transforming how people articulate and carry out their practices for good or for ill.

Because our articulations – theoretical or otherwise – at least partially constitute the reality social scientists wish to study, the subject-object distinction that seemingly works so well for natural-science runs into problems in social inquiry. Georgia Warnke (1987: 18–19, 27) recounts a good example of this regarding historical accounts of World War I. It was commonly identified as 'the Great War' or 'the war to end all wars' until the 1940s, and the war was perceived through the lens of that interpretation. When World War II occurred, however, this way of seeing the earlier war ceased to make sense and it came to be thought of as World War I. The significance of its events was transformed due to this new turn of events. Similarly, events in the second half of the twentieth century have led to World War II being called 'the Last Good War'. Future events will surely lead to new interpretations of that war as well.

Warnke's point is not that these wars only exist in the interpretations of historians and cultures. Rather, the point is that the past comes to be reconstituted in the light of current events and the interests and frame of reference of a particular community of interpreters at a particular time determine the significance or meaning of past events. Furthermore, the meaning those events have in turn determines how the events show up for the interpreters in their inquiry. This kind of situation, as we have seen, is fundamental to social inquiry, so there is no clear way to distinguish between the 'facts' of the matter and the ways they are interpreted. The interpretation of the inquirers determines what can count as a 'fact' in strong contrast with the kinds of facts we usually associate with the natural sciences (see Chapter 13). So objectivism's sharp distinction between the knowing subject and the object to be known cannot be made in the human sciences.[3]

Finally, implicit in this discussion is the fact that the objectivist view in social science presupposes the existence of an objective social reality. This reality supposedly stands independently of our conceptions of it and is governed by universal psychological, social and economic laws. However, all the evidence of our experience indicates that social reality not only is constituted by self-interpreting beings (social scientists included), but that reality is also reconstituted by us as we change our interpretations and understandings of things.

In the face of these and other problems, many seem to run in the direction of relativism as the only alternative (e.g, postmodernists and social constructionists: see Chapter 3, sec. 4). There is a strong temptation to embrace the view that there are no facts of the matter about social reality, that basically anything goes, that there are no universal truths, that social science is no surer than anyone's opinion. Objectivism assumes that the social world like the natural is composed of independently existing objects for us as subjects to know. But when we do not have such independent objects, we are only deceiving ourselves that we can somehow lift ourselves above our limited historical context and biases to clearly perceive the social realm as it is in itself. It seems natural then to adopt some variety of relativism given that we are forever locked into the play of insider's positions (hence, why so many postmodernists and constructionists are relativists: see Chapter 3, sec. 4).

Relativism also leaves us with a sense of loss about the social sciences. Where we were once looking for social reality, we only find perspectives and nothing solid or lasting. As well, relativism engenders cynicism and a growing sense of social inquiry's impotence to deliver genuine knowledge or solve real problems.

Moreover, many have followed Kuhn's radical claims regarding incommensurability of paradigms and irrationality in paradigm and theory choice (Chapter 1, sec. 2.3, 3). The implications of these radical claims are that research frameworks and theories in science ultimately can only be justified in some circular way – only on their own terms and not by appeal to any independent standards. Furthermore, given this circular support, there are no independent criteria by which to judge one paradigm or theory as better or truer than another. So in some sense the choice of frameworks and theories is more like a sophisticated matter of taste than of truth and evidence. While many may baulk at these implications in the natural sciences, when it comes to social inquiry, a number of people have thought these implications are on target. One only has to examine postmodernist and social-constructionist thinkers in the social sciences to see these attitudes (Chapter 3, sec. 4).

One way to put what many feel is at stake in this choice between objectivism and relativism is captured by what Bernstein calls the *Cartesian anxiety*.[4] '*Either* there is some support for our being, a fixed foundation for our knowledge, *or* we cannot escape the forces of darkness that envelop us with madness, with intellectual and moral chaos' (1983: 18). Certainty or utter despair seem to be our only choices. He goes on to say that:

> At the heart of the objectivist's vision, and what makes sense of his or her passion, is the belief that there are or must be some fixed, permanent

constraints to which we can appeal and which are secure and stable. At its
most profound level the relativist's message is that there are no such basic
constraints except those that we invent and temporally (and temporarily)
accept. (1983: 19)

In particular, for social inquiry, the absence of any outsider's perspective and
the failure of our methods to be truly value-neutral look to leave the door wide
open for an unbridled relativism regarding what to believe about the social
realm – 'It's all socially constructed!'

Why is relativism so attractive, or seem so inescapable, to many postmodernists and social constructionists (and others)? Guignon explains its appeal
this way. When it becomes clear that we can have no direct access to 'Nature
as it is in itself' distinct from our interpretations, we may experience a 'feeling
of loss' seemingly dictating that we are merely 'entangled in perspectives' or
that 'there is nothing outside the text' (1991: 96–98). Quite paradoxically, as
Guignon points out, this postmodern 'picture of our predicament as cut off
from Reality makes sense only because of the way it contrasts with the binary
opposition of self vs world it is supposed to replace' (1991: 98). In other words,
the relativist approach confusedly perpetuates the subject–object dichotomy it
is trying to replace!

The relativist is deeply wedded to the sharp contrast between inside and
outside, or between merely subjective and utterly objective. This picture of the
world is practically indistinguishable from that of the objectivist! Both divide
everything into the same two non-overlapping realms, while differing by giving
primacy to or accenting opposite sides of the picture. The relativist *defines* the
merely relative or subjective by contrast with something truly objective – even
though no such thing is supposed even to exist. Or, we might say that relativism
resembles the kind of terminal rebel against authority or the status quo that
would not know what to do if that status quo really collapsed. In any case,
strong relativist views do not seem effectively to revise objectivism and replace
it with something really more plausible. Rather, relativism actually *assumes* an
objectivist or foundationalist picture of what knowledge really is or would be
(Williams 2001: ch. 19) – it is just that no such thing exists, as its advocates
keep repeating over and over.

This basic problem with relativism shows up in different guises. It is as if the
relativist is deeply torn between (1) maintaining that all beliefs, truths, values
and norms are entirely relative and (2) insisting on the pristine, almost timeless
truth of its own doctrine. This split shows up in many relativist doctrines as

a deep divide between (1) the naive natives of various cultures, communities or eras who cannot help assuming the truth of their culture's worldview and validity of its moral code and (2) the enlightened relativist theorists who somehow stands apart from all these beliefs and values and can see through them. But this will not do at all. Over time, there is no reason why such natives might not question their certainties and adopt a somewhat different stance. Furthermore, relativist theorists really do not and cannot stand apart from cultures and beliefs. They have their own seriously held, taken for granted moral and metaphysical commitments which, as we have discussed, can be questioned only piecemeal, as situations arise that call for questioning, and cannot be all suspended or questioned at once. Relativists believe or assume that relativism actually undermines dogmatism and promotes individual autonomy, quite commonplace modern liberal values that they cherish and could not discard even if they wanted to.

If we were to drop the subject–object split, perhaps it might be possible to get beyond the Cartesian anxiety of either objectivism or relativism. A better alternative in this regard might be *contextualism*, where all beliefs, truths, values and norms are tied to the context or circumstances of inquiry and our projects in life, rather than to individuals, groups or cultures as the relativist maintains (Williams 2001: chs 13–20). The contextualist neither blindly assumes particular views are certain nor deems them all relative, but finds reasons in concrete contexts for questioning some views and values, engaging in dialogue with others or the past. Typically such engagement presupposes that some other views and values are not questioned at the moment while particular views and values are up for grabs and possibly revised. Otherwise, there would be no way to make sense of anything if all our views, beliefs and values are up in the air. For instance, a great deal of background knowledge, beliefs, attitudes and values must be taken for granted when I am evaluating whether my knack for being overly patient is an admirable character trait or actually is a besetting sin in many circumstances.

Contextualism, however, is consistent with there being genuine knowledge and truths that are not relativized to an individual, group or culture or even to a particular context of inquiry. Though the constraints on inquiry in a crime-scene investigation are specific to that context, for instance, the evidence uncovered leading unequivocally to establishing the identity of the guilty party produces knowledge and truth that hold in all contexts.

2. Objectivity without objectivism

By presupposing the subject-object ontology and epistemology, as both objectivists and relativists have, they are forced to view the subjective – feelings, values, interpretations, purposes – as being private, idiosyncratic and even arbitrary. The objective, in contrast, is supposed to be universal, absolute and lasting. Consequently, genuine knowledge must be objective – anything else is pseudo-knowledge at best. There is an assumption that truth is a matter of correct correspondence to or representation of an independent external reality. Moreover, there is a sharp separation between knower and known as well as between fact and value. So on the objectivist view, values, feelings and purposes must be treated as noncognitive emotional responses to our encounters with external realities or as private subjective preferences. The subject-object split forces us to view scientific knowledge as meeting these objectivist ideals for universality and value-neutrality, and never as subjective or biased.

The relativist stance also presupposes a subject-object ontology and epistemology. In contrast to the objectivist, the relativist maintains that facts about reality are not prior to and independent of interpretation. We only have unimpeded access to the subject and the subject's conceptions of and responses to the external world. So genuine knowledge, on this view, is always biased, always awash in our culturally conditioned perspectives derived from families, societies, faith communities, political parties and so forth. Indeed, the sense of loss that so many feel when they take the relativist position seriously depends upon this subject-object dichotomy. Put simply, relativism's critique of objectivism presupposes objectivism's commitments.

One striking similarity of these two polar-opposite positions is that both objectivism and relativism presuppose a subject-object ontology and epistemology. Both positions agree on the conception of objectivity as an outsider's perspective, free from the influence of all values, ideals and context. They disagree on the existence of this outsider's perspective. So both viewpoints share the same distorting picture of the world through their commitment to a subject-object ontology and epistemology. However, if there is no sharp subject-object distinction, no clear boundaries between facts and values, no punctual self as detached knower distinct from what is known, then neither objectivism nor relativism gain any purchase nor have any claims on us for allegiance.

Furthermore, just because there is no objective social order somehow standing independently of human beings does not imply that the social world is not real. The social order we create and in which we live is as real as anything there is. When social scientists theorize about the social world, they are participating in reconstituting that world, a world that really exists (one cannot reconstitute something that does not exist!).

Suppose we discard the assumptions of a subject-object ontology and epistemology. As emphasized earlier (Chapter 5, sec. 3), our everyday activity starts from concrete situations and concerns in the lifeworld – the practical stance, as I called it. We find ourselves already inhabiting this practical stance *before* we even consider the kind of theorizing in which we might engage. Our involvement in concrete contexts, with various practices and ways of seeing our situations, enables us to be actively engaged in the world. These contexts are laden with significance for us and pervaded by background knowledge that we can never fully articulate once and for all. Whatever theoretical stances we adopt always inhabit and are pervaded by these significances and background knowledge. This is the upshot of being self-interpreting animals coping in the world, but this upshot does not imply that everything is up for grabs, that it is all just interpretation and play 'all the way down' so to speak. Rather, the ordinariness of the lifeworld is the primordial ground on which we stand as we attempt to understand that lifeworld independently of whether we are looking for more practical or more theoretical understandings.

Our starting point has to be our everyday experience of ourselves and the world, the familiar sense of things we have prior to the imposition of theoretical concepts and scientific abstractions. After all, it is our experience of the human lifeworld that social inquiry sets out to explain. Certainly scientific research may contribute to discovering that our initial, pre-theoretical sense of things is mistaken, but it is important to get clear about what that initial experience is. Otherwise, social inquiry is not going to be able to account for what it set out to explain, namely, our actual, full-blooded experience of ourselves and our world.

This means that the subjective is not an arbitrary realm of reaction to objective realities. For instance, emotions are not merely reducible to stimuli and behaviour or raw affects that simply wash over us. Rather, emotions only make sense in relation to meaningful situations. And those situations are meaningful only in relation to our goals and aspirations, while those aspirations themselves are given shape by our emotions and the situations in which we find ourselves. So when we try to specify the objects of our concern, we find ourselves inextricably caught up in a web of meanings. There is a holistic mesh of experience-relative identifications which is not reducible to statements about objectively specifiable facts. The kind of objective account that presupposes the subject-object ontology and epistemology in its explanation of emotions and our sense of significance cannot escape this mesh of meanings and experience-relative identifications. Escape is impossible not because statistically significant correlations cannot be established; rather, because it is impossible to specify the terms of the correlation without relying on the very understanding of meanings that the outsider's perspective rejects.[5]

That feelings, meanings and purposes are not reducible to mere reactions to independent objective realities follows from the fact that we are self-interpreting beings. Because of this fact, humans must be understood in irreducibly evaluative terms (Taylor 1985a: 59–68). For instance, feelings embody judgements about situations. From this observation, Taylor argues that feelings also incorporate insights into what really matters to us in our lives. Our feelings have a hierarchical structure. There are the various first-order feelings and desires that come over us, such as a gut-level dislike of someone or a desire for sex. These basic reactions and urges are experienced directly, pushing us to act in particular ways. But there also are particular second-order feelings and desires ranging over and governing those first-order emotions and desires. These second-order motivations include such feelings as shame, remorse and pride, and such desires as the concern with maintaining our dignity or being a kind person. Such second-order motivations are 'higher' than our first-order desires in the sense that they play a crucial role in evaluating and regulating our first-order desires. For example, your spontaneous dislike for someone is overcome by the desire to be a kind and loving person. Or a physical attraction is reined in by your sense of marital loyalty. Second-order motivations are concerned with the qualitative worth of first-order desires and feelings, defining what is noble or base, deep or superficial, decent or sleazy, higher or lower. Therefore, you might resist spiteful feelings or vengeful desires because, from the standpoint of your second-order commitments, you find such responses unworthy, despicable, base and beneath your dignity.

These second-order motivations, Taylor argues, define a person's sense of the good, and this understanding of what is worthwhile in turn defines our identity, giving us a sense of purpose and direction. So, feelings 'incorporate a sense of what it is to be human, that is, of what matters to us as human subjects' (1985a: 60). Our second-order feelings and desires form a web of imports and meanings 'which resonate through our whole psychic life' (1985a: 60). Hence, part of what it is to have an 'identity' as a person is to try to articulate and clarify these defining motivations in the course of living out our lives. As Taylor puts it, 'the sense of imports that [feelings] incorporate has been articulated into our picture of our moral predicament, according to which some goods are higher than others, while still others are false or illusory' (1985a: 63). These 'strong evaluations' define our moral map of the world as well as giving us a sense of place and purpose in it (see Taylor 1989: 25–52). To the extent that we care about realizing these strong evaluations through time, they give our lives the kind of continuity and directedness characteristic of a well-formed narrative.

Objectivist approaches cannot provide a satisfactory account of such second-order motivations because objectivist accounts generally distinguish only pro and con feelings – basic attractions and repulsions – and limit themselves to identifying quantitative distinctions among the relative strengths of the feelings and desires. An objectivist approach, then, will see a clash of desires as similar to the conflicting pulls one might feel between two attractive options, where whichever desire is stronger wins out in the end. This is largely Hobbes' account of people as weighing up their desires and choosing their strongest preferences in the end (e.g., choosing the chocolate mousse over the tiramisu for dessert because one feels a stronger 'pull' towards it). What such approaches cannot account for are real qualitative differences in desires. Second-order desires are not simply stronger, but are distinctive in that they embody a sense of what is good or truly worthwhile, and so are definitive of one's identity.

But giving up the subject-object ontology and epistemology does not imply that we lose purchase on some form of objectivity. Recall the dialogical notion of objectivity sketched in Chapter 6. By honestly opening myself to what a friend or colleague has to say in a conversation about politics or religion, say, I can become aware of my own commitments and prejudices – perhaps for the first time or in a deeper way. Some of these commitments and prejudices may blind me to the truth of what I am trying to understand my conversation partner to be saying, while others may positively enable me to grasp the truth of what is being said. Either way, in the activity of conversation, I find that my understanding of the topic is deepened and broadened as well as my understanding of my own position and that of my interlocutor. I have gained a clearer picture of any situation.

Similarly for social scientists as they honestly and openly interact with the differing perspectives of their colleagues and rivals. These represent different insiders' perspectives on some feature of human activity and the more different perspectives that are genuinely brought into the conversation about the activity in question, the more complete will be our understanding of that activity. But this completeness does not aim at a final outsider's perspective as objectivism and relativism both would have it. Rather, it aims at a fuller, broader, richer understanding of the activity in question, of the various values and ideals at work in both the activity and the various perspectives on that activity. Furthermore, it aims at grasping the significance of this activity and what, if anything, we should do in light of these understandings. And we can make judgements about which understandings are more complete than others (just as we can grasp which friends have a fuller understanding of our subject of conversation than others). Moreover, the more complete an understanding is, the stronger its claim on us, obliging us to give up more incomplete understandings – even if these are our preference – for the more complete ones. This is authentic objectivity without objectivism or relativism.

Authentic objectivity implies that, as partners in a conversation, we are honestly engaged in hearing what others have to say, opening ourselves to truth revealed in their viewpoints. It further implies that we are able to take some form of critical distance on our own perspective so we can enter into and take seriously rival perspectives. Only in this way can we treat our own and other perspectives fairly or equitably. But none of this implies the value-neutrality at the heart of the outsider's perspective of objectivism and relativism. It only implies that to be authentically objective is to take an honest, critical stance towards our own and others's perspectives to the best of our abilities. In this way, we learn more about our own perspective and our rivals', as well as learning more about ourselves and our commitments.

3. Truth as disclosure

Finally, I want to make some remarks about truth in social inquiry. Truth in the realm of social science is similar to truth in the realm of natural science in at least one crucial respect: it is fallible or provisional, always subject to being overthrown in the course of inquiry that reveals new evidence and understanding. Truth claims always demand validation through the best evidence, reasons and arguments we can give in support of those claims, but are also always open to criticism and revision. In this way, for instance, the truth claims of Newton's mechanics were heavily revised in the light of lines of inquiry leading to the development of relativity theories and quantum mechanics. Nothing about steering a course between objectivism and relativism disturbs this important aspect of truth and its revisability.

As well, emphasizing the provisional nature of truth helps to make sense of standard practice in the sciences that would otherwise be difficult to comprehend. Before the advent of quantum mechanics and Einstein's theories of relativity, many physicists took Newton's mechanics to be an approximately true description of the workings of the natural world. But after these truly impressive twentieth-century breakthroughs in physical theory, physicists were faced with a choice: either consider Newton's mechanics to be false or consider it to only be valid for a sharply narrowed range of phenomena. Many physicists opted for the latter option, maintaining that Newton's mechanics is valid for contexts involving medium-sized objects that do not weigh too much and are not moving too fast. In this way, scientific truths have been revised and heavily qualified by contextual features of the world. We should expect nothing different from the kinds of truth social inquiry might reveal.

So truth, whether found in natural or social inquiry, is not some static picturing of an independent reality, a being *true of* that reality. Instead, truth is a faithful *presentation* of what reality – natural and social – is, a being *true to* that reality. Presentations are always revisable, multiply articulable and never final. Relativism holds no water here as there is something our presentations are true to – namely reality – but neither do we need objectivism to make sense of truth.

We do need to be prepared for truths uncovered by social inquiry to be less stable than those uncovered by natural science (see Chapter 16). After all, the persistent patterns and behaviours found in ths social realm are sustained by self-interpreting beings. As we change our interpretations and meanings, as we reshape our values, ideals and desires, as our feelings and ways of seeing things alter, we change our behaviours and alter or even destroy patterns in the social realm. So what is true about human behaviour today is not guaranteed to be true tomorrow, just as much of what was true about our behaviour in mediaeval times is not true of us now.

Suppose we stop thinking of truth as a static picture of an independent reality as both objectivism and relativism presuppose, and instead, conceive of truth as a faithful presentation of aspects of reality, where this presentation is open to modification as our context of inquiry and our purposes change. As an example, when a biologist puts a slide with a tissue sample under a powerful-enough microscope, the cellular structure of the tissue is disclosed. Or when an astronomer views a distant star or galaxy through a telescope, features of that star or galaxy are revealed that were previously unseen. Although what the truth of the cellular structure of the tissue or these disclosed features of the star or galaxy means requires further reasoning and thought on our part, they are nevertheless truths presented to us for our consideration.

Such a conception of truth opens the way to accounts of human activity that are revisable while not being merely subjective or relativistic. These would be accounts whose focus is to lay bare or disclose what is 'really happening' in the social realm as well as seeking to clarify these happenings and their significance for us. As discussed previously (Chapter 3, sec. 2; Chapter 16), the truths we encounter in the natural sciences largely involve only a single hermeneutic. Scientists must deal with the interpretations and meanings informing their research framework. Tissue cells, stars and galaxies have no interpretations or meanings of themselves and the world. In contrast, humans are self-interpreting beings, so social scientists must take into account both their own interpretations and meanings as well as those of the people they are studying. This complicates the disclosure of truth in social inquiry.

To show how complicated truth in the social realm can be, consider the following. A great deal of research in recent years (dozens of correlational studies, actually) have found a positive, moderate, statistically significant relationship between (1) scores on a variety of measures of common religious beliefs and practices and (2) scores on a number of different scales assessing mental and physical health or well-being (McCullough, Pargament and Thoresen 2001; Pargament 2001). What are we to make of these findings concerning religion and well-being? In what sense, if any, can we say that they disclose something true or valid about human life?

First of all, these findings are hardly value-neutral. The measures of religious belief and practice reflect the investigator's judgement as to what are normal or worthwhile religious activities and the scales of health and well-being employed reflect a researcher's opinion concerning what are desirable outcomes in living.

Second, it would be a mistake to construe these findings as showing a clear *instrumental* relationship between religion and well-being. Rather, we should think of these beliefs and activities on the one hand, and conditions of well-being or peace of mind on the other hand, as different facets or ingredients of a particular culture or way of life. They seem to go together to a modest extent as aspects of a particular way of being human at one point in time. We have to make up our minds about what we think about that way of being as a whole – there is no way to objectively or purely pragmatically evaluate it in terms of its 'results'.

I cannot stress enough how deeply value-laden such findings and any interpretation we place on them actually are. We can all imagine someone who values physical and social success or domination above all else in life. To this person such religious attitudes as acceptance or peace of mind would seem trivial or escapist, much mental turmoil might be interpreted as excitement or a sign of vitality, and high blood pressure deemed a badge of honour! In fact, many of us think that spiritual values like finding, at times, real meaning in suffering and adopting a minimally judgemental and forgiving attitude towards others have a great deal to recommend them, including the calm or accepting outlook on life they tend to foster. But no one can attain an outsider's point of view from which to demonstrate that this outlook is a good or worthy one. Even if one could reach that kind of purely detached vantage point, it would have little meaning. Such conclusions about what is truly significant or worthwhile have no real meaning unless they are worked out by individuals or a community in their struggle to discern things in a deeper or wiser way, a struggle full of surprises and at least some degree of 'learning through suffering' (in the words of the Greek poet Aeschylus).

None of this is to deny that these research findings concerning religion and well-being in our society disclose something interesting about human life. It is just that this research is in every way a living part of the human struggle for clarity, decency and wisdom. That struggle motivated and generated the research in the first place, and what sense or meaning we make of it will depend upon our vantage point and concerns at a given point in the struggle. This process of sense-making and interpretation is, I have argued, a two-way street. Social scientists interpret and explain human activity, but often their understanding (and, indeed, the very terms of their understanding) of this activity will change or develop in the process, just as partners in a conversation often influence one another's outlook and values in unpredictable ways. The same two-way process takes place between reported results and the way they are assimilated and interpreted by citizens, students and other social scientists. The meaning of these findings and the very realities of human activity or social life may alter as a result of how they are received and interpreted. We can imagine that secular readers of these studies on religion and well-being may be prompted to re-evaluate their opinion of religion as something usually backward or even harmful to human welfare. However, readers more sympathetic to religious values may be prompted to question some of their goals and ideals, as well. They may be prompted to wonder if the emphasis on health and well-being in this research and current religious culture perhaps blinds them somewhat to suffering and injustice in the world to which they probably should attend more pointedly, even at the cost of some of their comfort and security. Thus, the meanings we live by and our human-science accounts of them will mutually influence one another and change over time. This view of things places severe limitations on the traditional pretensions of mainstream social science to final or certain truths about the human realm. But it also reconnects us morally and existentially with our world, the world we are trying to understand. In return for accepting these limitations, we may gain a great deal in the way of meaningfulness and relevance in our pursuits.

4. Taking stock

> Our attempted definitions of what is really important can be called interpretations . . . and we can therefore say that the human animal not only finds himself impelled from time to time to interpret himself and his goals, but that he is always already in some interpretation, constituted as human by this fact. To be human is to be already engaged in living an answer to the question [of what is important or worthwhile], an interpretation of oneself and one's aspirations. (Taylor 1985b: 75)

Because of this irreducibly interpretive and meaning-laden character of human phenomena, only someone who is in on the forms of life and sense of meaningfulness suffusing this experiential lifeworld will be able to make sense of what such self-interpreting beings feel and do. Social science, understood as the interpretation of self-interpreting beings, is possible because the scientists doing the interpreting are themselves self-interpreting beings. They are genuine co-participants in a shared linguistic and historical world, and so are, to some extent at least, 'insiders' with a prior grasp of the meanings and evaluations they set out to interpret.

Viewed in this light, natural-scientific methods might best find their place in social inquiry as tools that researchers use to help uncover patterns and discern relationships among social features that might otherwise go undetected. Our experience of the lifeworld and our insight into human values, purposes and ways of seeing the world would then enable us to make sense of what such patterns and features mean and what, if anything, we should do about them.

However, the kind of humility that comes along with our human predicament – in particular, acknowledging that we only have access to insiders' views – counsels us to refrain from seeking the final truth of what we disclose about the social realm, partly because in the very act of disclosure, we change the very thing we are studying and find that we are often changed, as well.

Above all, we should think of ourselves as creatures in relationship – in relationship with one another, our social world, the past, and even the future. In those relationships, we depend upon and work with one another for a better, more authentic, or more decent life. For a social scientist, or any partner in such relationships, to achieve final or certain truth about their world or themselves would mean that they had stepped out of such relationships, attained a god-like status, and become a being quite superior to humanity as we know it. Every now and then, of course, someone pretends to such a superior status or knowledge. However, we have learned to see through such claims. At our best, we realize that the always tentative but (we hope) better or more insightful interpretations we make in social inquiry are like the understandings we arrive at or judgements we make in everyday life. We cannot make them alone. They are only works in progress, like our lives in general. They often require a measure of daring and risk to formulate, rather than hiding out in conventional wisdom or the 'common sense' of the day. And they require the humility to admit that we always have something more to learn.

A number of social thinkers (Habermas 1973; Taylor 1985b; Richardson and Christopher 1993) have made this point by insisting that to put social science in perspective we must re-imagine social science or social theory as a 'form of practice'. In actual practice or everyday life, we ruin everything if we pretend to an outsider's point of view or throw up our hands and fall into the cynicism or despair of 'nothing matters anymore' or 'anything goes'. Moving beyond objectivism and relativism means acknowledging that social inquiry is, above all, a form of practice. Seen in that light, social science can neither transcend the human situation nor escape its imperatives to try harder, love better, and see more clearly (even if always 'through a glass darkly'). But they can find their place and make their mark as one distinctive kind of voice in the conversation of humankind.

For further study

1. How do both objectivism and relativism presuppose a subject-object ontology and epistemology?
2. What do you think are the strongest arguments that can be made against objectivism and relativism? Evaluate these arguments.
3. Explain how it is possible to maintain viable notions of objectivity and truth without the subject-object split.

Recommended reading

R. Bernstein, *Beyond Objectivism and Relativism: Science, Hermeneutics and Praxis* (Philadelphia: University of Pennsylvania Press,1983).

J. Habermas, *Theory and Practice* (Boston: Beacon, 1973).

F. C. Richardson and J. Christopher, 'Social Theory as Practice: Metatheoretical Frameworks for Social Inquiry', *Journal of Theoretical and Philosophical Psychology* 13 (1993): 137–53.

F. C. Richardson, B. Fowers and C. Guignon, 'Social Theory as Practice', in *Re-Envisioning Psychology: Moral Dimensions of Theory and Practice* (San Francisco: Jossey-Bass, 1999), pp. 277–306.

C. Taylor, *Philosophical Papers*, vol. 2: *Philosophy and the Human Sciences* (Cambridge: Cambridge University Press, 1985b).

Notes

Chapter 1

1 Ontology deals with the properties, categories or other fundamental features of the world.
2 This would be one way that science's approval or value might be due strictly to criteria internal to its practices. Social constructionist thinkers (Chapter 3, sec. 4.1) often view science's approval as coming from social criteria having nothing to do with scientific practices.
3 The term 'positivism' refers to a so-called positive science dealing only with objective, verifiable facts. Generally, positivism maintains that sensory experience is the only means for producing knowledge about the world.
4 In the natural sciences, the practice of physics and other sciences requires extensions beyond the realm of first-order logic, but the needed extensions lead directly to problems regarding logical notions of completeness, decidability and other deduction properties. Simple examples show why it is reasonable to make these extensions. In order to represent properties of matter such as mass or charge as intrinsic, the use of at least second-order predicates with identity is required. Additionally many properties of classical physics take on a continuum of possible physical values requiring a formal language powerful enough to describe continuous functions of real numbers. A more complex example involves the mathematical language of physics itself. Although what mathematicians call real analysis appears to be expressible in terms of second-order predicates with identity, physics also makes use of mathematical concepts such as manifolds and the calculus of manifolds, both of which require going beyond second-order languages.
5 The act or process of logically deducing or otherwise reasoning to a conclusion from a set of premises or evidence.
6 The nature of this similarity relation between model and real-world system is hotly debated.
7 There are a number of situations where there may be no meaningful, working concept of insignificant (cf. Bishop 2006c).
8 Kuhn's use of the term 'paradigm' in *The Structure of Scientific Revolutions* is highly ambiguous (some have counted as many as 21 different uses in Kuhn!). The notion of paradigm as a collection of exemplars for problem solving is one very important sense of this term.
9 Efficient causation is typically taken to be the only form of causation in the sciences. The two key features characterizing efficient causation are (1) a transference of energy, momentum or some other physical quantity and (2) an antecedent relationship between cause and effect. This antecedence could be logical, that is, the cause precedes its effect in logical order, or temporal, that is, the cause precedes its effect in time. The temporal notion of antecedence has come to dominate the use of efficient causation in the sciences. A standard example in natural science contexts is that of a moving cue ball striking a

stationary eight ball, transferring energy and momentum, and setting the latter in motion. An example from cognitive science would be information input (via the senses, say) triggering processing units (located in the brain or wider nervous system), whose outputs, in turn, determine behaviours.

10 A formal cause (Aristotle, *Metaphysics* Book V, II; Slife and Williams 1995, ch. 4) is the form or structure of a process or event relating parts and wholes, guiding or constraining how parts can function in a whole (as in a blueprint for the construction of a house). Furthermore, this kind of constraining or regulation of parts takes place simultaneously in time, whereas, by contrast, efficient causation takes place sequentially through time.

11 Friedrich von Hayek (1967: 22–42) made an argument against the possibility of laws in the social sciences along the lines that agents and their actions are not significantly different from the objects of natural science except that the former are much more complex.

12 Many of them also insist that this is the only way to be 'scientific'.

13 Note that both interpreters and correlators might agree that the methodological conception is crucial to distinguishing science, but might disagree as to what methodologies constitute appropriate scientific practice. Or interpreters might maintain that the activity conception is more crucial than the methodological conception.

14 Taylor is largely silent on how correlators and interpreters can work fruitfully together, but we do not need to worry about this issue to see the big picture – the gap between the two approaches that Taylor is trying to bring out.

Chapter 2

1 He, perhaps, would not have acknowledged that there was a distinction between these two fields of knowledge as we think today.

2 This context-free emphasis foreshadows much of the thinking about science in the nineteenth and twentieth centuries as being concerned with knowledge that is independent of context.

3 There is a further problem for the metaphorical interpretation of Hobbes' 'scientific picture' of human behaviour. He maintained that metaphors were an abuse of language and tended to distort and mislead thinking (1994: ch. IV), so it would be odd for him to speak metaphorically about his scientific foundation for human behaviour. On the other hand, Hobbes crucially resorts to metaphors ('Leviathan', 'Behemoth') as the central organizing devices for his political work.

4 Indeed, Hobbes places great stress on the educative power of religion and universities as well as political and social institutions to encourage respect for law and authority that make neither explicit nor implicit appeals to self-interest.

5 Two notables worth mentioning are Robert Malthus (1766–1834) and Karl Marx (1818–83). Malthus, famous for his population arguments, studied and wrote on the perfectability of society, monetary issues such as the relationship between price and money supply (he is often acknowledged as England's first academic economist), rent, and the effects of free trade. Marx wrote extensively on social theory, political theory and economics. He pioneered class analysis, and undertook a detailed examination of capitalism.

6 Contemporary developments in 'econophysics' – the application of concepts and techniques from physics to the study of economic and social systems – can be viewed as striving to fulfil Comte's vision and attempting to render the study of such phenomena mathematically tractable.

7 In this sense, Durkheim follows the narrower interpretation of the Hobbesian picture of human motivation, namely that self-interest was the prime if not the only motivation for human actions.

8 Jürgen Habermas (1971; 1991), among others, has argued powerfully that rationalization and bureaucratization are actually repressive of human freedom and democracy as well as tending to undermine the ethical foundation of human relationships and society.

9 Weber's student, Joseph Schumpeter actually coined the term to refer to Weber's view.

Chapter 3

1 This chapter draws heavily on Frank Richardson's and Blaine Fowers' (1998) insightful identification and discussion of these five modes.

2 For Descartes, as for Hobbes, these reliable methods are largely rational/theoretical, whereas for Bacon and much of the modern scientific tradition they are largely empirical.

3 Additionally, I must also have some grasp of what voting is to participate in this practice.

4 Such 'neutral' principles actually represent a partisan commitment to political liberalism (Chapter 5).

5 Note the apparent mixture of both methodological holism and individualism here.

6 Or they perhaps serve to establish a new cultural regime for acceptable/unacceptable behaviour.

7 As we will see later, Kuhn (2000) challenges this characterization of natural science as somehow not crucially involving interpretation.

8 Unlike postmodern approaches, hermeneutics does not surreptitiously reproduce the subject-object split.

9 Indeed, hermeneutic social scientists would see conversation as the model for their interaction with any of the other four modes of social inquiry.

Chapter 4

1 In his own way, Durkheim raised similar concerns about the rise of self-interested action at the expense of social ties and mores.

2 Contrast this aspiration to autonomy and separateness in Western culture with the emphasis on harmony, civility and respect for hierarchy practiced in Japan. In their culture, these values are considered anything but subjective attitudes of individuals.

3 If people do not have this capacity to somehow step apart from these psychological forces and transform themselves, then psychodynamics is largely a manipulation technology, where therapists seek to 'push the right buttons' to get the underlying forces in a client to realign themselves to produce desired behaviours. This clearly allows therapists to approach their clients instrumentally, as things to be manipulated in the service of various ends of mental health (e.g., to exhibit acceptable behaviours).

4 This is an example where our theorizing about social practices and meanings does not merely describe these social realities, but fundamentally reinterprets them to be something other that what we take them to be. This feature of social-science theorizing is explored more fully in Chapters 10 and 11.

5 Indeed, primarily focusing on the most effective means implies that values such as justice and fairness are much less important!

6 Compare this instrumental picture of reason with the rational-actors picture in Chapter 10.

7 The instrumental picture can be unfalsifiable in another sense as well. Whenever evidence from psychological experiments, political action or economic performance of agents fails to live up to the descriptions and predictions of instrumental rationality, as is often the case, its proponents usually appeal to imperfections in the conditions to save the theory (e.g., lack of perfect foresight of agents, lack of knowledge of all the options, etc.). But this move clearly renders the instrumental picture of action immune to any contrary evidence.

8 Miller does seem to allow value judgements some role in justification of explanations taking place against a background of specific substantive principles in addition to background practices (1987: 113).

9 See van Fraassen (1993: 21–23) for a different line of argument leading to the conclusion that evaluative elements can never be eliminated from science. To his credit, Miller does hedge here in that he allows that explanations involving evaluative concepts may be appropriate for some explanations to have sufficient depth (1987: 112–13), illustrated by the following example.

10 Originally due to G. E. M. Anscombe.

Chapter 5

1 Contrast this with traditional Japanese village culture emphasizing consensus and unanimous decisions as the foundation for its social life (Smith 1959: ch. 5).

2 Moreover, Schumaker argues that neither evidence for possible genetic components of depression nor the fact that antidepressants are often effective in reducing depressive symptoms imply any causal link between biological features and depression. Rather, there is considerable evidence that shared meanings and more communitarian coping strategies can significantly raise people's threshold for depression.

3 See Sternberg and Ben-Zeev (2001) for descriptions of a number of such experiments.

4 Or on the descriptivist approach, should yield objective, accurate descriptions of motivations and actions.

5 So even in physics we do not have the context-free laws that are the aim of the universal-laws conception.

6 This is not to say that in the context of natural sciences (physics, say) that the theoretical stance cannot deliver truth (about the properties of electrons, say) in a way superior to other possible approaches to these domains. Rather, it is to say that our purposes are different in natural-science investigation in comparison with social inquiry.

7 Many results of the laboratory fail to hold when taken into the complicated, interrelated world outside the laboratory (Hacking 1992).

Chapter 6

1. I have hinted at the possibility that natural-science inquiry also is not value-free. Even so, one might think that values play no significant role in natural science as disguised ideologies play in social inquiry.
2. Examples of the kinds of self-correction mechanisms Nagel has in mind would be the reproducibility of experimental results by several different laboratories or peer review of scientific articles submitted for publication.
3. This suggestion amounts to a different conception of objectivity from that standardly associated with the natural sciences.
4. Perhaps this has occurred because our focus on efficient causation and instrumental action has tended either to exaggerate our individualistic rational mastery over events or to downplay ordinary conversation as merely the effect of more potent underlying causes. Or perhaps both, as when, highly inventive thinkers devise theories that tend to degrade the creative force and originality of human thought.
5. There is a worry that setting aside objectivity as the outsider's perspective means we must embrace relativism and reject any possibilities for genuine knowledge and truth. These worries are addressed in Chapter 17.
6. Although originally introduced in the context of social inquiry, we will see later that these three characteristics may also be found in natural-science inquiry (Chapter 16).
7. By sense or meaning being for a subject, Taylor does not maintain that people have to always 'get' or grasp the meanings of their actions. He simply means that meaning does not make sense apart from a subject capable of grasping or interpreting meaning, whether this grasping or interpreting is more or less confused or otherwise defective.
8. There is another way in which something might not 'make sense' or be 'nonsense'; namely, we could be asking wrong or inappropriate questions about the thing we are trying to understand.
9. It is worth pointing out that for someone's behaviour to be meaningful or make sense to them or to us does not mean that the behaviour has to be rational in some sense or be free of contradictions or confusions. Rather, as Taylor points out, 'the meaning of a situation for an agent may be full of confusion and contradiction; but the adequate depiction of the contradiction makes sense of it' (1985b: 24).
10. After all, the theoretical stance is really just a kind of stance a scientist might take for particular purposes to answer particular questions.
11. James calls it the psychologist's fallacy because he was a psychologist writing about psychology. But the form of the fallacy is quite general to the social sciences and could be called the 'social scientist's fallacy'.
12. Narrative accounts should not be viewed as a 'methodology' or technique for doing social science. To do so would be to decontextualize and distort narratives as well as the phenomena they imbue, divorcing them from the historically and socially embedded human interactions of which they are a constitutive part. It is also important to remember that a narrative account is one that respects the narrative structure of the lifeworld. This does not imply that the only such accounts are narratives of individual people. Explanations of

groups or societies and their dynamics can also be narrative so long as they respect the structure of the lifeworld.

13 For instance, as I watch the TV show *24*, I am in an ongoing conversation with agent Jack Bauer over uses and abuses of torture. And I discover and ponder my deepening conviction that torture is wrong in all circumstances. (Of course, Bauer's superiors often say that they disapprove of his methods, but that he is 'effective' at accomplishing his missions, a reflection of how far the instrumental picture of action and liberal individualism as ideals have seeped into our entertainment!).

Chapter 7

1 Methodological individualism also rules out Freudian explanations, where many of our beliefs are treated as rationalizations and our desires as sublimations. On these accounts, actions are really due to forces below the level of our conscious intentions and desires.

2 Understanding the thinking of individual criminals might provide insight into why they commit the crimes they do. But it may very well turn out that each criminal is as unique as his or her crime rendering it very difficult to find any generalizations.

3 For some discussion of arguments for and against reductionism in social explanations, see Kincaid (1986).

4 It is typical to call this a hermeneutic circle, indicating that meanings are refined and reworked as they cycle around between the individual and the social (or between the words and sentences). However, the image of the circle connotes something that has no direction or development, but meaning *does* develop in this process. Hence, my preference for a spiral to denote this development.

Chapter 8

1 In contrast, a non-hardy personality apparently would significantly lack these three components, but this leaves open an enormous number of personality variations that are ostensibly of low effectiveness in coping with stressful life events.

2 Doubtless meaningful involvements with others are interesting, but the emphasis on individuals and stressful events indicates this is not what the challenge component of hardiness is about.

3 Although no direct policies have been adopted as a result of Hardin's essay, his framework and arguments have shaped significant portions of public-policy debates on a number of related issues.

4 Indeed, conscious awareness of population effects has led to tremendous reductions in population growth in almost all industrialized countries, even to negative growth rates in some European countries. So the empirical evidence is inconsistent with the conclusions of Hardin's elimination argument, calling its underlying assumptions into question.

5 Tellingly, John Gottman, one of the most prominent marriage researchers, betrays this technical orientation in the title of his book: *What Predicts Divorce: The Relationship between Marital Processes and Marital Outcomes* (1994).

6 This is an example of the double hermeneutic at work, where the social scientists' supposed objectivity is heavily influenced by the cultural ideals of their society (Chapter 3, sec. 2).

Chapter 9

1 Joseph Rychlak argues that Freud's view of determinism and causation should be interpreted along the lines of final causation (teleology) as opposed to efficient causation (1979: 43–49). Perhaps ideally they should. But Freud insisted on determinism as an article of scientific faith, and most Freudians and many others who revised his views in the psychoanalytic tradition have held to this conviction (Greenberg and Mitchell 1983).
2 Again, humanist views like existential theories, are often too vague or lacking in accounts of agency apart from chains of efficient causes and effects. The characterization of hardiness (Chapter 8, sec. 1), which is based on existentialist approaches, is explicitly cast in efficient causal and instrumental terms, suggesting there is no significant difference on these points from mainstream approaches in psychology.
3 Some have thought the lifeworld picture is a better way to understand Freud's theory than the standard mechanistic account. The uncovering and treatment of a fixation from some previous life stage might be viewed as changing the past from the perspective of a present view of oneself. This might be understood as a mutual reshaping of the past and present.
4 While it is true that in the cognitive picture we can tell stories about deeper meanings regarding our relationships, these stories turn out to be instrumental as well, in that they are convenient fictions we tell ourselves, covering up the underlying, mostly unconscious calculations.
5 Our ordinary sense of purposiveness is included here, but note that while purposive states are intentional on the philosopher's view, not all intentional states are purposive on this view. The deeper philosophical problem here is 'How is the mind capable of having intentional states?'
6 Identifying the mind with the entire brain does not help because this simply restates the first step of the problem.

Chapter 10

1 Sometimes these units are referred to as *utils*.
2 There are further technical conditions needed to extend the theory to infinite sets of alternatives and to capture gambling behaviour, but we will ignore these here.
3 Some have questioned whether it is truly possible for agents to be indifferent, but perhaps all that is needed is that agents act as if they are indifferent in the case of equal preferences.
4 Technically, any order-preserving transformation of U would represent the agent's preferences equally well, so there is a potential problem with having a unique representation of agents' preferences.
5 The concept of a Nash equilibrium, which provides the standard definition of game-theoretic 'solutions', specifically exclude all forms of communication between the actors. These solutions do not work in cases where such communication takes place (Heath 2001). This clearly represents an extreme individualist requirement.

6 One might object, somewhat implausibly, that fun is a strategic consideration. More examples where even this kind of redescription are impossible are discussed in Chapters 11 and 12.

7 The concept of marginal utility is defined and illustrated in Chapter 12, sec. 1.

8 Popper took falsificationism to be a kind of marker distinguishing between science and pseudo- or pretend science. He famously argued that Marx's theory of history and Freud's psychoanalysis were unfalsifiable pseudo-sciences (Popper 1963: 33–38).

9 The supposed redescription does not look possible (Taylor 1989; 1995).

10 One can read Camerer and Fehr (2006) as doing exactly this task.

Chapter 11

1 The oldest recognized academic chair associated with the subject is the Johan Skytte Chair of Eloquence and Government at the University of Uppsala.

2 One might worry about what values inform this 'sense of importance' and whether political scientists can be merely descriptive with respect to these values.

3 A more recent influential movement within political science is the application of rational-choice modelling and the rational-actors picture (Chapter 10) to political inquiry (Chapter 11, sec. 4).

4 Or reflect the status quo by uncritically adopting the categories of the prevailing social and political orders under study.

5 The 'Chicago School' of rational choice is somewhat of an exception here as they do discount the role institutions play while emphasizing that political actors are largely egoistic in their motives and aims.

6 This is sometimes called a 'voter's paradox'. Stated most simply: one vote makes no difference to the outcome of an election. Hence, there is no incentive to vote, yet millions participate in elections.

Chapter 12

1 Note that if the processes of preference formation are deterministic, then individuals' choices are deterministic in this picture. This is an example of a free will–determinism dilemma in economics (Chapter 14).

2 Another difficulty with Friedman's view is his emphasis on predictive success. Many philosophers of science have pointed out a problem with only requiring a theory to make successful predictions of phenomena it was designed to explain. What is crucial to judging a theory successful is that it offers novel predictions – predictions going beyond the set of phenomena originally to be explained. Such predictions reduce the likelihood that the theory or model is ad hoc. On Friedman's view it is too easy to invent a theory merely to explain the intended phenomena. There are a number of ad hoc ways to build a theory that will 'get the predictions right'. But this tells us nothing about the theory's success, nor will the theory tell us anything about relevant related phenomena it was not designed to predict.

3 Ironically, natural scientists were not necessarily trying to avoid causal concepts and language.

4 If their preferences depend on irreducible social phenomena, then the rational-actors picture will violate methodological individualism (Chapter 7).

5 For good measure, a healthy dose of political liberalism (Chapter 5, sec. 1) is at work in the interaction between economics and public policy. So this vision of the good life is also advocated in the normal course of economic inquiry.

Chapter 13

1 Institutional review boards at universities and other institutions may add extra requirements (e.g., always requiring informed consent no matter what). And they can also deny experimental designs judged to violate ethical or other guidelines. Often universities and institutions will place tighter restrictions on research than professional codes to protect against potential law suits.

2 An institutional review board may make an additional assessment of harm or may simply accept the scientist's assessment.

3 As of 2002 the language of the APA guidelines still allow experiments like Milgram's although interpretations of those standards have changed such that institutional review boards generally will not approve such experiments. However, there is nothing preventing the interpretations of these standards from changing in the future so that such experiments become justifiable again (e.g., for national security or counter-terrorism research).

4 According to social historian Philippe Aries (1962), during the Middle Ages (a social kind constructed by historians) there was no concept of childhood. The ages of 4 to 12 were not considered to be life stages and there was no transition from weaning to the dress, responsibilities and roles of adults as we now conceive. At the end of the Middle Ages, due to changes in the roles and demands of adult life, 4 to 12 year olds were increasingly seen as not being ready for adult life. Instead, they began to be singled out for special treatment such that by the fifteenth century, there was a high interest in educating those falling in this age group, creating another distinct life-stage.

5 Our conceptions of natural kinds change over time (see Chapter 16, sec.2), witness the differing conceptions of the atom from ancient Greece to contemporary physics. Presumably, atoms as a kind have not changed over time once they came into existence in the very early universe. Planets, on the other hand, apparently are tricky as a kind, with astronomers recently redefining the kind so that Pluto no longer qualifies (Schilling 2006).

6 If the social scientist disapproves of these values, she can choose alternative categorizations. She might choose to distinguish between domestic partnerships of all types and single households. But as Root points out (1993: 169–70), this categorization will most likely not be effective for the social scientist's needs unless the society also accepts and uses the category. For instance, institutions are unlikely to keep records in terms of domestic partnerships versus singles, but perhaps only in terms of married versus unmarried, making it difficult to properly account for all forms of domestic partnership. To get the new categorization adopted would require the social scientist to explicitly advocate using the new categories, meaning she would be involved in advocating a change in values

and preferences. However, the social scientist cannot avoid supporting one set of values or the other: she either implicitly supports the values of the status quo, or explicitly supports the alternative values.

7 Consider the fad social kind soccer moms popularized in much mid to late 1990s political analysis and commentary on US elections.

8 Depending on the type of higher animals under study in biology, physiology, neurology and pharmacology, there might be the potential for causing harms due to research methodologies and data standards. These harms might occur in instances where higher animals would experience physical pain or other discomforts. (Much more controversially, if some higher animals have rights, they could be subject to other harms associated with violations of those rights.) But these would be some instances where natural science more closely parallels social science rather than the other way around. In general, natural science has no such parallels.

9 *Scientism* – the philosophical view that all there is to human beings and the world is what the physical, biological and other sciences tell us – certainly can touch all aspects of human beings. Richard Dawkins and Daniel Dennett are deft practitioners of scientism, but fail to see that it is a fully fledged philosophical position that receives little support from actual science.

Chapter 14

1 There is a further possible tension here in economics. To the extent that economic theories incorporate the rational-actors picture (Chapter 10), there is a potential conflict between rationality and determinism.

2 Compare these dilemmas with the postmodernist picture of individuals as totally determined by the historical flow of culture while these individuals simultaneously are assumed to have a radical freedom to step outside of or manipulate these same deterministic forces (Chapter 3, sec. 4).

3 For the most part they are simply too vague to make clear judgements as to whether they avoid free will–determinism dilemmas.

Chapter 15

1 Recall that the covering-law model only admits well-confirmed laws as appropriate for scientific explanations.

2 The idea that the universal-laws conception should be applicable to all sciences likely derives from a prejudice developed by taking physics to be the archetype for genuine science. But there is nothing about physics that implies any other sciences like biology, ecology, psychology or political science should somehow be concerned with universal laws.

3 There are some indications that causal notions need to be expanded to include formal causation in natural sciences like physics as well (Bishop 2006b).

4 Taylor's idea of correlators and interpreters working together (Chapter 1, sec. 4) might be understood along the lines suggested here. I should point out that Taylor is not advocating doing away with causation in social inquiry as some have charged (e.g., Martin 1994:

263–65). Rather, he is seeking to enrich our understanding of the social realm by encouraging us to break free from deploying predominantly natural-scientific and descriptivist modes of inquiry focused exclusively on efficient causation.

5 Recall Nagel's distinction in Chapter 6, sec. 1.

6 This is the kind of explanation in evolutionary biology that tends to promote views of genetic determinism.

Chapter 16

1 Much is made of prediction as a chief hallmark of the validity of a scientific theory in the natural sciences. However, if social scientists adopt this same attitude, then the stunning lack of successful predictions anywhere in social science looks to undermine the justification for social science.

2 Recent debates over the definition of 'planet' and the status of Pluto (Schilling 2006) are an interesting case to consider from Kuhn's perspective.

3 On the other hand, if natural sciences like physics also need to take other forms of causation into account like formal causation (Bishop 2006b), then this would make them more similar to social sciences.

4 Alexander Rosenberg (1995) and Kincaid agree on 2, but differ in their judgements over whether social science can be good science as currently practised. Rosenberg argues social science currently fails to meet such standards, hence is bad science. Kincaid defends the idea that social science can meet such standards.

5 No social-science theories exhibit the kind of empirical success Kincaid expects, so by these standards, social science would be judged as very poor science indeed.

6 Recall that we saw in Chapter 6 that objectivity for the social sciences should be reconceived dialogically. If the natural sciences are more meaning-laced as Kuhn seems to suggest, they may need to make use of this notion of objectivity as well.

7 One might object that natural science focuses on causal accounts, not interpretive ones; however, causal accounts are particular forms of interpretive accounts. Interpretation is inexorably involved in the proposing of specific causes as explanations for enduring patterns. Moreover, interpretation is involved in the debate among proponents of competing causal accounts (Miller 1987).

8 Recall from Chapter 2 that this was the attitude of Comte and Mill.

Chapter 17

1 These Enlightenment contrasts are largely due to exaggeration and misunderstanding of the two supposed oppositions (Gadamer 1975). For instance, even in the natural sciences, scientific reasoning is dependent on, not opposed to, traditions (Kuhn 1996).

2 Unfortunately, as we have seen, the kind of 'freedom' on offer in both viewpoints fosters isolation and undermines any sense of mutual obligation and commitment. It is impossible for a group of autonomous individuals to genuinely engage in cooperation, community and friendships as these forms of life involve precisely the kinds of mutual obligations and commitments that autonomy and hyper-individuality oppose.

3 If Kuhn is right, this distinction can be problematic in the natural sciences as well (Chapter 16, sec. 2).
4 Bernstein does not mean that this anxiety somehow begins with Descartes (Bernstein 1983: 16), but that Descartes articulates the anxiety in a particularly powerful way. Indeed, one can find such anxiety discussed in Plato and Augustine.
5 We saw examples of how our meanings, practices and articulations are co-constituting in Chapters 6 and 11.

Bibliography

Aries, P. 1962   *Centuries of Childhood: A Social History of Family Life* (trans. R. Bladick; New York: Alfred Knopf).

Auyang, S. 1998   *Foundations of Complex-System Theories: in Economics, Evolutionary Biology, and Statistical Physics* (Cambridge: Cambridge University Press).

Axelrod, R. 1984   *The Evolution of Cooperation* (New York: Basic Books).

Bacon, F. 2000   *The New Organon* (ed. L. Jardine and M. Silverthorne; Cambridge: Cambridge University Press [1620]).

Bandura, A. 1977   *Social Learning Theory* (Englewood Cliffs: Prentice-Hall).

1986   *Social Foundations of Thought and Action: A Social Cognitive Theory* (Englewood Cliffs: Prentice-Hall).

Banfield, E. C. 1990   *Unheavenly City Revisited* (Long Grove, IL: Waveland).

Barrett, W. 1978   *The Illusion of Technique* (New York: Anchor Press/Doubleday).

Becker, G. S. and K. M. Murphy 1988   'A Theory of Rational Addiction', *Journal of Political Economy* 96: 675–700.

Bellah, R., R. Madsen, W. Sullivan, A. Swidler and S. Tipton, 1985   *Habits of the Heart: Individualism and Commitment in American Life* (New York: Harper & Row).

Bentham, J. 1970   *An Introduction to the Principles of Morals and Legislation* (London: Athlone [1789]).

Berkowitz, P. 2000   'The Futility of Utility', *The New Republic* 222 no. 23: 38–44.

Berlin, I. 1962   'Does Political Theory Still Exist?', in P. Laslett and W. G. Runciman (eds) *Philosophy, Politics and Society, Second Series* (Oxford: Basil Blackwell), pp. 1–33.

Bernstein, R. 1976   *The Restructuring of Social and Political Theory* (Philadelphia: University of Pennsylvania Press).

1983   *Beyond Objectivism and Relativism: Science, Hermeneutics and Praxis* (Philadelphia: University of Pennsylvania Press).

Bishop, R. C. 2002   'Deterministic and Indeterministic Descriptions', in H. Atmanspacher and R. Bishop (eds), *Between Chance and Choice: Interdisciplinary Perspectives on Determinism* (Thorverton: Academic Imprint), pp. 5–31.

2003   'On Separating Predictability and Determinism', *Erkenntnis* 58: 169–88.

2005a   'Cognitive Psychology: Hidden Assumptions', in B. Slife, J. Reber and F. Richardson (eds), *Critical Thinking about Psychology: Hidden Assumptions and Plausible Alternatives* (Washington: American Psychological Association), pp. 151–70.

2005b   'Patching Physics and Chemistry Together', *Philosophy of Science* 72: 710–22.

2006a   'Determinism and Indeterminism', in D. Borchert (ed.), *The Encyclopedia of Philosophy* vol. 3 (Farmington Hills, MI: Thomson Gale, 2nd edn), pp. 29–35.

2006b   'Downward Causation in Fluid Convection', *Synthese*, in press.

2006c   'What Could Be Worse than the Butterfly Effect?', *Canadian Journal of Philosophy*, accepted.

Bourdieu, P. 1977 *Outline of a Theory of Practice* (Cambridge: Cambridge University Press).

Bruegmann, R. 2005 *Sprawl: A Compact History* (Chicago: University of Chicago Press).

Bruner, J. 1990 *Acts of Meaning: Four Lectures on Mind and Culture* (Cambridge, MA: Harvard University Press).

Brunner, K. 1969 ' "Assumptions" and the Cognitive Quality of Theories', *Synthese* 20: 501–25.

Camerer, C. F. and E. Fehr 2006 'When Does "Economic Man" Dominate Social Behaivor?', *Science* 311: 41–52.

Cartwright, N. 1989 *Nature's Capacities and their Measurement* (Oxford: Clarendon).

Cherlin, A. J. 1992 *Marriage, Divorce, Remarriage* (Cambridge, MA: Harvard University Press, revd edn).

Coles, R. 1987 'Civility and Psychology', in R. Bellah, W. Sullivan, and R. Madsen (eds), *Individualism and Commitment in American Life: Readings of the Themes of Habits of the Heart* (New York: Harper and Row), pp. 185–94.

Comte, A. 1974 *The Positive Philosophy of Auguste Comte Freely Translated and Condensed by Harriet Martineau* (New York: AMS Press [1855]).

1988 *Introduction to Positive Philosophy* (Indianapolis: Hackett)

Cushman, P. 1990 'Why the Self Is Empty', *American Psychologist* 45: 599–611.

D'Andrade, R. 1986 'Three Scientific World Views and the Covering Law Model', in D. Fiske and R. Shwerder (eds), *Metatheory in Social Science* (Chicago: University of Chicago Press), pp. 19–41.

Daston, L. 2000 'Can Scientific Objectivity Have a History?', *Alexander von Humboldt Stiftung Mitteilungen Sonderdruck aus Heft* 75: 31–40.

Dennett, D. 1987 *The Intentional Stance* (Cambridge, MA: MIT Press).

Descartes, R. 2000 *Philosophical Essays and Correspondence* (Indianapolis: Hackett).

Dewey, J. 1933 *How We Think* (Boston: Heath).

Dilthey, W. 1976 *Wilhelm Dilthey: Selected Writings* (Cambridge: Cambridge University Press).

Dreyfus, H. 1987, 'Foucault's Therapy', *PsychCritique* 2: 65–83.

Dreyfus, H. and S. Dreyfus 1988 *Mind over Machine: The Power of Human Intuition and Expertise in the Era of the Computer* (New York: Free Press).

Dunne, J. 1996 'Beyond Sovereignty and Deconstruction: The Storied Self', *Philosophy and Social Criticism* 21: 137–57.

Durkheim, E. 1950 *The Rules of Sociological Method* (trans. S. A. Solovay and J. H. Mueller; New York: The Free Press [1895]).

1960 *The Division of Labor in Society* (trans. George Simpson; New York: The Free Press [1893]).

Dworkin, G. 1989 'The Concept of Autonomy', in J. Christman (ed.), *The Inner Citadel* (New York: Oxford University Press), pp. 54–62.

Eckstein, H. 1975 'Case Study and Theory in Political Science', in F. J. Greenstein and N. W. Polsby (eds), *Handbook of Political Science*, vol. VII (Reading, MA: Addison-Wesley), pp. 79–138.

Elman, C. and M. F. Elman (eds) 2001 *Bridges and Boundaries: Historians, Political Scientists, and the Study of International Relations* (Cambridge, MA: MIT Press).

Elster, J. 1982 'The Case for Methodological Individualism', *Theory and Society* 11: 453–82.

1989 *Nuts and Bolts for the Social Sciences* (Cambridge: Cambridge University Press).

Elster, J. and O.-J. Skog (eds) 1999 *Getting Hooked: Rationality and Addiction* (Cambridge: Cambridge University Press).

Etzioni, A. 1994 *Spirit of Community: The Reinvention of American Society* (New York: Touchstone).

Fancher, R. 1995 *Cultures of Healing: Correcting the Image of American Mental Health Care* (New York: W. H. Freeman).

Flyvbjerg, B. 2001 *Making Social Science Matter: Why Social Inquiry Fails and How It Can Be Successful Again* (Cambridge: Cambridge University Press).

Foucault, M. 1979 *Discipline and Punish: The Birth of the Prison* (trans. A. Sheridan; New York: Vintage).

1980a *The History of Sexuality*, vol. I: *An Introduction* (trans. R. Hurley; New York: Vintage/Random House).

1980b *Power/Knowledge: Selected Interviews and Other Writings* (ed. C. Gordon; New York: Pantheon).

1982 'On the Genealogy of Ethics: An Overview of Work in Progress', in H. Dreyfus and P. Rabinow (eds), *Michel Foucault: Beyond Structuralism and Hermeneutics* (Chicago: University of Chicago Press), pp. 229–52.

Fowers, B. 1998 'Psychology and the Good Marriage: Social Theory as Practice', *American Behavioral Scientist* 41: 516–41.

Fowers, B., E. Lyons and K. Montel 1996 'Positive Illusions about Marriage: Self Enhancement or Relationship Enhancement?', *Journal of Family Psychology* 10: 192–208.

van Fraassen, B. 1990 *Laws and Symmetry* (Oxford: Oxford University Press).

1993 'From Vicious Circle to Infinite Regress, and Back Again', in D. Hull, M. Forbes and K. Ohkruhlik (eds), *PSA 1992, vol. II. Proceedings of the Philosophy of Science Association Conference 1992* (Evanston: Northwestern University Press), pp. 6–29.

Frank, R., T. Gilovich, and D. Regan 1993 'Does Studying Economics Inhibit Cooperation?', *Journal of Economic Perspectives* 7: 159–72.

Freud, S. 1964 *The Complete Psychological Works of Sigmund Freud*, vol. XIX: *1923–25) The Ego and the Id, and Other Works* (ed. J. Strachey; London: Hogarth Press).

Friedman, M. 1953 'The Methodology of Positive Economics', in *Essays in Positive Economics* (Chicago: University of Chicago Press), pp. 3–43.

1974 'Explanation and Scientific Understanding', *The Journal of Philosophy* 71: 5–19.

Fromm, E. 1969 *Escape from Freedom* (New York: Avon [1941]).

1975 *Man for Himself* (New York: Fawcett Premier [1947]).

Funk, S. C. and B. K. Houston 1987 'A Critical Analysis of the Hardiness Scale's Validity and Utility', *Journal of Personality and Social Psychology* 53: 572–78.

Furstenberg, F. and A. Cherlin 1991 *Divided Families: What Happens to Children when Parents Part* (Cambridge, MA: Harvard University Press).

Gadamer, H.-G. 1975 *Truth and Method* (New York: Continuum).

Geddes, B. 2003 *Paradigms and Sand Castles: Theory Building and Research Design in Comparative Politics* (Ann Arbor: University of Michigan Press).

Gendlin, E. 1999 'A New Model', *Journal of Consciousness Studies* 6: 232–37.

Gergen, K. 1982 *Toward Transformation in Social Knowledge* (New York: Springer-Verlag).

1985 'The Social Constructionist Movement in Modern Psychology', *American Psychologist* 40: 266–75.

1994 *Realities and Relationships: Soundings in Social Constructionism* (Cambridge, MA: Harvard University Press).

Giddens, A. 1976 *New Rules of Sociological Method* (New York: Basic Books).

Giere, R. 1999 *Science without Laws* (Chicago: University of Chicago Press).

Gigerenzer, G. and D. J. Murray 1987 *Cognition as Intuitive Statistics* (Hillsdale, NJ: Erlbaum).

Gigerenzer, G. and R. Selten 2001 *Bounded Rationality: The Adaptive Toolbox* (Cambridge, MA: MIT Press).

Gilligan, C. 1993 *In a Different Voice: Psychological Theory and Women's Development* (Cambridge, MA: Harvard University Press).

Girard, R. 1966 *Deceit, Desire, and the Novel: Self and Other in Literary Structure* (Baltimore: Johns Hopkins Press).

Gottman, J. 1993 'The Role of Conflict Engagement, Escalation, or Avoidance in Marital Interaction: A Longitudinal View of Five Types of Couples', *Journal of Consulting and Clinical Psychology* 61: 6–15.

1994 *What Predicts Divorce: The Relationship between Marital Processes and Marital Outcomes* (Mahawa, NJ: Erlbaum).

Gottman, J. and N. Silver 1994 *Why Marriages Succeed or Fail* (New York: Simon and Schuster).

Greenberg, J. and S. Mitchell 1983 *Object Relations in Psychoanalytic Theory* (Cambridge, MA: Harvard University Press).

Grüne-Yanoff, T. and P. Schweinzer 2005 'Game-Theoretic Models, Stories, and Their Assessment', Mimeo (unpublished).

Guerney, B., G. Brock and J. Coufal 1987 'Integrating Marital Therapy and Enrichment: The Relationship Enhancement Approach', in N. Jacobson and A. Gurman (eds), *Clinical Handbook of Marital Therapy* (New York: Guilford Press), pp. 151–72.

Guignon, C. 1986 'Existentialist Ethics', in J. DeMarco and R. Fox (eds), *New Directions in Ethics: The Challenge of Applied Ethics* (New York: Routledge & Kegan Paul), pp. 73–91.

1989 'Truth as Disclosure: Art, Language, History', *The Southern Journal of Philosophy* 28: 105–21.

1991 'Pragmatism or Hermeneutics? Epistemology after Foundationalism', in J. Bohman, D. Hiley and R. Schusterman (eds), *The Interpretive Turn* (Ithaca: Cornell University Press), pp. 81–101.

2002 'Hermeneutics, Authenticity, and the Aims of Psychotherapy', *Journal of Theoretical and Philosophical Psychology* 22: 83–102.

Guignon, C. and D. Hiley 1990 'Biting the Bullet: Rorty on Private and Public Morality', in A. Malachowski (ed.), *Reading Rorty* (Cambridge, MA: Blackwell), pp. 339–64.

Habermas, J. 1971 *Knowledge and Human Interests* (trans. Jeremy J. Shapiro; Boston: Beacon).

1973 *Theory and Practice* (Boston: Beacon).

1991 *The Philosophical Discourse of Modernity* (Cambridge, MA: MIT Press).

Hacking, I. 1991 'The Making and Molding of Child Abuse', *Critical Inquiry* 17: 838–67.

1992 'The Self-Vindication of the Laboratory Sciences', in A. Pickering (ed.), *Sciences as Practice and Culture* (Chicago: University of Chicago Press), pp. 29–64.

Hardin, G. 1968 'The Tragedy of the Commons', *Science* 162: 1243–48.

Hare, R. 1963 *Freedom and Reason* (Oxford: Oxford University Press).

Hareven, T. 1987 'Historical Analysis of the Family', in M. Sussman and S. Steinmetz (eds), *Handbook of Marriage and the Family* (New York: Plenum), pp. 37–57.

Harman, G. 1977 *The Nature of Morality* (New York: Oxford University Press).

Hausman, D. 1983 'Are There Causal Relations Among Dependent Variables?', *Philosophy of Science* 50: 58–81.

von Hayek, F. A. 1942 'Scientism and the Study of Man I', *Economica* 9: 267–91.

1967 *Studies in Philosophy, Politics and Economics* (Chicago: University of Chicago Press).

Heath, J. 2001 *Communicative Action and Rational Choice* (Cambridge, MA: MIT Press).

Held, D. 1980 *Introduction to Critical Theory: Horkheimer to Habermas* (Berkeley: University of California Press).

Hempel, C. G. 1965 'The Function of General Laws in History', in *Aspects of Scientific Explanation and Other Essays in the Philosophy of Science* (New York: The Free Press), pp. 231–43.

Henrich, J. 2006 'Cooperation, Punishment, and the Evolution of Human Institutions', *Science* 312: 60–61.

Hillman, J. and M. Ventura 1992, *We've Had a Hundred Years of Psychotherapy and the World's Getting Worse* (San Francisco: Harper San Francisco).

Hobbes, T. 1994 *Leviathan* (ed. E. Curley; Indianapolis: Hackett [1651/1668]).

1998 *On the Citizen* (trans. & ed. R. Tuck and M. Silverthorne; Cambridge: Cambridge University Press [1642]).

Hollis, M. and R. Sugden 1993 'Rationality in Action', *Mind* 102: 1–35.

Hoover, K. 2001 *Causality in Macroeconomics* (Cambridge: Cambridge University Press).

Horkheimer, M. 1974 *Eclipse of Reason* (New York: Continuum Publishing).

Hull, J. G., R. R. van Treuren and S. Virnelli 1987 'Hardiness and Health: A Critique and Alternative Approach', *Journal of Personality and Social Psychology* 53: 518–30.

Izawa, C. (ed.), 1989 *Current Issues in Cognitive Processes: The Tulane Flowerree Symposium on Cognition* (Hillsdale, NJ: Lawrence Erlbaum Associates).

Jaeger, C. C., O. Renn, E. A. Rosa and T. Webler 2001 *Risk, Uncertainty, and Rational Action* (London: Earthscan).

James, W. 1950 *The Principles of Psychology*, vol. 1 (New York: Dover [1890]).

Jones, L. G. 1997 'A Thirst for God or Consumer Spirituality? Cultivating Disciplined Practices of Being Engaged by God', in L. Gregory Jones and J. Buckley (eds), *Spirituality and Social Embodiment* (London: Blackwell), pp. 3–28.

Jordan, D., H. Montgomery and E. Thomassen (eds), 1999 *The World of Ancient Magic* (Philadelphia: Norwegian Institute at Athens/Coronet Books).

Kane, R. 1996 *The Significance of Free Will* (Oxford: Oxford University Press).

Karney, B. and T. Bradbury 1995 'The Longitudinal Course of Marital Quality and Stability: A Review of Theory, Method, and Research', *Psychological Bulletin* 18: 3–34.

Kelly, T. A. 1990 'The Role of Values in Psychotherapy: A Critical Review of Process and Outcome Effects', *Clinical Psychology Review* 10: 171–86.

Kerlinger, F. N. and H. B. Lee 1999 *Foundations of Behavioral Research* (Belmont, CA: Wadsworth).

Kincaid, H. 1986 'Reduction, Explanation, and Individualism', *Philosophy of Science* 53: 492–513.

1996 *Philosophical Foundations of the Social Sciences: Analyzing Controversies in Social Research* (Cambridge: Cambridge University Press).

King, R. 1973 *The Meaning of God* (Philadelphia: Fortress).

Kitcher, P. 1981 'Explanatory Unification', *Philosophy of Science* 48: 507–31.

1993 *The Advancement of Science: Science without Legend, Objectivity without Illusions* (Oxford: Oxford University Press).

Kobasa, S. C. 1979 'Stressful Life Events, Personality, and Health: An Inquiry Into Hardiness', *Journal of Personality and Social Psychology* 37: 1–11.

Koch, S. 1981 'The Nature and Limits of Psychological Knowledge: Lessons of a Quarter Century qua Science', *American Psychologist* 36: 257–69.

Kohlberg, L. 1984 *Essays on Moral Development* (New York: Harper & Row).

Kohut, H. 1977 *The Restoration of the Self* (New York: International Universities Press).

Kuhn, T. 1996 *The Structure of Scientific Revolutions* (Chicago: University of Chicago Press, 3rd edn [1962]).

2000 'The Natural and the Human Sciences', in *The Road Since Structure* (Chicago: University of Chicago Press), pp. 216–23.

Lasch, C. 1991 *Culture of Narcissism: American Life in an Age of Diminishing Expectations* (New York: W. W. Norton).

Lee, G., K. Seccombe and C. Sheehan 1991 'Marital Status and Personal Happiness: An Analysis of Trend Data', *Journal of Marriage and the Family* 53: 839–44.

Lee, T. D. and C. Yang 1956 'Question of Parity Nonconservation in Weak Interactions', *Physical Review* 104: 254–58.

Lester, R. A. 1946 'Shortcomings of Marginal Analysis for Wage-Employment Problems', *American Economic Review* 36: 62–82.

1947 'Marginal Costs, Minimum Wages, and Labor Markets', *American Economic Review* 37: 135–48.

Levi, I. 1986 'The Paradoxes of Allais and Ellsberg', *Economics and Philosophy* 2: 23–53.

Lewis, C. S. 2001 *A Grief Observed* (San Francisco: Harper Collins [1961]).

Lindberg, D. C. 1992 *The Beginnings of Western Science: The European Scientific Tradition in Philosophical, Religious, and Institutional Context, 600 B.C. to A.D. 1450* (Chicago: University of Chicago Press).

Lukes, S. 1968 'Methodological Individualism Reconsidered', *British Journal of Sociology* 19: 119–29.

1987 'On the Social Determination of Truth', in M. Gibbons (ed.), *Interpreting Politics* (New York: New York University Press), pp. 64–81.

McCarthy, T. 1988 'Panel Discussion: Construction and Constraint', in E. McMullin (ed.), *Construction and Constraint: The Shaping of Scientific Rationality* (Notre Dame, IN: University of Notre Dame Press), pp. 223–46.

McCullough, M. E., K. I. Pargament and C. E. Thoresen 2001 *Forgiveness: Theory, Research and Practice* (New York: Guilford).

MacIntyre, A. 1981   *After Virtue* (Notre Dame, IN: University of Notre Dame Press).

Mackie, J. 1977   *Ethics: Inventing Right and Wrong* (Harmondsworth: Penguin Books).

McMullin, E. 1965   'Medieval and Modern Science: Continuity or Discontinuity?', *International Philosophical Quarterly* 5: 103–29.

Maddi, S. 1997   'Personal Views Survey II: A Measure of Dispositional Hardiness', in C. P. Zalaquett and R. J. Wood (eds), *Evaluating Stress: A Book of Resources* (Lanham: The Scarecrow Press).

1999   'The Personality Construct of Hardiness: I. Effects on Experiencing, Coping, and Strain', *Consulting Psychology Journal: Practice and Research* 51: 83–94.

Malinowski, B. 1948   *The Sexual Lives of Savages in North-Western Melanesia* (London: Routledge and Kegan Paul, 3rd edn).

Markman, H., M. Resnick, F. Floyd, S. Stanley and M. Clements 1993   'Preventing Marital Distress through Communication and Conflict Management Training: A Four-and Five-Year Follow-Up', *Journal of Consulting and Clinical Psychology* 61: 70–77.

May, R. 1958   'Contributions of Existential Psychotherapy', in R. May, E. Angle and H. F. Ellenberger (eds), *Existence: A New Dimension in Psychiatry and Psychology* (New York: Basic Books).

Markman, H., S. Stanley and S. Blumberg 1994   *Fighting for Your Marriage: Positive Steps for Preventing Divorce and Preserving a Lasting Love* (San Francisco: Jossey-Bass).

Martin, M. 1994   'Taylor on Interpretation and the Sciences of Man', in M. Martin and L. C. McIntyre (eds), *Readings in The Philosophy of Social Science* (Cambridge, MA: MIT Press), pp. 259–79.

Marwell, G. and R. Ames 1981   'Economists Free Ride. Does Anyone Else? Experiments on the Provision of Public Goods. IV', *Journal of Public Economics* 15: 295–310.

Maslow, A. 1998   *Toward a Psychology of Being* (New York: Van Nostrand Reinhold, 3rd edn [1962]).

Mayer, S. E. 1998   *What Money Can't Buy: Family Income and Children's Life Chances* (Cambridge, MA: Harvard University Press).

Milgram, S. 1974   *Obedience to Authority* (New York: Harper & Row).

Miller, R. 1978   'Methodological Individualism and Social Explanation', *Philosophy of Science* 45: 387–414.

1987   *Fact and Method: Explanation, Confirmation and Reality in the Natural and the Social Sciences* (Princeton: Princeton University Press).

Mintz, S. and S. Kellogg 1988   *Domestic Revolutions: A Social History of American Family Life* (New York: Free Press).

Nagel, E. 1961   *The Structure of Science: Problems in the Logic of Scientific Explanation* (New York: Harcourt, Brace & World).

Nagel, T. 1989   *The View from Nowhere* (Oxford: Oxford University Press).

Ochs, J. and A. Roth 1989   'An Experimental Study of Sequential Bargaining', *American Economic Review* 79: 355–84.

Olson, D., D. Fournier and J. Druckman 1987   *Counselor's Manual for PREPARE/ENRICH*, (Minneapolis: PREPARE/ENRICH, revd edn).

Pargament, K. I. 2001   *The Psychology of Religion and Coping: Theory, Research, Practice* (New York: Guilford, new edn).

Parsons, T. 1937   *The Structure of Social Action: A Study in Social Theory with Special Reference to a Group of Recent European Writers* (New York: McGraw-Hill).

1959   *The Social System* (Glencoe, IL: The Free Press).

Polanyi, M. 1962   *Personal Knowledge: Towards a Post-Critical Philosophy* (Chicago: University of Chicago Press).

Polsby, N. W. 2001   'Political Science: Overview', in N. J. Smelser and P. B. Battes, eds., *International Encyclopedia of the Social & Behavioral Sciences* (Amsterdam: Elsevier), pp. 11698–701.

Popenoe, D. 1993   'American Family Decline, 1960–1990: A Review and Appraisal', *Journal of Marriage and the Family* 55: 527–55.

Popper, K. 1945   'The Poverty of Historicism III', *Economica* 11: 69–89.

1963   *Conjectures and Refutations: The Growth of Scientific Knowledge* (New York: Harper & Row).

1992   *The Logic of Scientific Discovery* (London: Routledge, [1959]).

Portis, E. B., M. B. Levy and M. Landau 1988   *Handbook of Political Theory and Policy Science* (New York: Greenwood).

Ragin, C. C. 2004   'Turning the Tables: How Case-Oriented Research Challenges Variable-Oriented Research', in D. Collier and H. Brady (eds), *Rethinking Social Inquiry: Diverse Tools, Shared Standards* (Lanham, MD: Rowman and Littlefield), pp. 123–38.

Rayner, S. 1986   'Management of Radiation Hazards in Hospitals: Plural Rationalities in a Single Institution', *Social Studies of Science* 16: 573–91.

Reichenbach, H. 1938   *Experience and Prediction* (Chicago: University of Chicago Press).

Richardson, F. C. and R. Bishop 2002   'Rethinking Determinism in Social Science', in H. Atmanspacher and R. Bishop (eds), *Between Chance and Choice: Interdisciplinary Perspectives on Determinism* (Thorverton: Imprint Academic), pp. 425–45.

Richardson, F. C. and J. Christopher 1993   'Social Theory as Practice: Metatheoretical Frameworks for Social Inquiry', *Journal of Theoretical and Philosophical Psychology* 13: 137–53.

Richardson, F. C. and B. Fowers 1998   'Interpretive Social Science: An Overview', *American Behavioral Scientist* 41: 465–95.

Richardson, F. C., B. Fowers and C. Guignon 1999   *Re-envisioning Psychology: Moral Dimensions of Theory and Practice* (San Francisco: Jossey-Bass).

Richardson, F., A. Rogers and J. McCarroll 1998   'Toward a Dialogical Self', *American Behavioral Scientist* 41: 496–515.

Ricoeur, P. 1992   *Oneself as Another* (Chicago: University of Chicago Press).

Rieff, P. 1959   *Freud: The Mind of a Moralist* (Chicago: Chicago University Press).

1966   *The Triumph of the Therapeutic: Uses of Faith After Freud* (Chicago: University of Chicago Press).

Rogeberg, O. 2004   'Taking Absurd Theories Seriously: Economics and the Case of Rational Addiction Theories', *Philosophy of Science* 71: 263–85.

Root, M. 1993   *Philosophy of Social Science* (Oxford: Blackwell).

Rorty, R. 1982   *Philosophy and the Mirror of Nature* (Princeton: Princeton University Press).

1985   'Solidarity or Objectivity?', in J. Rajchman and C. West (eds), *Post-Analytic Philosophy* (New York: Columbia University Press), pp. 3–19.

1987 'Method, Social Science and Social Hope', in M. Gibbons (ed.), *Interpreting Politics* (New York: New York University Press), pp. 241–60.

Rosenberg, A. 1995 *Philosophy of Social Science* (Boulder: Westview, 2nd edn).

Ross, L., M. R. Lepper and M. Hubbard 1975 'Perseverance and Self-Perception: Biased Attributional Processes in the Debriefing Paradigm', *Journal of Personality and Social Psychology* 32: 880–92.

Rychlak, J. 1979 *Discovering Free Will and Personal Responsibility* (Oxford: Oxford University Press).

1988 *The Psychology of Rigorous Humanism* (New York: New York University Press, 2nd edn).

Salmon, M. H. et al. 1992 *Introduction to the Philosophy of Science* (Indianapolis: Hackett).

Salmon, W. 1984 *Scientific Explanation and the Causal Structure of the World* (Princeton: Princeton University Press).

Samuelson, P. 1938 'A Note on the Pure Theory of Consumers' Behaviour', Economica 5: 61–71.

Sandel, M. J. 1996 *Democracy's Discontents: America in Search of a Public Philosophy* (Harvard: Belknap).

Savage, L. J. 1954 *The Foundations of Statistics* (New York: John Wiley).

Schafer, R. 1976 *A New Language for Psychoanalysis* (New Haven: Yale University Press).

1980 'Narration in the Psychoanalytic Dialogue', in W. Mitchell, *On Narrative* (Chicago: University of Chicago Press).

1981 *Narrative Actions in Psychoanalysis* (New York: Basic Books).

Schilling, G. 2006 'Pluto: Underworld Character Kicked Out of Planet Family', *Science* 313: 1214–15.

Schumaker, J. 2001 *The Age of Insanity: Modernity and Mental Health* (Westport, CT: Praeger).

Short, J. F. 1984 'The Social Fabric at Risk: Toward the Social Transformation or Risk Analysis', *American Sociological Review* 49: 711–25.

Shorter, E. 1975 *The Making of the Modern Family* (New York: Basic Books).

Siegel, L. 2006 'Thank You for Sharing', *The New Republic* 234: 19–23.

Simon, H. A. 1947 *Administrative Behavior: A Study of Decision-Making Processes in Administrative Organization* (New York: Macmillan 2nd edn).

Sjoberg, G. and T. R. Vaughan 1993 'The Bureaucratization of Sociology', T. R. Vaughan, G. Sjoberg, and L. T. Reynolds (eds), *A Critique of Contemporary American Sociology* (Dix Hills, NY: General Hall), pp. 54–113.

Skinner, B. F. 1965 *Science and Human Behavior* (New York: The Free Press).

1974 *About Behaviorism* (New York: Knopf).

2005 *Walden Two* (Indianapolis: Hackett [1948]).

Slife, B. and R. Williams 1995 *What's Behind the Research? Discovering Hidden Assumptions in the Behavioral Sciences* (Thousand Oaks: SAGE).

Smith, A. 1937 *The Wealth of Nations* (Modern Library; New York: Random House [1776]).

Smith, T. C. 1959 *The Agrarian Origins of Modern Japan* (Stanford: Stanford University Press).

Staats, A. 1991 'Unified Positivism and Unification Psychology: Fad or New Field?', *American Psychologist* 46: 899–912).

Sternberg, R. J. and T. Ben-Zeev 2001 *Complex Cognition: The Psychology of Human Thought* (New York: Oxford University Press).

Steuer, M. 2002   *The Scientific Study of Society* (Dordrecht: Kluwer Academic).

Stinchcombe, A. 1968   *Constructing Social Theories* (New York: Harcourt, Brace & World).

Sullivan, W. 1986   *Reconstructing Public Philosophy* (Berkeley: University of California Press).

Suppe, F. 1977   *The Structure of Scientific Theories* (Urbana: University of Illinois Press 2nd edn).

Taylor, C. 1975   *Hegel* (Cambridge: Cambridge University Press).

1985a   *Philosophical Papers*, vol. 1: *Human Agency and Language* (Cambridge: Cambridge University Press).

1985b   *Philosophical Papers*, vol. 2: *Philosophy and the Human Sciences* (Cambridge: Cambridge University Press).

1989   *Sources of the Self* (Cambridge, MA: Harvard University Press).

1993   'Engaged Agency and Background in Heidegger', in C. Guignon (ed.), *The Cambridge Companion to Heidegger* (Cambridge: Cambridge University Press), pp. 317–36.

1995   *Philosophical Arguments* (Cambridge, MA: Harvard University Press).

Teller, P. 2001   'Twilight of the Perfect Model Model', *Erkenntnis* 55: 393–415.

Thomas, G. 2005   'The Qualitative Foundations of Political Science Methodology', *Perspectives on Politics* 3: 855–66.

de Tocqueville, A. 1955   *The Old Regime and the French Revolution* (New York: Anchor [1856]).

Torretti, R. 2000   '"Scientific Realism" and Scientific Practice', in E. Agazzi and M. Pauri (eds), *The Reality of the Unobservable: Observability, Unobservability and Their Impact on the Issue of Scientific Realism* (Dordrecht: Kluwer Academic), pp. 113–22.

Tversky, A. and D. Kahneman 1981   'The Framing of Decisions and the Psychology of Choice', *Science* 211: 453–58.

Tversky, A. and R. Thaler 1990   'Preference Reversals', *Journal of Economic Perspectives* 4: 201–11.

Vaughan, T. R., G. Sjoberg and L. T. Reynolds 1992   *A Critique of Contemporary American Sociology* (Dix Hills, NY: General Hall).

Vogel, S. 1998   'Exposing Life's Limits in Dimensionless Numbers', *Physics Today* (Nov): pp. 22–27.

Wachtel, P. 1997   *Psychoanalysis, Behavior Therapy, and the Relational World* (Washington, DC: American Psychological Association).

Warnke, G. 1987   *Gadamer: Hermeneutics, Tradition, and Reason* (Palo Alto: Stanford University Press).

Watkins, J. W. N. 1957   'Historical Explanation in the Social Sciences', *British Journal for the Philosophy of Science* 8: 104–17.

Weber, M. 1949   *Max Weber On The Methodology of the Social Sciences* (eds & trans. E. Shils and H. Finch; New York: The Free Press).

1968   *Economy and Society* (ed. G. Roth and C. Wittich; New York: Bedminster, [1921]).

Weisstein, N. 1971   'Psychology Constructs the Female', *Social Education* 35: 362–73.

Whewell, W. 1858   *Novum Organon Renovatum* (London: J. W. Parker and Son).

Williams, M. 2001   *Problems of Knowledge: A Critical Introduction to Epistemology* (Oxford: Oxford University Press).

Williams, R. 1987   'Can Cognitive Psychology Offer a Meaningful Account of Meaningful Human Action', *Journal of Mind and Behavior* 8: 209–22.

2001   'The Biologization of Psychotherapy: Understanding the Nature of Influences', in B. Slife, R. Williams and S. Barlow (eds), *Critical Issues in Psychotherapy: Translating New Ideas into Practice* (Thousand Oaks: Sage Publications), pp. 51–73.

Winch, P. 1958   *The Idea of Social Science and Its Relation to Philosophy* (London: Routledge & Kegan Paul).

1977   'Understanding a Primitive Society', in F. Dallmayr and T. McCarthy (eds), *Understanding and Social Inquiry* (Notre Dame, IN: University of Notre Dame Press), pp. 159–88.

Wolin, S. 1972   'Political Theory as Vocation', in M. Fisher (ed.), *Machiavelli and the Nature of Political Thought* (New York: Atheneum), pp. 23–75.

Wylie, A. 1992   'Reasoning about Ourselves: Feminist Methodology in the Social Sciences', in E. Harvey and K. Okruhik (eds), *Women and Reason* (Ann Arbor: University of Michigan Press), pp. 225–44.

Yalom, I. 1980   *Existential Psychotherapy* (New York: Basic Books).

Yanchar, S. and B. Slife 1997   'Pursuing Unity in a Fragmented Psychology: Problems and Prospects', *Review of General Psychology* 1: 235–55.

Yankelovich, D. and W. Barrett 1970   *Ego and Instinct* (New York: Random House).

Index

CPSIA information can be obtained
at www.ICGtesting.com
Printed in the USA
LVHW081751140621
690189LV00011B/634

9 780826 489531